WITHDRAWN

BEFORE
HEAD START

HAMILTON CRAVENS

BEFORE
HEAD START

THE IOWA STATION &

AMERICA'S CHILDREN

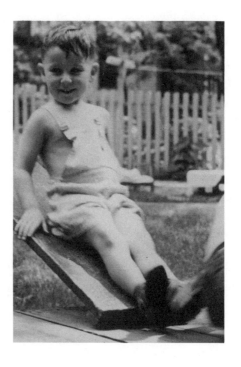

THE UNIVERSITY OF NORTH CAROLINA

PRESS • CHAPEL HILL AND LONDON

© 1993 The University of North Carolina Press

All rights reserved

Manufactured in the United States of America

Library of Congress Cataloging-in-Publication Data

Cravens, Hamilton.

  Before Head Start : the Iowa Station and America's children / by Hamilton

  Cravens.

       p.   cm.

  Includes bibliographical references and index.

  ISBN 0-8078-2092-X (cloth : alk. paper)

  1. Child development—Research—United States—History—20th century.

  2. Child development—Research—Iowa.   3. Iowa Child Welfare Research

  Station.   I. Title.

  HQ778.7.U6C73   1993

  305.23'1'0720777—dc20   92-44806

                                                                CIP

97 96 95 94 93   5 4 3 2 1

All photographs in the book are from the F. W. Kent Collection, University of Iowa
Archives, Iowa City, Iowa. They are reproduced here by permission.

FOR

Heather and

Christopher

CONTENTS

Preface   ix
Acknowledgments   xv
Introduction   1

CHAPTER ONE
A Problem of Definition   6

CHAPTER TWO
The Big Money   39

CHAPTER THREE
Inventing a Science   72

CHAPTER FOUR
Great Expectations   106

CHAPTER FIVE
The Science of Democracy   151

CHAPTER SIX
Individualism Reconsidered   185

CHAPTER SEVEN
The Perils of Professionalism   217

EPILOGUE
Toward Head Start   251

Note on Primary Sources   263
Notes   267
Index   317
A section of illustrations
follows page 142.

The child is father to the man; we become as adults what is established in us as children. Whatever its contemporary scientific validity or political acceptability, that old saw has fueled discussion and controversy in public life concerning the views that Americans have held of one another in society, economy, polity, and culture. Notions of childhood and child nurture have been directly linked to social action and thought in important ways. Thus childhood nurture as an intellectual and cultural construct occupies a central place in modern American history and plays a crucial role in social thought and public policy. Its ramifications have been large and extensive.

Historian Bernard Wishy has ably examined the American discussion of childhood nurture from the eighteenth to the twentieth century, when, as he put it, scientific and educational experts took over the culture's public discussions of child nurture and nature. The eighteenth-century Enlightenment made discussions of the nature of children and child development recognizably modern. Wishy saw the modern posture as assuming the innocence or moral flexibility of children and discussing their specific responses and experiences as they grew up. Gone were the ancient emphasis on moral depravity and the traditional abstractions on child behavior. In the nineteenth century Americans applied these modern perspectives to the problem of child nurture by attempting to find a reasonable balance between freedom and authority.[1]

In this book I discuss crucial aspects of the modern debates and discussions among twentieth-century scientific experts of child nature and nurture—of child development. My focus has been those actions and discussions that have preceded our own time and that ruled before our age's representative solution to the problem of childhood nurture, the federal government's Head Start program, and all that it symbolizes. More specifically, I have treated the years from the 1920s to the 1950s as a coherent era both in the history of American culture and the history of American child science and child-saving. Thanks to the vigorous new historiography in the areas of the history of women, child welfare, and reform, I have been able to focus not on the historical phenomena that some might imagine as the sources of these ideas and discussions, but on what the experts did with ideas about child nature and nurture once they got them. I have not assumed a "trickle-down" theory of the origins of ideas, according to which a scientific elite mints them and disseminates them throughout the culture; matters are always infinitely more complicated than that. And what the experts or technicians said and did seemed more than enough for one book, especially given the state of scholarly knowledge about the topic and related matters.

Initially my interest came from my efforts to explore once again the influence of evolutionary science in twentieth-century American culture.[2] Notions of heredity and environment provided the evolutionary theorist with general causal models of evolution. What, I wondered, was the role of notions about development in evolutionary theory? Eventually I recognized that these notions were fundamental to the question of speciation—the formation of species and groups and, therefore, of the complex relations between the individual and its species or group. Because so little has been written about these issues as a problem or series of problems in cultural history, a general book seemed inadvisable.[3] Rather, I decided to write about the field's most famous research institute in the interwar era, the Iowa Child Welfare Research Station, a research unit of the University of Iowa, which I hoped to show as a microcosm, as it were, of the larger story. This period was when it mattered to national culture that the Iowa station existed, when its identity was sufficiently singular to enable us to understand that larger culture; there was much about the station's relationship to debates and discussions in its field then that helped illuminate deep and profound issues in that age. Such cannot be said for the Iowa station's history since the 1950s; it therefore is not discussed in this book.

The Iowa station was the first research institute in North America, and perhaps the world, whose sole purpose was to conduct original scientific research on the development of normal children. It literally founded the field of child development. It was the guiding light for discussions in child development for almost a decade and a half. From the middle 1930s to the early 1950s, as the field jelled as a national scientific discipline with the full apparatus of a professional scientific subculture, the Iowa station maintained its eminence while becoming the field's maverick, its dissenter from the field's major and controlling hypotheses about the growth and development of human nature.

Central to child development's theoretical discourses and controversies was the question of the relationship between the individual and the group to which "science," or "society," or some other authority, had assigned the individual, whether the group in question was a gender, a race, a religious faith, a social class, or any other such "group." Naturally certain questions arose among practitioners in the field. To what extent was the individual's group member-ship definitive and restrictive of the individual? Could an individual be born into one "group" and through various means come to "belong" to another one that occupied a different niche in the social hierarchy? Or could an individual's own traits vary only within the expectations or means of the group to which he or she "belonged"? Was development, therefore, an automatic process, ema-nating from programmed natural inheritance and ineluctable social milieu? Could it be said that intelligence was inborn and fixed at birth, or could the IQ as measured "wander" in the same child from one test to another? Was the essence of child development the result of inner impulses interacting with certain postnatal circumstances—maturation, that is—or was it all existential experience, perhaps with some minimal maturation necessary to provide phys-iological and neurological support for the actions in question—learning, in other words?

These were some of the most fundamental issues that developmental scien-tists discussed in the era between the two World Wars. Those who came to dominate the field—the mainstream's champions—insisted that physical and mental development were predetermined, that the organism matured rather than learned, and that the ultimate reality of society and nature was that groups existed, and individuals existed only as members of the groups to which they "belonged." They were determinists, like most of their fellow citizens. As advisers and commentators on social and public policy, the field's majority counseled caution and a limiting of expectations. Development was an orderly, predictable process. Individuals in a particular group shared a certain common fate, subject only to minor variations within the range expected for that group. All was in balance, proportion, and symmetry. Not so of the Iowa scientists and a handful elsewhere in the country. They questioned the answers, the doc-trines, that the mainstream's advocates offered in technical and public discourse alike. They were not fatalistic conservatives. They saw much potentiality in children, especially in very young children. They were indeterminists: one could make a silk purse out of a sow's ear—and vice versa. Thus they challenged their contemporaries' all but universally accepted doctrine that group identity fixed the range of possibilities for each and every individual who "belonged" to that group. The social and political implications of their position were easy enough to understand. It constituted a direct challenge to the class and caste structure of the American social system and denied its naturalness and inevitability. Yet the Iowa scientists also believed, as did their opponents (and most of their fellow Americans), that the universe was an orderly, symmetrical place in which the whole was greater than or different from the sum of the parts, and in which all the parts were distinct yet interrelated. In a word, the Iowa scientists, no less than those they criticized, partook of their age's underlying holism.

Since the 1950s, however, we have lived in an age with radically different notions about the order of things—a new taxonomy of natural and social reality. Americans from all walks of life have insisted in many complex and often contradictory ways that there is no ultimate reality save the individual. Instead of perceiving the social system—or network—as a complex, intricate, and symmetrical entity in which all elements interact in balance and proportion with all others, Americans since the 1950s have assumed that the system is asymmetrical, unbalanced, dysfunctional, and constituted of very different parts; that each individual is distinct from all others; and that there is no larger whole. This model permeates our culture in widely disparate lines of activity, ranging from politics to popular culture and from science to social reorganization.

As these notions translated into social relations, Americans have acted and spoken as if the social system is oppressing or in other ways victimizing the countless and unique individuals in society. For the field of child development, the most obvious transformation of the post-1950 era was the sudden emergence of the notion of the child as an individual—often as a victim, as well—and not as a member of a particular group or setting that defined and limited possibilities and circumstances.[4] Suddenly the notion of the malleability of the preschool child as an individual who could "jump" from one group to another was an idea whose time had come. In the early 1960s some developmental scientists began to experiment as the Iowa scientists had with early childhood intervention; soon the politicians and the activists became involved. For better or for worse, the net result for public and social policy was the federal government's Head Start program. That program has remained, as one of the most perceptive developmental scientists, Professor Urie Bronfenbrenner, has said, the "rallying point" in the United States "around which you can ask who's taking care of kids." Head Start, and the individualistic, compensatory, and redistributionist assumptions that underlaid it, were unimaginable in the heyday of the Iowa Child Welfare Research Station. To explore these interesting problems before the 1950s, before our own time, has been my purpose here.[5]

ACKNOWLEDGMENTS

In many respects writing a book is a lonely enterprise. Nevertheless, any author depends on the support and kindness of others, and I am no exception to that rule. Numerous individuals have made my work easier than it would have otherwise been. Above all, Merle Curti, David M. Katzman, and Alan I Marcus have made many important contributions to my work over the years. In addition, they have been extraordinary friends. Marvelous as friends and colleagues as well have been Achilles Avraamides, Richard S. Kirkendall, Richard Lowitt, George T. McJimsey, and Andrejs Plakans. The members of my department's faculty discussion group, the Vigilantes, presided over by my special friend and colleague Robert E. Schofield, have read various pieces of this book with a vigilant eye and a sharp tongue; I appreciate more than I can say their various ministrations and benefactions. Alberta E. Siegel, Bernadine Barr, and the late Robert R. Sears have discussed the history and methods of their science with me with brilliance and patience; I am profoundly in their debt. Lee Cronbach enlightened me on several important scientific matters at a memorable lunch. Merle Curti, Gerald N. Grob, Mary O. Furner, Ellen Condliffe Lagemann, David M. Katzman, Richard S. Kirkendall, and Karl-Tilman Winkler made perceptive comments on what to do with the book's penultimate version, and, along the way, Paul S. Boyer, Stanley Coben, Carl Degler, and V. Betty Smocovitis have offered excellent suggestions and stimulating critiques. My debts to the work of other scholars in a variety of fields are considerable, and are acknowledged, however imperfectly, in the notes. In particular did I benefit intellectually from the work of a most able psychologist and historian of his field, the late J. McVicker

Hunt, even when I disagreed with him. In addition, I have benefited from the comments and criticisms of scholars who have invited me, sometimes more than once, to give seminars and public lectures at their campuses, including the University of Akron, the University of California, Berkeley, the University of California, Davis, the University of Göttingen, the University of Hamburg, Heidelberg University, the University of Illinois, the University of Iowa, Oregon State University, Stanford University, and the University of Washington. I am grateful to my auditors and critics for their interest and constructive criticism. I remain responsible for my own errors, to be sure.

I have also received some material support, including a leave from Iowa State University, two summers of salary support from the History and Philosophy of Science Program, National Science Foundation, and six months as a visiting scholar at the Hoover Institution and at the Humanities Center, Stanford University. I wrote important sections of the manuscript while teaching as George Bancroft Professor of American History at the University of Göttingen, Federal Republic of Germany, and as a visiting scholar in the Department of History and the Humanities Research Institute at the University of California, Davis, and the Department of History, University of California, Berkeley. I am especially indebted to the late Paul S. Hanna and to Gerald A. Dorfman, Bliss A. Carnochan, Roland Marchand, Clarence Walker, and Hermann Wellenreuther for many kindnesses. At Iowa State University, the office of the vice-president for research and of the dean of the College of Sciences and Humanities graciously provided grants in aid of research in various archives every time I asked; the Rockefeller Archive Center generously supported three of my research trips there; and the National Endowment for the Humanities supported interviews with Robert R. Sears through a Travel-to-Collections grant.

I am also indebted to numerous archivists, above all to Earl M. Rogers, curator of manuscripts at the University of Iowa Libraries, without whose help much of the story of the Iowa Child Welfare Research Station could not have been properly or adequately documented; Dr. Joseph Ernst and Dr. Darwin H. Stapleton, the directors, and the entire staff at the Rockefeller Archive Center, who made my research in their staggeringly rich collections as easy as possible; Manfred Wasserman, then curator of modern manuscripts, Historical Division, National Library of Medicine, who facilitated many matters; Roxanne Nilan, Stanford University archivist, and her superlative staff and her successors, who helped with documents and the oral history interviews with Robert R. Sears. Thanks also go to university archivists at the University of

Akron, the University of California, Berkeley, the University of Cincinnati, the University of Illinois, the University of Kansas, the Massachusetts Institute of Technology, the University of Minnesota, the Ohio State University, Teachers College, Columbia University, Toronto University, and Yale University. I am also indebted to the archivists at the Archives for the History of American Psychology, University of Akron, the American Home Economics Association, in Washington, D.C., as well as Dr. David Saumweber, archivist, and his superlative staff at the National Academy of Sciences, also in the nation's capital, and the archivists of the Yivo Institute, New York, New York. Also, I am grateful to the staffs of the libraries of Iowa State University, Stanford University, Georg-August University, Göttingen, Federal Republic of Germany, and the University of California, Davis, for many indispensable courtesies and benisons.

I am grateful to many individuals and repositories for permission to quote from the unpublished correspondence and records of persons and institutions involved in the history of the Iowa Station. I would like to thank the University of Iowa Libraries, Iowa City, Iowa, for permission to quote from unpublished correspondence in the University of Iowa Presidential Correspondence, the records of the Iowa Child Welfare Research Station and its successor, the Institute of Child Behavior and Development, and the Faculty Vertical Files, and for permission as well to use the pictures in this book from the Kent Collection, University of Iowa Archives. I thank the State Historical Society of Iowa, Iowa City, Iowa, for permission to quote from the letters of Cora Bussey Hillis, and the Rockefeller Archive Center, North Tarrytown, New York, for permission to quote from the records of the Laura Spelman Rockefeller Memorial, the Spelman Fund, the General Education Board, and the Rockefeller Foundation. For permission to quote from the Lewis M. Terman papers, I thank the Stanford University Archives, Stanford, California; thanks also go to the Stanford University Archives for permission to quote from the papers of Robert R. Sears and to David O. Sears for permission to quote from unpublished statements and correspondence of Robert R. Sears. For permission to quote from the papers of Florence L. Goodenough, I thank the University of Minnesota Archives, Minneapolis, and Mr. Lyman Moore; and for permission to quote from the published letters of Kurt Lewin, I thank Miriam Lewin and the Archives of the History of American Psychology. The Yivo Institute for Jewish Research, New York, granted permission to quote from the correspondence of Horace M. Kallen and Kurt Lewin located at that repository; I also thank Mary Catherine Bateson and Ann Brownell Sloane of the Institute for

Intercultural Studies, New York, for permission to quote from an interview with Margaret Mead and Cornell University Libraries, Ithaca, New York, for permission to quote from a letter by Livingston Farrand.

Certain passages have appeared in print before in briefer form and with different emphases. I wish to thank the following editors and publishers for their permission to use these materials again: "Child-Saving in the Age of Professionalism, 1915–1930," in J. M. Hawes and N. Ray Hiner, eds., *American Childhood: A Research Guide and Historical Handbook* (Westport, Conn.: Greenwood Press, 1985), pp. 415–88; "Applied Science and Public Policy: The Ohio Bureau of Juvenile Research and the Scientific Prevention of Juvenile Delinquency, 1913–1930," in Michael M. Sokal, ed., *Psychological Testing in American Society, 1890–1930* (New Brunswick, N.J.: Rutgers University Press, 1985), pp. 158–94; "Behaviorism Revisited: Developmental Science, the Maturation Theory, and the Biological Basis of the Human Mind, 1920s–1950s," in Keith Benson, Jane Maienschein, and Ronald Rainger, eds., *The American Expansion of Biology* (New Brunswick, N.J.: Rutgers University Press, 1991), pp. 133–63; and "Establishing the Science of Nutrition at the United States Department of Agriculture: Ellen Swallow Richards and Her Allies," *Agricultural History* 64 (Spring 1990): 122–33.

BEFORE
HEAD START

In 1909, Ellen Key's *The Century of the Child* appeared in English translation in the United States. Initially published in her native Sweden in 1900, and then in Germany and other Western countries, Key's volume was an artifact of its time. She argued that the twentieth century was destined to be the century of the child and thus sounded the tocsin for an increasingly popular social movement—child welfare—that was gaining moral authority and political clout throughout Western Europe and the United States. She offered a prediction and a motto for the child welfare movement of her age. The new century would witness the dramatic transformation of the circumstances of child life; as they improved, the race would progress. The child was the key to the future. And by racial improvement, she clearly meant a combination of eugenics, or the biological improvement of the species, and euthenics, or the bettering of the circumstances of life.

Born in a tiny hamlet in northern Sweden in 1849, the daughter of a wealthy landowner and a countess, Ellen Karolina Sofia Key was educated at home. Upon attaining her majority she chose for herself the career of a single woman intellectual, itself a small but increasingly common decision among some women of certain social, economic, and cultural backgrounds in the late nineteenth and early twentieth centuries. She taught in schools and workingmen's institutes. She ran classes for women in history and literature. Soon she turned to writing. In the 1880s she began publishing works on women's property rights; in the mid-1890s she published noted books on such questions as the rights of women, the importance of motherhood, socialism and the individual, and related social questions.

She was not afraid to express views that offended bourgeois or middle-class cultural sensibilities. Thus she believed that neither Christianity nor the traditional family would necessarily aid child welfare and racial progress. In *The Century of the Child*, she attacked conventional expectations of marriage and sex roles. Ultimately, she predicted that in the century of the child, the state and society would sanction the breeding and the training of the best possible offspring from the most talented and competent parents in each generation. In the ensuing progress of the race, mothers in particular had a vital role to play, for example, in teaching kindergarten for their children at home. By turns liberal and conservative in her nostrums, she nevertheless believed that the child should be allowed to learn for herself, so that the "highest result of education is to bring the individual into contact with his own conscience."[1]

Many educated women in Europe and America probably agreed with Key's prediction. Indeed, women seemed poised in several Western countries to push for the expansion of the powers of the state to assist "racial" progress, most commonly through child welfare, or what we would term the welfare state as it applied to women, children, and the family. In that sense, Key was fully in the mainstream of her time. And her notions of breeding a better race—popular eugenics, one might say—were less unusual among turn-of-the-century female activists than might be imagined.

Certainly Ellen Key's message resonated in the United States. Fundamental to nineteenth-century American popular folk beliefs were such notions as faith in racial progress through education, better breeding, and various physical, psychic, and other remedies. The whole question of the nation's melting pot, and thus of the assimilation of the "new" or "different" groups in the national population, boiled down to the issue of whether certain races could uplift themselves to the American or white, Anglo-Saxon, Protestant, middle-class cultural standard, as those who controlled society, politics, economy, and culture defined these matters.

In that era, the notion that different groups or races of peoples competed against other races and the forces of nature in the struggle for existence and progress was as American as that proverbial apple pie. Those who believed in absolute racial hierarchies posited scenarios in which the group or groups they favored always won, whereas those who believed all races had equal potentialities for racial accomplishment spun out theories in which matters depended more on the present than on the past. No less an advocate of turn-of-the-century multiculturalism than the black historian and sociologist W. E. B. Du Bois used notions of group or race progress and development in his famous monograph, *The Philadelphia Negro* (1899), in which he argued that the black race could pioneer the industrial cities and make them humane and democratic just as the white race had transformed the frontier into settled civilization in the century just ending. Female activists and writers embraced notions of group struggle and process as well, including Ellen Church Semple and her work on the influence of geographical factors in American history, Jane Addams of Chicago's Hull House and her hopes for a pluralistic American culture, and Ellen Richards and her campaigns for an Americanized human nutrition science and cuisine that would assimilate immigrants into American culture.[2]

In the late nineteenth and early twentieth centuries, more and more American women chose for themselves the kind of career that Ellen Key had. The selection of a profession, whether as reformer, doctor, nurse, scientist, or writer, for example, involved at least a measure of independence from tradition and custom. Female professionalism took shape as a parallel to male professionalism, as numerous scholars have pointed. And, as Key's own life suggests, it made sense to many such women to establish jurisdictional boundaries for feminine professionalism and activism, in what one scholar has dubbed a female dominion for reform within which concern over children would be paramount.[3]

Child welfare prospered as an integral part of the larger progressive movement in early twentieth-century American politics. The lion's share of activists for child welfare were middle-class women who had the luxury of time to pursue a career in reform, either through a fortunate choice in marriage or in a profession. At bottom, champions of child welfare stressed the amelioration of the conditions of child life through the expansion of the powers of the state, whether local, state, or federal, including the delivery of new kinds of social services for children in need of better health, education, and living conditions; the regulation of certain aspects of child existence, notably child labor; and, scarcely less important, the protection of mothers from the exigencies of contemporary society and economy.

Child welfare reformers also saw these problems through the prism of group or racial analysis, not necessarily with the hard-bitten sentiments of the racial bigot, but certainly with the conviction that the national population was constituted of many distinct groups or races and that each presented unique problems and challenges to effective social policies and programs. The child-savers focused their consideration and attention on groups of children that struck them as problematic—whose members suffered from various afflictions the child savers considered deviations away from or below the norms of middle-class, white, Anglo-Saxon, Protestant culture, including dependency, delinquency, "feeblemindedness" (called, in a different age, mental retardation), alcoholism, sex crimes, and the like. In reality only a thin line separated those who campaigned for Americanization of immigrants and nonwhites via the public schools—a vital strain of the progressive education movement—and those in the child welfare movement who wrung their hands in anguish over the subnormal and abnormal types or groups of children, each with its own distinctive affliction, all needing attention and ministration.[4]

The child welfare reformers achieved some victories in reform politics. Like their fellow citizens, they had much faith in the curative powers of institutions. It was hardly surprising that their major triumphs lay in the establishment or extension of institutions, whereas the realities of institutional life sometimes illustrated the maxim that there was many a slip between the cup and the lip. The juvenile court was an excellent example of this point. Established initially in 1899 in Illinois, the juvenile court idea rapidly spread to almost every state in the union before 1920. Yet the court's overall purpose—to rescue problem children from the harshness of adult justice and corrections—was more often frustrated than accomplished. The ethnic, gender, and class identities of the "delinquents" sometimes triggered discriminatory, arbitrary, and even abusive treatment from the staff members in the courts and justice systems in many cities.[5]

Yet by the end of the 1910s, child welfare reformers could point with pride to a number of solid accomplishments. On the federal level, they had successfully worked for the convening of the first of numerous decennial White House conferences on child welfare, which President Theodore Roosevelt hosted in February 1909, as the White House Conference on Dependent Children; for the establishment of the Children's Bureau, which had a minuscule budget and staff but the power to recommend all manner of child welfare legislation to the Congress; the enactment of a federal child labor law, which succeeded, only to be overturned by the Supreme Court in 1918; and the passage, in 1921, of the Sheppard-Towner Maternity and Infancy Act, which gave the Children's Bureau a law to administer, thus expanding its potential authority far beyond social investigation. In that sense, the Sheppard-Towner Act was a crowning victory for child welfare reformers, even though its substance was limited to the dissemination of well-baby information to expectant and new working-class mothers. In the states and the cities, child welfare reformers could point to a number of institutional accomplishments, the best financed of which were the public schools, which stretched from kindergarten to graduate and professional schools at the state university level. A number of states enacted various child-saving laws that addressed, however imperfectly, such problems as wages and working conditions for women, regulation of child labor, and pensions for widows and mothers and that expanded the legal rights of mothers, facilitating divorce and child custody cases. The states also passed public health measures covering pure milk, the registration of vital statistics, the dissemination of health care information, and the regulation of pure food and drugs; they also tried to create programs to cure mental retardation, delinquency, poverty, and the use (or abuse) of tobacco and alcoholic beverages by minors. Finally, some states expanded educational and cultural opportunities for women and children.[6]

These were impressive political accomplishments for the child welfare movement. Yet their larger circumstances and possibilities were soon to be transformed, and radically so. Scattered groups of scientists—doctors, nutritionists, psychologists, educators, and others—began to argue that the Progressive-era promise to modernize, rationalize, and make scientific all aspects of life should be extended to the whole domain of child welfare and, indeed, of the family itself. Perhaps the most noted scientist of that prewar era pushing for a science of the child was the president of Clark University, psychologist G. Stanley Hall, who had trained most of the first generation of child psychologists in America, including Henry H. Goddard of the Vineland Training School for "feebleminded" persons of all ages; Lewis M. Terman of Stanford University, who, with Goddard, was the most important American translator of the Binet-Simon intelligence test, soon an important weapon in the child scientist's arsenal; and Arnold L. Gesell of Yale University, a child psychologist and pediatrician who mapped out the development of the infant and young child through his scientific work. Before World War I, these and other child scientists could not be said to have constituted a coherent, self-conscious, intellectual, and professional community. And to the extent that the child scientists had mattered at all to the child welfare reformers, it was as ancillary advisers on mundane technical matters, as writers of manuals on how to feed the baby or to educate the child, or how perhaps to serve as an officer in a local child welfare society or even to give a polished, erudite banquet address on the scientific aspects of child welfare. In any realistic assessment of the balance of power of these two groups brought together in uneasy alliance, the activists clearly dominated the scientists. Child welfare was, after all, a woman's issue. And to the extent that child science existed, even for some years after World War I, it was an applied science whose lay constituents insisted on the most direct and immediate solving of social problems through the means—rational, logical, and, above all, efficient—of science. How matters would change after the 1910s is the subject of this book.

CHAPTER ONE

A PROBLEM OF DEFINITION

In early May 1900, the National Congress of Mothers (NCM) held its first genuinely national convention, in Des Moines, Iowa. Heretofore, this organizational progenitor of the National Congress of Parents and Teachers had been merely a creation of the alignment of particular local forces in Washington, D.C. Its founding genius was Mrs. Theodore Birney, who had persuaded numerous like-minded women in and around the nation's capital to join with her in launching a national crusade for the welfare of America's children. As Mrs. Birney and her associates put it, child welfare meant the constant struggle to uplift and to ameliorate all aspects of child life—education, health, nutrition, moral behavior, and racial purity. Such an endeavor had two foci: saving the children and educating the parents.

By the time of the Des Moines meeting, the fourth in the NCM's history, Mrs. Birney had attracted the support of Phoebe Hearst, the wealthy California philanthropist, for all the apparatus of a national organization, including funds for a national headquarters, a newsletter, an office staff, supplies, not to mention the costs of the NCM's annual meetings. The NCM had affiliates in perhaps twenty states. But these organizations, like the national office, were still essentially paper institutions—the creation of little clutches of determined individuals, not masses of members, in each of the union's commonwealths.[1]

Approximately a thousand persons registered for the Des Moines meeting. Perhaps another five thousand attended the reception that the progressive Republican reform governor, Albert Baird Cummins, held at his mansion for the congress. And clearly the Des Moines meeting was the NCM's most remarkable yet. In terms of the numbers of persons who registered for the meeting, of those who became members, of those who attended its parties and receptions, and even of the number of resolute recommendations the delegates enacted during their deliberations, the Des Moines meeting was indeed an important, formative event in the NCM's metamorphosis from local to national organization. The Des Moines meeting was the first away from the NCM's locale of Washington, D.C.; having met outside of the nation's capital for the first time, the NCM could now claim to have the status of a national organization.[2]

Instrumental in this transformation was a Des Moines matron and club woman, Cora Bussey Hillis. It was she who had brought the NCM to Des Moines and made the affair so overwhelmingly successful. Forty-two years old when the NCM met in Des Moines, Hillis was an early convert to child welfare, an important thread within the larger progressive reform movement. She and her husband, attorney Issac Lea Hillis, had lived in a fashionable neighborhood near the state capitol on Des Moines's east side since the 1880s. Both husband and wife were highly influential in Des Moines's social and political circles. The Hillises were good friends of Governor Cummins, for example, who had treated the NCM to such a gala reception at the gubernatorial mansion. A founder of the Des Moines Women's Club in 1886, Cora at first was interested in the promotion of high culture. But several family tragedies, including the eventual deaths of three of her five children, propelled her toward the child welfare cause and fortified her intense lifelong involvement in it.[3]

It was as a member of the fledgling Iowa Child Study Society, founded in 1897, that Cora Hillis was first exposed to child welfare as a social cause. The society's two hundred members met monthly to discuss child welfare issues, most often from the standpoint of how scientific child study would guide social amelioration. That era's high priest of scientific child study was G. Stanley Hall, president of Clark University and a pioneer of academic psychology. Hall taught that child psychology was fundamentally child biology. In the static hierarchy that was nature, organic structure was the basis on which mental life or consciousness occurred in all species, from the lowliest paramecium to that species that was positioned at the apex of evolution's pyramid: humankind. What Hall did was graft onto the new naturalistic psychology the standard maxims—and canards—of contemporary biology as understood by scientists and educated laypersons. And standing in for him in person were two emissaries from the world of science in the Iowa society, University of Iowa psychologists George T. W. Patrick, one of Hall's early doctoral students, and Carl E. Seashore, a warm admirer and flourishing experimentalist researcher. They constantly brought the ideas of the new evolutionary natural sciences to the mothers, ministers, teachers, and school administrators who constituted most of the society's membership.[4]

Characteristically, Cora Hillis threw herself so vigorously into the society's affairs that she found herself appointed its delegate to the NCM's third annual meeting, in Washington, D.C., in February 1899, scarcely a year after she had joined the Iowa Society. "There I heard presented by experts the problems of the children," she later remembered. "Then and there I dedicated my life to this service. . . . I was a mother. I needed what the Congress could give me."[5] While at the NCM meeting, she invited its delegates to meet in Des Moines the next spring.[6] She returned home, with her prize so audaciously seized, to marshal local forces to make good on her offer. She obtained formal invitations to the NCM from the governor, leaders of prominent fraternal, benevolent, and civic organizations, and "many other prominent men and women of the state," thus overwhelming any potential opponents with efficient aggression.[7]

Even before the NCM met in Des Moines, then, Hillis had already created child study and child welfare as statewide issues, thus going far beyond the Iowa society, which had never been able to broadcast its message beyond its own members. Indeed, Hillis had done much to stitch together distinct organizational parts that added up to a larger whole, or system, dedicated to child study and welfare. In this way she placed herself and her interpretation of the issues on the stage of statewide politics, certainly a larger one than Des Moines offered.[8] And it was at the NCM's Des Moines meeting that she found her voice as a crusader for child welfare. Her thesis was pure Stanley Hall: The child is father to the man; prevention is more important than cure. "We have long tried to reform the old drunkard, to cure the old criminal, to put crutches under the palsied," she declared to the delegates that May. "We would better begin at the beginnings, before disease, and drink, and crime, and wrong living, have wrecked human life."[9]

Over the next several years Hillis fashioned a political machine for child welfare that would have been the envy of any political boss. She worked relentlessly to make the Iowa Congress of Mothers a full grass-roots organization in the classic manner: from the top down. Using her statewide contacts in the Iowa Woman's Christian Temperance Union (WCTU), she gathered sufficient support for county affiliate organizations of the Iowa Congress in most counties. She was especially successful among the unorganized women in the rural areas, where her message of racial purity, moral rectitude, dynamic physical growth, and good health resonated strongly, and where in any case she had few strong rivals in women's organizations.[10]

She also involved the Iowa Congress in state politics, in particular using her national contacts in the child welfare movement, such as Hanna Schoff of Philadelphia and Judge Ben B. Lindsey of Denver, to push for the notion of a juvenile court in Iowa. Schoff and Lindsey taught her that juvenile offenders needed a justice system tailored to their special needs as children, as a special group in the larger national population. It took two years for the legislature to pass the measure, and it was permissive only: it permitted cities to establish such courts but without state appropriation. In the midst of the juvenile-court campaign, she was forced to take a respite for several years.[11] Her second son died; three years later, her nine-year-old daughter also died, and her father became an invalid. Aside from her personal tragedies, she found that her strong personality aroused considerable antagonism and rivalry in the various organizations that constituted the child welfare movement of Iowa, including the Iowa Congress of Mothers, which voted her honorary president for life on the understanding that others would take over practical direction of the organization. These were depressing times indeed for her.[12]

In February 1908 she attended the International Congress of Child Welfare in Washington. There she decided to dedicate herself to an idea she had first had in 1901, that of a scientific research institute devoted to the study of children. She had first thought of it as an analogue to an agricultural experiment station, even discussing her idea with officials at the Iowa State College of Agriculture and Mechanic Arts in nearby Ames. With a pat on the head, they told her that the college's mission was pigs, not people, and politely sent her on her way. The state university, in Iowa City, was more appropriate, they told her, for there the curriculum included people—and even Plato. Ever persistent, she tried again in 1904, when a new president was installed at Ames. Again she was rebuffed. Now, in 1908, at the International Congress, she discussed her idea with delegates, who all encouraged her to establish one at the state university. She remembered that this was when she committed herself to the task.[13]

In the end, her efforts succeeded in April 1917, almost exactly nine years to the month after she began her campaign for a child welfare research station at the State University of Iowa. She met with university officials to outline her plans. "I am so overwhelmed by the terrible human waste, by the thousands of defective, imbecile, blind, deaf, dumb, epileptic, abnormal and criminal children and the enormous sums spent annually in caring for these people, with so little to stem the tide," she told university president George MacLean, an old friend from the Iowa Child Study Society. She stressed that she well understood "that old methods of education do not fit men and women for parenthood or teachers for training the plastic child mind and body." Yet despite her entreaties to MacLean, Governor Cummins, and many other leading Iowans, her efforts were absolutely stalled until the middle 1910s.[14]

Three general factors were responsible for this delay. One was state politics. Like her sister states in the Middle West, Iowa had a one-party political system, with the Republicans dominant. By 1909–10 the Iowa Republican party, like GOP forces across the nation, were polarized into progressive and conservative, or "standpat," factions. The Cummins progressives wanted to expand the powers of the state government at the expense of the counties and the courthouse rings of politicos who controlled them. And the progressives made the University of Iowa their pet, seeing in its hefty expansion during the Cummins years to a budgetary and institutional equal of the Iowa State College the possibilities of full-fledged research and professional schools for the state's professional classes just as the Ames institution had its curricula and research operations for its agricultural and "courthouse" constituencies. Hillis had welded the child study and welfare cause to the university, not the college. Yet now Cummins left the governorship for the U.S. Senate, and leadership within the progressive wing correspondingly suffered. For the next several years the Iowa GOP was rent with incessant infighting between the Cummins progressives and the "courthouse" conservatives, each faction insisting that it alone had the expertise to run state government in the most parsimonious, efficient, and businesslike manner without increasing taxes.[15]

The second problem was the women's organizations. As they attracted more members, there were more conflicts over leadership and ideology. The practical result was stalemate here also, insofar as a child welfare research station was concerned. Suffrage was the divisive issue within the women's organizations. Hillis was indifferent to it, believing, in good nineteenth-century fashion, that women had more influence in politics posing as disinterested moral guides than as self-serving representatives of interest groups. This conception of feminine participation in politics was increasingly challenged in the early twentieth century, especially in the 1910s, as the suffragists altered their tune to win support. Thus the Iowa Congress of Mothers was deeply divided over suffrage, whereas the Iowa Woman's Christian Temperance Union and the Iowa Federation of Women's Clubs were strongly committed to suffrage. Like every other woman in politics, Hillis had to walk a tightrope. And she had many enemies; she struck many as overbearing, wealthy, and a haughty, disagreeable Des Moines clubwoman who was unwilling to compromise.[16]

And there was the university itself. For most of its history the State University of Iowa (as it was then known) had been an undistinguished and poorly funded institution with but a handful of publishing scholars, and which drew most of its students from the university's surrounding hinterland. It was certainly weaker as an academic research enterprise than the Iowa State College in Ames. It had no special research institutes at all, such as the experiment stations for agriculture and engineering at Ames, and it had no champions whatsoever in state politics until the Cummins progressives took power in 1901. Its extension service could not rival that of the state college; thus its external constituencies were severely limited.

But more was involved. Hillis's strongest opponent within the university was psychologist Carl Seashore, dean of the graduate college, who was the university's de facto president. He wanted a clinic or hospital for problem children within the university medical college. In 1909, when university president George MacLean tried to corral faculty support for Hillis's cherished station for normal children, Seashore blocked him. Seashore wanted to expand his psychology department into the medical school to study problem children, which aroused considerable opposition among the medical professors, who resented Seashore's imperialistic plans and imperious demeanor. Hillis firmly insisted that any child welfare station focus on normal children. Neither Seashore nor Hillis would compromise with one another. Nor did MacLean have the power to break the stalemate.

It was only when the distinguished botanist Thomas H. MacBride became university president that circumstances within the university became favorable for a child welfare station. MacBride, one of the university's few distinguished scholars, became president in 1914 as a stopgap measure. He knew he could undertake no important new programmatic ventures. But he seized every available chance to expand facilities for original research at the university. He was not especially interested in a child welfare research station, partly because it struck him as beneath the dignity of a pure research university to have such a thing, but he realized that Hillis was too powerful in state politics to be openly denied. He worked out a compromise between Seashore and Hillis. He promised Seashore he would work in cooperation with the medical school for a psychopathic hospital, the campaign for which succeeded in 1919. In return, Seashore would support the idea of a child welfare research station.[17]

Yet problems remained before there could be a political movement for the station. Hillis knew that most members of the women's groups were interested in the study of abnormal and subnormal children, not normal children. She aligned her views with those of her constituency, championing a station for the many distinct types or groups of "defective" or "abnormal" children. Hillis believed science existed to solve human social problems. To the extent that she had a conception of science at all, it was related to obvious areas of application—in the human sciences, in such areas as agriculture, medicine, and education. She had no interest in funding esoteric research in subjects that did not help solve human problems. She understood that scientists had to develop theories to explain events and their causes, and that such theories were useful in working out their social applications. And she revered expertise in all manner of activities—hers and the scientists'. But she firmly believed that the station should do practical work, as she thought that agricultural experiment stations, medical clinics, and schools did. And her followers in the women's organizations seemed to agree with her on most of these points.[18]

By this time Seashore had goals different from Hillis's. He wanted the station to focus on the normal, not the subnormal or abnormal, child. In Seashore's case, this twist, like earlier ones with Hillis, can be explained in part by his incessant warfare with her—both were domineering, obstinate persons. But Seashore knew that he could never sell his faculty colleagues, let alone President MacBride, on a research institute for abnormal or subnormal children, especially as his colleagues and MacBride were leery of the idea. It had to be a "basic science" institute to feed the faculty's pride in being in different fields from their colleagues at Iowa State College in Ames and in being in the same fields of knowledge as the faculty at such well-established universities as Harvard, Michigan, and Wisconsin. They hoped this would hoist the prestige of their struggling, underfunded, fourth-rate university.

Seashore had no desire whatsoever to play midwife to an institute for social amelioration. Nor, for that matter, did he want to echo Hillis and the women's groups. So he changed his tune. Now he argued for an institute that would probe the mysteries of child and adult development set within the theoretical framework of evolutionary natural science. Now that "abnormal children" would be studied in the proposed psychopathic hospital, he wanted the station's staff to probe the mysteries and insights that great scientists of body and mind had suggested since the publication of Charles Darwin's *Origin of Species* (1859). Now that "abnormal" and "subnormal" persons would be studied in the proposed psychopathic hospital, Seashore wanted the child research station's staff to study "basic science," whatever that might be; on these matters, Seashore was curiously inarticulate, perhaps because "basic science" was a new construct in the early twentieth century as technical knowledge began to crystallize into specialized disciplines in such fields as the useful arts, or technology, agriculture, and the other practical disciplines of the nineteenth century. It was clear, however, that Seashore wanted a child research institute that would do first-rate research and thus make his department and his university respected and famous in American science. In all of these grand hopes MacBride heartily agreed, and Seashore and Hillis, on the other hand, continued to argue with one another, thus lending their struggle of wills a substantive character. No longer was it merely that each played games to dominate the other.[19]

In late 1914 the wrangling over goals between Hillis and Seashore became public. Hillis argued for a model home in which two "defective" children from each of Iowa's ninety-nine counties would be raised and studied by the station's staff under controlled scientific conditions. Seashore was appalled by this technocratic anticipation of B. F. Skinner's *Walden Two* (1948) for several reasons, not the least of which was that it would not be an institution that he wanted to or even could control. He finessed the issue, however, by telling Hillis that her idea that the legislature would appropriate $100,000 annually for the station would mean that there would be enough funding for all priorities, basic and applied. He told her that the research station—meaning several research professorships that carried no teaching duties per se—came before her model home. Reluctantly she agreed. She had no choice; there would be no station at all if Seashore and MacBride did not support it before the legislature. But she fought back. She told them that the Iowa Woman's Christian Temperance Union would support the campaign only on her ideological terms, which was hardly the case, but neither Seashore nor MacBride knew that. Clearly, much would depend on how matters turned out, and what the balance of forces was when the station became a reality.[20]

The campaign that Hillis commanded in 1915 for the station was remarkable chiefly for its high public visibility. Together with her allies and Seashore she formed a vertically integrated statewide organization to convince the legislature to approve the research station and appropriate $100,000 per year for its support. She became the field marshal of the organization's many distinct constituencies. She sent out letters, even Christmas cards, to appropriate civic, business, and political leaders. She wheedled pledges from legislators, mayors, and other politicians. She plotted and schemed with legislative leaders over timing the bill's introduction and related tactical matters. And she enlisted the public support of the allied women's organizations, and of a number of news-papers, including the progressive Republican *Des Moines Register and Leader*, Iowa's largest-circulation daily. Probably her rhetoric jangled the nerves of some rural interests, as when she insisted that Iowa could pay as much for research on children as it did on cattle, hogs, and crops.[21] At a meeting with Hillis in Des Moines, Seashore repeated her litany, insisting that "facts, facts, facts about the child is to be the slogan of this child welfare campaign," charg-ing that "the question is, is the Iowa child as of great value as Iowa crops and Iowa cattle?"[22]

Hillis and Seashore buried their differences for the duration. They worked very hard behind the scenes to obtain pledges from legislators for the bill. Essentially the progressive statehouse Republicans supported the measure; they liked the notion of expanding the powers of the state as a general proposi-tion, and the idea of using modern, up-to-date science to study the child and social problems sounded very much with the times. The conservative, or "courthouse," Republicans—and their analogues in the Democratic party—were not opposed to the scientific study of the child per se so much as unwilling to allocate public funds for it through the state, thus revealing where the actual locus of conflict between these warring factions resided. Outright opposition to the notion of using science or some other kind of expertise was rare; one rural Catholic Democratic legislator did so publicly, saying that his own experience with raising a large family showed that this newfangled science, as distinct from centuries-honored tradition, was unnecessary, therefore trying to disabuse his colleagues of the notion of having the taxpayers fund it.[23]

Yet the effort failed in the 1915 legislative session. The research station did not, and never did, command much importance to most legislators, compared with such issues as funding the state highway commission or enacting state-wide prohibition of woman suffrage. Courthouse and statehouse politicians in both houses fought over these other issues. In 1915 highways were the big issue. The statehouse Republicans and their allies, the liberal Democrats, wished to expand the powers of the state highway commission so as to fund and build a system of state roads that would rival or even overshadow the county roads that the courthouse rings and their allies in local business communities favored. Millions of dollars in public monies hung in the balance, and attracted the interest of courthouse politicians and contractors as honey would bees. The research station had wide but superficial backing. Furthermore, vitriolic in-fighting between the university's champions and those of the agricultural col-lege broke out on a host of funding issues apart from the research station. The station proposal was doomed almost from the start. It became a hostage to other issues. The statehouse progressives dominated the senate. Hence the real battle came in the house, where the courthouse conservatives were strong. The proposal failed to win the necessary votes for passage. Its opponents initially insisted that the appropriation be cut from $100,000 to $25,000 per year, as a condition of their support. When the bill's supporters agreed, its opponents then renewed their attack, insisting that it was wrong to pay professors only to do research. And they hooted at the idea that the taxpayers should have to pay for any research on humans beyond research in a medical school. After the house vote, Hillis single-handedly engineered the bill's reconsideration. That failed. She did win more than enough pledges for its passage in the next session, two years hence, however.[24]

For Hillis and Seashore the next two years were difficult. Hillis had to extinguish brush fires within the women's organizations, as, for example, when some of her enemies in the Iowa Congress of Mothers tried to turn the campaign for the research station into one for an annual statewide series of baby health contests. By lining up powerful support within the Iowa Woman's Christian Temperance Union, always an organization in which she had great influence, Hillis was able to quash this and other rebellions against her queenly authority. And Seashore, the champion of "pure" scientific research, had difficulty in persuading faculty not to criticize the research station idea as demeaning to the university's lofty commitment to disinterested scientific and scholarly research. He won an ace in the hole with the appointment in 1916 of MacBride's successor as university president, Walter A. Jessup. A practical man and an educator, Jessup thoroughly embraced the notion of the public university as a service institution to the multiple constituencies of the state rather than a group of disinterested "basic science" researchers.[25]

The 1916 elections appeared a disaster for the research station proposal. On most important issues, the progressives lost to the conservatives in both the primary and the general elections. Thus the woman suffrage amendment to the state constitution lost narrowly, and most nominations in the primaries seemed to go to the conservatives, as when Lieutenant Governor William L. Harding, an avowed champion of courthouse interests and opponent of the state highway commission, easily trounced two progressive contenders for the Republican governor's nomination. And this pattern could be seen in races for the legislature as well. Harding also handily defeated his Democratic opponent, E. T. Meredith, Des Moines entrepreneur and publisher of *Successful Farming*, in the November general election. Meredith agreed with the progressive statehouse Republicans on most issues. The conservatives had seemingly won a complete victory.[26]

Hillis took an entirely different tack for the 1917 assembly battle. "We had better not say anything until we know 'who's who,'" she told Seashore before the elections. Thus she became a behind-the-scenes hustler, cajoler, and broker, using her rural allies in the WCTU and urban allies in the Iowa Federation of Women's Clubs to line up support among legislators regardless of their ideological affiliation. She made sure that there was a brief public campaign in a few newspapers. But in these and all other efforts she cut the research station issue loose from its progressive identity. Quite correctly, she understood that her greatest advantage was the research station's relative unimportance and irrelevance to most legislators. It was crucial to wait until the solons had exhausted themselves with larger matters, and then ram the bill through. And indeed, the whole agenda of the progressives in both parties was on the table in 1917. They fought with the courthouse conservatives over whether to return to the counties from the state such functions as building highways and printing state documents, among others; these involved millions of dollars in contracts for various entrepreneurial interests, including those who built roads or printed government notices in their newspapers or whose professional or business interests were regulated by the state, as in food processing or insurance. By comparison, a piddling $25,000 annual appropriation for a research facility for children seemed small potatoes indeed.[27]

To the session's midpoint, when the legislators took a week off to confer with their constituents, the courthouse factions appeared triumphant, especially in the lower house. But when the solons returned, the statehouse forces, dominant in the senate, enacted measures to safeguard the contested state offices and agencies and a bill that provided vast new monies for the state highway commission to spend in conjunction with the counties on state and county roads. Senators also enacted a whopping 41 percent increase in funds for the university and the agricultural college. The courthouse leaders in the house and senate speedily accepted the proffered olive branch. Obviously, money was a universal language. A few days later the bill establishing the station passed the lower house by a vote of seventy-nine to six and a unanimous vote in the upper one. Hillis's behind-the-scenes horse-trading had succeeded brilliantly.[28]

The law charged this, the first research institute in North America devoted entirely to the study of normal children, with three statutory responsibilities. First, its staff was to conduct scientific research on normal children. Second, its faculty was to train professionals in the new field of child welfare, which meant they would teach only graduate students. Third, its staff had the responsibility of disseminating the results of their research, and presumably that of other researchers elsewhere, to the public. The organization was given the name of the Iowa Child Welfare Research Station and located at the state university in Iowa City. Its director was a powerful officer within the university's structure, with the de facto status of a dean, for the director reported directly to the president. The annual appropriation was but $25,000, not $100,000, which meant that Seashore, not Hillis, had won, for there would be no model home, no demonstrations, and none of the other public extravaganzas Hillis so cherished. Indeed, there was nothing in the bill's language or provisions that had Hillis's imprint, save the generalized idea of a child research institute, which was no small contribution in and of itself. The station owed its existence to Hillis. She had fought for the idea for years. It was she, not the university professors, who got the bill enacted in the Iowa General Assembly. And she still had powerful allies in the women's organizations, who were the station's only important lay constituents. Whether she would be able to direct the station's development and influence its policies remained unclear, for nothing along these lines had happened as yet. In reality, Seashore now had a large opportunity to shape the station as he saw fit, partly through his own machinations, and partly because of the station's essential character as an academic and scientific institution. It would be several years, however, before that opportunity would be fully realized.[29]

The preponderance of scientific work on children, or, as it was more commonly known, child study, between the late nineteenth century and World War I focused on abnormal or subnormal children. Thus in that important sense, the Iowa station as Seashore had redefined it addressed the underlying issues of an era or a future that had not yet arrived, rather than those of the present and the past that Hillis conceptualized in her emphasis on the subnormal or defective types of children. Hillis's emphases mirrored late nineteenth- and early twentieth-century reformist child-saving and, ultimately, a taxonomy of reality that assumed the national population to be constituted of a hierarchy of distinct *groups*, each typified by a unique blend of characteristics. Seashore had pre-science. He pointed toward child study's future, and, in particular, to its new organizing conception, the normal child. To be sure, the normal child in Seashore's hands was a primitive construct, meaning only children of normal, middle-class Americans who had neither special abilities nor disabilities. But the notion of the normal child could be expanded deeply and applied widely.

And the political and cultural implications of the idea of the normal child could encourage, if not glorify, the study of conformity and utter conventionality in children—and, therefore, in adults.

The common topics of child study, old and new, were physical growth and child psychology. All child researchers, whether they studied normal children or not, took certain assumptions about natural and social reality for granted. In turn, these assumptions were drawn from the larger American culture. They assumed that the national population was divided into a hierarchical series of groups, or types, some superior to others, with the native-born whites of Anglo-Saxon Protestant ancestry at the pyramid's top. Within each group, or type, like begat like. In turn, variations among groups were more important than variations among individuals within a group. The rediscovery of Mendel's laws of heredity around 1900, and the manner in which scientists and champions of science commonly interpreted them, reinforced this larger model of natural and social reality.

The key to social perception and explanation in the later nineteenth and early twentieth centuries was the importance of group membership for the individual and of the relationships of the various groups in the population to one another. Thus it made sense for those interested in children to divide them into different types or groups—the dependent, the delinquent, the immoral, the feebleminded, the psychotic, and so on. This kind of group taxonomy was pervasive in American culture during this era, as in references to the different types or groups of children. Some who studied children attributed the causes of group differentiation to heredity, others to environment, just as was the practice for discussion and explanation of groups in the national population more generally. Whether nature or nurture was primarily responsible for the differential evolution of types, the causes of the present taxonomy resided entirely in the past. Put another way, the causes of the present lay in the past—a profoundly historical notion of natural and social reality.[30]

For scientists interested in human nature and conduct as understood through the laws of evolutionary natural science, this theory placed a great emphasis upon the structure of the organism and of the type or group to which it belonged. Thus the founders of American physiological psychology had stressed the neurophysiological structure of the human species and its evolution from those of the lower animals. William James's *Principles of Psychology* (1890) set the intellectual framework for that nascent discipline for several decades. James shackled the individual to the standard forces of evolutionary natural science, heredity, and environment, and assumed that an adequate social psychology was contained in the natural history of the individual's neu-rophysiological development because the individual belonged to a type that bred true. Humans did develop habits from their innate instincts, and these were responsive to life experiences, but they were usually formed rapidly in childhood.[31] For some years, those who wrote about the psychology of the normal child followed James's example. E. A. Kirkpatrick published an early textbook, *Fundamentals of Child Study* (1903), which had more than a dozen printings in prewar America. Kirkpatrick was a much revered and respected professor of child pedagogy. He insisted that the processes of child and human development were those of the working out of the various instincts of the race, and of the development of patterns of habits and consciousness based evolved mental structure.[32]

It was probably G. Stanley Hall of Clark University who did the most of any scientist in late nineteenth- or early twentieth-century America to promote the scientific study of the child. Hall was a pioneer of the infant science of experi-mental psychology. As president of Clark and professor of psychology, Hall was in a strategic position to push his own ideas and to cultivate lay constitu-ents. By the early 1900s he had trained a growing number of doctoral candi-dates who went on to take appointments in chairs of educational psychology or pedagogy in various normal schools or public colleges and universities. Hall was well known in the women's clubs as an authoritative speaker on child study. He had given a key address at NCM's first annual convention in Washington, D.C., in 1897;[33] indeed, his address at the 1906 Saint Louis Congress of Arts and Sciences had inspired Cora B. Hillis to become a full-fledged champion of child welfare.

Hall's message was ultimately biological and evolutionary in character. It had two general themes. One was that physical development was the basis of sound mental development. Thus he stressed proper health, growth, diet, and the like. He called for studies of the physical growth of children, of their health in the public schools, and of their muscular development. Above all, he was concerned to identify the norms or standards of development and of capacity of mental powers and physical strength. His conceptions of health and develop-ment as physical led to his conceptions of mental health, which likewise had a biological grounding.

The other general theme of Hallian scientific child study revolved around the mental, emotional, and psychological aspects of child behavior. Here too he was concerned with normality, with standards and norms of behavior. Hall's notions about psychology were thoroughly entrenched within contemporary biological theory. Using the hoary recapitulation theory from nineteenth-century biology, Hall insisted that the individual as embryo, child, and adult passed through the sequences of evolution itself, from the forms of the simplest species to the most complex ones at the apex of the evolutionary pyramid. Hall shared with other contemporary psychologists the belief that the causes of human thought and conduct were psychobiological rather than cultural, and he argued that the child was father to the man. His genetic or developmental psychology presumed an evolutionary hierarchy for the history and development of a mind that passed through definite stages, including those of the various animal species, then the primitive races, then the child, the woman, and finally the man, of the superior white race. Each benchmark constituted a distinct phase in psychic evolution. From his point of view, such phenomena as insanity or defect mattered too, for the abnormal or the subnormal mind could instruct us in the normal patterns of growth and development. Thus it was important to study diseased and defective minds. They would show the scientist how and why nature went off the straight and narrow path of normality.

In this emphasis, Hall connected powerfully with those middle-class, white, Anglo-Saxon, Protestant Americans who were concerned with the "submerged tenth" or the "other half" of turn-of-the-century American society, those individuals or types of individuals or groups whose members were criminals, delinquents, dependents, alcoholics, prostitutes, mental defectives, the insane, and so on. And most workers in the field followed Hall's powerful, compelling message.[34] In the pictures of natural and social reality that they borrowed from the larger American culture and from the culture of science, the child psychologists also assumed that natural and social reality was hard, indeed three-dimensional, and this was the way to visualize psychological structure. Their notions of causation were mechanical. They thought of causal factors as binary opposites, such as heredity and environment.[35]

All who wrote about child psychology and normal children knew one obvious fact: children grew. It was their task to figure out how and why growth occurred. In the early 1900s, few theories had been developed beyond those of unfolding development "explained" by appeals to historically oriented schemes of biological and psychological evolution. There was awareness that there were distinct growth processes in the child. Thus one of Hall's most industrious doctoral students, Lewis M. Terman, took as a research problem precocity or prematuration in the normal child. Precocity was troublesome, for it meant unwholesome development. Terman scoured the European and American literature on the problem. He concluded that there were many different processes of development and growth in the normal child that had to be kept in balance if the child were to become the normal type. His own research on the problem convinced him that, as a general rule, to the age of ten years, the child should be far more occupied with the physical, not the mental, aspects of his or her existence, in order to encourage the volitional powers before puberty. Such activity was indispensable, for only "a strong will can guide the human bark through the storm and stress of adolescence."[36] Terman did more than call for a static and symmetrical balance of the many different processes of growth in the child. In his doctoral dissertation he took up the problem of mental capacity and how to measure it. He summarized the results of his many tests of fourteen boys, seven bright, the others decidedly not, by saying that psychology now must follow biology's example and "become increasingly dynamic" in its orientation. Structure might well be less important than function. Yet Terman did not throw structure out of consideration. He concluded, rather, that any science of the child should emphasize the functions that different structures permitted; for example, it was his "impression" that native endowment was more important than training as a determinant of the intellectual rank of the boys in his study.[37] As another of Hall's students, Henry H. Goddard, put it in an address before the American Philosophical Society in 1912, mental traits were inherited, according to the ratios announced by Gregor Mendel. Goddard was one of the rising American researchers on children. He was director of psychological research at the Vineland Training School, an institution for feebleminded persons in Vineland, New Jersey.[38]

By the early twentieth century, researchers interested in children had available three distinct techniques of measuring growth in children. The oldest and most familiar was the measurement of physical growth. Customarily, doctors and anthropologists did this kind of investigation. In the late nineteenth century, for example, a Massachusetts physician, Henry Pickering Bowditch, studied growth in the height and weight of almost 25,000 children in the Boston area for the Massachusetts Board of Health. In his study he attempted to establish different average measurements for different "nationalities"—or groups—in the sample.[39] Columbia University anthropologist Franz Boas made numerous contributions to the improvement of technique and statistical measurement. He also worked on problems related to growth and development. In one study he argued that a child's developmental stage at a given point in time depended chiefly upon the factors which caused acceleration (or retardation) of the whole body, so that all measurements would accelerate or lag in relationship to the norms, if the individual deviated from the norms. In a later and better-

known study, Boas argued that the head forms of second-generation immigrants more closely approximated the head-form measurements of native-born
Americans than of subjects of their parents' countries.[40]

Bowditch and Boas addressed the problem of physical development from
the same general perspective. They asked whether there were specific physical
types—or groups—in the larger national population. Bowditch believed a hierarchical taxonomy of such groups existed; the traits of each group were stable;
and each group or type had a distinctive array of characteristics. Historians
correctly have interpreted Boas's conclusions as suggesting he did not believe in
a hierarchy of races, that he did not view the characteristics of a group as fixed,
and that he used his findings to undercut contemporary scientific and popular
racism. It also was true that Boas's view of physical anthropology and human
development was dynamic and functional, rather than static and "formalistic."[41] Yet the Boas of 1904 or 1911 was not the Boas of a later era. In the early
1900s he perceived the national population as comprised of different groups.
For Boas, *group* and *type* were virtually synonymous terms. As was characteristic of that age, he formulated the problem of causation in a binary fashion, that
is, environment versus heredity. And his notions of body build, physique,
indeed of physical reality itself, were literally three-dimensional, rather than
multidimensional. Thus he stressed that second-generation immigrants approached a common American type and had a uniform American face. His
ultimate taxonomy of natural and social reality differed little from Bowditch's
or others' of that time.

A newer technique of measuring growth in children was the scaled mental
test. Henry H. Goddard and Lewis M. Terman adapted Alfred Binet's measuring scale for American children. In the 1910s they tried it out on various
populations or groups in America and not only translated it into English but
transformed it into an instrument with purposes different from those Binet
intended. Binet had developed the device as a consultant for the Parisian
school system as a way of measuring how prepared or unprepared working-
class children were to be integrated into the public schools, whose pupils to this
point had all come from the middle and upper classes. The Binet test was a test
of how *educationally* backward children were and whether they needed compensatory education before being placed in the schools.

It is noteworthy that the Binet test was thoroughly an artifact of its time.
Binet too thought that individuals existed only as members of the groups to
which they "belonged" in nature and society, just as Terman, Goddard, and
Hall did. This was manifest in the very construction of the Binet test itself. The

test, as both Binet and his American interpreters designed and used it, was predicated on the assumption that individuals existed only as members of biological and cultural groups in the larger population. Binet and his collaborator, Theodore Simon, assumed that for any chronological age represented in their mental scale, the questions were "standardized," or selected, so that one-fourth of the examinees for that age group would fail because of stupidity, one-half would pass because they had normal intelligence, and the highest one-fourth would score above the average because of their superior intelligence. In all such examinations, whether given to *individuals* one at a time, as with the Binet test, or to *groups* of persons, as with the tests given to recruits in the U.S. Army in World War I, the assumption remained the same: individuals could be classified according to particular groups (and, thus, mental levels) to which they naturally belonged. Mean IQs were calculated for such groups and remained highly constant on retesting—purely as the result of the way the tests were constructed and their results were derived and interpreted. Nevertheless, researchers now had apparent evidence, according to the way reality was understood in that age, that the IQs of individuals were fixed, when all they had proved was that the tests would reproduce the same approximate group means when repeated. Here the assumption that individuals existed only in groups powerfully shaped the Binet test—and, on a practical level, made it a successful instrument for its time.

Binet considered his technique a tool to help uplift children from one social class to another. He did not regard intelligence as a fixed trait in an individual or believe that a narrow range of mentality predetermined the IQs of all individuals within a particular biocultural group in the population. His American followers, however, thought of the Binet test as a device that would distinguish differential levels of innate intelligence among groups, as well as between individuals in particular groups. They conceived of these measurements as reflections of group characteristics, even when they claimed to be measuring the differences among individuals. By standardizing the Binet test first upon normal children, they established a typology of American child intelligence. Such normal children were also of middle-class background and northwestern European ancestry—they belonged to one or more groups in the national population. Hence, in the hands of the Americans, Binet's diagnostic device, designed to uplift individuals and break down artificial social class barriers, and to use public education to do so, became a rather different social and psychological technology. It became an instrument based squarely on the assumption of *group* determinism. Ultimately, Goddard was interested in defining levels of mental retardation—"feeblemindedness" in contemporary parlance—and Terman was concerned with normal and above-normal children. They thus went about their tasks somewhat differently and devised tests that differed technically. Their general procedure was the same, however. They interpreted the Gaussian bell-shaped curve to mean that there was a natural hierarchy that would be borne out by the distribution of what was measured. Then they employed the Gaussian expectation of normal or average to define and adjust the difficulty of the several questions for each chronological age.

In the event, Goddard's scale was the first published, and it did not survive more than a few years because it could not make what psychologists thought were justifiable discriminations among levels of intelligence above the chronological age of twelve. Terman's test, developed over several years, became known as the Stanford-Binet, and, as such, was one of the most widely used and well-known American intelligence or mental tests. It was directed toward making discriminations of mental levels of "normal" children up to a chronological age of sixteen years. In Terman's hands, and in those of the growing number of specialists in psychometrics throughout the country, it became a social technique that demonstrated, to those who believed in it, that innate intelligence, the presumptive attribute so measured, was distributed in essentially infinite gradations up and down a hierarchical pyramid, from absolute imbecility to absolute genius, with the great mass of individuals (née types or groups) clustered within a predefined range of intellectual "normality." In a very real sense, the shift from Goddard's focus on the subnormal minds to Terman's emphasis on normal and above-normal minds was indicative of the new emphasis on the normal child which the Iowa station so well represented.[42]

The third method of measuring growth in children was the science of human nutrition, which had been first developed in Europe and America in the later nineteenth century. Nutritionists then were commonly physiologists or biochemists, or both, with considerable training in analytic chemistry. They were interested, broadly speaking, in why particular species grew, what combinations of foods made them grow normally, and in how to make them grow soundly in the most efficient manner possible. Some were interested in animal nutrition and marketed themselves as contributors to the new field of agricultural science; they fed all manner of foodstuffs, including materials we would classify today as inedible (at least by humans), to the various species of livestock in a campaign to find the least expensive and most nutritious typical foods that would contribute to animal growth and, thus, the largest return on the owner's investment. By the early 1900s this "racial" nutritional work for animals had reached a dead end and disappeared for a generation.

But "racial" human nutrition studies, which such pioneers as Max Rubner at Munich and W. O. Atwater at Wesleyan or Ellen Richards at the Massachusetts Institute of Technology developed in the 1880s and 1890s, continued into the new century, until the 1910s. Indeed, Atwater was able, through his machinations at the United States Office of Experiment Stations in the Department of Agriculture, to stimulate and have underwritten a national effort to collect information, known as "dietaries," on the consumption of various foods by particular ethnic and racial groups in the American population, all to discover what the least expensive and most efficient typical diet was for each "race" in the American population, so that these groups would stop spending lavishly on foodstuffs and be able to live on the kinds of wages the workers and peasants of Europe did. Thus would American capitalism be rescued from the avarice and greed of American workers, Atwater insisted; Richards simply thought it appropriate to Americanize the immigrants through the use of an "American" diet.[43]

By the 1910s the human racial nutrition movement had collapsed, in no small measure because, of its most powerful leaders, Atwater was dead (of stomach cancer) and Richards, offended by Atwater's success in isolating her and other women chemists from the human nutrition campaign, had gone on to found home economics as a new professional field for women. Certainly, belief in innate racial differences had not suddenly evaporated among American citizens. In the new decade there was an attempt to place human nutrition studies on a new basis. Those who were most closely associated with this new science were commonly biochemists attached to medical schools or to land grant colleges with agricultural experiment stations. A major architect was E. V. McCollum. What McCollum and his professional colleagues attempted to do was to redefine the organism, human or animal, as a machine that consumed fuel. For them the vital question became what specific chemical ingredients combined to produce the most efficient fuel. Notions of efficiency and growth underwent some changes from the original tests at the University of Wisconsin Experiment Station in 1906 to the late teens and early twenties, by which time McCollum was a professor at Johns Hopkins University. But McCollum and his colleagues provided a method—the measurement of growth—as well as an experimental animal, the white rat, and a search for the right combination of substances that would fuel maximum growth. As had Rubner, Atwater, and Richards, scientists in this field assumed that there were distinct groups in the population, and that individuals did not exist apart from the groups to which they "belonged" naturally and culturally. The levels of discourse and methods in this field were somewhat alien to the majority of child scientists, who were most often psychologists, however. Clearly, by the early twenties, the science of nutrition had yielded the discovery of a number of growth-causing substances, first known as "vitamines," later simply as vitamins, and workers had begun to identify substances, whether singly or in combination, which accelerated or retarded growth. Ultimately acceleration and retardation were relative terms; there was an implied standard of normal growth and development through stages.[44]

Methods and procedures were one problem. Definitions and conceptions were quite another, although in the grand scheme of things, they were obviously related and interdependent. To about 1910 most who called themselves students of the child—perhaps *scientist* was too strong a word for some of them—stressed the subnormal and the abnormal child as objects of investigation and interpretation and ignored the normal child. At the same time, the traditional experimental psychologists who held professorships in the nation's major universities and colleges still emphasized adult psychology—the states of consciousness of the normal adult human mind. Only with the publication of British psychologist William McDougall's *Introduction to Social Psychology* (1908) did the interests of traditional psychologists shift away from the adult mind. McDougall popularized the instinct theory as human social psychology, according to which human institutions and established patterns of behavior could be traced back to instincts that had been useful in the struggle for existence in the evolution of the race. For McDougall, instincts possessed an inherited emotional core for the individual as well as for the group or race; indeed, such innate equipment was a part of the group's inheritance. Although he wrote from a slightly different point of view than did Hall—one that was less out of date in biological circles—McDougall helped encourage American psychologists to turn to genetic psychology, if not with an explicit derivation from Hall's rather overly clever and unscholarly schemes, then certainly with a new attention to those "types" in the grand scheme of human evolution that Hall had highlighted: animals and children.[45]

Thus, when younger scientists in the field began discussing the normal child within the context of the evolution of the human mind from its animal precedents, as they began to do in the 1910s, they sent a signal that Hallian genetic psychology was being incorporated into mainstream academic psychology. These younger scientists cast aside the recapitulation theory, and other such elements of nineteenth-century biological theory that Hall had grafted onto his notions about the evolution of mind, in the new definitions and conceptions of the field that they were working out in that decade. Thus consider the definitions offered by Arnold Gesell and Bird T. Baldwin, later among the most eminent of the first generation of child psychologists in America. Gesell founded an important clinic at Yale, and Baldwin was the Iowa station's first director.[46]

In 1912 Gesell, with his wife, Beatrice Chandler Gesell, published a textbook, *The Normal Child and Primary Education*, in which they attempted to reconcile various contemporary currents of thought on the subject. They defined the normal child in two ways, one familiar, the other novel. The normal child could be called a type, they insisted, even though "at present we have more adequate pictures of types of subnormality than we have of normality." Those who are normal, are so; and most children were normal. This simple, uncomplicated statement noted that there were various types of children. Most types fell into the abnormal or subnormal categories, and there was but one type of normal child, which included most children.

The other definition that the Gesells fashioned outlined a research agenda. The normal child, they declared, should approximate the "ideal" rather than the average, meaning that "the higher and stronger norm of normality the better for the race." The ideal child was that individual who lived up to the highest potentiality of his group or type. In the language of the population geneticist (who did not yet exist, of course), the Gesells had defined a typological rather than a quantitative notion of the normal child. Average was not sufficient. Each child should develop to the utmost. This was, of course, a very convenient assumption for professionals engaged in the training of elementary school teachers, since the achievement of the ideal as distinct from the average could be accomplished only by a professional caste—the schoolteacher. What was the content of a science of the normal child? Here the Gesells fell back upon the traditions of academic psychology and the kind of child psychology that G. Stanley Hall had preached. "The present is born of the past and the past abides in the present, and to understand the present we must appreciate the past," they declared, thus insisting upon a profoundly historical and evolutionary framework from which to define any type of child, normal or not.[47] After discussing the theory of evolution, including the evolution of minds and instincts, the Gesells examined those various activities in which young children could be expected to participate at elementary school, including drawing, dramatic expression, reading, handwriting, outdoor play, speech, and the like, and showed how the primary teacher could bring out in each child the utmost expression of the appropriate instinct for each activity. Put another way, the Gesells looked back from the psychology current in 1912 for the content of child science. Theirs was a historical conception of development, in which the causes of the present were in the past, and in which human development unfolded as the consequence of the evolutionary structures of body and mind.[48]

Bird T. Baldwin, a professor of psychology at Swarthmore College, offered a transitional definition of the normal child. Unlike the Gesells, his point of view was dynamic and quantitative, rather than typological or idealistic. In 1914 he published a general summary of his intensive research on growth in normal children. Ultimately, Baldwin was interested in understanding the relationship between physical and mental growth in normal children. His research program was cast in terms of a binary formulation. Yet his definition of the normal child was hardly so constricted. Any child has five parallel, or interrelated, ages, Baldwin insisted: a chronological age, signifying the span of life; a physiological age, indicating stages of physical growth and maturity; a mental age, manifesting the development of certain instincts, capacities, and mental traits; a pedagogical age, denoting school progress; and a moral age, meaning normal moral and religious judgments. In a normal child, he declared, all these ages balanced one another; the normal child was thus a symmetrical and dynamic whole. Baldwin's definition thus looked beyond the static, three-dimensional, and binary worldview of his professional contemporaries. It suggested a world of fluctuation and balance, of proportion and adjustment, of no certain absolutes but of interactions and contingencies of the many different yet interrelated factors in the making of the normal child. The normal child was defined as the composite balance of numerous factors.

Baldwin's notion was unusual for American culture in 1914. It bespoke the language and perception of an age not yet quite born. It was the function of the rest of his career to work out that definition in all its dimensions. Operationally, Baldwin was still rooted in that earlier (and present) world. He defined his research project as the study of physical and physiological growth and mental growth of 1,000 boys and 1,000 girls. He amassed 43,840 physical measurements and 21,683 academic marks, which he believed fairly represented physiological growth and mental development of these 2,000 normal children. Eventually he hoped to show that the growth curves, physiological and mental, paralleled one another and thus plotted out the laws of growth in the normal child. His conclusion at this juncture was more immediate. Chronological age, he insisted, was a poor guide to the placement of children in particular grades in schools. Rather, he insisted, "our school systems, public and private [should] be graded on the physiological age and the accompanying stage of mental maturity of boys and girls in place of chronological age, as is now done."[49]

And, indeed, in most respects, Baldwin had not departed from the assumptions of child psychology of the last quarter century. He thought of the growth curves as linear, and of their relationships as binary, of correlations between this measurement and that as a means of calculating a child's growth at a particular point in time. He still believed the child was the father to the man, that the causes of the present rested entirely in the past. If he did not endorse enthusiastically the hereditarian emphases and typological notions of other child psychologists, such as Hall, Terman, and Goddard, he did not question them either. Indeed, he thought that the physical and physiological measurements and processes were the fundamental baseline for understanding the child, normal or not. If he was willing to admit some sense of dynamism and functionalism into his notions of human development, he was not willing to go further in this regard than were such savants of mental science as Terman. Such were the two definitions and conceptions of the normal child before Seashore's.

The constituencies that participated in public discourse about American children in the late nineteenth and early twentieth centuries showed great concern for dependent children—the abnormal, the subnormal, the delinquent, the impoverished, and the like—and paid relatively little attention to normal, middle-class children. Americans from many walks of life then assumed that normal children, raised in good, sound, white, Anglo-Saxon, Protestant homes, would grow up to be good citizens and contributors to the nation's economic progress. Those from bad circumstances, whether strictly those of environment or of biological inheritance, seemed troubling and problematic in the extreme. By the early 1900s these unfortunate classes of people seemed to present daunting challenges to the stability and prosperity of American civilization, insofar as many members of and participants in white, middle-class, Protestant American culture were concerned. It was from perceptions of reality such as these that the child welfare movement of the late nineteenth and early twentieth centuries was forged.

Examples of this generalization from that era abound. The legal system defined the relations between adults and children from a protective point of view. According to those who held this perspective, there were in society a multiplicity of types of children, each type representing a specific problem of degeneracy, delinquency, dependency, or other such ills. Child welfare advocates thus tended to focus on this problem or that. Relatively few were "generalists," at least to the extent that they tended to create distinct organizations for each problem, as in the instance of one of the earliest, the New York Society for the Prevention of Cruelty to Children, founded in 1874 as the result of benisons initially concerned with one individual. As the states in the later nineteenth and early twentieth centuries reshaped or expanded their institutions for children, they tended to make them far more specialized than had been the case in the mid-nineteenth century, for example, in the newfound distinction between industrial schools for delinquents and custodial institutions for the mentally retarded, or "feebleminded," in that era's jargon.[50]

Many leading advocates of child welfare came from the ranks of social work, a new field that was taking shape in the later nineteenth century as an expert profession. Typical of many child-savers was Hastings Hornell Hart. Hart began his career as a Congregational minister. Soon bored with that profession, he became a social worker and rapidly made himself well known in his field. For a decade and a half he was an administrator in the Minnesota State Board of Charities and Corrections. Here he gained much experience in working with dependent and delinquent children. After a stint with the Illinois Children's Home and Aid Society, which he made into one of the best such organizations in the country, he moved to the Russell Sage Foundation in New York state in 1909 and organized its child-saving department (and work), making it into one of the best in America. His perspective was always that of the child-saver, never the child scientist. He wished to extract the many vulnerable types of children from the dangerous environments in which they lived. Prevention was the key to child-saving, he argued endlessly, thus sounding the same refrain that Cora Bussey Hillis had over and over again.

Another leading child-saver was Julia Lathrop, daughter of a prosperous family of Illinois abolitionists and reformers. Her career included working at Jane Addams's Hull House settlement in Chicago and giving determined, principled service on the Illinois Board of Public Charities. Although she concerned herself with a variety of issues that had little or nothing to do with children, child welfare was always a major commitment for her. She was influential in the creation of the Cook County Juvenile Court, the nation's first. As the first chief of the federal Children's Bureau from 1912 to 1919, she struggled with a grossly inadequate budget to work up investigations of the conditions and circumstances of child life as the basis for recommending policy measures to public institutions, especially state bureaus and the Congress. If Hart did little research that did not have an immediate objective, neither did Lathrop. In

Lathrop's case, however, institutions that she nurtured did some investigations of child life.[51]

In these years child welfare leaders did much to involve public and private institutions in child-saving. These activities were as varied as the culture itself. Often reformers less well known than such stars as Hart or Lathrop would focus on a particular issue to the exclusion of others. Rudolph R. Reeder, for many years superintendent of the New York Orphan Asylum, sought to improve asylums for orphans via the cottage plan. A homelike atmosphere would be created in each cottage; children would be grouped as if members of the same family, with a matron in charge, provided with all the amenities of home that could be replicated with the available funds. He believed that such a material home environment would cause all behavior problems that orphans usually manifested to evaporate.[52] Or consider the example of William R. George, an upstate New York businessman who founded a rural community or colony for urban problem children in the belief that the rural surroundings would help save these unfortunates from lives of desperation.[53]

Nor was this all. There were increasing numbers of experiments with various techniques to solve problems after the turn of the century, a phenomenon not unrelated to the McKinley Boom and the generally prosperous times. Numerous variations were attempted with regard to the problem of foster care, even though the central trend drifted smartly toward the model of the foster home, with adoptive parents whose circumstances and personas were superior to those of the natural parents. Blood would tell: that was the underlying belief. Child-savers and other reformers attempted to persuade legislators, governors, congressmen, senators, and mayors to do a variety of good things for the children, including various programs to assist families in need of welfare services, including public health, housing, improved working conditions, and mothers' pensions, among others. One of the great changes of the early 1900s was the vast increase of the intervention of the states in all aspects of public life, including both the market economy and the social order. An obvious example of this trend was the expansion of involuntary public education. But there were others as well, such as the enactment of laws to protect children against abuse, desertion, and other family problems.[54]

Most of these reform activities proceeded with a minimum of investigation beyond the demonstration of a need for the changes being called for. That is, reformers and child-savers did not, as a general rule, foster research on children and the circumstances of their lives as a scientist might investigate the laws of nature—from the standpoint of the intellectual curiosity of the investigator.

Rather, the child-savers, to the extent that they sponsored or favored research at all, were concerned to show that a problem existed, and that there was a demand for their solutions and remedies. Thus what emphasis there was in the general area of children tended to have a strongly didactic or engineering focus, that is, the application of knowledge to problems at hand. Perhaps that engineering focus was appropriate for the age, given the fact that engineering as a series of academic and research disciplines was taking shape in American society and culture in the early twentieth century.

Yet child-saving institutions did permit research to go ahead, if only at a snail's pace. The Cook County Juvenile Court, founded in 1899, came to offer a context for research on children that was unusual compared with most juvenile courts of the 1900s and 1910s. Thus it was possible for reformers and experts to cooperate. Commencing in 1908, the English-turned-American alienist Dr. William Healy came to work at the court, thanks to a generous five-year grant given by Ethel S. Dummer, a Chicago philanthropist. Healy subjected children referred to his clinic to all manner of tests and examinations. Over time and with more research, he found contemporary theories of delinquency and criminality, especially those that stressed the force of innate factors, too simple. What happened to children now mattered as much as what had taken place in the past, Healy and his associates began to conclude. His method was that of the child psychiatrist and the individual patient. He and his associates gathered both case histories and test results so as to draw as multidimensional a portrait of their charges as possible. Initially they had thought in terms of binary opposites, but in the later 1910s and beyond, they simply thought of infinite factors and of a whole that was greater than or different from the sum of the parts. In 1914 Healy's operation became the Psychopathic Clinic of the Juvenile Court of Cook County. Thereafter, its funding was entirely public. Dummer retired from the field of financing Healy's enterprise. Healy and his associates, particularly Augusta Fox Bronner, whom he eventually married, published a steady stream of articles, pamphlets, syllabi, books, and other materials, all about so-called bad children. The juvenile court gave them access to a research population, a crucial advantage for carrying on investigations. Even before Healy and his associates moved to the Judge Baker Foundation in Boston in 1917, they had concluded that the causes of delinquency, dependency, and other problems that children experienced were primarily emotional, not biological. They might as well have agreed with Cora Bussey Hillis and said, as she often did on the hustings, that an ounce of prevention was worth a pound of cure.[55]

Henry H. Goddard was probably Healy's only serious competitor as a researcher on children in the early 1900s and 1910s. Goddard's work at the Vineland Training School made him a star among those few scientists who investigated the circumstances of children. Born of a rural Quaker family in Maine in 1866, Goddard was among the first of Hall's doctoral students in psychology at Clark University. He imbibed his master's psychobiological schemata.[56] Chance attendance at a meeting of the New Jersey Association for the Study of Children and Youth, in Trenton, in late March 1900, brought Goddard into contact with others interested in child and childlike minds, including E. R. Johnstone, of the Vineland Training School. At the association's 1901 annual meeting, Johnstone, Goddard, and others formed the "Feeble-Minded Club" to facilitate the study of these unfortunates.[57] Goddard's career was born; he cast his lot with Johnstone, who raised sufficient funds by 1906 to make Goddard the first director of research at the Vineland Training School. The school, founded in 1890, was a private institution, chartered under the laws of New Jersey as an eleemosynary and charitable institution governed by a private association of perhaps 250 individuals in Pennsylvania, New Jersey, Delaware, and surrounding states. Its purpose was to provide a lifelong institutional environment for those persons who were so deficient that they could not take care of themselves in society. Yet the school received public funds, in addition to the shares of stock individuals purchased; these public monies were capitation grants for residents of the various states. In effect, Goddard had enormous freedom to conduct research on this virtually unknown mental phenomenon. He trained teachers of "special" students, as the feebleminded were sometimes called, during the summers at Vineland and, after 1908, at New York University too.[58]

In an application to the Carnegie Institution of Washington in 1908, he proposed to expand his research with mental defectives to investigate parentage and inheritance, prenatal conditions, measurements of physical growth, diet, nutrition, metabolism, psychology, and, finally, anatomy and neurology with his more than four hundred charges in the school. In this way he outlined his conception of how to approach the problem of mental defect and how to grasp its underlying realities. "The greatest problem of science today," he wrote, "is the relation of structure to function." The institution's trustees rejected his application. In time, the Vineland Association, the fund-raising agency of the relatives of the inmates, gathered enough money for a modest endowment that permitted Goddard to expand his research work there.[59]

From 1909 to the mid-1910s Goddard focused his considerable energy and enthusiasm on the problem of the relationship between mental defect and juvenile delinquency. Convinced that the feebleminded or mental defective constituted a type, or a closely related series of types, he was recruited into the eugenics movement by its high priest, Charles B. Davenport, director of the Eugenics Record Office and of the Station for Experimental Evolution at Cold Spring Harbor, on Long Island. Davenport convinced Goddard that mentality was inherited according to the Mendelian ratios; from this Goddard surmised that feeblemindedness behaved like a recessive unit of inheritance.[60] The other instrument Goddard found useful in his long-term investigation of the relations between mental defect and juvenile delinquency was, of course, Binet's mental test.[61] Goddard's interpretations of Mendelian heredity and of the Binet test as proving that intelligence was inherited according to the Mendelian ratios helped shape his notions and work on delinquency and mental defect.[62] At an international congress in Brussels in 1910 he reported on the important researches he had initiated on the physical growth curves of ten thousand feebleminded American children whose abnormality or subnormality would be of the highest scientific value for contributing to a greater understanding of the normal child. One could study human mental and physical growth as manifested in the arrested stages of the inmates.[63]

At the 1910 meeting of the Feeble-Minded Club, now redubbed the American Association for the Study of the Feeble-Minded, Goddard presented a three-part typology of mental defect, based on his version of the Binet test with the Vineland inmates. Those who tested below the mental age of three he called idiots; they were not capable of ever caring for themselves and had to be permanently institutionalized. Next came the imbeciles, who tested between three and seven years in mental age. They too could never be released. Finally came the higher grade of mental defectives, who tested anywhere from eight to twelve years in mental age, that is, close to almost normal. They could be trained to do many routine tasks in society and could pass for normal to all save the expert. This highest group he proposed to call morons, from the Greek *moronia*, meaning "foolish or deficient in moral judgments." This was precisely what distinguished this group from the other defectives, on the one hand, and from the normal or above-normal persons on the other. And it was this group that was chiefly responsible for all or nearly all juvenile delinquency, and for much criminal behavior among adults as well.[64]

Within a few years Goddard was publishing a series of studies that seemed to show that it was the morons who were indeed culpable as a group or class in the national population for most crime and social problems.[65] Perhaps his works that won the most attention were *The Kallikak Family* (1912) and *The Criminal Imbecile* (1915); these were lurid, melodramatic works, in which he claimed that mental defect was inherited and that it was the root of all evil, for mental defectives, if left to their own devices, would ineluctably do wrong.[66]

Thus Seashore's attempt to focus the new Iowa Child Welfare Research Station on the normal child was audacious, if for no other reason than, as scarce as scientists who worked on any aspect of child life were, those interested in the normal child were even more rare. It was not for some time before he could rest easy, and foil Hillis entirely on the matter of the station's foci and activities. Meanwhile, an organization had to be created and staffed, and work had to be initiated. So Seashore began. During the spring of 1917, Seashore and President Jessup scoured the country for an appropriate director. Among others they invited to apply were Lewis M. Terman, whom Hillis admired, and Arthur J. Todd, a social worker at Minnesota. Neither was interested. Finally they appointed Bird T. Baldwin, whom the Harvard comparative psychologist Robert M. Yerkes had recommended to his good friend Seashore. Initially, Jessup and Seashore had their doubts; so did Hillis.[67]

Yet Baldwin turned out to be just what Seashore and Jessup wanted. Born in Marshalton, Pennsylvania, in 1875, and a Quaker, Baldwin attended Swarthmore and Harvard, where he met Yerkes, whose version of genetic psychology, in contradistinction to Hall's, included the study of the normal as well as the subnormal or abnormal or defective child. Baldwin was interested in the relations between physical and mental growth. In his dissertation, finished in 1905, he marked out a fresh path that few followed. Unlike most scientists of the day, he did not leap from a presumed physical structure to an assumed mental life. He took rigorous anthropometric measurements of children, distinguished by sex and race, and then attempted to correlate these with measures of chronological and physiological age, school age, and the like. He did not compare presumed racial types, after the current fashion among his professional colleagues. Instead, he attempted to correlate measures of thousands of individuals. Above all, he was committed to the development of the science of the normal child. In a very real sense, he was, along with Terman, the only midcareer scholar who could have taken command at the Iowa station.[68]

Baldwin arrived that September. Immediately he outlined the station's potential research program, listing twenty-eight possible projects to President Jessup. He appointed a research professor of nutrition, Amy L. Daniels, of Wisconsin, who had taken her work with the distinguished biochemist Lafayette B. Mendel of Yale. She was interested in the dietary factors that produced growth in mammals. Baldwin also appointed Ellsworth Faris, a former missionary and graduate of the University of Chicago, as professor of sociology. He put graduate students in charge of research projects in corrective speech, physical measurements, and mental testing.[69]

Starting in January 1918, Baldwin and his assistants began giving systematic physical and mental examinations to any and all "normal" children whose parents brought them to the station, all to gather research data otherwise difficult to obtain. Cora Hillis attempted to persuade Baldwin to organize a national survey of child welfare, a task that was far beyond the station's resources. He talked her into organizing volunteers from the various women's groups to survey the health and well-being of Iowa children in wartime.[70] Over the next year volunteers recorded physical and dental measurements of approximately 140,000 Iowa children, an activity that the station could proclaim as its participation in Children's Year, which President Wilson had just proclaimed.[71] Baldwin tried to keep Hillis satisfied in other ways too, for example, launching a lecture series in which he and Daniels gave talks about the station's activities around the state.[72] Yet Hillis remained anxious that the legislature would not continue the station if immediate demonstrations of the improvement of the conditions of Iowa children were not made. It was especially difficult while the world war was on and Baldwin was serving in the army, for the station seemed to make no progress as Hillis defined that term. Yet projects were completed. Baldwin returned from war service in the fall of 1919.[73]

Hillis brought the station another windfall in 1919. That spring she learned that the national board of the Woman's Christian Temperance Union allocated $150,000 over the next five years to support child welfare activities begun during Children's Year. Seashore and Faris pleaded with Hillis to apply for funds, which she did. The plan of research involved investigating the effect of "harmful substances" on children, including alcoholic beverages, tobacco products, coffee, and hot chocolate. With her superlative connections in the state and national WCTU, Hillis successfully lobbied national WCTU officers, who voted $50,000 over five years to the station. They accepted Baldwin's condition that the station be thoroughly independent of the WCTU—"full control, no strings," as he wired Hillis hours before the directors met.[74]

In March 1920, national officers of the WCTU came to Iowa City to work out specific agreements for the grant. Suddenly they had a different agenda. Even Hillis was surprised. The WCTU officers now insisted that the grant's major purpose was to establish a Department of Eugenics at the station. It should be a fully recognized academic unit within the university. Its work would bear directly on child welfare research, and include, they continued, such possible subjects as the impact of heredity and environment upon the development of normal children, the proportional distribution of "normal" and "inferior" children in the population, investigation of recommended mental, moral, and physical traits of suitable marriage partners, and the formulation of "norms and standards of child development for young fathers and mothers." Research on harmful substances was also permitted. Baldwin delicately finessed the issue. So long as the station's faculty was to have complete intellectual control over its research agenda, a point the WCTU officers agreed to, Baldwin was amenable. He was relieved also to discover that his guests did not accept the kind of ultranationalistic and racist eugenics then being peddled by the leaders of the scientific branch of the eugenics movement. To women in the WCTU, eugenics did not mean sterilization of unfit races, and the like, but socialization into proper habits of health, diet, and sobriety for the young, plus a need to watch out for partners of the opposite sex who came from the wrong side of the tracks, had peculiar relatives, or otherwise did not conform to community standards of "being nice."[75]

The arrangements concluded, Baldwin began a search for a research professor of eugenics. At first he contacted Harry H. Laughlin, a mediocre biologist and protégé of the eugenics propagandist Charles B. Davenport. When he discovered the eugenicist's scientific standards were too shoddy for his taste, he jettisoned Laughlin's candidates, telling Jessup and Hillis that finding a competent scientist in human genetics was a tall order.[76] Eventually Baldwin offered the appointment to Phineas W. Whiting, who had been trained in entomological genetics at Harvard and Pennsylvania. Whiting had superb scientific credentials, Baldwin told Jessup. It took longer for Baldwin to inform Jessup of Whiting's research speciality, and small wonder. Whiting was interested solely in the inheritance of certain patterns of veins in the wings of a given species of wasp. Baldwin told Hillis that Whiting was the best available scientist, period. She accepted Whiting, but not without hesitation. Whiting arrived in Iowa City in August 1921, almost two years after the WCTU voted the grant.[77]

The WCTU grant marked a turning point for the Iowa station. It probably constituted the largest private gift the university had ever received. It added 40 percent to the station's research budget, and almost matched the $13,500 per year that Seashore, as graduate school dean, had available in uncommitted research funds of all sorts for the university's 202 faculty and approximately 400 graduate students. And the grant's value as recognition of the station as a scientific enterprise of national orientation could not be overestimated. The grant undermined Hillis's authority with regard to the station. What power she had as the broker for the grant was diminished by the grant itself and the WCTU's anointment of the station. Having once succeeded as a winner in national competition for distinction, the station could do so again.

By 1921, the problem of definition that had embroiled activists and scientists interested in the child—normal or otherwise—had not yet been resolved. But in 1921, unlike the situation a decade before, there was at least an institutional as well as an intellectual alternative to the notion that child-saving simply was all there was to concern for the child, and the corollary that the proper focus of attention was anything but the normal child. It was still permissible and conceivable that one could investigate the many distinct types of abnormal and subnormal children. But it was at least equally, if not more, conceivable that one could create a profession and a discipline of the normal child. And that was precisely what happened in the 1920s. Whether, in fact, that profession and discipline of the normal child would carry on the attitudes and policies of child-saving remained, of course, an open question.

CHAPTER TWO

T H E   B I G   M O N E Y

At World War I's end, child welfare activists in America could point to several important victories. They had succeeded in recruiting the federal government as an important player in their affairs. The first White House conference on children, officially known as the White House Conference on the Care of Dependent Children, and held in January 1909, placed the matter of care for dependent children on the national agenda, just as the Children's Bureau, founded in 1912, helped create a national forum for discussions of the circumstances of child life, especially child labor. Yet the role of the federal government was to remain limited in the interwar years; it was to serve as a coordinator, a bully pulpit (in Theodore Roosevelt's happy phrase), and a forum or arena in which national issues were aired, and the various interests were to resolve their differences. Social and public policy were not dependent for articulation and resolution on a large, centralized, federal bureaucracy; rather, state and local government, often acting in concert with citizen constituencies, the relevant professionals or experts, business enterprises, and, in particular, a new institution, the philanthropic foundation, were to work together to hammer out solutions.[1]

Of course, charity was hardly new in the 1910s and 1920s. As Merle Curti and Roderick Nash have pointed out in their seminal study of philanthropy and higher education, the new foundations of the early twentieth century were the institutional innovation made possible by the accumulation of vast fortunes by such businessmen as Andrew Carnegie and John D. Rockefeller in the post-Appomattox decades. The new foundations acted as buffer and broker between the benefactor and the institution so blessed; a new class of administrators, program officers, and trustees, sometimes referred to as "philanthropoids," gathered information, conducted surveys, evaluated applicants, and allocated the funds. Trustees of the new foundations often promoted experiments and changes in social and public policy, usually with the advice of the professions, all to inform public policy and to propose solutions.[2]

Throughout the twenties the new foundations underwrote all sorts of public policy initiatives in national culture, seeking to bring various interests and distinct yet interrelated elements of the body politic into a new era of cooperation. The solution of social problems was no longer a matter of this interest versus that, as was true in the late nineteenth and early twentieth centuries, but of seeking a middle way, through the construction of an elaborate network that included professional experts, private foundations, local authorities, the press and even that new artifact of popular culture, the radio broadcast, private corporations, and, when necessary, the national government. This strategy of the twenties, which historians have sometimes identified as consensus and coordination, became the new ideal of public discourse and action. The new foundations played a crucial role in those fields in which it could be claimed that expert knowledge mattered or could make a difference, and supported the development of that knowledge in academic culture—especially at the public and private research universities. When child welfare became a target of foundation intervention in the twenties, the central issue was whether the scientific experts would dominate the field to the exclusion of concern for the welfare of children. The Iowa station was to play an important role in that question.[3]

The WCTU Jubilee Fund's grant marked a watershed in the Iowa station's history. It signified that the station was a national institution, and, because of the WCTU's prestige in child welfare and women's issues, conferred prestige on the station. This approval made it possible for Baldwin to seek other national support for the station's work. Baldwin had a fondness for costly projects. He prevailed on Cora Hillis to raise more money.[4] Neither President Woodrow Wilson nor the Children's Bureau responded to her pleas. Seashore and Baldwin wanted a permanent endowment for the station, with no strings attached. In these discussions Baldwin talked about a large building with many offices and work spaces, as well as funds earmarked for long-range, complex research projects. Seashore assured Hillis that such notions would benefit an "institution of national character."[5] Hillis was as skeptical of Seashore as ever. But she wrote several friends in her efforts to find money. Among those whom she contacted were influential officers at the Rockefeller Foundation and the Commonwealth Fund.[6] At her suggestion, Baldwin submitted tentative proposals. He told President Jessup that among his first priorities was securing an endowment of $1 million, preferably from the Rockefeller Foundation; Jessup tartly responded that he could appeal to the foundation, not through the Iowa State Board of Education (the university's trustees) because the university already had other large grants pending on behalf of the medical school there. Baldwin did not take Jessup's hint to delay his application.[7]

In late 1920 Baldwin asked Cora Hillis to write to the Rockefeller Foundation on the station's behalf. She did so. George E. Vincent, the foundation's president, was a childhood friend; it was he she wrote. Vincent had taught sociology at the University of Chicago before going to the Rockefeller Foundation. He was interested in reform through social science methods; he believed child welfare a worthy goal.[8] At the same time, Baldwin wrote W. S. Richardson, then director of the Laura Spelman Rockefeller Memorial, to ask whether the station's programs fell within the memorial's jurisdiction. John D. Rockefeller, Sr., had founded the memorial in 1918 in memory of his late wife. Its mandate was to spend its funds to benefit women and children.[9] That December Richardson told Baldwin that the memorial's policies had not yet been defined. Hence it was "not [yet] possible to state whether this will come within the scope" of the memorial's plans, he told Baldwin. Then, in March 1921, Vincent finally responded officially to Hillis's inquiry; the Rockefeller Foundation had decided not to support the field of child welfare. But the foundation's trustees had warmly recommended that area for support to the memorial.[10]

In the spring of 1921 Seashore was in Washington, serving that academic year as chairman of the National Research Council's Division of Anthropology and Psychology as well as chair of the division's Committee on Child Welfare. This was a crucial appointment, for the chairmen of the council's divisions recommended research projects (and researchers) to the various foundations for support. Thus, Seashore discussed proposals for the station with foundation officials in New York. Simon Flexner of the Rockefeller Foundation and Max Farrand of the Commonwealth Fund were especially receptive to child welfare.[11] They insisted that a million-dollar endowment for the station was impossible. Flexner opined that the memorial, not the foundation, would support child welfare, but not for at least a year.[12]

Seashore took Baldwin to see Flexner and Farrand in New York City. When Farrand at the Commonwealth Fund said he would consider an application immediately, Baldwin returned to Iowa City and drafted a request for $100,000 over four years. This plan was entirely a research program. There was no mention of an endowment. Baldwin asked that the money be pooled with the station's budget, to accelerate research already underway in nutrition, child health, and physical and mental measurement, and to start new projects, including a metabolic ward for nutritional research and a preschool to study children directly.[13] In February 1922, Barbara S. Quin, a member of the fund's board of directors, visited the campus for several days. She inspected the station's facilities and discussed matters with Baldwin, Seashore, Jessup, and others. Baldwin thought the interview went badly. Quin had said that the fund was reluctant to make large awards to state universities. Nor was the Commonwealth Fund especially interested in underwriting "basic" research in the sciences. Baldwin groused to Jessup that Quin had "little appreciation of real research."[14] In late March the trustees rejected the proposal. As Baldwin explained the situation to Jessup, the fund had but $58,000 to distribute among forty-eight applications. Several weeks later, in explaining the fund's decision to Hillis, Baldwin said that it was a "form of pseudo-educational politics."[15]

What Baldwin decried as questionable politics was simply the consequence of the Commonwealth Fund's trustees' deciding not to support what Baldwin wished to do. Obviously, child welfare was no longer the unified reform movement or field of endeavor that it appeared to have been before 1920. With different constituencies crystallizing within the larger field, a divergence in patronage patterns was hardly astonishing. The Commonwealth Fund moved toward the medical and psychiatric, rather than the scientific, aspects of child welfare. Hence, that decision left the Laura Spelman Rockefeller Memorial as a possibility for large grants to child science—and to the Iowa station. Even before the Commonwealth Fund rejected his proposal, Baldwin had submitted a large proposal to Richardson at the memorial. He asked for a mere $100,000 over four years to support his work on mental and physical growth in children.[16]

Richardson demurred again, insisting that the trustees had not yet established policy. That was technically true, but more was involved. The trustees liked to try a new prospect with a small grant before investing larger sums. Richardson interviewed Baldwin at the memorial about future prospects.[17] Through Hillis, Baldwin discovered that some of the trustees were especially interested in the study of rural communities. Hillis had been a member of the United States Commission on Country Life, which her good friend Theodore Roosevelt had appointed slightly more than a decade before. She understood and was sensitive to the notions that gave the ideology it represented impetus, shape, force, and content. For once, Baldwin listened to her carefully. He soon came to appreciate the concern for the deterioration of the countryside that marked the Country Life movement's ideology, its concern that racial stocks being left there were inadequate and needed to be uplifted in one way or another.[18]

Baldwin now played his trump card: Hornell Hart, one of the station's first doctoral graduates and the son of prominent social worker Hastings Hart. Hornell's interests combined rural sociology and rural social work. He had studied sociology and social welfare at the University of Wisconsin. His favorite teacher was the flamboyant sociologist Edward A. Ross, the progressive reformer and immigration restrictionist. Ever since the early 1910s Ross had pushed a racial interpretation of America's past and present that was congratulatory to the "Anglo-Saxon" stocks but to no others.[19] Hart had written his dissertation at the station on the consequences of the migration of "superior" people from farm to city. He argued that the better economic opportunities of the city and town would attract the best people from rural areas, and rural communities would deteriorate. No one on the Country Life Commission could have said it more colorfully than Hart.[20]

While in New York at the memorial's offices, Baldwin learned that a brilliant young psychologist, Beardsley Ruml, would succeed Richardson as director. This was no mere game of musical chairs, for Ruml's appointment signified that the memorial was reorganizing its priorities. Born in Cedar Rapids, Iowa, in 1894, Ruml graduated from Dartmouth College in 1915 and won his doctorate at the University of Chicago at the age of twenty-three. Already he had published a book and seven articles on psychometrics. Ruml's mandate was to organize a plan for the memorial's funding of basic and applied social science. He perceived in Hart's rural-child survey the basis of a larger and more ambitious research project. He told Baldwin that a reorganized program involving as many of the university's offices and resources as possible would receive a sympathetic hearing from the trustees. Baldwin returned to Iowa City. Over the next six months he worked out a new proposal. This time he asked for only modest support. Its thrust would be a comparison of the advantages and disadvantages, from the standpoint of child welfare, of residence in "modern" and "traditional" communities. In July, Ruml spent several days in Iowa City. He was given a complete tour of the facilities of the station and university. He discussed the proposal extensively with Jessup and Baldwin, making many suggestions so that the trustees would accept it.[21]

In November 1922, the memorial's trustees awarded the station $22,500 over three years.[22] The project involved a multidisciplinary comparison of 500 children in each of two contrasting townships in Johnson County, Iowa—the county in which the university was located. One township possessed most, if not all, the attributes of a "modern" community: a consolidated public school system; a large proportion of its workforce engaged in nonfarm labor; private and public health institutions and resources; and what Baldwin considered a vigorous community life—active churches, parent-teacher associations, civic organizations, and municipal recreational facilities. The other township had none of these attributes. Here, then, were two populations of children, ranging in age between birth and eighteen years, as the center of an intensive, multi-disciplinary investigation. Each of the one thousand children would be studied from the standpoints of social environment, heredity and eugenics, school standing, physical, medical, and dental health, nutrition, physical and physiological age, and, last but not least, intelligence as measured by intelligence tests, with particular attention not merely to "normal" children but to those with "abnormal" traits, whether above or below the "average." Furthermore, this would not be a one-man show. The trustees demanded teamwork and institutional involvement. The station's staff would be involved, and the funds would permit the appointment of extra personnel to help carry out the investigation. The university's faculty in "collateral" departments and schools, including education, medicine, dentistry, corrective speech, and sociology (meaning social work), would also participate.[23]

Ultimately, the amount of the grant was unimportant. What mattered was that a relationship had been established between the station and the memorial. This had important consequences for both institutions. The WCTU grant had provided national recognition and legitimacy for the station. Presumably, that endorsement influenced Frank and the trustees on the station's behalf. Now the station had taken a far more important step. No longer would it have to depend upon citizen movements and patrons alone for direct support. It had cachet in the burgeoning world of "national"—that is, New York—large-scale philanthropy. It had found a national patron that was committed to research in ways Baldwin could accept and Jessup could defend to university faculty. To an extent heretofore impossible, the Iowa station was emancipated from direct face-to-face politicking with its lay constituents. That became important to the station's history. From the memorial's perspective, the Iowa appropriation provided an opportunity to invest in an academic child welfare enterprise. The station was America's only publicly supported research institute devoted to child welfare. The trustees' ultimate ambitions were to install pilot projects in child welfare research so as to inspire state and local governments to imitate them, and thus in time to stimulate the founding of such institutes in every state. Funding the Iowa station in 1922, even before the memorial had a plan, made sense, for this was a trivial sum indeed, a mere $7,500 out of the memorial's annual resources of approximately $4 million, through which to gain understanding about what a child welfare research institute was and what it could and could not do.

The memorial's grant to the station suggested that its own policies were undergoing an inner evolution. Ever since it had been founded in 1918, the memorial's trustees wrestled with the ambiguity of the memorial's mandate to improve the lives of women and children without restriction. So the trustees marked time. They gave large sums to charities in the New York area—almost $3.3 million to social welfare organizations and another $692,754 to public health organizations from 1919 to 1922. They also contributed over $1.5 million to overseas emergency relief, and but $50,500 to scientific research.[24] Between 1919 and 1922 the trustees gave away more than $13 million to a multitude of charitable organizations concerned with the welfare of women and children. They were painfully aware that they were carrying out a holding operation. The coherent program they wanted would accomplish more than the mere maintenance of the current expense budgets of certain philanthropic and helping institutions. They pined to underwrite innovative social experiments and to influence public policy.

Ruml's appointment as director of programs in 1922 signaled that the trustees had decided to embark on such a comprehensive program. They knew that Ruml and his associates would outline a systematic and appropriate program in social and public policy. Ruml wanted fresh ideas on how the memorial could usefully expend a million or so dollars a year for the benefit of the children, as the trustees desired, and still create imaginative, experimental projects.[25] Ruml himself had some ideas on the matter. He was mainly interested in developing the social sciences as "basic" sciences, wanting to put large sums of money in ambitious cross-disciplinary research projects in these fields at major universities across the country. Hence, he began to look around for someone who could handle the child study and child welfare part of the memorial's mandate.

In the spring of 1923 Ruml found his man. He appointed as associate director of programs Lawrence K. Frank. Frank had many ideas about child study, child welfare, the education of parents, and the ways in which science could improve the family as a social institution in modern America. Frank had had a rather painful childhood. His parents separated when he was six. Thereafter he lived in penurious circumstances. His mother moved from Cincinnati to Buffalo; when he was an adolescent, she moved him again, to New York City, and to a boarding house in Greenwich Village, where the boarders' rents paid for a roof over the Franks' heads. Lawrence adapted. He was a bright, intellectually curious child who read voraciously. At Columbia he majored in economics. Among his favorite teachers was John Dewey, whose work introduced the young Frank to the blossoming New York progressive education movement, which was the left wing insofar as the national movement was concerned. Frank was influenced by the works of many progressive and radical intellectuals of the day. Aside from Dewey, perhaps the most important intellectual influence on him was Thorstein Veblen. If Dewey taught Frank that human progress consisted of the application of individual intelligence upon problems of survival value, he learned from Veblen that human nature and institutions were related; to change the latter held out the promise of altering the former.

When Frank graduated from Columbia College in 1912, he went to work for the New York Telephone Company as an economist, calculating rates, managing budgets and accounts, and performing similar tasks. Yet he always maintained an activist streak. In college Frank had worked for several municipal reform organizations, which enabled him to meet many political and social reformers such as Frances Perkins, Franklin Roosevelt's secretary of labor. While serving as an economist for the War Industries Board during World War I, he met the famous Columbia economist Wesley Clair Mitchell, famous even then for his studies of business cycles. Through Wesley he met Lucy Sprague Mitchell, Wesley's wife. The Mitchells opened Frank's eyes to the countless ways that social science, if applied to social problems, could lead to a better and brighter tomorrow. As Wesley taught Frank about economics and social reform, so Lucy introduced him to what would be his lifelong field of expertise: child study and the family.[26]

Lucy Sprague Mitchell was a leading figure in Gotham's progressive education circles. In 1916 she founded the Bureau of Educational Experiments, later known as the Bank Street College of Education. There she began what was arguably North America's first preschool laboratory, in which children learned to be socialized outside the home. Frank's ripening friendship with the Mitchells converted him to the cause of progressive education. He now perceived in education the means of wholesale and systemic social reconstruction and amelioration, broadly defined to include the education of parents in the private home as well as children in the public school. And he was impressed with his first child's experiences in Lucy's preschool; progressive education apparently offered many possibilities.[27]

In 1920, the Mitchells helped Frank win appointment as business manager for the New School for Social Research. Now he had an academic platform from which he could operate as an intellectual and reformer. In the several articles he published over the next several years, he argued, as befit a disciple of John Dewey, that social reconstruction and salvation could come through education. He insisted that education focused merely on the schools would be insufficient to reform society. The school, he insisted, depended on the larger society that surrounded it. What took place in society—meaning family and community, chiefly—determined the school's health and success. Hence the obvious corollary to progressive education in the public schools as agent of democratic social change was parent education in the home. Parents must be trained as children were to acquire pragmatic, Deweyite methods of intelligent problem solving in raising their children. Parent education, literally, was both formal instruction of parents in classroom settings and dissemination of information to parents through various instruments of the mass media. And what information would parent educators impart to their multiple constituencies but the latest and most up-to-date results of child science as unearthed by the child scientists.

In this way, a reasonable, well-informed electorate would be trained. The quality of American politics would be upgraded. So would the character of family life. Application of social science methods to family and community problems, Frank believed, would eliminate social problems. Clearly he was interested in research on children. But research had to have social applications. Frank fully embraced the lusty positivism of the age; he believed that science could be positively true. Social science properly applied, he argued, would uplift and improve the social order. He wanted nothing less than to alter the very nature, the social roles and the social values, of the American family, which, in his opinion, was too traditional. It had to be rationalized and modernized—brought into congruence with modern science and learning. That he believed his particular nostrum of child study and parent education would do the trick hardly needs saying.[28]

Frank's reputation within New York intellectual and reform circles soon brought him to Ruml's attention. In the spring of 1922 Ruml appointed Frank as a part-time consultant. Frank's assignment was clear. How could the memorial discharge its mandate with regard to child study and child welfare? Over the next several months Frank investigated all of the facets of the problem that he could. He submitted a long memorandum for the trustees to Ruml that fall.

In his memorandum, Frank argued that at least $2 million a year was available for further appropriations for child study and related issues. Frank addressed himself to the question of large-scale policy, not, as he put it, for a year, but perhaps for a decade, during which time $20 million might be available. If the memorial's interest was in investing in child welfare with the goal of reaching remote ends, the difficulty was that science knew so little. The "great practical need for greater knowledge concerning the forces that affect the behavior of individuals and societies is definitely recognized by the ablest leaders of social welfare organizations," he wrote, yet such work "is largely controlled by tradition, inspiration, and expediency, a natural condition in view of our ignorance of individual and social forces."[29] The conditions for social science research in the United States were deplorable. Only major intervention by foundations could correct the situation.

Frank argued that the memorial had to support the social sciences adequately so that practical, scientific solutions to the urgent problems of women and children could be devised. The first order of business, then, was to select several promising universities that were capable of benefiting from major grants for social scientific research. Ideally this would mean founding several social science research institutes. Frank pointed to the Iowa station as an excellent model in the child welfare field. Then he suggested a child welfare institute at Teachers College, where the children in New York City could be systematically studied. Universities in large cities could start long-term investigations of the urban context of child and family life, and other universities, such as the state universities of Iowa, Michigan, Wisconsin, and Illinois, could study rural children and family life. Such a program depended upon the training and placement of sufficient numbers of competent scientists—thus the need for the memorial's largess.[30]

The trustees considered Frank's scheme sufficient basis for further discussion. Very likely Frank's proposal, considered as it was a month before the rural child grant to the station, legitimated that proposal to the trustees. Over the next year and a half Frank surveyed the possibilities of implementing his program at a number of universities and colleges. As the memorial's official report for 1923 acknowledged, the memorial had not yet committed itself to a well-defined program, "yet certain selections have been made, from among the many possible and desirable fields, of opportunities for service which are now to be thoroughly explored." In particular, special attention was focused on "child study, recreational activities, social science, and to the forward-looking, experimental work of social welfare organizations."[31] By the end of 1923, the memorial was making several exploratory grants, on a small scale, to various institutions, as the basis for judging whether child study could develop.

Teachers College and the Yale Psycho-Clinic received small awards, and Frank also recommended several experiments in parent education.[32]

In 1924, the trustees came to accept, in bits and pieces, Frank's general program for child study and parent education. In late February he presented an overall plan for discussion. Child study and parent education were now intimately related; by sponsoring them both, the memorial would be "promoting child welfare of a preventative nature," he declared.[33] The trustees gave Frank license to develop his ideas in more detail. In late May he appeared again before the trustees. After reiterating his thesis that the objective of child study and parent education was "the welfare of the child through the education of the parents," he argued that the science of the child must be integrated "so that the various functions and needs of the child are met as a whole and not through a separate attack on health, nutrition, behavior, and so on." The central question was admittedly complex. How could a sufficiently catholic parent education program be created that was acceptable to the "varying capacities and intelligence of the different groups and classes of parents" and that could be implemented through local agencies with the least amount of additional facilities and institutions?

Frank insisted that first the memorial had to recruit the state universities. After all, they were the leaders of public opinion in their localities. Some would have research centers, after the Iowa model. A far larger number would have parent education centers whose staff would disseminate the new research. Extension and operations would distribute information and offer various classes, workshops, and other programs. In these ways parents could be reached directly. Federal funding through such legislation as the Smith-Lever Act of 1915 would provide additional support and legitimacy. And the various lay constituencies would have to be organized politically; eventually the states could absorb the costs of these experimental programs, so cultivation of lay constituencies was essential.

Naturally, only a few institutions, selected for their strategic importance, could be funded. The memorial was supporting only a few experiments; ideally, they would encourage local funding and widespread imitation. Nor were all universities equally desirable. Much depended on local circumstances, such as faculty enthusiasm and expertise, and strong lay support too. Frank understand that the scientists required free access to a research population, as did the parent educators. He suggested that in each center, whether for research or for parent training, there be "set up a laboratory in the university or college . . . in the form of a nursery school." Such a preschool had several advantages, including ease of research, of training teachers in child study, and of serving as a demonstration institute for parents. In this way parents might be convinced to establish a network of cooperative nursery schools throughout the state. And the nursery school would focus the university's attention upon child study. Because the university was the leader of public opinion in the state, the entire program for each state could diffuse the gospel of social reconstruction through child study and parent education to its citizens.[34]

In October, Frank again appeared before the trustees. Now it was a matter of discussing particulars, of being concrete. He stressed again the necessity of creating several research centers, for the present diversity of opinion and chaotic nature of the human sciences was due, "in large part, to the absence of careful investigation." Furthermore, parent education depended upon the best scientific research. It had to stress all aspects of child and family life. Its interdisciplinary character was indisputable, beyond serious debate. And staff at research centers had to accept "application" as well as "basic research" as integral parts of their institutional goals. Parent education was simply indispensable. He pointed out how to use existing governmental machinery, such as the maternity educational programs supported by the federal Sheppard-Towner Act of 1921. Rather offhandedly he suggested that it might be effective for the memorial to invest in a popular magazine whose pages were devoted to scientific parent education.[35] This organizational blueprint thus outlined a balanced, symmetrical whole that was greater than or different from the sum of the parts, for it included a variety of elements that were distinct yet interrelated, including public and private institutions, and for-profit and not-for-profit ventures. In such a pattern, it was the whole, not the parts, that attracted the most attention.

A nasty squabble in Iowa over the politics of child welfare and of the rivalry of the state university with the State College of Agriculture and Mechanic Arts provided Frank with his first opportunity to devise a child research and parent education program within a definite academic context. In the 1923 legislative session, opponents of Hillis within the women's organizations combined forces with champions of the Ames institution to force passage of state matching monies for the Sheppard-Towner Act, which Congress had passed in 1921. They did so as implied criticism that the station was more interested in "pure science" than in helping Iowa children. That November, the governor, who warmly supported the university and the station, appointed a Child Welfare Commission, charged with the responsibility of studying "abnormal children," as a gambit to deflect criticism of the station. He appointed a prominent and well-respected Des Moines legislator to direct the commission. The anti-Hillis and anti-university forces did not fall for the ruse, however. In the 1924 legislative session, ostensibly devoted to revision of the Code of Iowa, these groups tried to embarrass the governor by denying any funding to the commission.[36] Baldwin intervened on the commission's behalf. He wanted the station to lead and coordinate all child welfare matters in the state. By arguing that the station and commission had different mandates, Baldwin persuaded the solons to give the commission as much as half the loaf it had requested.[37]

Other problems crystallized. In February 1924, Baldwin had approached the memorial for a small grant to launch a parent education program for the station. May Pardee Youtz would be trained as a field organizer in parent education at Columbia's Institute of Child Welfare and the Merrill-Palmer School for a few months. The memorial would support her training and two years of her work through the university extension service. Her work involved establishing parent education classes through the university's extension service all over the state and recruiting the staff, including herself, to run these (usually) evening classes. The grant was small: $9,500 for two years. Frank and Ruml assured the memorial's trustees that this experiment at Iowa would generate between fifteen and thirty parent-training child study groups in the state's rural and urban communities. From the station's perspective, the organization of child study groups in the commonwealth's varied communities was a boon. It placed much of the station's public-relations responsibilities on a routinized and impersonal basis, and permitted the station to invent formal constituencies. Frank and his associates saw the grant as a test of Baldwin's intentions and an experiment in its still-evolving plans for experiments in child study and parent education. By the fall, Youtz was organizing study groups all over the state. She was an extraordinarily effective apostle of the new scientific gospel of child development. She had a genuine flair for disseminating that ideology in ways highly attractive to her lay constituencies. Throughout the school year, then, parent education classes met in such communities as What Cheer, Brooklyn, or Podunk Center, on such subjects as being a new mother, preparing your child for kindergarten, the advantages of a preschool program, the healthy child, and the like.[38]

The next step occurred with the more ambitious proposal Baldwin submitted in early 1925 to expand the station's research resources. That proposal centered on the novel idea of a home preschool laboratory. Baldwin had begun the original nursery school in the fall of 1921, essentially with the WCTU funds. The preschool enrolled youngsters from ages two to six, at first either in the mornings or the afternoons. By 1924 there were three preschools, but in all cases children were day students, and the environment was that of a school, not a home. Baldwin was quite interested in what factors constituted a home, as distinct from a school, environment; hence, he proposed the idea of a home preschool laboratory in which children of various ages would live and learn round-the-clock for periods of time up to a year. The preschool was crucial to the station's work: it provided the only free access, on a continuous and systematic basis, to children as subjects in various research projects.[39]

Baldwin soon discovered that he had to promise more than an expansion of the parent education program to win further support from the Laura Spelman Rockefeller Memorial. At first he and Frank disagreed. Frank insisted upon the necessity of a statewide program. In such a plan there would be distinct yet interrelated roles for each of the specific institutions involved in the larger whole of child study and parent education. The station would act chiefly as a center for research, consultation, and general coordination. Thus the differences between Baldwin and Frank involved something other than the alleged conflict between basic and applied work. Baldwin wanted a strongly centralized statewide program, if statewide program there must be, in which the station (and Baldwin) would literally direct and coordinate all the distinct elements. In this hierarchical blueprint of centralized monopoly, all elements were unique and thus controlled from a centralized center for maximum efficiency; it was a system of disparate, efficient parts. In many respects, Baldwin was simply following widely adopted practices of organizational reform and structuring in American society and culture since the 1870s. It was the way universities, colleges, and corporations had been constituted. Clearly, it was omnipresent within the structures and processes of the academic scientific professions.

Frank challenged Baldwin with a new model of oligopoly, decentralization and federalism for a statewide plan of child study and parent education, in which the whole was greater than or different from the sum of the parts. Baldwin's monopolistic model assumed the necessity of centralization because of the uniqueness and distinctiveness of each part of the whole. Frank's plan was predicated on a different market model in which there were a number of interrelated elements, each suited for a different role, each interactive with most or all of the others. Frank's model assumed a certain latitude for each of the distinct parts, because in the larger whole or system of systems there was dynamism yet also balance, proportion, and symmetry in all relations between the parts. In Frank's plan each part of the larger whole was distinct from all others; yet all were indivisibly connected to one another and the whole itself. In a word, Baldwin thought of a single head for a hierarchical *system*, and Frank insisted on a system of systems, a *network* of interactive, balanced, and interdependent yet distinct systems or parts. The Iowa Child Welfare Research Station's role was carefully defined. It would be the center for graduate training and original investigation. It would also be responsible for general coordination of the program and for consultation with those involved in its various activities. In a word, it would be a brain, but not a head.[40]

Thus the station would have its own parent-training program expanded. No longer would May Youtz be alone; she would have salaried colleagues. The 1925 grant awarded $10,000 a year for three years for experimental demonstration centers of parent education in three "typical" Iowa cities, Des Moines, Council Bluffs, and Mason City, implemented through the extension service, with the other half of the costs being borne by each city's school system. Here Frank assumed that the state university had as its major constituencies the urban professional classes. If they could be won over to the gospel of child study and parent education, in time they would insure that the new programs would be taken over by their school system en toto, and the memorial could retire from the endeavor.[41]

Frank carefully restricted the station's grants to its distinctive activities. Thus he did not even permit Baldwin to apply through the station for funding for the other two public institutions Frank deemed integral to the whole statewide program, Iowa State College of Agriculture and Mechanic Arts, in Ames, and Iowa State Teachers College, in Cedar Falls. Frank insisted that when officials at those institutions were ready to submit their own applications, they should do so directly to the memorial. Frank literally imposed his scheme upon all interested parties.

Even before the station's grant was made, Frank was already negotiating with Anna E. Richardson, dean of the Division of Home Economics at Iowa State College. Indeed, she gave him the information he used to structure the statewide program. Faculty from both state colleges, upset that they might be left out, complained to the State Board of Education, whose members governed the three state institutions.[42]

In early March 1925, Frank interviewed Richardson at Ames. She wanted child study and parent education within home economics, not psychology. She thought the nursery school should be upgraded into a training laboratory for prospective mothers, as 80 percent of home economics graduates became homemakers after graduation. When she suggested that Iowa State College could organize the rural communities through its extension service, Frank pounced on her idea, as he saw the Ames school as central to any statewide plan. May Youtz had shown that rural communities were interested. Iowa State could follow up. Frank thought Baldwin wanted all child study and parent education under the station's firm control. Apparently too, Baldwin resented the home economists' invasion of turf he thought the station's.[43] In late March Frank saw Baldwin in Saint Louis and told him of the memorial's—or Frank's—terms for any further funding. All three institutions must be involved; each was to have its own designated yet interrelated functions and roles.[44] The grant to Iowa State College provided $7,500 annually for three years. It underwrote an expansion of child study and parent training to several hundred home economics majors and the organization of study groups for mothers in rural communities.[45]

The statewide plan now materialized. The State Board of Education, following Frank's lead, made the station the program's coordinating center for child study and parent education but prescribed the roles of the three public institutions "to prevent duplication . . . and to insure the highest degree of efficiency and cooperation."[46] Thus would there be balance, proportion, and symmetry in the larger system or network. Although Baldwin and Richardson had some initial difficulties in negotiating the distinctive roles of their institutions, these were resolved soon.[47] It took another year, the fall of 1926, before the state teachers college was integrated into the program. All three institutions had their distinctive yet interrelated roles. The station was to organize the cities for parent education. The state college in Ames was to create support for parent education in the rural communities. And the state teachers college in Cedar Falls was to train the teachers of child study and parent education, both on campus and through its extension service. Each institution had its own distinctive yet interrelated role in the larger plan—in the larger whole.[48]

The final step in the construction of the statewide plan was taken in the fall of 1926, with the creation of the Iowa State Council on Child Study and Parent Education. The state council became the official coordinating body for the entire program. It was a private organization. But its definition as a private organization did not prevent its integration into a larger whole with other private and public institutions. In the larger organizational scheme, the state council stood above the station. It represented all elements. It had representatives from the three state institutions, from the urban school systems with demonstration projects, and from selected private civic organizations, including the Iowa Woman's Christian Temperance Union, the Iowa Federation of

Women's Clubs, the Iowa Parent-Teacher Association, the Iowa Chapter of the American Association of University Women, and the Woman's Division of the Iowa Farm Bureau. The first three of these private organizations had been integral parts of Hillis's lobbying coalition of a decade before. Above all, the state council sought to represent all three state institutions in ways that would suggest maximum cooperation and minimal competition.[49]

Yet the state council could issue no embargoes on action by any of the three institutions. Even before the council was officially organized, the station was deploying new techniques of reaching its constituencies, as when Baldwin inaugurated a series of radio programs over the university radio station in February 1926. In time, this became formalized as the Radio Child Study Club, broadcast over all three institutions' radio stations, presenting a different speaker each week from one of the institutions. For a nominal fee, listeners could join the club and receive pamphlets and other reading material through the mail. Here was an important tool for parent education. Literally, parent education was no longer restricted to evening classes. The mass media, in this instance the combined facilities of the radio stations of the state university in Iowa City and the state college in Ames, thus supplemented the extension services of both institutions and blanketed the state with a coordinated curriculum of courses. Every week a program was broadcast in the early afternoon, timed for mother's maximum convenience, and aired again in the early evening, so that father could listen too.[50]

Doubtless the most visible event with which the State Council on Child Study and Parent Education was associated was the annual summer conference it sponsored beginning in 1927. The station had always had some kind of summer program, and this event became the precedent for its role as continuous host for the conference. The purposes and themes of the station's earlier summer programs varied, but they always combined some graduate instruction in nutrition or child psychology for public school teachers or graduate students with a short conference, as on physical growth for public school nurses. In 1925, for example, the station offered six-week courses in child development for the first time. Mothers from Iowa and other states enrolled. They brought their preschool children with them, lived with them on the campus, and, as a part of their instruction, observed them "scientifically" in the preschool. National experts also gave public lectures.[51]

The state council's annual summer conference carried on the station's tradition, but enlarged and modified it according to the statewide program's dicta. The station always hosted the affair on the Iowa City campus. The council sponsored the conference, acting as the public representative of the statewide program. The station handled the details. Every summer hundreds attended. Many came as representatives from various organizations committed to the gospel of child study and parent education, others as professionals from various fields in developmental science, and still others as interested individuals. Usually five or six national authorities in the fields of social work, charities and corrections, mental hygiene, child development, and parent education gave public addresses. The council held its annual business meeting. If the station was thus now forced into a new set of institutional relationships with diverse elements, its prominence as the pioneering institution in the field locally and nationally could nevertheless not be denied.[52]

Thus in the middle and late 1920s the implementation of the organizational relationships mandated in the new statewide plan—Frank's invention, really—forced a qualitative change in the character of relations between professionals and their constituencies. The techniques of professional-client relationships—the radio broadcasts, the parent education groups, and the summer conference, in this instance—were formal and impersonal, fully mechanisms of contemporary mass culture. Personal and informal contacts and relationships, such as friendships between individuals and presentations before local groups, did not end. Rather, they were overshadowed by the new structures, mechanisms, and processes of mass culture.

Of course, these institutional structures, mechanisms, and processes were hardly unique to child study and parent education, the prairie commonwealth, or higher education. They were part and parcel of the American mass culture and existed, as it were, cross-sectionally, across the culture itself, or were in the process of crystallizing. Parallel transformations had commonly occurred across the country, as if the culture had traversed a gigantic chasm from one age to another. Thus, officials at institutions of higher learning were now seeking to invent impersonal mass constituencies, themselves comprised of such differing yet unified components, by means of recombining in new mixtures such social techniques as alumni associations, extension programs, and athletic programs. In this way would new sources of public and private support be created. From this point of view, the transformation of America's public and private institutions in the 1920s was characterized by the invention of new publics and constituencies through the techniques of mass culture and advertising. That the station—and the state council—sought to create loyalty to a specific program of education, rather than to a particular brand of coffee or cigarettes, seemed almost beside the point.[53]

Yet child study and parent education were not commodities that all wanted to consume. The parent education program stimulated considerable interest in child study and parent education groups. Demand exceeded supply. Child study and parent education had their strongest appeal to fiancées, wives, mothers, aunts, and grandmothers, not to prospective grooms or fathers or uncles or grandfathers or older brothers or other males in the family. It scarcely mattered whether the feminine enthusiasts of child study and parent education lived in city or country—given organizational activity and the stimuli of appropriate ideology in a particular setting, there would always be a response from mothers or mothers-to-be—but the amount of education a woman already had constituted a powerful precondition for interest in child study and parent education.

The new field was exciting to college women. Child study became a roaring success at Iowa State College. Within the first full year of the child study program there, the program included a required course in preparental training in the nursery school for all senior women in the college. In Dean Richardson's words, this gave the women "the fine ideals of wholesome family management" as well as experience in the "care and management of the child of pre-school age." The nursery school enrolled thirty-two preschool-age children. In design and curriculum, the Ames preschool closely resembled the station's preschools, with the important exception that the Ames preschool was a teaching, not a research, operation and an integral part of the home economics curriculum. It was also a "hands-on" training laboratory, in one of the most revered rhetorical traditions of land grant colleges. One field worker, Alma H. Jones, offered all extension classes. She could not keep up with the demand for her services. During her first year, she organized thirteen distinct groups in as many communities, with a total regular or attending membership of about 250 mothers. She also trained new leaders for these groups. Women with some college experience dominated these groups; most of the rest wanted their children to attend college.[54]

The Iowa station's experiences in attracting constituents for child study and parent education differed only in detail. By the spring of 1927, May Youtz had organized forty-four parent-training groups. In the larger cities, fathers as well as mothers sometimes attended. Some notion of the differential appeal of child study and parent education can be grasped from the experiences of the programs in Des Moines and Council Bluffs. The station's demonstration program in Des Moines organized thirty-two parent education groups and enrolled more than 600 parents. The capital city had a large proportion of white-collar professionals and businessmen in its labor force. Many of these individuals had attended college. Many, too, lived in the city's affluent, middle-class neighborhoods west of the Des Moines River. Of course, child study and parent education did not appeal to all white-collar burghers, nor to all who had some college education. Groups in working-class neighborhoods were fewer in number and smaller in average attendance than those in the middle-class neighborhoods. Apparently the one common denominator among all constituents, actual and potential, was interest in and commitment to education for one's children, although it would be dubious in the extreme to assume that all such persons took an interest in parent training. Child study and parent education seemed an adjunct or aspect of the growing national interest, regardless of an individual's social class or caste, in public education.

The Council Bluffs field laboratory program's history suggested as much. It was Frank who had literally jammed the notion of a field laboratory in a working-class city such as Council Bluffs down Baldwin's throat. From Frank's Deweyite left-liberal perspective, that the masses could be aroused to good social policies through rational appeals to their intellects dictated this arrangement as self-evidently valuable. Hence, Council Bluffs was a test case of Frank's common sense. Many of its workers labored in the railroad yards and the Omaha slaughterhouses and stockyards. By the later 1920s employment was not as steady as it was in Des Moines, surely a reflection of the ballooning agricultural depression of those years. Council Bluffs had fewer study groups as a proportion of the population than did Des Moines. Average attendance was barely eight mothers per group, slightly less than half the average of the Des Moines groups. Also fathers, as a rule, did not attend in Council Bluffs. The Council Bluffs field worker reported that much of her time was simply spent in persuading the city's major church, school, benevolent, and social leaders to support the program in the city.

No such problems confronted the child study and parent education leaders and organizers in Des Moines, where civic and public school leaders, with support from the business community, took the initiative in backing child study and parent education. It cannot be said that every white collar, college-educated parent in either community—or in any community, for that matter—embraced the new gospel of parent education and child study. Obviously many did not. Probably a majority were indifferent. By the same token, the overwhelming proportion of those who were committed to child study and parent education were drawn from that middle-class stratum, not from that of the working class. The differential appeal of parent education and child study seemed akin to the appeal of education more generally to Middletown's "business" and "working" classes in the twenties.[55]

In reality, the station had been thrust from a local to a national stage, with important consequences. An event symptomatic of the shift, although not related to it causally, was Cora Hillis's tragic death in an automobile accident in August 1924, as Baldwin and Frank were working out their complex negotiations over the station's future. Once the station had won support from the memorial, Hillis's potential influence, always problematic from the station's founding, slowly evaporated. If Hillis and Frank believed in the amelioration of the lives of children and regarded a science of the child as a means to an end, important differences between them nevertheless remained. Hillis's world was that of the upper-middle-class midwestern gentry, her politics those of the Woman's Christian Temperance Union and the Republican party. She could— and did—organize powerful political coalitions, although not without considerable resentment and jealousy, to be sure. She was no intellectual, nor was she confined or disciplined by the customs of American science and philanthropy.

If Frank had a larger view than Hillis of how the discipline and profession of child development and parent education could develop within the context of American institutions, and was able furthermore to engage in intellectual play with the child development scientists, he was nevertheless bound by certain realities no less than was she. He could influence the proposals that scientists brought forth to him for brokering with the trustees. He could and did have an effect on trustees and scientists in his middle-man role. But ultimately he could only facilitate negotiations. What the principals did, despite Frank's frequent attempts to be a principal himself, was something that was beyond his control. Now local constituencies were, at most, a secondary worry; more crucial was competition from other emerging institutes and centers of professional competence and performance.

In the spring of 1927 Baldwin again approached the memorial for what was to be the largest round of appropriations for the station and the statewide program. The negotiations were not completed until the next March. Insofar as Frank was concerned, the paramount issues were the shape of the statewide program and the balance of support between research and parent training. Baldwin and Jessup acceded. The memorial awarded the station $818,000, on an ascending scale for the first four years, then with tapering appropriations, over the last six years, on the assumption that the state would assume an increasingly large share of the total costs. Of the $818,000, $530,000, or almost five out of every eight dollars, was allocated to sustain the home preschool and to create an entirely new infant laboratory. There had never been adequate cooperation from the medical school, insofar as the station was concerned, in supplying a regular and sufficient flow of infants for scientific study. This had crimped research professor Amy Daniels's nutrition investigations. Ostensibly, the new infant laboratory would make use of orphans who could be studied in the new laboratory without legal problems—or friction from the medical school. Another $104,000 was granted for various cooperative projects between the station and other university departments for specific research projects. Of the remainder, $144,000 was assigned to support an undergraduate program in child study and parent education in the college of education, and $40,000 to pay the salary and expenses of an executive secretary for the state council.[56]

In separate negotiations—which Baldwin endorsed—the memorial awarded $16,000 over a fifteen-month period to the Des Moines public school system to continue its parent-training program, and $30,000 to Iowa State College on a diminishing schedule through 1933 and $15,000 to Iowa State Teachers College on a similar basis through 1931 to continue their roles in the statewide program.[57] The other urban field laboratories were not renewed. No further appropriations were contemplated.

Now Baldwin had a statewide program—not one he would have designed, to be sure, but one he had come to accept. Its most important element, insofar as he was concerned, was the substantial expansion of the station's research capacities and resources. Virtually all involved agreed that the program's weakest link was to the state teachers college, whose participation seemed justified more on the basis of abstract symmetry than on any other. On the other hand, child study at Ames was so successful that a department of child development, organized in 1929, more than held its own in attracting students and off-campus mothers through the college's effective extension division. Thus on the Great Depression's eve, the Iowa station had vastly augmented its resources and responsibilities.

In the middle 1920s Frank invented a national institutional network for what he believed would be the science of child welfare and the gospel of scientific parent training. Over a period of five years, he persuaded the memorial's trustees to disburse large sums of money to those ends. Thus in 1923 they allocated but $105,250, the next year $494,500, an almost fivefold increase, and in 1927 and 1928 about $3,700,000.[58] By December 23, 1928, the memorial's investments in child study and parent education amounted to more than $5.5 million. If the sums Frank recommended never comprised more than about one-third of those Ruml used to underwrite "basic" social science research projects, and if the memorial's support of child study and parent education paled by comparison with the amount of funds available to researchers in such well-established fields as astronomy, physics, chemistry, agriculture, and engineering, they were nevertheless ample enough to have enormous consequences for the child sciences. The memorial's intervention was emblematic of a new age of American technology and science, in which gigantic foundations could create possibilities for whole new fields of work and alter the circumstances of investigation and professional discourse in older sciences.

In the hierarchical blueprint of institutions of child study and parent education that Frank had presented the trustees, the research centers stood at the top. He had hoped to install or further encourage research centers in public universities in several regions of the country as the best guarantee of the diffusion of the ideas of child science and scientific parent training in the short run and the implication that the states should take over financial responsibility for the centers once the memorial's support ended. Yet Frank was virtually forced to underwrite research centers at Columbia and Yale universities, with results he eventually found disappointing.

It was probably inevitable that Frank would have to include Teachers College at Columbia in his plans. Teachers College was arguably the nation's most important center of progressive education sentiment and practice. In any event, there were simply too many ties between Columbia and the several Rockefeller philanthropies. In early 1924, Frank persuaded James E. Russell, dean of Teachers College, that the college should undertake a survey of Hope Farm, a rural child welfare organization near Verbank, New York. Several months later Frank told Russell that the memorial might consider supporting a major child welfare research institute at the college. Frank hoped thus to combine research and parent training through an alliance between the college and Hope Farm, using the memorial's funds as the glue.[59] At first Russell was wary. In canvassing his faculty, he discovered considerable enthusiasm for the idea. Most important, Edward Lee Thorndike, arguably his most eminent researcher, gave it a ringing endorsement. In April Russell applied. He proposed that the institute's research and training functions would mesh with the college's main goal of training teachers.[60] Frank wanted more. He suggested that the institute conduct research on the nonscholastic interests of children, that it become a bibliographical center in the field, and that it serve as the organizational hub of demonstration projects such as Hope Farm. Russell capitulated. In May, the trustees awarded Teachers College $265,000 spread over five years.[61]

The Teachers College Institute of Child Welfare never achieved the high goals Frank had hoped for. It was two years before the permanent director, Helen T. Woolley, arrived, and, in the interim, the institute could do little more than mark time. Chiefly, the staff administered clinical examinations to children.[62] Nor did matters improve after Woolley arrived. Although she threw herself into her work with energy and imagination, she fell victim to a recurring mental illness; her unavoidable absences made matters at the institute rocky indeed. In 1929 she was replaced.[63]

Subsequently, the institute became what Russell had initially recommended, a training center for teachers in the preschool and parent education. More complications than merely leadership problems were involved. Costs, and therefore budget requests, escalated astonishingly, despite the staff's best efforts to be frugal. New York prices were very high, which constricted the potential Frank thought existed for the institute.[64] Institutionally, Teachers College was the wrong place from which to elaborate his plans; it had no tradition of or interest in either research or public outreach. As Frank ruefully put it in lamely recommending yet another emergency appropriation to the trustees, Russell's attitude, and that of his faculty, was that "Teachers' College is running this Institute for the Memorial."[65] By late 1926 Frank had accepted, reluctantly, Russell's conception of the institute as a teacher training institution.[66] Frank had made several tactical errors in negotiations. He was naive and gave away too much leverage. He had not insisted upon cost sharing from Teachers College, nor that institute staff (save for the director) be regular college faculty, nor that the funds be held back until a director was hired. In other words, he had not given Russell any reason to consider the institute an integral part of Teachers College.[67]

Nor did the fruits of his negotiations at Yale please Frank more. Since the early 1920s Ruml had discussed with President James Rowland Angell establishing a major psychological research institute at Yale. Angell had been one of Ruml's teachers at Chicago, and they occasionally attended Yale football games together.[68] In 1924, Ruml and Angell closed the deal for an institute of psychology, to operate for at least five years. The institute's research professors would be Robert M. Yerkes, the animal psychologist, Raymond Dodge, a physiological psychologist, and Clark Wissler, an eminent anthropologist. At no point did it occur to Angell or Ruml to include Arnold Gesell in the institute, even though Gesell was then a rising star in child development and psychology.[69] Nor did Gesell identify with the new institute. Psychologists and child developmentalists thought of their fields as different. And Gesell always wished to run his own operation.[70] He received two small grants from the memorial in 1923 and 1924. In early 1925, when he applied again, Frank intervened. He insisted that Gesell's program be placed within the institute.[71] Unwittingly, Frank had engineered a shotgun wedding. Yerkes, Dodge, and Wissler had no wish to work with Gesell; indeed, none of the four men wished to work with one another in any meaningful sense. As Yerkes remembered it three decades later, "Instead of the single agency for psychological and anthropological research which the announcement seemed to imply, and instead of the unitary team of investigators, there developed four virtually separate and almost independent centers . . . of research, each with its special staff group."[72] Nor did Ruml, as the man responsible for the institute, protest. The four scholars went their own way.[73] Gesell won more support from the memorial, with Frank's endorsement, as a child development specialist, and, of course, Ruml was the patron of Yerkes, Dodge, and Wissler, through his own social sciences grant empire.[74] Frank had to settle for a one-man show in child development at Yale because his hands were tied. Gesell was a productive researcher, but the parent-training program he ran did not match Frank's large ambitions for that enterprise.

Frank had a much freer hand at the universities of Minnesota and California, the two state universities besides Iowa where he acted as programmatic and financial midwife for research centers in the 1920s. In both cases he combined research and diffusion in the proposals. If the structures he helped build did not fulfill his hopes entirely, that merely testified to philanthropy's limited influence upon academic scientific institutions. He considered Minnesota a possible host for an institute for several reasons, including its active social work program and its child guidance clinic. Also he thought the Iowa station needed a friendly competitor in its own region.[75]

In early 1923 he interested Lotus D. Coffman, the university's president and a college classmate, in an institute. Coffman appointed a faculty study committee. Initially, some professors objected, especially in the newly established psychology department.[76] By early 1924, the committee had approved the idea, and within a year the institute was functioning. In contrast to the Teachers College institute, the Minnesota Institute of Child Welfare made all its professional faculty regular university faculty. Furthermore, faculty in collateral departments could teach courses in the institute in return for research time and funds. The university made the Institute of Child Welfare a regular university department and provided all normal privileges and maintenance. In effect, the institute was an integral unit of the university, and the university had a substantial investment in it.[77]

Frank had but one objection. He told Coffman that the parent-training plans were "not sufficiently developed . . . to indicate the kind . . . and method of operation which you propose to set up." A more elaborate program that "should lead to a future organization which will have its roots in local agencies and existing machinery of the state, county, or city" was now the condition of the grant.[78] Coffman responded immediately, pointing out that a large parent-training program should not be implemented until university extension staff had enough experience with small experiments to devise an effective and economical statewide program. Frank had no choice but to yield. The trustees awarded $245,000 over five years for the Minnesota institute.[79] Clumsily, Frank promoted his own candidate as director, but his counsel was ignored.[80]

The Minnesota institute operated smoothly. Appointed director was John E. Anderson, assistant professor of comparative psychology at Yale and one of Yerkes's protégés, who by all accounts was an effective administrator as well as a productive researcher. He surrounded himself with able colleagues, such as anatomist Richard Scammon and psychometrician Florence L. Goodenough.[81] The institute's on-campus courses became heavily subscribed. Five hundred undergraduate students used its laboratory school each year. The faculty were productive researchers. If the parent-training centers throughout the state did not reach the many thousands Frank had blithely assumed would be possible, nevertheless, the center's teachers had busy, crowded schedules. Frank could never quite understand the local problems of parent training in Minnesota, including such astonishingly elementary obstacles to statewide meetings as winter storms. Ultimately, Frank had his own expectations and paid little attention to local realities, or dismissed them as the rationalizations of uncreative faculty.[82]

In contrast, the founding of the Institute of Child Welfare at the University of California, Berkeley, was tumultuous indeed with a dash of burlesque. There were certain parallels between the Iowa and the Berkeley institutes. Like Iowa, Berkeley had its child welfare movement and its Cora Hillis, except the California citizen reformers never bothered to ask the university faculty whether they wanted an institute. The California Congress of Parent-Teacher Associations was one of the largest state PTA associations in America. Thanks to its effective legislative lobbying in prewar times, it was one of the most powerful forces in California politics. Josephine Rand Rogers, a San Jose matron and power within the congress, led a Hillis-style political crusade for a research institute, save that her minions included thousands rather than hundreds. In early 1923, she and her supporters persuaded the legislature that such an institute would terminate poverty, crime, delinquency, and countless other forms of social degeneracy. The solons voted the $500,000 annual appropriation she requested. So far, university faculty and administrators sat on the sidelines as spectators. When a legislative committee visited Berkeley to discuss establishing the institute with university officials, various professors gave the assembly members such conflicting and possessive schemes that the disgusted legislators returned to Sacramento and rescinded the appropriation.[83]

Indeed, faculty opposition was the chief obstacle to an institute for the next four years. Frank knew of the fiasco with the legislature. In 1924, Jean Walker, a psychologist connected with the university, asked Frank if the memorial was interested in establishing a nursery school at Berkeley. He demurred, unless it involved also a "well-rounded program for the promotion of research in child growth and development," and he implied that rival Stanford University was under serious consideration at the memorial.[84] Frank's threat galvanized the California administrators to express interest in an institute at Berkeley. In March 1925, Frank visited Berkeley for a week to discuss the idea with administrators and faculty. Two months later they submitted a tentative proposal. Although Frank wanted an institute at Berkeley, he was disappointed that the plan did not provide for interdisciplinary research with a finely balanced, symmetrical concordance of disciplinary expertise applied to complex, intricate problems. He played a waiting game and set the plan aside. He told the graduate dean that he and his colleagues should "get acquainted with" the other institutes, so as to avoid "a simple laboratory scheme."[85] Many faculty found Frank's remarks bewildering.[86]

Administrators now realized that they had to start afresh. Within another year, the special faculty committee had studied the other institutes and prepared itself in other ways to draft a new and potentially fundable proposal.[87] Yet the prospect of interdisciplinary research caused so much contention and opposition among professors not on the committee that further progress was delayed for another year. In the spring of 1926, Frank successfully negotiated with officials at the California Department of Public Instruction for a three-year experimental program in parent training, and Dr. Herbert R. Stolz, a rising star in pediatrics who had a strong interest in parent education, became the director of the program, which was based in Sacramento. Clearly, Frank wanted California in his evolving national plan; he goaded the Berkeley faculty into approving a research institute on campus.[88] In late 1926, Frank reopened negotiations at Berkeley. The next spring, with not a little pushing and shoving, he had the plan he wanted. The Institute of Child Welfare would do the kind of balanced, symmetrical, interdisciplinary research that Frank so clearly cherished. And it could not avoid parent training. Frank insisted that the university and state programs be merged into one unit, so that child research and parent training would be carried on together. The Berkeley institute won $290,000 over a six-year period, and the parent-training program boosted the entire appropriation another $22,500.[89]

The Berkeley institute rapidly became a major center of child research and parent education. Herbert R. Stolz, who had run the state parent-training program, became the institute's director, dividing his time between administrative chores at Berkeley and Sacramento and a supervisory role at parent-training centers throughout the state. Harold E. Jones, a capable young Columbia University psychologist, was appointed the institute's director of research at Berkeley, and took direct charge of all on-campus activities. Happily, Stolz and Jones worked well together as a team. Stolz was especially gifted at human relations. He and Jones were fully committed to interdisciplinary research, and thanks to their strong intellectual leadership, launched a large number of significant research projects.[90]

Of particular importance from the beginning were the Berkeley Growth Study and the Guidance Study, which Nancy Bayley and Jean Walker Macfarlane began in 1927 and 1928, respectively. Bayley came to the institute in 1927 as a research associate to direct an intensive developmental study of 125 normal babies born of English-speaking, white Berkeley parents. The study was to be multifaceted and balanced among a wide variety of factors, and focused on the first year of life. Rapidly, Bayley and her assistants found that there were more questions than answers; once they had decided to extend the project beyond its original terminus, the "pattern became established of an open-ended, continuing study of growth."[91] The next year, Macfarlane and her associates initiated what they believed would be a limited study of the efficacy of parent training. What began as a quintessentially Frankian research project became in short order just as open-ended and longitudinal as Bayley's, as Macfarlane and her associates discovered that it was an exciting scientific research project in personality development. Ironically, the original question of the effectiveness of parent education was soon put aside when it became clear that there was no answer to the question.[92] And it was a further paradox that within the structure of the institute itself, members of the institute staff did not automatically become members of departments, as was the case at Minnesota. Bayley, for example, never became a regular faculty member of the university. Macfarlane already was when she began her Guidance Study. Obviously academe did not energetically welcome women to faculty ranks then. These structural problems, however, did not seriously interfere with the institute's research productivity, which soon became legendary.[93]

Not all sites were so favored. Frank always insisted that there should be only a handful of experiments at a few strategic points. Thus he rejected overtures from officials at the universities of Nebraska and Montana and from Swarthmore College for parent-training or nursery school programs.[94]

In other instances the investments Frank negotiated took advantage of a particular line of work already underway. Thus in 1924 he discussed the possibilities of funding two small experiments in parent education with officials of the Merrill-Palmer School in Detroit, Michigan. The school had opened in 1921. It was funded by a $3 million bequest from the will of a local philanthropist, Lizzie Merrill-Palmer. The school's purposes were multiple—to teach young girls and women to be homemakers and mothers, but also to conduct research in child development and parent training. By the mid-1920s it had some thirteen specialists in child psychology, nutrition, household management, and nursery school administration on its faculty. Students came from other colleges for a term or so of course work, for which they received credit in their home institutions. One experiment involved getting the memorial's support to disseminate improved methods of parent training to a marginal community, the other a demonstration project in parent education for mothers who had problems with their children. The memorial acceded.[95] Frank also invested in Mills College, in Oakland, California, to test the viability of a nursery school and parent training in a first-class women's college. He thought the experiment a roaring success. By the beginning of the nursery school's fourth year, the college had a full-service department of child development.[96]

Frank also established a statewide plan for New York on the Iowa model, as if to atone for his negotiations with Teachers College. In late 1924 he began talking with certain home economists at Cornell University. He discovered that they were already teaching child study and wanted support to develop a parent education program. Frank was pleased to discover there were no arms to twist in Ithaca. In the next year the memorial made a substantial grant to Cornell to start the Department of Family Life, Child Development, and Parent Education. The department appointed a staff that included a professor of parent training as well as teachers and helpers for the nursery school, engaged the services of a pediatrician, and developed field organizations in university extension. The university put up matching funds, but the legislature refused to fund the program in their next session.

Frank was not easily discouraged. In 1929 he convinced officials of the New York State Department of Education to lead and coordinate the program, now expanded to a glorious size. Cornell would train the professionals in the field, offer residential courses, conduct some research, and carry on its excellent extension work. The State University of New York at Albany would educate nursery school teachers, as would the Buffalo State Teachers College. And the Albany Board of Public Education would operate an experimental nursery school in the city's public schools. This intricate, symmetrical program got underway in 1930. The funding was for five years. Only Cornell's participation thereafter seemed assured. Frank seemed not to mind. He had his statewide program.[97]

Frank also invested in parent education and child study programs at the universities of Georgia and Cincinnati. These were tests of how well the gospel of child study and parent education might fare with city people, southern whites, and southern blacks—traditional objects of Rockefeller concern and charity. The eventual result was no different from that in any other place in the country. Child development scientists were always happy to accept money so that they could go about their own business. As for reaching the lower classes and the uneducated, and converting them to scientific parent education, there were no surprises either. Frank was preaching to the converted: educated, white, middle classes in all cases.[98]

But Frank's reach—and grasp—extended further. In the spring of 1920, the National Research Council's Division of Anthropology and Psychology created a Committee on Child Welfare, of which Baldwin became chair, apparently by default. Customarily, the creation of divisional committees was a signal to the nation's scientific establishment that corporations and foundations should invest in research in the committee's subject matter. Baldwin tried as hard as he could to use his status as chair to raise funds for the station. Until the memorial was ready to proceed in the mid-1920s, no such funds were forthcoming.

And Baldwin had to overcome another obstacle. His colleague Carl E. Seashore worked very hard behind the scenes to block funding of child welfare and development research through the National Research Council. Seashore feared that child development might siphon funds from traditional psychology. In 1924 Baldwin capitalized on the appointment of Robert S. Woodworth as divisional chair, for the Columbia University psychologist fully supported child development research. Woodworth had more important connections in the scientific community than did Seashore. This turned matters around. Traditional interests could no longer throttle the committee. Baldwin and Woodworth engineered the committee's renaming as the Committee on Child Development, thus rescuing the field from progressive reform activism and taxonomizing it as a field in science. Woodworth took other steps as well. With his Columbia professorship, he had important connections to the power centers in American science and philanthropy, access that neither Seashore nor Baldwin, as professors at the State University of Iowa, ever could have. Woodworth's prestige did much for the nascent field and helped run interference for it. And Woodworth understood how to create a professional subculture for a new field of science. Thus he told Frank at the memorial that he was canvassing some 1,200 scientists to discover who was interested in developmental research on children and animals. About one-third responded, of whom 129 declared that they were working on child psychology.[99]

Woodworth was a sly fox. By his actions he virtually dared Frank to invest in the committee and its constituents. Thus he made an end run around traditional psychologists and their control over the National Research Council by inviting Frank to intervene. Frank, of course, was waiting for such an invitation, and it served his purposes well that it was a distinguished professor at Columbia, a favored institution within Rockefeller philanthropy, who chaired the renamed (and reinvented) Committee on Child Development. Frank could not have resisted the temptation to intervene in any event, but now the circumstances could not have been more auspicious for him. In 1925 the Laura Spelman Rockefeller Memorial funded the first of four Committee on Child Development conferences. Held over the next seven years, these conferences enabled the most active researchers in the field to meet face-to-face—mostly for the first time—to interact intellectually and professionally, to work out the field's intellectual boundaries, and to engage in various activities that would provide strength and cohesion for this latest professional scientific subculture. Starting in 1926, the committee awarded postdoctoral fellowships in the field that the memorial had funded. The next year the committee began publishing a sorely needed bibliographical journal. In 1933, at the last committee conference, through a highly complex process, the committee became a scientific society, the Society for Research in Child Development (SRCD). The SRCD was soon publishing three journals in the field and holding biennial meetings. It was perhaps testimony to the actual vitality of interdisciplinary scholarship in the interwar years that it was not until after World War II that the SRCD became financially independent of the NRC and of foundations—and then promptly almost went out of business.[100]

Frank also attempted to sustain a national lay constituency for child study and parent education. Through truly heroic negotiations he arranged to have the memorial purchase large blocks of shares of stock in *Parents Magazine*, a highly successful, "slick" magazine. This would be the capstone of the parent education movement, an attempt to provide national inspirational leadership for what remained, in the main, local and regional movements. In this particular scheme, the stock was given to the four research centers—Iowa, Minnesota, California, and Yale—and the dividends were supposed to go to the research centers to support research. Frank hoped in particular that these monies, thus under the research centers' control, could pay for new, innovative projects that might be too unorthodox to win funding from more traditional sources.[101]

On January 3, 1929, the memorial was consolidated with the Rockefeller Foundation as part of the general reorganization of Rockefeller philanthropy, thus ending a decade and more of sometimes chaotic entrepreneurship among various program officers. The new reorganization of Rockefeller philanthropy, its instigators hoped, would bring balance and proportion to the relations between the various elements and interests in the larger whole. The Laura Spelman Rockefeller Memorial's trustees voted some $10 million to continue child study and parent education through a new Rockefeller philanthropy, the Spelman Fund. In the months before the general reorganization, Frank had carried out a final round of negotiations on the memorial's behalf for long-term, massive grants to the research centers in child study, as he had with Iowa; Teachers College won $0.5 million, Minnesota slightly more than $700,000, and Gesell's work was continued at Yale through another gigantic plan, the Yale Institute of Human Relations.[102]

Frank had indeed stitched together a complex unity, a professional scientific subculture with many distinct and interrelated parts or elements. As a typical construct of its age, this institutional entity combined the public and the private, the academic and the philanthropic, the layperson and the expert, the national, regional, and local, all into a network of complex, interrelated, symmetrical yet distinct elements, a whole that was greater than or perhaps different from the sum of its parts. Perhaps what held all the parts together in that sphere of activity within the larger national culture was that special attitude in those years that there was something important, vital, even compelling, about the notions of saving children and improving family life through the promises and techniques of the new social sciences. Of course, such a hope could be interpreted in at least two ways: giving a priority to the saving of children or valuing first and foremost scientific investigation and method. As the profession of child development crystallized, and as workers thus turned to the invention of a scientific discipline and its attendant ideology, popular and technical, in the decade or so after Frank began his labors, that issue, which had taken a particular configuration in the pre–World War I years, was to emerge again. And the Iowa Child Welfare Research Station was to play a major role in these events.

CHAPTER THREE

INVENTING A SCIENCE

On a Friday evening in early March 1923, the Mothers and Parent-Teacher Association of Mason City, Iowa, sponsored a program of entertainment and edification at the Washington Elementary School. As earnest parents continued to file into the auditorium at about 7:45, suddenly the lights went out, thanks to a jinxed transformer. It was not until "well after 8 o'clock" that an electrician from a local firm, the Peoples' Gas and Electric Company, corrected the difficulty. The program then began with a rendition of "Winken, Blinken, and Nod" by members of the Matinee Musicale Club. In response to sustained applause from the audience, club members sang, as an encore, "Lullaby and Good Night." Next, Mrs. Harlan McMillian ascended to the stage with her piano accompanist, Mrs. Hazel Patton. Mrs. McMillian's first violin solo, "Gavotte," by a seventeenth-century composer, was followed with an encore, "Valse-triste," by Jean Sibelius, to "unstinted applause." Then the audience was treated to a reading, "The New Piano," by another Mason City matron, Mrs. E. E. Geeting, who reportedly left her listeners in stitches as she delivered it in her "finished manner and with a perfect 'Minnesota' accent." Her encore was "Any Mail for Murphy?" in which her child impersonation was executed, according to the newspaper reporter, with "matchless realism."

The speaker who edified rather than entertained that evening was Bird T. Baldwin. He addressed the assembled crowd on the station's latest researches and their implications for school and home. He argued, as he had in 1914, that the child had five ages beyond the chronological, all of which had to be in balance and adjustment if the child were to be considered normal. Of all six ages, the chronological signified the least. He pointed to research that demonstrated, for example, that physical and mental growth curves were parallel in the child and thus intimately related, part of a larger, symmetrical whole. The mental depended upon the physical, *physical* in Baldwin's usage meaning anatomical and especially physiological growth. This research had important implications, he insisted, for the proper placement of children in the school grades best suited to their actual, as opposed to their mere chronological development. Baldwin also discussed the preschool laboratory, where sixty children between the ages of two and four were observed with the best available methods of science. Above all, science had its applications.[1]

Public relations was a central element in Baldwin's routine as the station's director in these early years when there was no institutional mechanism to perform these tasks. There were, as yet, no conferences or summer courses, let alone a statewide parent-training program or the Radio Child Study Club of the middle and late twenties and thirties. Between 1920 and 1925 he spoke at least forty-seven times before lay and civic groups such as the Mason City association, not to mention giving almost as many addresses of a more technical nature before professional and scientific organizations. Inasmuch as his views can be accurately ascertained from newspaper accounts, he shifted in the themes he took up in these years from emphases on the body, on conservation of the race, and on physical and physiological maturation, to the relationships between physiological and mental growth, to the importance of personality and social development as compared with the intelligence quotient per se, and to his increasing, if not fully elaborated, sensitivity to nonorganic factors in child and human development. He argued that a child's basic nature and attributes were established by the time he or she entered public school, thus the major importance of a child's proper development during the preschool years. And he insisted that child science had to be developed and managed by experts, meaning professionals trained in science. By the same token, the responsibilities of parenthood in today's modern, complex, technological society were such that parenthood must become a profession. The old cut-and-fit techniques of the past, the traditional folklore and wisdom, would no longer suffice.[2]

Baldwin's popular notions of child science did not differ markedly from his scientific ideas. The shift in his thinking was representative of shifts in the field itself. At the time, all that Baldwin and his professional colleagues understood was that theirs was a science in infancy, that in most respects it had no independent existence as a science or a discipline apart from those fields in which specialists worked, such as child psychology, embryology, pediatrics, physical growth, nutrition, and the like. Indeed, there was no such thing as a science of the child when the Iowa Child Welfare Research Station was founded. Rather, a handful of scientists merely engaged in a few displays of technical competence here and there.

Thus Baldwin and his colleagues could invent a science of the child by default. It was not until the late 1920s that the other child welfare institutes were fully functional and were producing quantities of data through their investigations. Above all, child science had no grand underlying theory as yet, no fundamental mainstream assumptions or principles that would guide, nay compel, workers in the field to interpret discoveries in particular ways. Nor was there yet theoretical or methodological content distinctive to child science that distinguished it from its antecedent and founding fields of psychology, physical growth, physiology, pediatrics, and the like. Baldwin wanted his field to be as professional and scientific as possible; questions of social application, as, for instance, Hillis's concerns, mattered less to him.

From the field's institutions and history some clues existed for the invention of this new science, such as the conflict between Baldwin's and Frank's blueprints of state plans of child study and parent training, or the training that most in the new field had in psychology, education, and medicine. Psychology was the major training ground of most developmentalists, and their work reflected their background. They pursued normative research, producing reams of data on the norms—including the group measurements—of the subjects of their investigations to find out how the "typical" normal child acted, behaved, thought, felt, and related to others. At least initially, they brought the group orientation of their prior training into the new work without betraying the slightest sign that they understood the larger implications of their actions.

In the station's early years, Baldwin influenced the station's intellectual direction more than had any other single person. As director, he held a dean's rank and reported directly to the president. Jessup guided Baldwin's political and public relations activities on the station's behalf, but he did not interfere in the least with Baldwin's ideas. And within the station's ranks, Baldwin was the dominant intellectual figure. No member of the faculty, no graduate student, and no staff member remained at the station for all of his eleven-year tenure. The only faculty member who even approached his quantity of published works was Amy Daniels. Together they were responsible for most of the station's publications from 1917, when he was appointed, until 1931, when the last work undertaken under his influence and guidance was published. In that period, the station's staff published 161 distinct works, including monographs, research articles, abstracts of research reports read at professional conferences, textbooks, reviews of the professional literature, statements of professional or disciplinary theory, and popular articles on the station directed toward its patrons and constituents. Excluded from this list are extension bulletins, pamphlets, service publications, brochures, advertisements of curricula and conferences, master's theses and doctoral dissertations. Of the 161, 125 were reports of original investigations and 36 were statements about the station and its activities. Baldwin wrote 82 of the total, including all but 2 of the popular statements, and Daniels 35 original papers and 2 popular pieces. No other member of the station's staff, faculty, or graduate student population published more than 13 distinct works. When appointed at Iowa, Baldwin was a specialist in education and educational psychology, with a special interest in the physical growth of children. Of the 45 publications on his curriculum vitae in 1917, at least a third were concerned with the profession of public school teaching. His most substantial research publication was the massive monograph, published in 1914, dealing with physical measurements and school marks of certain groups of children. And, indeed, in the 1910s, it was that work, and his article in *Popular Science Monthly*, that constituted his credentials as a researcher on the normal child.[3]

Baldwin's problem, and that of the station, was precisely that of the pioneer who must create a cultural construct de novo. It was not true, of course, that accepted facts about normal children did not exist in American scientific culture in 1917. Facts existed in such widely scattered fields as child study, pediatrics, physical education, nutrition, and, above all, in the rapidly growing field of mental measurement. But it was to be no simple task to gather "old" facts together, rename than as "new facts" within the confines of the new science, and then proceed to discover more new facts, so as to imply that the new science did exist and that it was growing, progressive, and useful.

Almost certainly Baldwin did not realize that his early activities as director constituted the turning of old facts in other sciences into new facts in his new science. He did precisely that when, for example, he had a graduate student ransack the European and American scientific literature for references appropriate for the new science of normal children. The annotated bibliography of 911 items he included in the massive monograph he published in 1920 on physical growth was another example of appropriating materials from preexisting fields for a new field, as was his course on child welfare, which he taught in the spring of 1918; he simply incorporated, lock, stock, and barrel, the literature of physical anthropology and of psychological processes into that of the new science of child development.

Nor was this all. He foraged for facts any way he could. Thus he announced a free baby examining clinic. Parents could bring their offspring for physical measurements. The quid pro quo was that the anxious parents received expert advice on whether their children were normal, and the station won the right to take semiannual measurements of the same children, thus systematically multiplying the station's inventory of information over a period of years. Like his national colleagues, Baldwin believed that the crucial years to study were the first six or seven. And he knew also that without access to a research population of living, normal children, relatively little experimental or observational work could be done at the station.[4]

The world war interrupted the station's activities. Baldwin served as a major in the U.S. Sanitary Corps, and was stationed at Walter Reed Hospital, where he was assigned to devise and apply techniques for occupational therapy for wounded soldiers. He appointed the station's sociologist, Ellsworth Faris, as acting director for the duration of his absence, from March 1918 to August 1919, while the station marked time.

Probably the station's most important accomplishment during the war was its participation in the survey of Iowa children from April 1918 to April 1919, at the behest of the Children's Bureau. Hillis had wanted full cooperation with the bureau, whose officers wanted to collect socioeconomic data about poor and unfortunate children. Baldwin, who wanted information of a more scientific character on normal children, won the struggle. Iowa women's groups and other civic organizations provided the volunteers, hundreds of them, for the work. The Iowa survey canvassed some 140,000 children and "cooperated" with the U.S. Children's Bureau, which meant simply a doff of the hat to the bureau. Baldwin told Jessup, "a survey of the homes, schools, and institutions [of Iowa] is opportune and thousands of people can be made to work for us."[5]

The survey did not work out as Baldwin had hoped. Volunteers did not turn out in sufficient numbers, and most of the children examined were older than seven years, too old to conform to the age group he thought fundamental to study.[6] He did publish a handbook of carefully spelled-out instructions on how to take the semiannual measurements of height, weight, and breathing capacity of children between the ages of five-and-a-half and eighteen years, and on how to derive the norms of growth for height and weight by sex and year. He stressed that only competent professionals could take the measurements and derive the norms; these complex and intricate matters were best left to either members of the station's staff, or, if they were not available, science teachers or medical inspectors in the public schools. Citizen volunteers received no direct mention in Baldwin's pamphlet for the simple and obvious reason that there was no role they could play in the survey except to help the professionals when asked. This was hardly democratic or popular science. Expertise mattered above all else. Eventually, data on the 140,000 children were collected and put into useful form. Baldwin was able, upon his return from the army, to incorporate it into his own work on physical growth.[7]

In Baldwin's absence there were other projects. Amy Daniels arrived in September 1918. After some initial difficulties, she and her assistants began work.[8] Her early endeavors included projects in corrective speech, a survey of first-grade pupils in nearby Cedar Rapids, a survey of musical talent that Seashore conducted, and continued measurement of the intelligence and physical growth of a group of normal children in the university elementary schools. She also continued work on several bibliographies of books and articles on children from the scientific and social policy perspectives—gathered, of course, from the bibliographies of preexisting fields.[9]

When Baldwin returned, he addressed the problem of gaining access to large numbers of normal children for research purposes. He won permission from Seashore to give mental and physical tests to all normal children referred to or enrolled in university clinics, hospitals, and schools and to deposit the data in the station's archives. He also arranged to have mental tests given to normal and borderline children referred to the Des Moines Health Center, which had ties with the university medical school and the psychology department's mental hygiene clinic. Baldwin was anxious to gather as much research data as he could; as he told Hillis, it was "absolutely essential that the Station have some source material of its own on which to work and as it is now carried out we have no direct control over children any place."[10] And no wonder. The data came in slowly; the station's staff had managed to collect systematic measurements in the infant examination clinic on only about four hundred children in the first two years of the station's history.[11]

Over the next two years Baldwin succeeded in gaining regular access to normal children for research purposes. No longer did he have to content himself with improvisations and half-measures. In the end, it was the WCTU money that made the first preschool laboratories possible. How and why this occurred might seem peculiar at first, for the funds were supposed to support a professor and department of eugenics and to support investigations on the effects of such harmful substances as cocoa, tobacco, and alcoholic beverages, on children. Yet it was not so difficult as it might have appeared. For the women of the WCTU, and, one suspects, for a lot of Americans who were not scientists, the term *eugenics* did not mean sterilization of the unfit, tracing out family lines for various dysfunctional traits, and the like. Rather it meant the improvement of the conditions of child and family life; often such persons used it interchangeably with the term *euthenics*, which, to members of the eugenics movement, meant improvement of the environment, not of the germ plasm. So eugenics did not have the dreadful connotations to many Americans as it did to a handful of scientists and activists, despite the presentist arguments of some historians to the contrary.[12] And Baldwin had been able to prevail with the WCTU officers on the point that the $50,000 should be pooled with the station's resources and support an expanded program in child welfare and science with no strings attached.[13]

The WCTU funds enabled Baldwin to fulfill his plans. He appointed more research assistants, as well as Lorle I. Stecher, his research associate, who proved an able collaborator. Stecher began by taking charge of the station's mental and physical measurements. The assistants collected semiannual measurements of physical growth, as a continuation of the wartime survey, albeit on a much reduced scale. Baldwin then accessioned these measurements for his own research, which he thought of in grand terms; he wanted to construct growth curves as linear—as replicating the life cycle. When he talked about the five ages of the child, he nevertheless did research only on binary comparisons between physical and mental growth. And he thought that all normal children varied within the mean for one type of child, the normal child. He began to beat the drum for a new kind of institution, the preschool laboratory. In a popular pamphlet, for example, he argued that the most far-reaching use of the WCTU funds for the station would be this observational school, "where the nutritional, physical, mental and social environments of each child" could be rigorously studied to produce "specific results of great value to the state at large."[14]

It was not until mid-October 1921 that the preschool was completed and could actually open its doors to its first class of children ages two to six. As always, Baldwin had had a number of grander ideas.[15] In the end, a four-room building, meant to be temporary, was constructed that summer. Baldwin kept Hillis informed about its progress that spring and summer, so that she would be reassured—and pacified.[16]

Initially, only sixteen children were to enroll in the preschool for three-and-a-half hours each weekday morning. The number of interested parents grew quickly. By January there were twenty-four pupils divided into morning and afternoon sessions of equal length. In the preschool, care was taken to create a child-sized environment in the furniture and other equipment. Activities were planned with the children's interests in mind, to be sure, but also with a keen eye toward the kinds of routine and utility necessary for scientific observation. If the ultimate public justification for the preschool was, as Stecher explained to a local women's club, to teach the children how to be sociable and how to get along with their peers, the preschool was first and foremost a scientific laboratory, even if games were played, refreshments served, naptimes observed, and windows adorned with gay chintz curtains. Reams of data were processed and collected; certain measurements were taken, and a student observer wrote in a logbook the seemingly important acts that signified something about each child's development. Whether physical and mental growth were correlated was a major scientific issue in the preschool's early years that interested Baldwin immensely.[17]

Soon the number of sessions was extended to two each in the morning and the afternoon, serving forty-eight, not twenty-four, pupils. Parents in Iowa City and its immediate environs clamored for space for their children. The preschool's pupils were typically members of the business and professional families found in such small midwestern communities as Iowa City. Faculty children were especially numerous. Among the preschool's first class of twenty-four were twenty children of university faculty, including Patricia Baldwin, daughter of Bird Baldwin, and Arthur M. Schlesinger, Jr., son of Professor Arthur M. Schlesinger, Sr., then a rising star in the field of American history. The preschool's routine was highly popular with the children. They were taught to take care of many of their own needs, such as putting on or taking off their coats, getting their own drinks, buttoning their shoes, and spreading butter over their bread. The sessions were divided into a half-hour period of individual play, followed by an hour of group play, the purpose of which was to encourage the children to respect the rights of others and to obey adult authority. Individual play might include being on the sandpile, playing with certain toys, sketching pictures, and the like, and group play might involve singing, artistic work, stringing popcorn, modeling with clay or plasticine, and so on.[18]

This play was not without larger purpose. Beyond the staff's balanced and symmetrical routine of regular mental, medical, and physical measurements, the children were observed, and their behavior systematically recorded. The staff conducted this scientific work from within the intellectual framework of traditional psychology as adapted to children. They emphasized group life and the child's adjustment to it. Indeed, in numerous instances, staff followed up observations in the preschool with observations in the home. Staff members took all aspects of the individual child into account, including intelligence quotient, personality, coordination, ability to get along with others, and willingness to obey the rules. Each child could be an individual so long as this individuality did not disrupt others. The staffers viewed the child as an atom added to that larger combination of distinct, individual atoms, the sum of the preschool's pupils.

Since each child was tacitly understood as but a variation of the normal child, naturally it occurred to no researcher at the station to investigate the other side of the coin, the impact of the group, and its dynamics, upon each and every other child, save from one perspective, that of whether the child was normally progressing for his or her age toward that ultimate standard of completed development, "adult behavior." Indeed, much of the emphasis in the observations was precisely upon cognition, upon mental development without regard to nuances of learning theory, either in a formal, scholastic sense, or even in the sense of general intellect. Nor was there any interest in elaborating Baldwin's dictum of 1914, that there were six ages of the normal child that were in perfect balance and proportion to one another. The major emphasis in all work was binary, usually the physical versus the mental. Any notion of multiple, interdependent, and interrelated factors, as suggested by Baldwin's formula, did not yet exist among the station's researchers—including Baldwin—as an operational assumption in research. Clearly the content of child research had altered since 1900. But the larger and deeper assumptions of the science had not yet changed.[19]

Baldwin gained much from the preschool. Now he had his research population. Henceforth the station could generate original investigations, not to mention professionally marketable data, without recourse to other sources. The collection of old facts from the bibliographies of preexisting disciplines, and their transformation, as if by magic, into new facts by their inclusion in the station's library and bibliographies, continued apace, if for no other reason than to give graduate assistants chores to justify their stipends. But now genuinely new facts could be found, processed through scientific method into data, and these data, in their manufactured state, could be proclaimed as part of the station's own research activities. Baldwin was immensely pleased and excited.

Furthermore, he had played his hand well insofar as the station's diplomatic relations with interests within and without the university were concerned. He had not alienated the university faculty. Fears of a reform-school clinic, first aroused in the legislative campaigns, existed no longer. The preschool itself was enormously helpful in that regard. And this circumstance also checkmated Seashore's behind-the-scenes efforts to undercut Baldwin's authority. The WCTU gladly accepted the new uses of their money. When national president, Anna E. Gordon, visited the campus in September 1921, she gushed poetic over the new facility for the little darlings. Hence there was little that Hillis could do. Baldwin was finally learning faculty and interest-group politics, but it had been a struggle for this gentle and somewhat naive Quaker unused to such domineering and autocratic persons as Seashore and Hillis.[20]

In the early 1920s Baldwin was primarily interested in finishing his work on physical growth and its relations to mental development. When he spoke in public, he took care to accentuate the remedial aspects of the work. He spoke before the women's club of Waterloo, Iowa, arguing that the human body should be conserved. He stressed how many defects in otherwise normal schoolchildren the station's workers were finding in their surveys, and how costly and inefficient these problems were to family, community, school, and the nation at large.[21] Sometimes he spoke as if race and nationality were vital, real categories. He was still in a transitional stage of his thinking, with no sense of contradiction at all, and thus took a variety of tacks. In the fall of 1921, when he gave a paper at the Second International Congress of Eugenics, he argued that physiological, not chronological, age was the proper key to understanding growth. He was fascinated, too, by the prospect of being able to predict development from such a baseline. In his address before the Eugenics Congress, he stated that comparisons between individuals assumed a strict linear form, and measurements were based on the assumption that the body could be viewed, from the exterior, as a three-dimensional form. Processes and forces could be considered binary and conflictual. Obviously, here he was not thinking in terms of multiple, interactive factors as constituting a larger symmetrical whole, as his 1914 definition of the normal child would have implied. Yet on other occasions he invoked the newer point of view.[22]

To address the problem of how to create and disseminate data about the normal child, Baldwin established a monograph series for the station, the University of Iowa Series in Child Welfare. The early volumes emphasized, in various ways, the new science and its applications. The series' first volume was his magnum opus, the summation of his decade of research on the physical growth of normal children. His major concerns were to derive national norms or standards of physical growth and the lawful principles of physical growth for normal children.

The book was an expansion of his 1914 monograph, together with data acquired since. Now he had data on children from infancy to age eighteen. The groups of children had been measured adventitiously, that is, they did not constitute a longitudinal sample of the same individuals (and groups) measured at different and consecutive times; the notion of longitudinal studies, as that would come into play in the field, had not yet been devised or articulated. He argued that one of the great advantages of his data was that it had been collected in sufficiently different states, especially New York, Pennsylvania, Maryland, and Iowa; his data were "national," and he could define "national" norms of physical growth at various stages of the life cycle through adolescence. He established a series of principles of physical growth, by age and sex, and, to some extent, by race. In turn, he claimed that these defined the various growth patterns for these different types of normal children. By deploying particular instruments and gaining certain key measurements, the child scientist could determine that growth was lawful for each individual within the group to which he belonged. Most striking were the differences between boys and girls; girls tended to mature physiologically earlier than boys. Even then, however, adolescence meant more irregularity, more spurts and jumps, for boys as well as for girls. Growth curves of related individuals were parallel, even when siblings were of the opposite sex, meaning that family heritage mattered.

Above all, Baldwin insisted, mere chronological age was a poor guide to understanding physical growth. More important—and revealing—were anatomical and physiological ages. Anatomical age was a measure of the maturation of the skeletal structure. Physiological age, on the other hand, meant the measurement of the maturation of physiological processes and the organs responsible for them. Breathing capacity, he insisted, was one universal criterion of physiological age, regardless of the group or individual studied. Other manifestations of advancing physiological age were related to the onset of puberty, with the enlargement of the genitalia, the growth of body hair, the beginning of the menses in girls and the presence of sperm cells in penile secretions of boys, and so on. Thus far, Baldwin had sketched in a considerable amount of information and interpretation concerning the physical growth of normal children. He had certainly gone far beyond the prewar notions of the child, with that heavy emphasis on the abnormal or subnormal child.[23]

He gradually shifted his angle of vision. On the most obvious level, he grew more and more interested in problems of the relations of physical and physiological development with mental development of normal and superior children, and less and less interested in physical and physiological development as such. In 1922 he and Lorle Stecher published a preliminary study of the correlations between anatomical, physiological, and mental indexes of growth in individual children. They found that girls matured more rapidly than boys, and, moreover, superiority in one index was matched by superiority in others, in the same individuals. Baldwin and Stecher raised critical questions about the Stanford-Binet intelligence test, essentially on technical grounds. They wanted to know if there were safeguards against such methodological flaws as whether children benefited in their scores from retesting. They neither questioned nor challenged the notion that the IQ was inherited.[24]

Baldwin soon became involved in two projects that enabled him to explore the relations between physical and mental growth. The superintendent of the Cleveland, Ohio, public schools appointed Baldwin a consultant on that very question for children in the Cleveland public schools from kindergarten through junior high school. Baldwin selected 3,500 pupils and gave them physical, medical, dental, nutritional, and mental examinations, together with certain physical tests as further measures of physiological growth. He also administered a battery of intelligence tests. Here he was obviously thinking of multiple factors, although not yet of multifactorial measurements, as if all variables were interdependent. His overall argument was that those who were physiologically advanced should be promoted or demoted to a grade level congruent with their development, on the theory that mental development awaited physiological development. He also thought in terms of race and ethnicity: different groups in Cleveland, such as Hungarians, white Americans, black Americans, and so on, appeared to have different norms of development.[25]

His conclusions had been similar when he worked with Lewis M. Terman at Stanford on the physical growth aspect of Terman's Genetic Studies of Genius project, launched in 1921 with funding from the Commonwealth Fund, on one thousand California children whose IQ scores were in the genius range. Terman's was the nation's first true longitudinal project in the social and behavioral sciences. He wanted to show that these California geniuses were advanced in physical and physiological as well as intellectual measures. Good things seemed to go together, the argument ran. Baldwin's conclusions easily fit within Terman's larger hypotheses.[26]

Yet Baldwin had a broader vision than that of a mere psychometrician interested in the measurement of innate IQs. He noted in passing that the Cleveland project verified the assumption that the child's capacity for education was not limited to a few school subjects but included other phases of mental development, "such as the aesthetic and emotional life and the child's capacity for physical and social growth."[27]

In 1923 and 1924, Baldwin emphasized these themes increasingly. When he declared that factors other than innate intelligence and class standing, such as physiological, social, and ethical development, must be considered in school placement, or when he told the superintendents of Iowa's charitable and corrections institutions that a child's character could not be ignored and a simple IQ score was not an adequate measure of the complexity of any child, he was in fact moving from one bundle of basic assumptions and preoccupations to another. He brought the same message to lay and civic and parents' groups in Minneapolis and Saint Paul, Minnesota; Philadelphia, Pennsylvania; Clinton, Sioux City, Dubuque, and Brooklyn, Iowa; Rochester, New York; South Bend, Indiana; Tulsa, Oklahoma; Emporia, Kansas; Wilmington, Delaware; and New Haven, Connecticut; among other communities.[28]

Clearly by the mid-1920s Baldwin had incorporated child welfare into the science of the normal child, or child development, as it was becoming known. He had become closely tied, in an ideological sense, to the left wing of the progressive education movement, centered as it was in New York. Increasingly, he wanted child science to help children. But unlike Cora Hillis, he wanted the science and its applications to remain firmly in the hands (and heads) of the professionals, the experts. The crystallizing synthesis, at least at the Iowa Child Welfare Research Station, included the development of a science and of its social applications, or, perhaps, of a science and its social technology.[29] This was, after all, an age when many Americans believed technology could be used to solve social problems.[30]

This belief was evident in the nutritional work of research professor Amy L. Daniels and her associates. The strong tone of social application in her work was typical of that of her scientific colleagues in nutrition nationwide, that of uncovering the principles of proper nutrition for the healthy, normal infant and child. She defined her experimental subjects, rats and infants, as complex, multifaceted organisms that consumed a variety of substances. She wanted to identify and classify whether these materials were beneficial to growth and, therefore, to good nutrition. The rules of proper nutrition presumably held for most species; the trick was to uncover the proper chemical reactions, and, thus, the particular laws of nutrition. She explored the most nutritious methods of food preparation, for example, whether canned and dried foods contained sufficient quantities of the antineuritic vitamin (thiamin).[31] In another study, she ascertained the antineuritic and growth properties of orange juice for infants.[32] Daniels assessed the nutritional value of lard and cottonseed oil, of heat-treated milks, and of yeast as a source of the antineuritic vitamin.[33] She and her helpers explored growth and milk in a more complicated experiment involving rats and infants, probed the nutritional value, for human infants, of milk in goats and cows and of evaporated milk, and even conducted an intergenerational study of the value of cow's milk for rats.[34]

According to Daniels and other nutritionists, growth was a linear process, an unfolding into the present and future of the forces of the past and the present. Daniels insisted that proper nutritional intervention was helpful and curative. She was no deterministic pessimist, nor did she evoke the notions of late nineteenth- and early twentieth-century nutritionists that different groups or races in the human population typically required different diets. Nutritional science had changed since the late nineteenth century from racial analysis into an optimistic social technology. Accordingly, she stressed the centrality of intervention in the present. But there was more. She and her coworkers in the new science of nutrition also assumed that proper growth and nutrition resulted from a multitude of interactive factors, and that nutrition, whether from the standpoint of the food or the organism, had to be thought of in terms of discrete yet interrelated parts that as a sum were different from or greater than the larger whole. Mere reductionist, mechanistic, and static analyses would not do. An integrated, dynamic, and holistic perspective was essential.[35]

A similar tone pervaded other investigations at the Iowa station in the mid-twenties. Natural and social reality were complex, dynamic, intricate, and interrelated, constituted of many distinct yet interactive elements. Balance, symmetry, the correlation between the micro and macro visions—these were the qualities of the taxonomy of reality. From slightly different perspectives, Frank Horack, a political science professor, and A. Ione Bliss, a graduate student in the station, published brief monographs in which they assessed the legal protections afforded children in Iowa and national law. They found Iowa statutory protection sorely lacking, at least as compared with the standards established by the federal Children's Bureau, and not addressing the needs of normal children, either.[36] Graduate student Sara Stinchfield found all manner of speech problems among samples of schoolchildren at the university elementary school and in Pittsburgh, Pennsylvania. She insisted that most problems were functional, not structural, and had biological, physical, cultural, and even individual causes, and were therefore curable.[37] Clara Town surveyed first-grade children in nearby Cedar Rapids to see how well the home had prepared the children for school. Her results were highly negative—which was hardly surprising, given the station's developing ideology that preschool was good for children as well as convenient for child researchers. She also challenged the argument of many mental testers that a child's intelligence determined his or her socioeconomic level in life. Rather, she insisted, the reverse proposition was more clearly the case. Her radical statement was not echoed by her local or national colleagues.[38]

Any possibility that the station might have turned into a center of eugenics nostrums and bromides was rapidly disappearing. Phineas W. Whiting, the station's research professor of eugenics, came and went within four years; he worked mainly on his own research on venation in wasp wings and refused to be a noisy eugenics propagandist, thus saving the station much potential embarrassment. In fact, in the few public statements he did make about human inheritance, he argued along with other up-to-date geneticists that nature and nurture were intimately integrated in dynamic, symmetrical, and balanced interaction in all biological inheritance, including that specifically of humankind.[39] The station's sociologist, Hornell Hart, concerned himself more directly with problems that eugenicists liked to discuss, notably the alleged decline of the "quality" of "racial stocks" in the countryside. And indeed, this was the original trump card Baldwin had played with the memorial's officials. But Hart kept his rhetoric comparatively cool. He did publish studies that could be interpreted as eugenic in orientation, but they were demographic rather than racial, *racial* meaning notions of racial differences shaping public policy. In any event, by 1925 he, like Whiting, had left the station for presumably greener academic pastures.[40] Thereafter, there was no mention whatsoever of eugenics research, the eugenics professor, or the department of eugenics, as specified in the WCTU grant, in any form at the station. It was as if these things had never existed there.

Indeed, notions of the taxonomy of natural and social reality were changing in the mid-1920s. In 1926 Ruth Updegraff, a doctoral candidate at the station, published her first scientific paper. She had studied psychology at Vassar College with Margaret Floy Washburn, a distinguished scientist who worked hard to train women to take their places, such as they might be, in American scientific institutions.[41] Updegraff was fortunate indeed. She moved from traditional adult psychology to child psychology, a new field in which she knew there were professional and intellectual opportunities.[42]

The scientific problem Updegraff addressed was on the nature of finality in melody. She defined melody as a succession of musical sounds felt to constitute a unity. This unity, in turn, implied an interrelationship, a completeness and a coherence as a symmetrical whole. Unity signified relationship and finality. From a scientific point of view, the problem of melody thus became that of explaining how a series of tonal stimuli could excite a feeling of unity among those who heard them. The traditional view of psychologists of music, set out in the early 1900s, was that related tones were only those that shared a technical relationship according to their rates of vibration. Only those vibrations whose relations could be expressed or represented by the prime numbers one, two, three, five, and seven, and their composites, could stimulate a feeling of relationship among auditors. According to this view, music constituted a system in which the parts added up to a whole, no more and no less.

More recently, some had questioned this theory. They insisted that their experiments, modeled after those upon which the traditional definition had been based, had shown that a feeling of the finality of melody was acquired, learned by listeners as the result of social experience. In this new view, melody consisted not of a system divorced from social experience; it was an integral and yet distinct part of a larger balanced whole, constituted of social experience and melody, a holistic symmetry that was greater than or different from the sum of its parts. Updegraff then asked which approach was correct: was the feeling of tonality physical or psychological, and to what extent?

In her experiment, she employed longer series of notes than the traditional three, which she airily dismissed as not worthy of the term *melody*. For tonality to be a factor in melody, more than three notes were required. Three notes could, for instance, be harmonious, as in a triad. But that was no test of melody. And if the three tones did not constitute a chord, melodic unity would not result. Updegraff presented four distinct series of notes to three groups of listeners. In the first, eight had definite musical training, and seven had none. The next was a group of children, aged four to six, from the station's preschool. The third was a group of American and Chinese students. The results with the preschoolers were ambiguous. Those with the others were not. Finality seemed determined by the influence of the falling inflection, of the interval—not the note—and of the suggested tonality of the melody. In other words, the experiences of the listeners mattered, not the mathematical (and physical) relations of the notes and their vibrations. The results with the American and Chinese students appeared especially telling, for they heard both Western music, designed as vertical and harmonious, and Chinese music, always horizontal and nonharmonious. Their reactions underlined the importance of social experience.[43]

Updegraff's paper suggested that child science was expanding and changing at the Iowa station by the mid-1920s. She had taken a small component of traditional adult psychology and had appropriated it through her work into her science.[44] Yet more was involved than what might be presumed to be a linear accumulation of "new" facts (even if they were largely old ones rechristened as new facts) for the discipline. The traditional view that she revised of finality in melody was predicated on a different taxonomy of natural and social reality, in which music existed as an entirely natural construct and in which the distinctive element constituted the larger whole, a system unto itself. Her notion of natural and social reality was predicated upon the idea that the natural and the cultural were distinct yet inseparable elements bound together into a balanced, functional, unified whole that was either greater than or different from the sum of its parts. Not surprisingly, she thought of her work as addressing only narrow issues within the discipline; indeed, she cited the recent work of a young behaviorist as inspiration for her experiment.[45] Clearly, however, the pictures of natural and social reality current in the early 1900s were simply not, for her, a useful point of departure. Thus her paper marked a dramatic change from a worldview in which nature and culture were antagonistic to one in which they were interrelated.

By the middle twenties the Iowa station's staff had generated new facts from old facts and had processed an ever-growing mountain of data through various scientific methods, thus inventing a science of the normal child. They had also articulated notions and practices of the relations between professionals and laity in the field that would secure the professionals' ambitions. And they had not abandoned the goals of child welfare and the amelioration of the circumstances of child life. These were not small accomplishments. Yet the ground would continue to shift under everyone's feet for a few more years, especially as more institutions in the field geared up and their staffs began to function. Within another five years, the Iowa station was still first among equals. But the science as well as the profession of child development had taken on definite shape, and certain assumptions undergirded what might be considered the mainstream of the profession—and the discipline.

Updegraff's investigation foreshadowed her adopted science's intellectual horizons. Her paper represented a holistic perspective, a rebellion against the reductionist notions of the psychology of music of the late nineteenth and early twentieth centuries. By the same token, the notion of the normal child, so underdeveloped in the 1900s and 1910s, became the holistic alternative to the reductionist notions of the subnormal and abnormal types of children of the early twentieth and late nineteenth centuries.

As historian of biology Garland E. Allen has brilliantly argued, the revolt against the mechanistic and reductionist point of view in the biological sciences after the 1910s marked a transformation in attitudes about the relations of the whole and the parts in organisms. Those embracing the older mechanist and reductionist perspectives did not regard the interaction of parts as capable of generating any new characteristics to any one component. Thus, mechanists believed that studying interactions mattered as much as examining parts in isolation. For holistic materialists new characteristics of parts were precipitated from interaction that were qualitatively different from the old.[46] A parallel perspective resulted from the resolution in the 1920s of the important controversy over heredity versus environment, from a model of heredity over environment to one of heredity and environment, from nature over culture to nature and culture, from a static to a dynamic symmetry.[47]

Another manifestation of the crystallization of the new, holistic worldview and its specific importance for the emerging field of child development was the abrupt disappearance of the prewar structuralist typology of subnormal and abnormal children. It was replaced by the functionalist notion that most children were normal and required only normal circumstances and perhaps a few modest adjustments here and there. Thus subnormal and abnormal children evaporated, and normal children were suddenly everywhere, as if a sorcerer had conjured them up. This was even—or especially—the case with those self-appointed therapists and psychiatrists who had drawn attention to the many afflicted and compromised types of children in the first place. Thus consider the mental hygiene movement as replacement for the earlier eugenic concern for juvenile delinquency. In the later 1910s the Commonwealth Fund of New York sought to invest large sums in what were initially eugenic surveys of "inferior stocks" in many of the states. As assembled in a larger plan, the Commonwealth Fund subvened the Johns Hopkins University psychiatrist Adolf Meyer, among others, to spread the ideology of mental hygiene. At first mental hygiene pertained to the psychotic, not merely the neurotic. Meyer believed the mentally ill were responsible for most of society's problems.

Increasingly in the 1910s Meyer taught that the individual must be apprehended in a holistic, not a reductionist, manner; it was society's responsibility to encourage the dangerous individual to undergo that kind of therapy that would permit his or her adaptation to society's norms of conduct and values. Original nature and social milieu were thus interrelated in the individual's process of continual adjustment to society and its expectations. Mental hygiene became a parallel to public health. As the ideas of what mental hygiene could do were expanded in the later 1910s, the Commonwealth Fund, together with the National Committee for Mental Hygiene, initially planned a gigantic assault on the problem of juvenile delinquency. In January 1921, at a major conference, those invited by the fund and the committee worked out the particulars of the campaign to address and to cure the individual delinquent child. The conferees believed that mental deficiency and abnormality caused most, if not all, social problems.

Yet within a few years the whole program had been transformed into a holistic attack on the problem of adjustment of the normal child to society's expectations. Almost entirely vanished, as if by magic, was the "typical" individual juvenile delinquent, as prewar terminology would have had it. Meyer and his associates now defined the normal child as a dynamic entity, a whole in which there were many interdependent and distinct parts that functioned together. If they were aware that they had changed their ideas so drastically in a few years, they gave no sign of it. The binary distinctions between good and bad children, once so crucial to their plans and ideas, simply evaporated. Now mental hygienists argued that all children were essentially normal, save for the few afflicted ones. Each child differed from all others in many ways but was also an element in a balanced, dynamic psychosocial whole that included kin, peers, and acquaintances, among others. Children could not be understood in isolation from their larger milieu, for the good and simple reason that they could not exist apart from it; they had no identity apart from that larger, symmetrical whole to which they belonged. And they were most certainly not divisible into distinct or unique categories and types.[48]

Nor was this the only example of the disappearance of reductionist typologies for holistic models of the normal child. From the Vineland Training School in New Jersey, Henry H. Goddard went on to become director of the Ohio Bureau of Juvenile Research in Columbus, in 1918. The bureau was fully an institution founded to diagnose the causes of delinquency among the state's most difficult and incorrigible convicts from its system of juvenile courts, the assumption being that scientific investigation of individual types would yield answers to pressing social problems. Yet by 1921 Goddard was singing a different tune. Delinquency could be prevented, or, if manifested, cured, in all but a few cases, for most children were normal and required only a little attention and mild therapy. Goddard had made a career proclaiming the permanent differences among the various types of subnormal and abnormal children in the national population as the ultimate cause of social problems. He did not change his mind because of the straightforward accumulation of evidence; he and his associates at the bureau suddenly began asking different kinds of questions than they had before.[49]

Not unexpectedly, the general categories of scientific notions about children that had existed from the late nineteenth and early twentieth centuries underwent major transformations in the 1920s and early 1930s. New holistic notions of growth and development of body and mind took shape in these years, chiefly, the maturation theory and the idea of the innate intelligence. It was that high priest of behaviorist psychology, John B. Watson, who made the initial contribution to the evolving theory of maturation in the 1910s. The maturation theory, as fully articulated, assumed that the individual's development followed those parameters laid down by the species' genetic endowment, and that events in the individual life cycle took place as the individual's many distinct yet interrelated parts ripened and were "ready" for action. In his work with animals and infants while he was a professor at Johns Hopkins, Watson worked out a holistic theory of interaction between the organism and its environment that has often been interpreted as suggesting Watson believed in the environment over inheritance.

Watson's legacy was complex. In both *Behavior* (1914) and *Psychology from the Standpoint of a Behaviorist* (1919), he argued that animals and humans possessed innate mental structures that contributed the foundation for behavior such as reflexes and instincts, as well as for broader tendencies toward complex behavior. In his model of the organism as a whole greater than or different from the sum of its parts, as the individual developed, its mute, "empty" anatomical structures, themselves a part of the species' native equipment, would "ripen"; as they did, specific environmental stimuli would "awaken" them, and they would begin to function. Tellingly, Watson left the brain out of this formulation. The entire body was involved in the most simple actions. All parts were symmetrically and intricately interdependent with all others. Qualitatively new reactions might well take place as a result. Watson was very interested in developing the conditioned reflex in animals and human infants, and in working out the average amount of time in which an individual member of a particular species could learn to perform a particular act. Watson was a determinist and a holist. The stimulus-response formula in his hands was a rigid mechanism involving genetically programmed structures that were aroused by environmental stimuli, but clearly the social milieu did not exist as it would for those who believed in the efficacy of such environments. And his interest in group averages showed his belief that the individual's development as an individual over time did not matter; it was the group, not the individual, that was central to his model.[50]

Leonard Carmichael, a young animal psychologist, and George E. Coghill, a distinguished neuroanatomist, took further steps in working out this new holistic, symmetrical, functionalist, and interactive maturation theory. By doing so, they appropriated much of Watson's legacy, including his interpretations of the stimulus-response mechanism, of the importance of the "mute" or "empty" genetic endowment of behavior patterns, of group over individual performance, and, in general, Watson's holistic determinism, his sense that the whole was balanced and symmetrical because it was constituted of many distinct yet interrelated factors. Carmichael, an instructor at Princeton, published an interpretation of the controversy over heredity and environment that evinced his belief that the nature-versus-nurture dichotomy was sterile and outmoded. In effect, he attacked reductionism as useless. Heredity and environment worked together; the one was inconceivable without the other. All manner of factors interacted. They were the distinct yet interrelated parts of the larger whole.[51]

Carmichael applied the dynamic holistic view to a series of experiments with certain species of frog and salamander embryos. He proved, at least to his generation's satisfaction, that embryonic behavior was the result of the interaction of all factors, that it developed rather quickly—as the organism's nervous system matured—and that external stimulation had but an initiatory role in maturation. The "internal stimulation and response of the nervous system must . . . be initiated by environmental stimulation," Carmichael affirmed; but once the stimulus had aroused the mute behavior pattern in question, development and maturation could occur for some time in "relative independence of external stimulation," thus confirming Watson's "empty innate structure" model of the organism.[52]

Coghill, a researcher at the Wistar Institute in Philadelphia, already had a distinguished career in neuroanatomy when he published a series of lectures at University College, London, delivered in 1928, as *Anatomy and the Problem of Behavior* (1929). For a quarter century he had worked on the neurological development of the salamander *Amblystoma*. In his early years, he had interpreted the amphibian's growth from the reductionist perspective of the late nineteenth and early twentieth centuries, in which the various parts all developed and then integrated themselves into an accumulated unity. By the mid-1910s, however, he began to argue precisely the reverse: preneural structures as a dynamic whole integrated the various parts of the developing neurological system, or system of systems—a network of balance, dynamism, symmetry, and interactionism.

Coghill's thesis was that the living body was an integrated unity from the beginning of life. Various parts of the organism were always under the control of the organism as a whole. The living body was no mere quantitative sum of its parts. It was different from or greater than such a mere accretion. In his first lecture, Coghill insisted that the animal's behavior patterns developed in an orderly, predictable sequence that was entirely congruent with the development of the nervous system and its parts. In other words, there was complete coordination between the inner nervous system and the animal's actions. Total integration was, therefore, the key to development. He also argued that physiological processes followed precisely the order of their embryological development in all functions. Furthermore, behavior always developed through the systematic expansion of a perfectly integrated total pattern. In the organism as a whole, individuation of parts happened. Thus partial patterns had their own degrees of distinctiveness. Yet all separate elements were integrated into the larger whole.

In his second and third lectures he concerned himself with organizational questions regarding the nervous system's development. How did the conduction paths acquire their definite functions? The embryo was perfectly and symmetrically integrated before it had a central nervous system. The organism as a whole navigated the development of the parts. The prior structure led the emerging structures and integrated them into the larger system simultaneously. All was fixed and predictable. In his third lecture, Coghill discussed how preneural growth and differentiation in the nervous system worked within the system as an entity. Two points needed emphasis. The total pattern grew as a perfectly integrated unit. At the same time, parts or partial systems grew and became differentiated with distinct form, shape, and configuration. From the start, however, there was always organic unity. Thus, Coghill concluded, *Amblystoma* developed from the extension of the total pattern and not—as had been thought previously—through the emergence of separate and isolated parts that became integrated afterward.[53]

Thus Carmichael and Coghill brought together the various elements of a maturation theory that Watson, they, and others had worked with into a larger and logically consistent theory. From that point on, workers in animal psychology had a model to apply to animal behavior. Thus a whole school of thought persisted for some years on various kinds of instincts, such as the pecking instinct in chicks. And Carmichael himself became a psychological or behaviorist embryologist.[54]

It was perhaps not at all surprising that one of Hall's most prolific students, Arnold L. Gesell, took up the maturation theory in the interwar years and elaborated upon the fresh holistic interpretation that Watson, Carmichael, and

Coghill had pioneered. In 1911, as a medical student at Yale, he opened his psycho-clinic, which he ran as a diagnostic clinic, but by the early 1920s Gesell was doing research in child development. He was primarily interested in maturation, and in the depiction of the various stages of that process typical for the species in general. He did for human infants what Carmichael was doing for baby animals: mapping out their psychological and behavioral development and linking it to the emergence of definite innate structures within the organism.

In several works, such as *The Mental Growth of the Preschool Child* (1925) and *Infancy and Growth* (1928), Gesell described at some length the processes of maturation and growth, which he patterned directly after the ideas of Carmichael, Coghill, and other animal developmentalists. The organism's unity was reflected in the differentiation and maturation of the various parts of the nervous system and the body. The great principle of maturation was total integration—complete symmetry, balance, and order. Like his predecessors, he was a holistic and a determinist. Neither the fetus nor the infant exhibited adventitious behavior. "Never does the picture of normal behavior become as diffuse and formless as a drifting cloud," Gesell wrote in 1929. "Even the random movements of the month-old child are not utterly fortuitous." Maturation, he insisted, was the regulatory mechanism within the developing organism. Growth was so intricate a process that it required powerful restraints, internal rather than external, which conserved the balance of the total pattern and the growth trend's direction. Otherwise, there would be chaos. Growth occurred because of the interaction of internal and external factors. He insisted that "growth is a function of the organism rather than of the environment itself. . . . These manifestations come from inner compulsion and are primarily organized by inherent inner mechanics and by an intrinsic physiology of development."[55]

Gesell and his associate, Helen Thompson, studied what was probably the most influential of the early human maturation studies, that of identical twins. Each twin acted as both a control and a practice on alternating sets of skills for the other. Gesell and Thompson insisted that their work with twins demonstrated conclusively that maturation was far more important than practice or learning; the twins could not do certain tasks until their nervous systems had matured to the point at which they could support such activity.[56]

Other child psychologists championed the maturation theory also. Their customary experimental technique was to identify a skill, use experimental and control groups, and ascertain if a particular task could be permanently mastered by the experimental group in advance of the presumed requisite development. Workers at the Institute of Child Welfare at the University of Minnesota, at the Institute of Child Welfare at Teachers College, and at the Institute of Human Relations at Yale all did such studies and pronounced the maturation theory correct. A child could not acquire a skill before he was ready, they insisted. Learning always fed this ripening of neurological structures—not environment or individual action. These studies, and their imitators, tested motor skills and abilities, ranging from rote memorization to playing the piano.[57]

In this way the maturation theory took shape and became an integral part of developmental science, or of child development. It assumed that in development, environmental stimuli awakened the genetically predetermined mute anatomical structures that governed species-specific patterns of behavior, as with Carmichael's frogs and Coghill's salamanders, and that no structure "awoke" before its predetermined moment in the developmental sequence specific to its species. This was group determinism with a vengeance.

The corollary to the maturation theory in developmental science was, of course, the notion of the fixed IQ. The American versions of the Binet mental test as those two star pupils of Stanley Hall, Henry H. Goddard and Lewis M. Terman, created them, were based the assumption that the test's standardization on white, middle-class American children of northern and western European extraction made it a valid instrument for the measurement of intelligence of other ethnic groups in the national population. Other assumptions in the American versions of the Binet test included the belief in innate intelligence, the relative fixity or constancy of the intelligence quotient, and the importance of group over individual scores.[58]

After the early 1920s, Goddard and Terman gravitated toward perspectives on these matters. Goddard was an ally of Woodrow Wilson in New Jersey progressive politics, and kept his liberal ties intact with Ohio's James Cox when he came to the Bureau of Juvenile Research; he was forced out of the bureau in the aftermath of the Republican landslide in 1920 and became a professor of clinical and abnormal psychology at Ohio State University. There he worked out a new nondeterminist perspective on mental problems that stressed the importance of the individual and of the cultural milieu. On the other hand, Terman maintained his faith in the doctrines of innate intelligence and the fixed IQ. As he put it in 1921, that "rough prediction is now possible on the basis of intelligence tests."[59] Or, as he declared in an argument with a self-pronounced antideterminist on intelligence tests, if there was anything that the science of psychology had demonstrated in the last quarter century, it was that native differences in intelligence were real and fundamental. Terman consistently supported liberal and reform causes in American politics; he was a liberal Republican who had voted for Bryan and the two Roosevelts for the presidency. He had no difficulty whatsoever reconciling his political and his scientific and educational views; he insisted that "the one purpose of intelligence tests in the schools is to aid us in making the most of every child, the dull as well as the bright."[60] His Genetic Studies of Genius project became a justification for arguing that geniuses were superior people in all respects—and that genius was inherited. He considered them society's natural leaders.[61] The genius project became an important prop for the fixed-IQ theory in the interwar years.

In the later 1920s and on into the 1930s, though, Terman and his associates broadened the study to include many social as well as mental and physical characteristics. By 1930 three large volumes had appeared. In the first, Terman and his associates published the results of their initial investigations of mental and physical traits of geniuses. They argued that geniuses had superior ratings in every characteristic evaluated—physical, mental, moral, and social. Good things went—or matured—together. The second volume, published in 1926, was a retrospective assessment of geniuses in the past, an attempt to estimate their IQs from the biographical sketches his research assistants had gathered from anecdotal "historical" accounts.

The third volume, published four years later, was a full articulation of the notions of maturation, innate intelligence, and holistic materialism. The perspective was, quite literally, cross-sectional rather than longitudinal. That is, Terman and his coworkers examined this large sample at various junctures over time. Each measurement was, in effect, like a group portrait. Individuals were assumed to belong to the group—defined as geniuses—and their variation took place only within the expected and predictable norms for that group. The idea of following individuals over time would have struck them (and, as we shall see, did strike them) as nonsensical. All individuals existed within the group. Terman thought only in terms of group averages, means, and medians. For the individual to exist apart from the group to which "nature" or "science" had assigned that person would not have made sense to Terman. Here then was the fully articulated maturation theory as applied to mind as well as to instinct or reflex. Only groups could exist; individuals did not.[62]

Generally speaking, most psychometricians in the 1920s and 1930s believed not simply the doctrine of innate intelligence, but also its corollary, the fixity of the intelligence quotient: The IQ was constant from birth to death. The ways in which the Binet test was constructed and used encouraged this belief by the larger culture as well. Sometimes, however, psychologists gave contrary findings. In 1925, Helen Thompson Woolley, then a child psychologist at the Merrill-Palmer School, reported that many children in the Merrill-Palmer nursery school, when considered as individuals over time, had different IQs on retesting, a result that implied that the IQ was unstable. She supplied group averages of both rises and falls in IQs upon retesting. She also discussed what happened to individual children over time. Woolley was chiefly interested in pointing to the effects of nursery schools, which, she insisted, could boost the IQ if their curricula were sufficiently richer than an average home or preschool. She declared that there was enormous growth occurring in children's minds between the ages of two and four or five. An enriched nursery school curriculum could make an enormous difference.[63]

Psychologists Helen Barrett and Helen Koch of the University of Chicago made even more spectacular claims a few years later. They chose for their subjects preschool-age children from orphanages and placed them in a preschool, assuming that there were sufficient qualitative differences between the environment of a state orphanage and a preschool to stimulate as much growth in mental ability as could be done, or to validate the hypothesis, which Terman and others advanced, that the inmates of state orphanages were all innately inferior in intelligence to normal, middle-class children. Using experimental and control groups, Barrett and Koch found a substantial rise in mental age after six months in group scores among the children in the experimental group, thus undercutting the customary argument that the IQ was fixed. George Stoddard knew of this work almost right away; he was one of the few experts in child development who took it seriously.[64]

Most mental testers and child development specialists strongly objected to these arguments, claiming that such reports were unscientific. Given the state of technical knowledge then, they had a point. The IQs of individual children from school age to adulthood had been shown to be fairly constant upon retesting, a fact that had given great support to the notion that the IQ was fixed at birth or even innate. Very few psychologists had systematically studied the suitability of IQ tests for very young children. There was one version of the Binet, the Kuhlmann-Binet, which its champions declared could be used to ascertain accurately the IQs of children of preschool age. But most testers believed that the IQs of children of such tender years were too unpredictable to be measured with any confidence, and, furthermore, were subject to such statistical phenomena as regression to the mean and problems with sample selection.

And there were many who argued that in the first year of life, only sensori-motor, not cognitive, development took place, with the clear implication that what the IQ tests measured did not yet exist. And when psychologists such as Woolley reported that the IQs of preschool-age children varied enormously, mainstream developmentalists took that as evidence not of the possibilities of individual development, as Woolley argued, but instead as further confirmation of the pitfalls of testing the IQs of children prematurely.

Florence L. Goodenough, one of Terman's star doctoral students, reacted critically to Woolley's arguments. In 1925, when the Institute of Child Welfare opened at the University of Minnesota, she joined the faculty. Goodenough heard her master's voice loud and clear on the IQ's stability and on physical and mental maturation. She began a study of two groups of set pairs of children. Her procedures differed from those of Woolley or Barrett and Koch; unlike Woolley, Goodenough did not track the scores of individuals over time, and unlike Barret and Koch, her subjects were normal, middle-class children, not orphans, whose home environment could be expected to be similar to that of the nursery school and radically dissimilar from that of a state orphanage. Her purpose was to examine the permanent IQ gains, if any, that the preschool's curriculum had on children who attended. She selected two groups of children, so that each child in this experimental group was "paired" in socioeconomic traits with a child in the control group. Children in the experimental group attended the preschool. Those in the control group did not. By spring 1926, well before the experiment ended, she declared in a report to director John E. Anderson that the study's results "do serve to call attention to a number of spurious factors which may operate to give an appearance of such effect." Goodenough was interested only in group measurements. In a stance typical of those in developmental science's intellectual and ideological mainstream, she dismissed as anecdotal and unscientific any measurements of individuals.[65]

In 1931 Goodenough and Anderson published their seminal *Experimental Child Study*, less a textbook for students than a handbook for researchers. In it, they welded together the various elements of what might be dubbed grand theory in child development, including maturation, the IQ's constancy, the symmetrical interaction of multiple and interdependent factors—the entire holistic blueprint of child development. The deterministic thesis they advanced was not original with them. In effect, they had inherited models of reality in which all was symmetrical, holistic, and multifactorial from antecedent workers in the life sciences. This book was a blueprint for determinism.[66] Goodenough and Anderson insisted that development was always orderly.

"Practically, as well as theoretically, the law of the *constancy of developmental order* is of the greatest importance for the study of child development," they wrote. "Consider, for example, what would happen to the ordinary mental test if it were actually necessary to try out individuals on all possible kinds of performance. A lifetime would hardly be sufficient to complete the task." In brief, the viability of child science as science depended on the notion of unfolding regularity and symmetry of development itself.[67]

The IQ constancy thesis gained support from other scientific sources in the late 1920s and early 1930s. Since the early 1900s psychologists had known that results of various tests on the same individuals had shown high statistical correlation with one another. This encouraged belief among psychologists in the English psychologist Charles Spearman's notion of a single factor for intelligence, which he called *g*, for general intelligence. Many assumed that *g* was a Mendelian unit-character. But with the decline of late nineteenth- and early twentieth-century reductionist notions of reality, so went the early Mendelian single factor–single trait schemes. The new age of holistic interaction and dynamism demanded more ornate theories of Mendelian inheritance, which had emerged by the early to middle 1920s, but also multiple-factor theories of intelligence to complement them. In 1928 the University of Chicago psychologist and statistician Truman Lee Kelley proposed precisely such a multiple-factor theory.[68] And in 1933 Robert Thorndike of Columbia published an evaluation of various studies of retests of persons given mental tests. Although his data did not include retests of young children, as Woolley's study had, the general conclusion that he and most of his readers drew from his discussion was that the IQ was highly stable upon retesting; for his subjects, all school age or above, the correlations fell over a five-year span from a +.89 to a +.70, a very high Pearsonian positive correlation that underlined the IQ's constancy.[69]

A group of psychometricians at the Institute of Child Welfare of the University of California, Berkeley, provided the most direct evidence of links between the assumptions of the regularity of innate development and the stability of the IQ. In 1928, Nancy Bayley began what was to become one of the institute's three celebrated longitudinal research projects, the Berkeley Growth Study. She selected a group of seventy-four newborn infants, chiefly white and middle class, from the community. At first she intended to limit the project to the first year of life and to study the infants holistically, from every conceivable angle of vision. The project eventually became an open-ended permanent enterprise at the institute.

In 1933 Bayley published an interim report on her subjects' mental growth.

She took for granted the notion of regular, predictable maturation in all aspects of growth and development, including intelligence. She insisted that Spearman's reductionist theory of *g* was simply inadequate. It could not explain the multiplicity and complexity and interaction of all the factors of mental growth. Mental growth, she found, was a highly intricate process—or series of processes. Growth was quick in the early months, decelerated after ten or so months, and again increased after fifteen or more months. With growth came variation within the group; as the children grew older, they differed increasingly in their performance at all age levels. She found no consistency whatsoever in the children's test scores over a long period, but the scores of other "adjacent" tests correlated rather highly. Development in the first eight months was largely sensorimotor. And there were negative correlations between the children's test scores and their parents' educational levels in these early months. With time, as the cognitive and intellectual aspects of mind developed in serial fashion, such correlations increased dramatically. Bayley's work confirmed the assumption that one could not test the IQs of infants because their mental growth was all sensorimotor, the antithesis of the intellectual and cognitive aspects of mind that the intelligence tests supposedly measured. The first year could not be used to predict the later years, save in rare cases of horrific abnormalities. It should be noted also that Bayley used group averages, means, and medians. At no point did she trace the development of single individuals or focus on the stability of their IQs. Like Terman, she made group measurements.[70]

Revealing too were the conferences of the National Research Council's Committee on Child Development, which were held in 1925, 1927, 1929, and 1933, by invitation only. Debates over two major substantive issues rippled through all of the discussions and papers. One was whether the blueprint for the field should be reductionist, hierarchical, static, and structural, or holistic, symmetrical, decentralized, dynamic, and interactive. The latter position prevailed always. In the earlier conferences in particular there was much discussion over whether typologies were useful—whether one could think of *types* of children, as had been so common before the 1920s. The all-but-unanimous answer was negative, that children represented a multiplicity of groups—sometimes the term *population* was used in the delegates' understanding of contemporary population genetics. The new perspective was holistic, not reductionistic. The other major issue that arose time and time again in the conversations and discussions at the four conferences was precisely the meaning of group identity for the individual. Almost without exception, the conferees declared, or at least did not argue with, the notion that an individual always shared the characteristics of the group to which he or she "belonged" and could vary only within the norms of that group. This was deterministic thinking; of that there was no doubt, whether one was a social scientist arguing the importance of the social milieu or a biological scientist stressing the importance of biological factors. There was a notable dissent from this orthodoxy, and it came from the new director of the Iowa Child Welfare Research Station, George D. Stoddard, who argued that development was not predetermined and the IQ was not fixed at birth. For evidence, he pointed to Helen T. Woolley's 1925 study.[71]

In 1931 and again in 1933, Clark University psychologist Carl Murchison published a *Handbook of Child Psychology* in two editions. It was a compendium of state-of-the-art essays on special topics within child psychology. In the first edition, Murchison published articles on a wide range of topics, including the conditioning of the emotions, children's drawings, various amusements, morals, and the like, but also on such natural-science problems as learning, twin psychology, physical and motor development, and so on. In this edition, the chapters did not advance from one set of developmental problems to another. Murchison thought of the field—as did his referees and advisers—as a scattershot of discrete problems, many of general interest and applicability, such as emotional conditioning, others rather narrower, such as studies of gifted and retarded children. If he had an underlying theme it was the progression from chapters concerned with natural-science problems to those on the applied social sciences, psychiatry, and clinical psychology. Furthermore, the authors did not adhere to specific assumptions and the announcement of laws of child development, after the fashion of Goodenough and Anderson's *Experimental Child Study*. And Murchison included all sorts of authorities who could not be expected to agree with one another on many issues.

The second edition was markedly, indeed dramatically, different. The volume was organized like a manual of the various topics and problems of maturation, from the development of animal and human fetuses to the neonate, to the normal child in all of its multiple and interactive dimensions, shapes, proportions, characteristics, and so on. Ultimately, the edition was an argument for the maturation theory and the notion of the fixed IQ. Carmichael wrote the first chapter, on maturation, and made many references to the work of Coghill and others who agreed with this perspective. This edition was not a collection of state-of-the-art essays in which the field was an aggregate of many distinct and separate problems; rather, the field was now viewed as a complex unity of many different yet interrelated dimensions, factors, proportions, and characteristics. That was Murchison's new message; it was hardly original with him, of course, and it had highly conservative sociopolitical implications, on at least two levels. First, child science was an affair for the pros, not the citizen activists, and second, knowledge of the child made sense, for it showed that intervention, or interference, in the functioning of nature and culture made relatively little difference on many matters.[72]

It is difficult to ascertain at precisely what point the workers at the Iowa Child Welfare Research Station began to march to a different beat from their national colleagues. All accepted the underlying holistic taxonomy of reality. But through a process that remains partly in shadow, the Iowa workers began to stress certain points that in one way or another undercut or qualified the determinism of the majority of their scientific and professional colleagues.

In 1924 Baldwin and Stecher published the field's first general text, *The Psychology of the Preschool Child*. Much of what they said emanated from the new ideas of the 1920s concerning children. They were fully at home with the new notions of dynamic, functional, interactive, holistic perspectives. Yet they also reported on the researches done at the preschool laboratories. They insisted that they were interested in measuring the development of individuals, meaning individual children, mentally and physically. In one sense, the children they studied belonged to a selected group. They were the offspring of middle-class, white, Anglo-Saxon, Protestant midwestern gentry, businessmen, farmers, and university professors, among others.

For Baldwin, these were simply normal children, simply the creatures in which crucial events took place. He was interested in studying development of mental and physical *processes* in individuals; individuals qua individuals, with distinctive and definite traits that distinguished themselves from one another, held no interest for him whatsoever. Such asymmetricality would have obscured the larger whole in which the processes were presumably taking place. His assumption that individuals were interchangeable was, however, fully within the mainstream of his profession and his culture. But his interest in processes and events, rather than in groups and their traits, marked him off from most in his science and his culture. Maturation of the group (and individual) held little interest for him. It was the developmental processes that were important; and they were not tied to any group, experimental or "natural." Thus Baldwin edged away from mainstream views—probably without fully realizing it.

Furthermore, Baldwin had severely devalued the importance and relevance of the problem that had so interested him, that of the relations of physical to mental development. Physical development took up only one short chapter. And he and Stecher revealed another dissent from the majority point of view as it was emerging in the field: IQ was but one trait of mental development that interacted with all others. Baldwin and Stecher defined child science as holistic and interactive, but there was more than a whisper of indeterminancy in their arguments and presentations. Growth might not have a predetermined direction. There might be a role for chance and happenstance.[73]

Other projects at the Iowa station explored aspects of child psychology besides the IQ. Intelligence was but one part of child psychology, went the underlying argument, and many other factors seemed to influence it. This stance turned the arguments of a Goodenough or a Bayley upside down. Some of these studies focused on children's abilities to use form boards, play materials, vocabularies, personality development within social milieu, group dynamics, motor coordination, and the like.[74]

By the middle to late 1920s Baldwin himself was becoming increasingly critical of the IQ as the only measure of child mentality. In 1926 and 1927 he told a variety of public groups that if heredity constrained a child's opportunities, training and environment were nevertheless highly important factors in conditioning personality and character in the early years. A child was a "changing, complex unity," as he put it in an address in Philadelphia in 1926. A few months later he attacked the heredity-versus-environment dichotomy as meaningless. He insisted that the true view of the matter was that both were involved in each other, in an intricate and symmetrical whole that was greater than or different from the sum of the parts. He also argued here and there that the profession of child development and the preschool nursery could do much to assist children with their special problems. Experience and training would shape actual behavior. In 1927 he argued for the establishment of a nationwide system of preschools, attached to the public schools, to train children to live up to their full capacities.[75] In 1928 he severely criticized the twenty-seventh *Yearbook* of the National Society for the Study of Education, whose major theme was the role of inheritance in intelligence. The *Yearbook*'s editor was Lewis M. Terman. Not surprisingly, most contributors insisted that intelligence was innate and developed normally with other characteristics of the person. Baldwin slashed away at the notion that the IQ was all there was to intelligence. He virtually declared IQ tests meaningless misrepresentations of mental complexity, thus opposing majority opinion in the field. And in what was to be one of his last important public addresses, in Toronto, Canada, under the auspices of the Canadian National Committee for Mental Hygiene, Baldwin argued that a nationwide system of preschools could prevent juvenile delinquency, the causes of which were located entirely in the first seven years of life.[76]

In 1930, the first major investigation executed at the station with the Laura Spelman Rockefeller Memorial's support, *Farm Children: An Investigation of Rural Child Life in Selected Areas of Iowa*, was published. The project had focused on comparison of two rural communities, one modern, progressive, and prosperous, the other, decidedly well-off in economic terms but suffering from all manner of community disintegration and difficulty. Baldwin had won a supplementary grant from the memorial in 1925 to carry on the work when Hart left. Two assistants, Eva Abigail Fillmore and Lora Hadley, wrote up the materials that Baldwin had collected. In a very real sense, *Farm Children* was a statement of the emerging scientific and public policy ideology of the Iowa station in the late 1920s.[77]

It had been Baldwin's idea to select the second community for comparison. Evidently, Baldwin had realized early on in the project that there was not one type of rural child and had deliberately broadened it in the middle 1920s to include all manner of comparisons of children in physical, mental, social, educational, and other aspects. Each individual would be examined so that the slight variations within the type could be cataloged and the type as type could be interpreted.

Indeed, for a research project initially and later predicated on the typological thinking so characteristic of the late nineteenth and early twentieth centuries, the book as published in 1930 seemed rather peculiar. If its tone and explanatory agenda maintained the point-by-point comparisons of the progressive and stagnant rural communities that Baldwin had promised Frank, and if the cascade of facts seemed to point to the importance of salvation of community through the science and technology of progressive education, the book nevertheless denied both typological and deterministic thinking. If it was true that Homeland, the culturally impoverished community, and Cedar Creek, the modern town, had resulted from the many distinct yet interrelated factors of their mutual (and, to some extent, shared) pasts and presents, it was also true that, at bottom, they were rural communities that taught a lesson for today. The children raised in them were not typical rural children. In fact, the concept of rural children as a type or a group of closely related types was meaningless. Children were simply found to differ according to the influences around them, the most important of which were emotional, psychological, mental, and spiritual; in that sense, there was no such thing as socioeconomic forces, as contemporary political, social, and economic public discourse assumed there was. If members of the community did not take an active role in the improvement of the community, conditions for each child to live up to his or her potentiality were slight indeed. But as the history of Cedar Creek showed, all that was needed for a brighter tomorrow was scientific truth and the commitment to reform and to improve.[78]

By the early 1930s, then, the Iowa Child Welfare Research Station was clearly entering a new phase of its history. Its workers had begun to embrace some interesting and unorthodox views. In particular, they had shifted the locus of concern in child science from deterministic to indeterministic notions of the meaning of group identity for the individual, insofar as their own work was concerned. Whether they would be able to shift that locus of concern in their field of science as a whole was, of course, a question that remained to be answered—and that had crucial implications for the fate of child welfare, as distinct from child science. If the new pessimism and determinism in child science were also manifest in public policy discourse, then there seemed little opportunity for Cora Hillis's dream to come true, on whatever terms that could and would have taken place in the decade of the Great Depression.[79]

CHAPTER FOUR

GREAT EXPECTATIONS

On Monday morning, May 14, 1928, President Jessup telephoned Beardsley Ruml at the Laura Spelman Rockefeller Memorial in New York. He wanted Ruml's advice on a successor to Bird Baldwin, who had died five days before of a freakish infection. "You ought to have a man," said Ruml. "Yes, we don't want a woman for the job," Jessup replied. "We must have a man." Ruml recommended Herbert R. Stolz, the director of the University of California Institute of Child Welfare, who was interested in physical growth and in parent education. "I hate to take him out of California, but I think he is the man for you," Ruml added.[1] Jessup's negotiations with Stolz and other outside candidates failed, and he appointed George D. Stoddard, one of Seashore's protégés, as the station's acting director.[2]

Stoddard was a bright young man. Born in Carbondale, Pennsylvania, in 1897, he graduated from Pennsylvania State College in 1921 with a degree in chemistry. He studied psychology with Theodore Simon, Alfred Binet's collaborator on the Binet test, at the University of Paris for a year. Stoddard won his doctorate in psychology with a specialty in educational testing in two years at Iowa. When he came to the station from the university's Department of Psychology, he jumped from assistant professor of psychology to professor of child welfare, and had already published fifteen research articles and coauthored a major study on academic tests for high school students. He was also one of the architects of the Iowa Placement Tests, which became nationally recognized as pioneering attempts to measure what school pupils of various grade levels had learned. Stoddard took very seriously the original intention that Binet and Simon had for education and intelligence testing—that of diagnostic tools to help children live up to their full potential, not of instruments to determine a fixed, inborn intelligence.

To those who did not know him, however, Stoddard appeared to be nothing more than a research scientist with little or no interest in social amelioration. Certainly he struck Mrs. S. E. Lincoln, a prominent Des Moines clubwoman, that way. It could be argued that Lincoln was Cora Hillis's successor for the Iowa station's lay constituencies. Lincoln was a mover and a shaker in the Iowa Congress of Parents and Teachers, and was heavily involved as well in parent education in the capital city. She had important connections with many components of the Iowa State Council of Child Study and Parent Education.

That fall Lincoln did something that Cora Hillis might have done. There were rumors aplenty within the statewide parent education movement that President Jessup would appoint Stoddard as permanent director for the station. Lincoln regarded Stoddard as nothing but a scientist—as did many other activists, apparently. She wrote to Beardsley Ruml and Lawrence K. Frank at the Laura Spelman Rockefeller Memorial to complain about the station and to ask them to intervene to set matters straight. She raised two issues: A mere researcher like Stoddard did not have the vision to run the Iowa station as first and foremost a service organization to its statewide citizen constituencies. President Jessup, too, cared only about the university and its research station; he was indifferent to the needs and wants of the ordinary citizens who had made both the station and its research possible. But she went a step further, suggesting that the memorial's staff pressure President Jessup to appoint a woman to succeed Baldwin. A woman could do the job just as easily as a man, Lincoln argued, then nominated her own candidate, May Pardee Youtz, the station's director of parent education.

Ruml and Frank responded in different ways to the issues Lincoln raised. Ruml was decidedly hierarchical in his views and was not thrilled, as Frank was, by the prospects of citizen involvement in social science. Condescendingly and disingenuously, he told Lincoln to contact President Jessup directly, as, he sniffed, it "would be extremely inadvisable for this Memorial to make any suggestions to him of a positive character with respect to this or any other phase of the management of the Research Station." Ruml thus spoke as the high-and-mighty professional to the lowly client. Frank on the other hand, revered expertise but not the expert. He thought well of Stoddard and told Lincoln that he was "confident that the work will go on under adequate leadership because the very significance of the task [parent education] demands it."[3]

How matters had changed. What began as a woman's crusade with women's and children's issues at the forefront had now been domesticated within the structures and processes of essentially male-dominated institutions. Yet Frank and Lincoln got what they wanted in George D. Stoddard. He turned out to fulfill their fondest dreams—and much more besides. In July 1929, his appointment became permanent.[4] Stoddard was much closer in his notions of the balance between the claims of scientific professionalism and social activism to Frank than to Ruml—or to Baldwin. As matters turned out, he combined research and social activism to pursue his own political agenda, for the politics of the American nation no less than for the tiny professional scientific subculture of child development.

Stoddard became director under happy circumstances. Until the mid-1930s the station was protected from the Depression's consequences. This was a golden age of growth and increasing fame for the station. The memorial's huge grants provided financial stability. In 1924–25, the station had an income of approximately $49,750, including the final $5,000 WCTU payment. The next year the state's annual appropriation ballooned from $25,000 to $35,750, and rose to $40,750 in 1929–30. In 1927–28, Baldwin's last year, the station had slightly over $71,000 available, $35,750 from the state, slightly more than $30,000 from the memorial, and the balance from other sources. In 1929–30, the first year of the memorial's large grants, the budget was $157,300, of which but $40,750 was the state's share, about $114,370 the memorial's, and the rest from other sources. The budget declined to just over $149,000 two years later, and to $134,000 after four years.[5]

The station's staff grew as well. In 1930, for example, seventy-four persons held appointments, including two professors, two associate professors, three assistant professors, eleven research associates, thirty-two research assistants, nine teachers, and fifteen technical and clerical staff members. In 1934, the station's personnel had risen to ninety-eight, including two professors, three associate professors, five assistant professors, eleven research associates, forty research assistants, nine assistants, nine teachers, fifteen staff members, an executive secretary for the Iowa State Council on Child Study and Parent Education, and a secretary. The memorial's funds supported this expansion, which occurred chiefly at the lower ranks. As the memorial's funds diminished in the mid-thirties, Stoddard reduced salaries to save as many positions as possible. He made several shrewd key faculty appointments, including Ruth Updegraff, Ralph Ojemann, Orvis Irwin, Wendell Johnson, and May Pardee Youtz at the junior ranks, and Charles H. McCloy as associate professor in physical growth to replace Baldwin. Updegraff ran the nursery school and did research in child psychology, Ojemann pioneered in research on parent education and family life; Irwin was the station's specialist in infants; Johnson researched stuttering; and Youtz *was* the statewide parent education program, period—none others could duplicate her magic with the people. Perhaps Stoddard's greatest coup, though, was his appointment of the brilliant German psychologist and émigré Kurt Lewin as full professor.[6]

An enlarged staff made possible higher productivity in graduate teaching and research. Counting all those who won graduate degrees through 1928 as having been in Baldwin's era, and those through 1942 as in Stoddard's, the station awarded 7 doctorates and 15 master's degrees during Baldwin's tenure, and 68 doctorates and 136 master's degrees in Stoddard's. Thus in Stoddard's era, the number of graduate degrees conferred increased more than ninefold, and the graduate student population apparently increased even more. About half of the 151 doctoral and 260 master's degrees that the station conferred through the middle 1960s were awarded during Stoddard's tenure.

Stoddard's years as director were crucial for productivity in research, too. From 1917 through 1928, the station's staff—mainly Baldwin—wrote 144 research publications. From 1928 through 1942, the station's staff published 603 research works, of which 586 were studies carried out under Stoddard's intellectual leadership. A far higher percentage of faculty and graduate students published in Stoddard's than in Baldwin's days. Thirteen faculty wrote 357 of these works, or slightly over 60 percent; and graduate students and research associates wrote the rest. Between 1917 and 1965, the station's staff wrote over 1,200 research publications; about 12 percent appeared during Baldwin's tenure, about half in Stoddard's era, and by 1950, when Stoddard's successor, Robert R. Sears, left Iowa, the station's staff had published another 13 percent of the 1,236 research works in question. During his time as director, Stoddard was the most prolific faculty member, with 63 publications to his credit. Beth L. Wellman was second, with 42 works. Orvis Irwin and Amy Daniels tied for third place with 36 each. Ralph Ojemann had 30, Howard Meredith 27, Kurt Lewin 18, and Harold M. Skeels 16. No other faculty member at the Iowa station in those years had more than half a dozen research publications. Of the sixty-eight doctoral students in Stoddard's years, twelve published nothing before they left the university, ten published 1, fifteen published 2, and eight published 4 works, with four other graduate students with as many as 8 to 10 works to their credit. Three doctoral students—Howard Meredith with 27, Ruth Updegraff with 22, and Harold M. Skeels with 16 publications—were sufficiently productive and central to the station's programs to be appointed as regular faculty.

The station's research priorities changed. To be sure, Stoddard retained

Baldwin's emphases on preschool education and intellectual development—on the IQ, in short. Research in personality and in social psychology declined in quantity but probably rose in quality, thanks to Kurt Lewin and his students. Nutrition, physical growth, and general child psychology declined dramatically. And parent education—the field Lincoln feared would disappear—jumped dramatically from 2 to 73 publications.[7]

Like Baldwin, Stoddard kept the station's research programs focused on the first seven years of childhood, believing, as Baldwin did, that these years were key to all future development. Both were committed to the dynamic, symmetrical, holistic sense of the order of things in their historical era. Stoddard continued Baldwin's preferred starting point for all investigations, the *individual child*, in sharp contrast to his colleagues across the county, who just as naturally began theirs with *groups* of children. Neither Baldwin nor Stoddard perceived any difficulty whatsoever in embracing a holistic taxonomy of reality and insisting at the same time that the individual was the point of departure for investigation and interpretation. What Baldwin began, Stoddard continued and expanded. Under Stoddard's leadership, the Iowa station became the leading challenger of the field's twin theses, the maturation theory and the idea of the fixed IQ. Baldwin had, for the most part, hewed to an apolitical or nonpolitical line in his public persona as director. Stoddard threw himself into contemporary politics as a liberal supporter of the New Deal and of the left wing of the progressive education movement, whose patron saint was John Dewey. In certain respects the Iowa station retained its position of eminence, of being primus enter pares, in its field of science, and became endlessly controversial in others.

Under Stoddard's intellectual leadership, the station's staff attacked grand theory in developmental science, the maturation theory and the notion of the fixed IQ. In the thirties the station's scientists carved out a new pattern of interpretation that differed sharply from that of the majority of their colleagues in child development. Like their contemporaries in science and society then, they believed in a world of dynamism, fluctuation, and movement, in which the all-symmetrical whole was greater than or different from the sum of the parts, and in which each part of the larger whole was distinct yet intimately related to all others. Yet they shifted the locus of attention and explanation in two ways.

While always embracing that blueprint of a dynamic whole or system of systems with its intricate, symmetrical internal architecture of its many parts, the Iowa scientists nevertheless disputed that this system of systems, this network of incalculable complexity, was driven in a particular direction by necessity, final causes, the forces of nature and society, or any other deterministic power or mixture thereof. The pathways of development were not necessarily linear, foretold, or predestined; they might be presumed to fall within a given range, so that there was some order, not total chaos, in natural and social events. Some of the causes of the present were in the present, in other words, and some were in the past. In brief, they believed that it was possible to embrace holism and indeterminism.

Another important way in which the Iowa scientists parted company with their colleagues was to insist that within this world of fluctuating movement, complex interrelations among the parts, and all the rest, it was possible to intervene in the system, to isolate an element within it, and to subject that part to examination and, often, reconstruction or change. The Iowa scientists believed, as their colleagues and fellow citizens did, that all elements within the larger whole belonged, naturally and appropriately, in one group or another, and that every category had its own locus within its system and within the larger network. But the Iowa scientists believed that the individual part could nevertheless be plucked, so to speak, from its group, and ministrated to, and that should that part fail, any other one could substitute. That is, the Iowans believed that the group determinism of their professional colleagues was in error. And they wrote much that was critical of that perspective. But they also believed, with no sense of paradox or contradiction, in an individualism in which, within limits, each part was distinct yet ultimately the same as any other part. The universe was, in brief, symmetrical; asymmetry was literally unthinkable.

The scientists at the Iowa Child Welfare Research Station investigated many aspects of physical maturation and development, including physical growth, nutrition, the development of motor and cognitive skills, and, especially, infant development. They probed two related issues. Was there a necessary and ineluctable direction to development? And did beings learn from the exigencies of the moment or, as their intellectual inspiration John Dewey might have put it, from the application of intelligence and reason on a specific problem? Or was it all, as Watson, Coghill, Carmichael, Gesell, and their followers had it, a matter of the ripening of empty anatomical structures in response to situations in a larger, systematic, dynamic, and yet predestined system?

The nutritional work that Amy Daniels and her associates did at the station did not support the maturation theory. Thanks to the memorial's last grant,

Daniels finally had adequate facilities and sufficient research assistants. Although developmentalists across the country were beginning to act as if nutrition was not a component of the science of child development, Daniels and her associates nevertheless offered interpretations of animal and infant nutrition that shed light, however indirectly, on maturation.[8]

Thus Daniels and her associates explored the role of various nutrients in the growth of rats and infants. Much of the work on rats centered on the part milk played in nutrition. In one series of experiments, for example, they explored the causes of high mortality of the suckling young of milk-fed mother rats. They made some fresh discoveries in this series. For one thing, they found that the suckling young's high mortality was not caused by a deficiency in the antineuritic vitamin in the milk fed to the mothers. They also discovered that temperature and aeration were important factors in determining the degree of destruction of the antineuritic vitamin in milk. These results were contrary to accepted professional opinion. In a follow-up, Daniels and her assistants fed groups of infant rats evaporated and dried and partially skimmed milk. All females bore young. Some survived. Daniels and her associates concluded that it was the lack of vitamin F that stopped lactation and caused the deaths. In yet another study, they insisted that lack of vitamin F caused abnormal glandular development. The thymus was much smaller, and the thyroid much larger, than normal. Other unfortunate results of a deficiency of vitamin F in the mothers' diets were found in the suckling young rats. In a later investigation, Daniels and her colleagues discovered by weighing the hearts of rats in which anemia had been induced that a cardiac hypertrophy, or abnormal enlargement, had resulted. In a complex investigation of the nutritive causes of congenital debility in the suckling young of milk-fed rats, they found that manganese deficiencies in the mothers' diets caused high mortality among the suckling young.[9]

The work with infants focused on a variety of nutritional problems. As with the investigations with rats, Daniels and her coworkers sought to identify the most efficacious balance of particular nutrients insofar as maximum growth was concerned. The chief difference between the experiments with rats and infants was, of course, that only rats could be used to trace negative and lethal influences. They discovered, for example, that a balance of calcium and phosphorous in the feeding mixture was essential to prevent rickets, and that the secretion of creatinine in infancy was related to the ingestion of protein. They also investigated the minimal calcium needs of normal children fed an otherwise adequate diet; the retention of a balance of calcium, phosphorous, and nitrogen in diets differing in the amounts of calcium; as well as the retention of manganese, iron, and copper. In a subsequent study of the causes of anorexia in children of preschool age fed different diets, they found that high proportions of cereal foodstuffs sometimes caused anorexia. That is, too much bulk made it difficult for some children to absorb other important nutrients. They also devised a new method for measuring the necessary amount of protein for preschool children.[10]

In mid-November 1931, Daniels summarized her group's findings at the National Association for Nursery Education, in Philadelphia, Pennsylvania. Drawing on data broadcast at the 1930 White House Conference on Child Health and Protection, she reported that 6 million American children were improperly nourished, 1 million had damaged hearts, and 95 percent of the nation's 45 million children suffered from dental caries. American children must be brought to adequate nutritional standards, she argued. Inadequate diet resulted from incorrect nutritional information. The key to proper nutrition, development, health, and eventual maturation was a properly balanced diet in which all elements were distinct yet interrelated. Thus Daniels insisted that development was not predetermined. The allegedly orderly sequence was anything but automatic or inevitable. Deficiencies and imbalances could cause serious difficulties, including nutritive disasters and even death.[11] She agreed with other leading nutritionists that heredity limited growth but insisted that these restrictions were broad indeed. Daniels and her coworkers at the Iowa station thus undermined the maturation theory. And they focused on the individual, not the group, in developmental thinking.

Nor was this all. Stoddard made sure that the station's preeminence in the field of physical growth continued. He made two important appointments, Charles H. McCloy, in physical education, and Howard V. Meredith, one of Stoddard's doctoral students. Meredith became assistant professor in 1935. Until McCloy and Meredith came in 1935, the station's work in this field constituted finishing the work Baldwin did with students and publishing it.[12] Meredith made his debut on the faculty with several publications. In one he demonstrated how inaccurate professionally accepted standard physical measurements could be. He took fifteen of these standard measures of twenty-five white eight- and nine-year-old boys from the Iowa City public schools. Using professionally accepted standards of rigor with each measurement, Meredith reported that when he rechecked them, he found some measurements reasonably reliable, others ridiculously inaccurate. He concluded that both a more sophisticated idea of what good measurements were and better techniques were essential. In a separate study, Meredith and Stoddard reviewed the field's literature and found it constituted of "a large body of inconclusive findings, suggestive leads, and inviting hypotheses [that] await further research."[13]

When Stoddard became director, he made sure that Baldwin's data files were preserved and that, if anything, the pace of collecting measurements was quickened. Stoddard groomed Meredith to use this material for a fresh program in physical growth. Meredith made a number of departures from pre-1920s physical growth and maturation studies and, for that matter, from those contemporary with his own work. He took as dissertation topic the problem of the rhythms of physical growth in boys. He insisted that his sample was but one physical type, and that there were many different types of normal children, certainly a novel refrain in the 1930s, unless one were intimately acquainted with the arcane arguments of European and American population geneticists. Meredith reinterpreted Baldwin's data and fashioned a new argument from it. The data, collected over the last fourteen years, consisted of 93,232 measurement values of eighteen distinct physical measurements of 1,243 white males from birth to eighteen years. He noted that the population was homogeneous with regard to geographical location, somewhat diverse in ethnic background, and advantaged with regard to economic and cultural factors. And its members had characteristically normal body builds.

Thus Meredith defined the body in ways very different from prewar notions—it was a holistic and diverse entity constituted of many distinct and interrelated elements. Given the population's homogeneous character, he continued, it was not surprising to find much overlap in individual and group growth curves, as, for instance, for stature after the age of six. For the group as a whole, there were at least four phases of alternate quickening and slowing of growth for eight of the eighteen distinct measurements. Yet, he cautioned, growth was not linear or, more precisely, unilinear. Nor was it automatic or predetermined. For individuals from ages six to eleven, individual curves of development rarely crossed, proof of his larger thesis.

In other words, individuals grew as individuals, even within a larger and reasonably well defined population or group. And it was foolhardy indeed to predict a person's stature between the ages of eleven and eighteen. Thus Meredith departed from orthodox maturation theory in fundamental particulars. He defined types as relatively specific; he even seemed to regard his classifications as hypotheses rather than as natural types, thus departing from the work of most of his colleagues across the nation. Also he stressed the individual within the group, rather than group averages. Finally, he was highly distrustful of the unilinear patterns of growth that most developmentalists seemed to cherish so fondly. The next year one of his doctoral students, Bernice Boynton, published a parallel study of girls from the same data and came to similar conclusions.[14]

Meredith turned to new problems. He and his students investigated changes in growth of the proportions of the various elements of the body. With Virginia B. Knott, a graduate student, Meredith studied growth patterns by using the thoracic index, a ratio of the breadth to the depth of the thorax. The data used in the study were 2,037 paired measurements for width and depth of the thorax in 557 males and 1,631 paired measurements for like dimensions of the thorax on 448 females. The sample or population was relatively homogeneous; all were white Christians of northern or western European ancestry. Meredith and Knott found considerable complexity. Patterns of growth existed within the group, but they were not simple or linear. Mean thoracic index for males and females increased from three months to five years, with the greatest period of increase between three months to two years. During the sixth year, males and females showed a minor decrease in mean thoracic index. Yet variation among individuals in thoracic index betrayed no consistent trend toward either increase or decrease.[15]

In a follow-up study, Meredith and Knott investigated the developmental direction from embryo and fetus to birth to six years. The basic data they used were approximately 3,500 measurements each for width of hip, chest, and shoulder, and for stem length and for stature. Developmental direction, they argued, was far more complex than had been previously imagined. Different parts of the body grew at different rates in various periods in the life cycle to age six. The direction of development was not a simple linear curve, as orthodox developmentalists said it was. Yet it was always whole, unified, never asymmetrical; on that point Meredith and Knott were resolute.[16]

Meredith and Knott used the skelic index, a ratio of the length of the lower extremities divided by statuary height, to probe individual and group growth patterns for about 1,100 infants and preschool children of both sexes. Again they found a highly complex series of patterns. In another project, Meredith and Boynton studied the transverse growth of the extremities, about which little was known. The data consisted of 2,373 measurement values from 771 Iowa City white females and 2,897 measurement values from 1,013 Iowa City white males aged birth to 18 years, for arm, forearm, thigh, and leg girth. The forearm circumference of females was less than that for males throughout the entire age interval studied, whereas thigh circumference of females was greater than that of males after two years. In general, absolute variability was least for the forearm, intermediate for the arm and the leg, and greatest for the thigh, whereas relative variability was least for the forearm, intermediate for the leg, and greatest for the thigh and the arm.

Individual differences were great, they found, even in so homogeneous a population. Some six-year-old males and females had larger girths of both upper and lower limbs than did some eighteen-year-old males and females. Obviously, growth and development for individuals and for this relatively narrowly selected population followed highly complex and particularistic patterns. For both sexes, the annual percentage movement curves for all girths experienced an initial rapid descent during the first year following birth, and a second maximum at age three. For children from age five on, the curves resembled two roughly concave arcs, with maximum growth between eleven and thirteen years for girls, and thirteen and fifteen for boys. At eighteen years, the growth rate was negligible for females, and 2 percent for males. Indeed, growth for individuals was not predictable at important points in the life cycle—as from age eleven onward. There was simply too much variation among individuals.[17]

Meredith was a maverick in his field. He and his coworkers challenged the maturation theory as applied to physical growth at virtually very point. They criticized the notion that all growth curves were linear, that individuals could vary only within the range of possibilities permitted by that species' endowment, and that growth meant merely an increase in size and development, the predetermined differentiation of organs and functions. In one of the few self-consciously theoretical publications he permitted himself, Meredith insisted that physical growth was "the study of changes taking place in the size, complexity, the proportions, and the texture and pigmentation of the body between the beginning of embryonic life and the close of senility." Order, not chaos, typified development, he insisted; it was even more complex, more interrelated, more intricate, more dependent on the present as well as the past, and more symmetrical, than his national colleagues might have imagined.[18]

Even those presumably dry-as-dust factual studies he directed had powerful and contrary theoretical statements embedded and often disguised in his arid writing style. In one study he offered complex measurements of head and neck, trunk, and lower extremities, or total stature, which he gathered from Iowa City children from ages seven to seventeen. That he took—and showcased—such complex measurements was his way of rebuking his professional colleagues. He criticized his colleagues' work, for instance, the Harvard Growth Study that Walter F. Dearborn and his colleagues had conducted. The study was flawed, Meredith claimed; it lacked methodological rigor, and its central argument, that growth was linear and predetermined, was simplistic and erroneous. Meredith also investigated the physical measurements of poor white Alabama girls and compared them with middle-class white Iowa City girls of comparable age. The Alabama girls were individually and collectively a smaller group by age. Meredith concluded they constituted slightly different populations or types. In another project, Meredith and a student subjected eight standard generalizations about the neonate in the specialist literature to verification by the data they had collected. They concluded that half of the generalizations were wrong. Meredith used measurements of individuals, not of groups—a cause of the difference, to be sure. Individual variation was a fact of nature, he insisted; it could not be ignored or swept under the carpet. Group averages were a poor and inappropriate substitute. There was too much variation among individuals in any group no matter how that group was defined.[19] In these and other ways, Meredith directly challenged the maturation theory's assumptions.

In 1936 McCloy published an intensive monograph in which he spelled out reliable measurements of the bony framework, or gross form of the skeleton. These more than thirty distinct measurements would be crucial for any generation of raw data for the calculation of normal weight for body build. He settled on several, including standing height, chest circumference at the level of the xiphoid cartilage (the posterior section of the sternum), and hip width at the epicondyles of the femur. McCloy made corrections for fat. He used multiple regression equations to figure the normal weight of an individual for that person's distinct body build. From these methods, he insisted, it was possible to generate tables and other representations of growth and development for the many distinct body builds of the human species. Indeed, to overlook individual variation was a serious mistake.[20] Thus he agreed with Meredith's challenges to the maturation theory.

One of McCloy's graduate students, Eleanor Metheny, also took on the maturation theory. She argued in the journal *Human Biology* that established authorities seriously erred by insisting that measurements need be taken only every three years. Too much change occurred in any individual in so long a period. In determining the normal weight for any given body build, the older age-height-weight tables—such as Baldwin's, for instance—were simply not useful for any body types save that of the "normal child," which was but one type among many. Furthermore, such tables made no allowances for individual differences, which were assuredly wide. There were many different kinds of body builds and many individuals. McCloy's four measurements yielded fairly accurate representations of the gross skeletal form, Metheny continued. In yet another project, McCloy, Metheny, and Knott argued that with the use of multiple regression equations from these data, the normal weight could be predicted for an individual of a given body build. It was possible to study deviations from normal in terms of body build as distinct from average or normal types.[21]

Everett L. Marshall, another of McCloy's students, used multiple-factor theories of statistical inference to interpret physical growth. From 850 white boys six years of age or less, he compiled approximately 15,000 measurement values. He had calculated these measurement values from a series of eighteen anthropometric factors that he had arranged in four groups of factors. He concluded that one such group of factors was related to growth in subcutaneous fatty tissue. In the rest of his article he simply presented these very complex measurements. In another investigation, Marshall compared the accuracy of four standard methods of determining physical stature. He measured the same seventy-seven individuals with all four. The results were uneven. Those obtained with the now-traditional Thomas Wood–Bird T. Baldwin age-weight-height tables and those with McCloy's table were in reasonable accord. But those taken with more commonly used tables were so inadequate that a person could be ranked subnormal on one and average on another. Marshall and Metheny published other studies critical of commonly accepted measuring devices and procedures. Knott criticized the reliability of numerous standard anthropometric measurements. Metheny published a study of breathing capacity and grip strength of preschool children.[22]

All this work shared certain common assumptions. Development was a complex process; great oaks from little acorns did not grow. Designation of groups was, at best, highly arbitrary. Individuals existed; it was essential to plot the intricacies of their development. Above all, the individual—or the larger population, for that matter—was best understood as a holistic, symmetrical unity of many diverse yet interrelated structures and processes, a whole that was perforce greater than or different from the sum of the parts. In none of their arguments did they appear to perceive any conflict between individualism and holism.

The memorial's last grant had funded an elaborate infant laboratory, which permitted a new departure, the investigation of infant behavior. Orvis C. Irwin was appointed to direct this program. He had taken his doctorate at Ohio State University with Albert Paul Weiss, a brilliant, prolific behaviorist who published almost forty articles and several books before his death in 1931 at the age of fifty-two. Weiss as behaviorist was no believer in the "empty organism" theory that most behaviorists who followed John B. Watson's lead embraced. In his wide-ranging work, Weiss sought to create a behaviorist interpretation of psychological processes and events that admitted contingency, variation, and choice in the organism. From Weiss, Irwin learned of the importance of "mass activity," the undifferentiated activity of the infant at birth and even in the fetal condition that at later points in development would become more specialized and differentiated as the organism as a whole developed. Weiss helped shift the locus of professional concern from group to individual, and from determinism to indeterminism, departing from the Watsonian stimulus-response formula. Yet Weiss embraced the larger symmetrical, holistic blueprint of natural and social reality.[23]

Irwin brought this perspective to the station's infant research program. Initially, Irwin probed the phenomenon of motility, or body movement, of infants. He used a two-dimensional stabilimeter and a polygraph for several determinations and measurements. He found sharp individual differences in body motility soon after birth that seemed more striking than any presumed central tendency according to standard developmental grand theory. And, if there were wide individual differences in motility, all seventy-three infants studied demonstrated at least some movement. The earliest fluctuations in movement, before the fourth or fifth day, seemed not significant, entirely random and happenstance. In a different experiment, he found low correlations between individual physical traits and individual differences in body motility; the former could not be deployed to explain the latter. He also discovered that individual differences in motility were not due to such factors as wakefulness, body temperature, and nutritional status. There was, not unexpectedly, a strong relationship between hunger and increased body motility.[24] Motility, an expression of mass activity, could not be closely correlated with most other developmental characteristics. In many respects it was the result of the organism as a whole and had, as it were, a life of its own, its own blueprints, large and small, and its own intricate and complex symmetry—or symmetries.

Irwin also attacked important elements of the maturation theory. Initially he ran two experiments to test behaviorist John B. Watson's argument that fear was one of the three innate responses of newborns. First he tested the phenomenon of body startle, an involuntary newborn reaction in which the body jerked together; the arms extended and returned, with a flexing of the elbows, in a clasp to the trunk; the fingers extended, then clenched; and the legs moved similarly but less violently. Watson and others interpreted body startle as the basis of fear in children. Irwin placed twelve infants, six male, six female, on the stabilimeter and noted the time it took each to react to a loud tone. He measured the length of time for the reaction. He found no sex differences; more importantly, the babies did not cry as Watson had claimed. In the second experiment, infants were dropped two feet and caught. The infants did not, as a rule, cry. Again, they criticized Watson's argument: fear was not innate; an important element of the maturation theory was wrong.[25]

In other investigations Irwin and his associates attacked Watsonian orthodox behaviorism, with its associated notions of an "empty organism" and predetermined movement through the interaction of innate anatomical structures and environmental stimuli. They discovered that infant reactions to light and sound stimuli were extremely specific, not a continuous series. This cast considerable doubt on the validity of the idea of predetermined development.[26]

Irwin and T. W. Richards, one of his doctoral students, took Watson's explanations to task. Richards published several studies of hunger in the newborn infant—Watson had argued, after all, that hunger was one of the three innate responses of infants. In particular, Richards criticized Watson's notion that a simple stimulus did not produce a reasonably well defined response. Watson's interpretation of the events surrounding and leading up to hunger in the newborn was totally inadequate. It was untrue that external stimuli merely "awakened" mute anatomical structures and spurred on maturation through its manifold "stages." Richards examined peristaltic gastric activity in newborns, an activity that definitely increased with time after feeding, thus suggesting that a simple stimulus had produced a definite response. Yet this was not the case. Gastric activity was not related to the infants' behavior as measured on the stabilimeter. Indeed, the infants' thrashing was not related at all to their gastric activity. This flatly contradicted Watson's argument that they were causally linked. Richards also noted that there were wide differences in individual infants in all sorts of behavior, bodily and gastric, external and internal, as it were. These events seemed not related at all. What orthodox developmentalists had insisted was virtually stereotypical behavior in infants, Richards and Irwin found to be unrelated. If anything, the events seemed random, and there were no convenient group designations that made these events more understandable, such as sex, race, ethnicity, age, physical status, birth weight, type of feeding, and so on. Richards insisted that Watson and his followers were careless indeed not to distinguish between gastric and more general bodily activity, to the point that they misinterpreted so deceptively simple a series of events as hunger, which was not reducible to a mechanistic stimulus-response formula. There were too many events in the infant's life to be so simply explained.[27]

In several other studies, Irwin and his coworkers found widespread individual differences in body movements, with the clear implication that much activity was spontaneous, discontinuous, and disparate, even in the same individuals.[28] In an investigation, with M. A. Wenger, of the conditioned reflex, Irwin argued that conditioned reflexes first appeared on the fourth day of life. Great variability characterized the responses and their latencies. Internal inhibition of responses seemed an artifact of the experiment rather than a genuine accompaniment of conditioning per se. Again, development was not smooth, automatic, mechanical; it could not be explained in reductionist terms, or as the consequence of the action of particular anatomical or genetic structures. It was characterized by mass activity, was highly flexible, and was the result of the action of the entire organism in response to its milieu.[29]

Irwin had a theoretical axe to grind. He used his organismic hypothesis to attack orthodox behaviorist maturation theory in the pages of the prestigious *Psychological Review*. He insisted that from the structural point of view, the organism differentiated into cells, tissues, organs, and structures, all the time maintaining its integrity as a whole and existing as an environment for the body organs, tissues, and cells involved in behavior. On the functional side, the organism as fetus and newborn exhibited spontaneous, primitive, and largely undifferentiated behavior—a matrix of behavior, in fact—which he termed mass activity. Mass activity was at its maximum during the first fetal months, and during the uterine existence, the differentiation of activity into definite patterns began to take place. After birth, the processes of differentiation proceeded with increasing degrees of specificity, definiteness, and precision of pattern, until they approximated what would be called adaptive behavior. This was a process involving the whole organism, in which the whole was greater than the sum of its parts. Behavior was not simply a question of a series of continuous, programmed responses from specific cells, neurons, and others parts of the body to specific environmental stimuli. Rather, the organism as a balanced, well-integrated whole "sought out" responses variously and in a somewhat adventitious manner. Much more was involved, then, than a mute organism mechanically responding to stimuli because of its distinctive, innate endowment.[30]

Almost immediately Irwin was criticized. In the 1933 edition of Murchison's *Handbook of Child Psychology*, Leonard Carmichael, now at Brown University, disputed Irwin's arguments. Irwin and Carmichael debated learning versus maturation. Irwin insisted that much was contingent and random, and organisms learned as they developed, whereas Carmichael argued that all organisms followed definite patterns of integration in the neatly synchronized patterns of interaction of innate "empty" structures and environmental "stimuli" to produce the awakening of the individual during development. In particular, Irwin questioned maturation theory at its most crucial point, the connections alleged between internal structures and external stimuli; so did Richards in his questioning of Watson's formula of hunger responses. Writing as Watson's intellectual descendant, Carmichael insisted that such orderly developments had to be determined in advance. In effect, Carmichael and Irwin fought over determinism and indeterminism as appropriate models of reality.[31]

Irwin attacked the maturation theory in other ways, too. Several years later he criticized Ivan Pavlov's theory of conditioned reflex as both reductionist and mechanistic, attacking the Russian physiologist's turn-of-the-century assumptions as well as the determinism of contemporary maturation theory.[32] The infant was not a passive organism upon which the forces of nature and nurture acted, as the maturation theorists would argue. Rather, he pointed out, infants were active, even wiggly, bundles of mass activity. In several studies of infant speech sounds, he offered new methods of observation and measurement. He insisted that speech patterns, like all other patterns of behavior in young infants, showed that each and every baby was an individual who could not be pigeonholed into specific group categories. On the basis of other investigations he insisted that intellectual development in babies was not stereotypical; the IQ was not fixed at birth.[33]

Researchers at the station also explored the development of motor skills and coordination in very young children. All of the work, especially in the later 1920s and early 1930s was explicitly normative; that is, the researchers sought to uncover the norms of growth and motor development. James Allen Hicks, one of Beth L. Wellman's first doctoral students, carried out a complex series of experiments on the effects of systematic practice on preschool children. The problem he posed was whether maturation of motor control and generalized exercise was more important than specific practice in the ability to perform various physical acts. He used the control group method, then just coming into vogue in the field, and confronted the learning-versus-maturation debate head-on. He divided sixty preschool children ranging in age from two years, seven months to six years, five months into control and experimental groups, matched as closely as possible for age, sex, mental age, and other variables. Children in the experimental group practiced for eight weeks the four motor skills tests he devised. Those in the control group did not. In the end, Hicks argued that specific practice—learning, that is—was much less important than the general maturation of motor control and generalized exercise in the children's success or failure in passing the tests. Thus, Hicks took the side of orthodox maturation theory. He also plotted group averages rather than individual performance.[34]

Yet most of the work at the station that focused on motor skills and coordination pointed in the opposite direction, toward learning rather than automatic maturation. In her work on handedness and eyedness, Ruth Updegraff had a specific agenda: the importance of learning over maturation. She insisted that training and learning might well have much to do with these phenomena. If children as young as two years old exhibited a preference for one hand or the other, the degree of preference still varied with the individual. Development was neither automatic nor programmed. If there was a native tendency in the individual to prefer one hand over the other, a large minority of individuals nevertheless seemed to change their preferences over time through training or, perhaps, the happenstance events of their lives. This was true of ocular dominance, Updegraff insisted. Unilaterality was the strong preference for dominance by the right or the left hand or eye. As such, it was a direct corollary of the notion of genetically predetermined development. Yet "the most plausible hypothesis at present" was that of unilaterality as "varying in degree" and with "different manifestations of dominance, of which handedness and eyedness are only two."[35] Other investigations of physiological development done at the station in the early 1930s made much the same theoretical point.[36] In another study of maturation versus learning, Beth Wellman and a graduate student found that the most important indicator of proficiency was age, not sex or any socioeconomic categories. The individual developed according to his or her own life experiences, and the ultimate reality of nature and society was the individual, not the group.[37]

The station's workers also researched problems in mental and cognitive development. Here again they shifted the locus of concern to the individual from the group, disputing their colleagues' determinism. They embraced the larger holistic, dynamic, and symmetrical taxonomy or blueprint of natural and social reality in which their colleagues believed. Lois Z. Smith and Genevieve L. Harter pointed out that the preschool child varied according to his or her mental ability in grasping abstract concepts. Harter insisted that a child needed much overt trial and error to solve a series of nonverbal performance tests.

Therefore, she concluded, mental development was not an automatic unfolding or maturation of innate potentiality that epiphenomenal stimuli awakened
in proper sequence. Mental or cognitive development involved considerable
learning by an active individual child.[38] In an ambitious study of a child's ability
to pronounce English language sounds at different ages, Wellman and three
associates studied 204 preschool children. They found that the learning of
speech sounds progressed at astonishing rates at each age they studied, that is,
from two to three, from three to four, from four to five. By the age of five years,
the normal child was able to produce the standard 133 speech sounds of the
English language of which adults were capable. Wellman and her colleagues
insisted that the ability to produce speech sounds seemed primarily a matter of
physiological and chronological maturation, not mental maturation or age,
social milieu, and the like. In other words, some aspects of development could
be thought of as maturational; others could not.[39]

Mental and physiological maturation, declared Wellman and her colleagues,
were not necessarily closely related. Development's complexities could not be
reduced to a simple nature cum nurture formula, with its emphasis on heredity
and the consignment of environment to the mere role of catalyst. One researcher scrutinized the criticisms children made of one another. The older the
children were, the more critical they were of one another. This observation
suggested that some social traits were more related to chronological than mental age. In a more intensive project, investigator Olive J. Grigsby probed the
verbalized conceptions of relations children had of time, space, number, part-
whole, discordance, and cause. She selected as her subjects eighty-three children from the ages of two to six. She found that gradations in sophistication
were more closely related to mental than to chronological age. Other studies
indicated that language use and grammatical competence owed more to chronological than mental age, but, at the same time, the age of five years seemed the
important benchmark for normal children.[40]

The study of child personality and behavior had begun at the station before
Baldwin's death. Baldwin was strongly committed to these investigations as a
way of promoting the notion of the whole child and as a criticism of contemporary psychometrics. These were studies of individuals interacting with one
another; as such, they were not studies of group dynamics such as those that
Kurt Lewin initiated in the later 1930s at the Iowa station. Rather, they were
pioneering efforts in personality theory. In one way or another, these early
studies focused on the complexities of the social milieu surrounding the child.
They were predicated on the belief that the child no less than the adult is the

product of that milieu of notions, beliefs, and actions. Although these studies were not necessarily opposed to the maturation theory in all cases, they offered little aid and comfort to it.

In 1930, Esther Van Cleve Berne published a pioneering personality study focusing on domination. Her concerns were as much methodological as substantive. She sought to understand the holistic pattern of elements or components of the child's environment and the relationship of each to the child's behavior. Above all, she attacked what she termed the crudities of John B. Watson's stimulus-response formula. She wanted to identify normal behavior—in this case, the normal wants of the normal child. She observed seven children in the 1926 summer preschool for slightly more than 540 hours, and other children subsequently for another 1,000 hours. She took notes on behavior in all situations in the preschool—free play, organized play, lunches, and naps. She defined social behavior as that any individual child made in response to the behavior, including verbal behavior, or even to the presence, of other persons. Nonsocial behavior was what was left, meaning largely individual behavior, such as sleeping or eating. She then categorized the various patterns of social and nonsocial behavior to ascertain what wants the children sought to satisfy in each instance. The children seemed animated to act socially to satisfy the desire to observe others from a distance, to cooperate with others, to conform to notions of their own identity, to assert control of themselves, and to promote their superiority. In a nutshell, sometimes children wished to dominate, at other times to conform, and on still other occasions to steer a middle path between dominance and conformity.[41] In this way, Berne addressed an issue that had preoccupied Baldwin in the middle 1920s, whether very young children had distinctive personality traits that projected into the school years and beyond into adulthood.

In other experiments, station researchers observed children with play materials, chiefly clay and blocks; the scientists investigated the stimuli that produced cooperative and isolative behavior. Clay encouraged children to play together. Blocks did not.[42] In a further extension of Berne's study of cooperation and domination, Ida Gaarder Mengert used ten pairs of preschool children to identify overtly friendly and overtly unfriendly behavior as ranked by adult observers. Her purpose was methodological, to test the techniques of adult observation. Her hope was that her methods could be translated into a form that parents and nursery school teachers could use to influence child behavior.[43]

Perhaps the most intensive study of personality done at the station in the early 1930s was Wendell Johnson's *Influence of Stuttering on the Personality.* Ultimately, he was one of the most distinguished researchers in speech pathology in the world; for a time in the 1930s, Johnson held joint appointments in speech and child welfare. His study was a landmark in speech pathology, literally reorienting or even reinventing the field. He studied by the case method eighty stutterers, ranging in age from seven to forty-two years and averaging almost nineteen. Sixty-one were male, nineteen were female. He prepared intensive case histories, gave them speech clinic examinations, obtained autobiographies and personal documents, administered a mental hygiene examination, interviewed them at length, and placed them under extensive observation. A former stutterer himself, Johnson studied his subjects' attitudes and adjustments to various situations in their lives, at home, in school, on the job, and in all manner of social situations. What were the stutterers' attitudes toward the act of stuttering itself? Toward themselves and others? What were their fantasies, wishes, and personality problems?

Johnson defined stuttering functionally, not structurally. It was not a trait unto itself; it was a distinct yet interrelated part of a larger, dynamic, symmetrical whole. Nor was it primarily the physiological and biological aspects of stuttering that mattered to him in this study. He wanted to know what the impact was of the stutterer's social milieu upon his personality and behavior, or, put another way, what stuttering meant to the stutterer in various social situations. Johnson's thesis was that the great problem was not stuttering per se as an act, but the "part which stuttering plays in the stutterer's life." Johnson disputed the assumption that stutterers were in some sense abnormal persons, afflicted with peculiar problems besides stuttering itself. Stutterers were relatively normal and well-adjusted persons save for the impact of stuttering upon their lives. The therapeutic regimen he recommended to cure stuttering was to build confidence in the stutterer. This could even include some training in corrective speech.[44]

In the middle 1930s Johnson published the results of an investigation of stuttering from the physiological and physical point of view. Thus he discussed the apparent relationships between stuttering and handedness; he insisted these were highly complex. Stutterers differed from normal speakers because, relatively speaking, they lacked unilaterality of motor-hand control. In a general way, it seemed that stuttering was closely related to the processes of physical maturation. Inheritance was also a factor. Johnson did not repudiate his earlier studies of stuttering in its social milieu. Rather, he attempted to comprehend stuttering as a complex natural and cultural phenomenon resulting from the interaction of many discrete yet interrelated factors. Stuttering was not determined by inheritance but appeared to be a complex trait resulting from the interaction of many discrete factors. Johnson was no determinist. Nor did he think of physical maturation as a simple process of the awakening of responses by environmental stimuli. Much, much more was involved.[45]

As late as the middle 1930s, the station's investigators were not probing the dynamics of small groups or evolving a distinctive way of holistically explaining the behavior of individuals in group situations that was distinct from the older static, atomistic traditions of psychology. Some were aware of the need for such theoretical and methodological work, like the staff member who attempted to devise a methodological technique for studying the entire social situation; yet this work was not yet true group dynamics.[46] In 1934, however, Lois M. Jack and six associates published five related studies in which they addressed small-group dynamics and statics as distinct from individual behavior—and opened up the whole field of the psychological study of group dynamics in America. They were especially concerned that their techniques of observation of data could be verified, and that their notions of units of behavior were realistic. The most important theoretical argument was Jack's notion of ascendant behavior as the response from the totality of the group situation, not from the individual conceived as a psychological datum. Ascendant behavior was the pursuit of one's purposes against interference from others in the social situation and, indeed, directing the behavior of all other persons in that situation. Jack constructed two experiments. In the first, she and her colleagues studied differences in ascendant, moderately ascendant, and nonascendant behavior; they found a host of explanations for each, including lack of confidence or confidence, obviously crucial variables for ascendant and nonascendant behavior. In the second experiment, they trained nonascendant children to compete with ascendant children. In other words, training or learning for the individual and the group mattered much.[47] One could not use simplistic maturation schemes. The "natural" limits to such situations were very broad indeed.

If there was a predominant view among workers in child psychology and behavior in the middle 1930s at the Iowa station, it was that the individual, not the group, was the field's unit of analysis, and that psychological and intellectual factors, not ineluctable social forces or group identity, were responsible for the making of behavior patterns of all kinds. Yet their notions of the individual, or of individuals, seemed in retrospect curiously generic, bereft of any particularity, distinctiveness, or asymmetry; if in one sense individuals appeared distinct, the symmetry of the whole made them appear interchangeable.

On occasion, the conflict between the mainstream or orthodox position among developmentalists and that of the Iowa workers came clearly into view. Evaline Fales and LaBerta A. Hattwick drew diametrically opposed conclusions from their studies of sex differences. Fales had taken her doctorate from the California Institute of Child Welfare and had won appointment at the Iowa station. Hattwick, on the other hand, was a doctoral graduate of the Iowa station and now worked in public nursery schools in the Chicago suburbs. Fales investigated quiet and vigorous activities in boys and girls, preschoolers all, paired by gender and age, who represented a definite mixture of social and economic backgrounds in the San Francisco metropolitan area. On the basis of her rating scales, she argued that the conventional view, that boys were more active than girls, was flatly contradicted by her results. The mean scores for these traits were identical for boys and girls. And the results of individual scores showed wide variability and an almost complete lack of sex-typed behavior. In her study of 283 boys and 296 girls, Hattwick reinforced the conventional view. Fales looked at individual as well as group scores; Hattwick did not. Therein lay the chief intellectual difference between the two studies.[48]

Criticisms of the notion that group identity defined all traits and patterns of behavior of individuals emerged in other quarters from the station's scientists as well. Ruth Updegraff, never a shrinking violet on such matters, took Florence L. Goodenough and John E. Anderson, both of the Minnesota institute, to task for what she called their sterile idea of the environment in their *Experimental Child Study* (1931). She attacked their notion that the material aspects of the home environment and the family's abstract socioeconomic occupational levels were formative, causal forces for the development of the child. The most important aspects of the home environment, she tartly insisted, were not its physical or socioeconomic characteristics. What went on in the the home— what mental events took place, what psychic reactions individuals had to one another, that is—mattered much more. She argued that such views as Goodenough's and Anderson's were antiquated, for they ignored the new work in the field of personality theory and such specific psychological processes as identification and projection. She insisted that a fruitful approach would be to have children in the preschool laboratories act out their attitudes with puppets, dramatic play, and specific toys. That approach was just as important as understanding that the environment was essentially psychological and intellectual, not the result of ineluctable social forces and psychobiological processes and structures. As for the home, it was "the resulting behavior within the family group and the interplay of attitudes within the family which constitute the real core of the problem."[49]

Here again the Iowa scientists' ideas differed from those of their national colleagues concerning child social and individual psychology. In the view of Goodenough and Anderson, and thus of the profession at large, individuals were the results of social and psychobiological processes—they were manifestations, as it were, of larger forces beyond their control. Their traits and patterns of behavior were fixed within certain rather narrow ranges, which natural and social forces had established for the group to which they belonged. For the Iowa workers, the individual was the real datum of child science. Groups existed when researchers constructed them for purposes of study. And there were natural groupings in nature and society, although they had relatively broad limits. The orthodox view was static in the sense that it was subtly but powerfully deterministic. The Iowa workers were moving their view toward a not always openly articulated position of indeterminism, and of a focus on the individual, not on the group. It should be clear that not all workers at the Iowa station necessarily agreed with one another, especially on matters of detail and emphasis. Nevertheless, the interpretations they gave of child behavior and development offered a far more liberated vision of the possibilities of child and social life for the American nation than did those interpretations of the work of the vast majority of their professional colleagues throughout the nation. And the arguments that the Iowa scientists made had definite implications for social and public policy, especially toward children and the family. They made a simple point: Science showed that social intervention could make a beneficial difference. Their professional critics, by and large, denied that thesis. At some level, the differences between the Iowa scientists and their critics had to do not merely with arcane points of science, but with large questions of social and public policy. The Iowa argument was ultimately one for responsible, science-based social amelioration—a social technology, in other words.

This outlook was true with those who worked in the station's programs in mental hygiene and juvenile delinquency. Harold H. Anderson ran the latter effort as a statewide program with large administrative responsibilities. His ideology was that of the national mental hygiene movement, save that he placed the individual front and center in his concerns. His thesis was that mental conflicts caused social problems, not the mainstream thesis that social forces caused social problems. In a talk before state corrections officials in 1934, for example, Anderson insisted that nothing was "static about the child or his environment," for they were two activities that were constantly affecting one another.[50] Those who worked in delinquency studies took a position very close to Updegraff's. Social forces did not matter; mental conflicts did. The interactions of individuals, both one on one and in groups, mattered the most. As early as 1931 Elizabeth Skelding Moore had insisted that there were no certain links between personality, on the one hand, and socioeconomic and home environment, on the other, in explaining child behavior. Environment was not some static and inevitable force. It was the mental and emotional relations of individuals that were always dynamic, interactive, interrelated, and in flux.[51] In the later 1930s, Newell C. Kephart and H. Max Houtchens, inspired by contemporary psychiatrists, used word association tests for diagnostic purposes. They found the behaviorist stimulus-response theory of Watson and others lacking; Kephart and Houtchens's results suggested that association was a mental process, and disturbances in the tests resulted from disturbances of the process rather than, as the Watsonian formula would predict, from a specific situation presented to the subject's mind by a particular word on the test.[52]

The Iowa station became increasingly noted in the early to mid-1930s for its work on the inconstancy of the intelligence quotient. It was rapidly becoming an idée fixe among most scientists, whether they were developmentalists or not, that the IQ was fixed in individuals at birth, and that the variation within groups had certain limits, probably because of the force of heredity and environment interacting together. There were numerous reasons why almost all mental testers believed that the IQ was fixed; indeed, the preponderance of evidence in the interwar era supported that proposition. Quite apart from the deterministic and hereditarian beliefs that most scientists shared on the nature of human nature then, there were certain technical reasons why most scientists, regardless of their broader views, found the argument that the IQ was fixed upon birth persuasive.

It is useful to review those reasons here, for they enable us to comprehend the station's later history in this field of research. As Binet tests of one version or another had been standardized in America, or adapted to American children, psychometricians found that, with Binet and Simon, performance on a test increased with chronological age, thus establishing a link between chronological and mental age and giving rise to German psychologist Wilhelm Stern's very notion of the intelligence quotient, or the ratio of the mental to the chronological age. Second, psychologists found in their own investigations of the Binet tests that mean or average IQs for *groups* of children, upon retesting, appeared highly constant. This was, of course, a mere artifact of the construction of the Binet scale itself. It was designed to insure that, for each age group, one-fourth would be too stupid to pass, one-half would pass within a middle range, and one-fourth would excel; these results produced a normal curve. The children on whom the American Binet tests were standardized, and who were thus tested in countless studies of the utility and accuracy of the Binet test, were middle class, white, and of northern or western European extraction, and they stretched in age between the first grade and adulthood. The test was thus culturally and socially restricted. And when the testers examined *individual* children, they found the IQs of their charges constant upon retesting also; as before, though, their subjects were white, middle-class children, of Anglo-Saxon, Protestant extraction, and they were no younger than age six. Thus the standard kind of retesting of IQs to establish IQ constancy did not cover all kinds of cases, but it did embrace those American psychometricians studied: white, Anglo-Saxon, Protestant, middle-class, and school-age children. It occurred to almost no one what might happen if such an instrument was administered to a population with radically different characteristics.

Additional evidence seemingly confirmed the thesis of the fixed IQ. The results of other tests of learning and education had high statistical correlations with IQ scores in individual and group comparisons, which most scientists then interpreted as further confirmation that the IQ (and intelligence) were biologically inherited. And IQ scores seemed to correlate with other measures of success for individuals and groups, which again served to confirm deterministic arguments about human intelligence. That something other than biological factors might be reflected in these studies simply never occurred to most scientists in the field. Such considerations were simply not a part of their professional discourse. And there was very little evidence before the later thirties to suggest that the IQ was anything other than constant, except for the Woolley and the Barrett and Koch investigations, whose argument was that the IQ changed, and dramatically so, in very young children in preschools and orphanages. Helen Thompson Woolley, of the Merrill-Palmer Institute, and the first director of the Teachers College child welfare institute, studied middle-class tykes in a preschool, and noted the enormous gains in IQs that individual children in the preschool made on retesting; Florence Goodenough, among others, ridiculed her work. Helen E. Barrett and Helen Koch, of the University of Chicago, studied working-class orphans in 1930 and insisted that individual inmates in such institutions had highly variable IQs on retesting. It is noteworthy that no one else in the profession replicated the methods or the angle of vision of either the Woolley or the Barrett-Koch studies, and no one gave Binet tests to *preschool* age orphans, as Barrett and Koch did, until the Iowa scientists began their work. This was not a good omen for the Iowa station's work on the IQ.[53]

Stoddard and Wellman worked together to challenge these doctrines. Stoddard played the role of the public advocate and theoretician for the work, whereas Wellman gathered the data and presented it in scientific forums. The data came from the station's preschools, and the pupils were almost entirely from white, middle-class homes in Iowa City and its environs.

Baldwin had been interested in the problem of mental growth. In the last year or so of his life, he had criticized the idea that a child's mind was innate. Wellman and Baldwin were engaged to be married when he died, and Wellman probably carried on Baldwin's criticism into work she and, eventually Stoddard, did on the IQ. Wellman published a brief report in 1928 on the testing of psychological processes that had been carried out at the preschool since it had opened in 1921. She insisted that the station had in its files some 21,000 measurements on all kinds of mental abilities, including perception of form, shape, size, color, motor control, learning, intelligence, vocabulary, memory, speech development, and emotional development, among others. Obviously here was an avalanche of data waiting to be used.[54] She did not address the question of whether the IQ was constant or not; apparently she had not advanced that far in her thinking. After Stoddard settled in, he and Wellman discussed the data. Soon the idea took hold. At the 1931 National Association of Nursery Education conference, Wellman reported on work done at the station on psychological measurements of children. Parenthetically, she remarked that the station's preschool children had gained significantly in IQs from fall to spring, but not from spring or summer to fall. She argued this gain was due to attendance at the preschool.[55]

Over the next several years Wellman worked on the problem intensively. She did not have access to longitudinal data in the important sense that a longitudinal project was never formally established at the station, as had been done at Stanford, for example, with Terman's genius project. Ever since the station's preschools had opened, however, staff workers had amassed an avalanche of routine physical, mental, and medical measurements on the pupils. This fact gathering was done to uncover the norms of child life and development from as many different angles as possible. Some pupils remained in the preschools a brief time. Some continued in the university's elementary and high schools. Others did not, and left at various junctures. Hence, the children constituted a pool from which records could be retrieved for analysis and interpretation. Yet individual children could not necessarily be tracked throughout their individual life cycles, as many left the preschools and university schools. Wellman was forced to use data historically, literally to reconstruct her data after the fact.

Thus her study differed in some particulars from a true longitudinal study, such as those at the Berkeley Institute of Child Welfare.

In a preliminary report, she argued that all children gained while attending the preschool and university schools. The mean IQ on the first test for all 1,333 children was 100, for 1,027 children on second and third tests was 119, and for 574 children on fourth through seventh tests was 124. The greatest advances were made by children starting below average, who gained twenty-eight points if they persisted through thirty months and five tests. Next came those who initially tested in the average range, who gained twenty-two points if they persisted through forty-two months and seven examinations. The very superior children gained far less, and those in the genius range made no appreciable gains whatsoever. She concluded that attendance at the preschools explained the gains made. The longer a child attended these enriched schools, the larger the gains for those below average and average according to initial tests. Within certain limits, and for children of somewhat superior native endowment, she insisted, "intelligence is modifiable by environmental conditions."[56]

Two years later Wellman published more results. Her work involved more than using existing data files. She presented information on three groups of children—a transfer group, a continuous group, and a nonpreschool group. Seventy-seven had attended the preschools but had subsequently transferred and were retested several years later. She was able to match thirty-five of the transfer children with the same number of children continuously enrolled in the preschools or the university schools. The transfer children gained, on the average, 9.2 IQ points while in preschool or university schools, that is, from an average of 108.4 to 117.7 IQ points. Again she found the same pattern as before, that those who initially tested lowest gained the most, and those with initial high scores gained the least. Four to eight years after they had left Iowa City, the transfer children had made no further gains. Indeed, she insisted, their ultimate average gain was slightly less than when they had departed, 8.9 IQ points in slightly less than fifty-five months. Those continuously enrolled in the university schools gained a startling 17.0 IQ points, on the average, in barely more than fifty-one months. There seemed to be no other difference between the transfer and continuous children that would account for their differential gains. Those who did not attend either the preschools or the university schools, sixty-eight children, did not gain; indeed, on the average, they lost slightly more than 1.0 IQ point.

Wellman then made a highly important distinction between the performances of individuals and of groups. The failure of the transfer children to gain after they left Iowa City and of the nonpreschool children to gain at all confirmed the commonly accepted view that the IQ tended to remain the same, or nearly so, over a period of years. Such might well be the case for groups of children. But it was not true for individuals *within* groups. Wellman underscored a distinction between group averages, which applied to no particular individual, and individual test scores, which applied to actual persons. She noted that all children who attended the schools did gain, with a mean gain of around 11.0 points—a group measurement from which she could not emancipate herself. She came very close to saying that individuals, not groups or typologies, were what mattered in her analysis; indeed, it was the changes in the scores of *individual* children to which she referred, as a careful reading of the text makes clear. But she did not make that leap.

Rather, Wellman insisted that the gains should be understood in terms of their sheer direction, rather than the actual amount of change, and thus muddied the waters and confused her national colleagues. The problem had nothing to do with her lack of professional ability. Instead, she had observed events that professional culture, ideology, and fact processing all told her were not supposed to happen. It is difficult to escape the conclusion that she could not translate her results into the discourse her contemporaries used. If individuals were truly the center of attention, as she and her colleagues insisted over and over again, she could nevertheless identify no singularity, asymmetry, or even distinctiveness to the individual children in her study. Like her soulmate Stoddard and her other Iowa colleagues, she assumed that they were studying the variables for mental events within the minds of individuals. But these children were, by their definition, highly interchangeable individuals; it was their mental processes and events, not their psychobiological nature (as their critics would have had it), that mattered. Literally, there was nothing tangible about them. And when she said that it was the sheer direction upward of her subjects on retesting that mattered, this statement was incomprehensible to the majority of her professional colleagues, nurtured as they were to think about group measurements and coefficients of correlation, not to mention group determinism. It was probably not easy for most of Wellman's contemporaries to square a belief in group determinism with her point that it was the sheer direction of the IQ scores on retesting, not the actual scores themselves, that was important. Nor was that all. That there might be mental events apart from the natural and social forces that were presumed to create reality was, to most Americans then, if they thought about it, third-rate Kantian or Hegelian idealism. That Wellman's argument was also in some sense the individualistic (and equally out of phase with its time) stuff of John Dewey, who seemed to have no direct connections with the Iowa scientists, is another issue entirely. It was hardly surprising that Wellman and her colleagues had enormous difficulty in making that distinction between group scores, which measured a group at a point in time, and individual scores, which tracked specific persons over time. After all, if all individuals were truly *interchangeable*, or if they had no distinction, why did it make sense to draw attention to them in the first place?[57]

In their work on the physical and mental development of the child in the 1930s, then, the researchers at the Iowa Child Welfare Research Station had sketched out a mosaic of interpretation in which the child was an active individual, blessed with multiple gifts and different from every other child. The members of the staff were not members of a tightly organized school. But they had obviously become an intellectual community in which certain assumptions unified most of the community's members to conceptualize problems from certain perspectives that were not the dominant view in their field.

The man who helped bind them together as an intellectual community in the 1930s was George D. Stoddard. He broadcast the station's political doctrines in plain language because he had large political notions and ambitions for America's children and his science. At the twentieth anniversary celebration of the Iowa station's founding, held in the spring of 1937 at the Iowa City campus, Cora Bussey Hillis was celebrated as the woman whose singular vision had created the station and guided its work. Only in the most indirect sense was that the case. Clearly she cared for children. But her visions were those of a bygone age and stressed notions that few, if any, of the Iowa station's scientists thought sound, at least as scientific ideas. The Iowa station's ideological singularity in the profession and discipline had begun haltingly, through Baldwin's efforts. Stoddard and his colleagues amplified and extended that intellectual identity. It was Stoddard's grand visions and great expectations that came to matter, not Hillis's, and they were as obviously out of tune with the dominant orthodoxy in the field as with Hillis's motions about the child. Stoddard agreed with Hillis that children should be "saved." That was the extent of their consensus.

Stoddard greatly facilitated the station's intellectual and ideological unification by his own public activities. Some idea of his political prominence as advocate of nursery schools by the mid-1930s can be gleaned from a survey of the field's literature. Between 1919 and late 1934, American specialists published 840 works in the field of nursery school education. Six were published before 1922. Half appeared after 1929. Of the twenty-nine individuals who wrote 5 or more contributions in the field, Stoddard was the third most prolific, with 15 pieces, just slightly behind Arnold Gesell, with 16, and Mary Dabney Davis, nursery school specialist at the U.S. Department of Education, who had 18.[58]

Stoddard unified politics and science. Alone among institute directors in his field in the thirties, he consistently spoke out for child welfare, and, indeed, made that crusade his main professional activity. It was crucial to the nation's well-being that child development be used to upgrade and ameliorate the lives of children, he insisted. There were children who suffered from poverty, racism, poor educational opportunities, and a host of other identifiable social and economic problems. Direct intervention in the system, or system of systems, no matter how complex they were, must be done. People must be saved; that was the point of his activism. The ultimate remedy, he argued in true Deweyite fashion, was education. The nation's entire educational system should be restructured top to bottom. He almost alone among his national colleagues saw the need, based on the research of his colleagues at the Iowa Child Welfare Research Station, for a national system of nursery schools.

Stoddard argued that the nursery school was the basis of all future educational progress for the individual, and it was on behalf of individuals that he urged intervention in the system. Once better education was generally available, then there would be social progress. A democracy depended on an educated citizenry. Most of his national colleagues denied his premise that the nursery school could boost the IQ. The nursery school merely socialized the child and affected its personality; no larger gains were possible. But Stoddard was a maverick in this, as in other matters, and was unrelenting on the benisons of education, including those of the preschool, for society. As commencement speaker at the university in 1932, for example, he insisted that the most important limits upon education were those Americans imposed upon their educational institutions and, thus, upon themselves and future generations. He conceded that biology severely limited mentally retarded persons. Yet most persons of normal and above normal intelligence restricted their own opportunities and failed to realize their enormous potentialities. The educational system did not bring out the individual's maximum potential. Activism, reform, intervention, the unification of democracy and culture, progress—these were his watchwords no less than John Dewey's.[59]

Indeed Stoddard called for a national system of nursery schools well in advance of the results of any scientific program at the station to assess their impact upon children. In 1929, for instance, he called for the creation of half-day nursery schools. In his presidential address at the National Association for Nursery Education in 1931, he argued for a universal nursery school system to educate the nation's 5 million children of preschool age. He pooh-poohed the usual objections to nursery schools, that they were expensive and that parents distrusted them. It was far cheaper, fiscally, socially, and in every other way, to nip problems in the bud with high-grade nursery schools, he argued. Furthermore, Stoddard continued, whenever parents sent their children to nursery schools, they were pleased with the results. An investment of half a billion dollars a year in a universal system of nursery education would reap rich rewards in the future by preventing social problems; by training the young to be constructive citizens, it would even create wealth.[60] At the 1933 conference, Stoddard went even further, arguing that it would take too long to establish universal nursery schools if professionals waited for the ordinary citizen to become convinced and agitate for the proper legislation. The professionals must become activists, he declared, certainly not a mainstream view among professional scientists.[61]

The opportunity seemed to exist for a national system of nursery schools. Stoddard was an enthusiastic New Dealer; Roosevelt's programs energized him and gave him hope. In October 1933, Harry L. Hopkins, administrator of the Federal Emergency Relief Administration (FERA), agreed to an emergency program in education as a way of reducing the unemployment rolls and dispensing relief monies that Congress had appropriated. It was a quintessential New Deal idea; Hopkins wanted mainly to provide instant relief for the unemployed and the vulnerable. The program was organized as a typical New Deal measure on then contemporary notions of the relations of the federal government, the states, and the various interested parties, including private philanthropy and the professions—in other words, a larger whole constituted of discrete yet symmetrically interrelated parts. FERA would provide lump sums for each mandated part of the program. The states, acting through their governors, relief administrators, and superintendents of public instruction could apply for FERA funds, provided they could demonstrate that the funds would provide employment. Five of the six components of the program—adult literacy, vocational education, vocational rehabilitation, general adult education, and nursery schools—were not part of the states' existing public educational systems. The sixth, the reopening of rural schools closed because of the declining tax revenues, was a standard feature of American education. And that, in a sense, told the tale. While the FERA program might be viewed as an attempt to innovate in public education, what mattered to the decision makers at FERA and in the Congress was to spend money for unemployment relief and yet respect the rights and prerogatives of the states.

The General Education Board (GEB), a Rockefeller philanthropy, became involved too. The GEB's trustees wanted to launch a series of grants in the general area of American education, including child development, but emphasizing the adolescent, not the young child. The trustees and their advisers believed that in the present economic emergency, adolescents were potentially tempted toward socially unappetizing career and political choices. In particular, were they alarmed by the rise of authoritarian regimes in Europe and their efforts, like the Hitler *Jugend*, to mobilize youth in their service.

Lawrence K. Frank became the program officer for the GEB's child development program, in October 1931. His general task was to administer a grant program on adolescence. By adapting his brand of Freudianism to the interpretation of social events, he was able to steer the program in the direction of the behavioral, rather than the social and economic, sciences. When the chance presented itself for him to sponsor a federal nursery school program, especially with the help of his friend and ideological soulmate George Stoddard, he could not resist. His opportunity to intervene came when it became clear that neither FERA nor any other federal agency, such as the Office of Education, could afford to fund the administrative personnel for the FERA program in the states and local school districts. FERA funds were limited to the employment of teachers and other necessary persons, chiefly construction workers, who would make the program viable. Through a complicated process that Frank masterminded, the GEB made available $350,000 for 1934–35 to the states that applied for the FERA program funds, so that the states could appoint functionaries. In December 1934, the GEB raised the amount to $500,00 and extended the grant's duration to mid-1936.[62]

In early November 1933, a few days after Hopkins approved the educational program, Stoddard announced that Iowa would apply for funds from the emergency nursery schools program. This was impressive testimony to Stoddard's political clout in state government and educational circles. By January 1934, Stoddard had arranged for Harold H. Anderson at the station to be made the program's regional adviser for Iowa, Kansas, Nebraska, and Missouri. Stoddard's influence in Washington was obvious, too. The emergency nursery schools were intended for children from the most destitute families, not from middle-class families. Here was the social intervention that Stoddard had argued for, and the recognition of asymmetry in the supposedly smoothly functioning social system, although it is unlikely that contemporaries grasped the latter point. Symmetry, after all, was what made sense then.

Almost immediately, thirty-six groups in twenty-nine Iowa communities applied for nursery school funds. Iowa's share of federal funds for nursery schools was $35,500 a month; the four states together received $135,000 a month. The approved nursery schools used, not surprisingly, the station's own nursery school curriculum. Construction workers, hired through the Civil Works Administration offices around the state, remodeled buildings of various sorts into nursery schools. Anderson expected to keep the teacher-pupil ratio fairly low, at ten pupils per teacher. Unemployed bus and taxi drivers would be hired on relief funds to transport the children from home to nursery school and back again. In this new system, the parts functioned to enhance the larger whole. The costs of the hot noon lunch, the cod liver oil, and the orange juice would also be borne by relief funds.[63] By the late spring of 1934, approximately 2,500 emergency nursery schools were operating in thirty-six states, providing full day care to approximately 50,000 of the nation's neediest children and employing approximately 10,000 adults as teachers and occasional or part-time workers.

On May 21, 1934, Stoddard spoke at the White House on the nursery schools in the emergency education program. Warmly and enthusiastically, he cataloged the many benefits that the schools were already providing. The schools reduced unemployment, facilitated the wholesome development of underprivileged children, helped parents meet their offsprings' nutritional, physical, and social needs, and served as a demonstration to the entire nation of the utility of nursery schools. And, he charged, it was foolish to insist that the country could not afford such a program; far more was spent every year on automobiles, cosmetics, and tobacco than could ever be spent on the most elaborate educational system. "We should not talk glibly about not having the wealth to do what we think ought to be done as long as such conditions are the rule," he exclaimed.[64]

Stoddard had taken the station to heights of national political and scientific recognition that Hillis could not have imagined. He also fused child welfare and child development in ways that had not occurred to Baldwin, and that he probably would have disliked. Baldwin wanted to make science more important than child welfare and social activism on the part of the professionals. Stoddard, on the other hand, insisted they were equally important. He never forgot Hillis's maxim—keep the vision—which she had repeated in countless letters to university presidents, legislators, citizen groups, to anyone who would listen, and to some who would not. Stoddard added a populist flair when he strove to keep the vision close to the people and to assert that the experts were useful to the people, not the reverse. His expansion of the station's parent education programs to fuse child development and child welfare was a parallel effort to his national campaign to establish nursery schools.

He had in May Pardee Youtz a parent education field-worker of legendary charisma and effectiveness who led parent groups with genuine inspiration and influence. When Stoddard appointed Ralph H. Ojemann to work in parent education as an organizer and researcher in curriculum, he chose perhaps better than he knew, for Ojemann quickly demonstrated a genuine talent for working with lay citizens in the parent education movement.[65] Youtz and Ojemann made a highly effective team. She was the more practical, or, more precisely, the less academic, member. She could develop rapport with local citizens and distill the sometimes complex findings of child science into simple yet precise statements parents could read and understand. In 1932 she published a textbook for parent education teachers in the field that demonstrated a genuine flair for responsible scientific popularization.[66] In the thirties she was constantly in the field, working with teachers and running classes of her own. Ojemann fulfilled different roles. Stoddard, who believed the mass media useful,[67] worked with Ojemann from a research project on the proper components of a parent education curriculum that the latter was developing to found the Radio Child Study Club in 1932. The club became the central part of the station's statewide parent education program. Broadcasts were made over WSUI and WOI, the radio stations of the State University of Iowa and the Iowa State College of Agriculture and Mechanic Arts. Every other week a speaker would discuss a particular topic. Each program would be broadcast twice, so that fathers could listen, too. The study group members would discuss each topic with the aid of curriculum materials assigned in advance and available from the public library. As Anderson coordinated the nursery schools and the statewide program in mental hygiene for the schools, and as Youtz worked with the station's constituents in person, Ojemann directed the club and conducted an ambitious research program in parent education. By the fall of 1935, the fourth year of the club's operation, it offered distinct eight-week courses on infants, preschoolers, school-age children, and adolescents. More than two thousand parents in 150 clubs throughout the state participated.[68]

By the middle 1930s there were signs of problems ahead. The most pressing to Stoddard and his colleagues at the station stemmed from the confluence of two circumstances, the fiscal and budgetary reductions triggered by the deepening economic crisis and the tapering off of the memorial's grants. In the latter half of the 1930s and beyond, a new series of challenges arose, some of which were not fiscal at all but had to do with the station's new and singular intellectual identity in its profession and science, which Stoddard had done so much to encourage. And the Depression's stark social and economic realities made the question of child welfare even more pressing than it had heretofore been. If there were some promising developments from Stoddard's point of view, like the FERA program, such programs were a trifle compared with the scale of the problems children faced, and he knew it. That perception may well have driven him and his colleagues to make all the more vigorous the challenges that they presented to their colleagues and fellow citizens.

Cora B. Hillis, ca. 1920

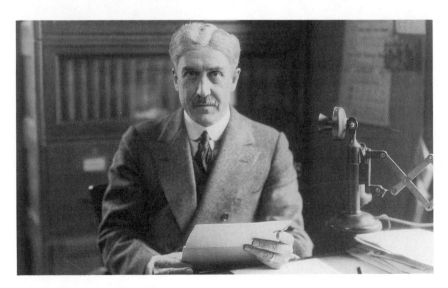

Bird T. Baldwin, ca. 1924–25

George D. Stoddard in the late 1930s

Kurt Lewin in 1936

Robert R. Sears in the early 1940s

Children taking part in an experiment on teaching them to modify assertive behavior, 1941. Doctoral student Gertrude E. Chittenden is taking notes.

Story time at Preschool Laboratories, 1930s

Organized play time at Preschool Laboratories, late 1930s

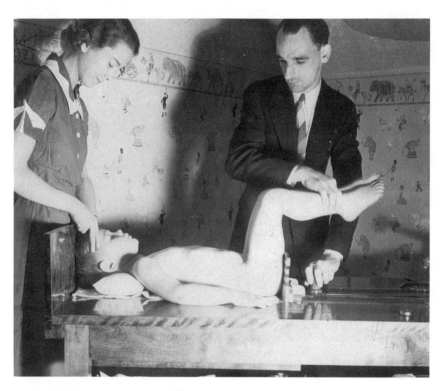

Howard V. Meredith and an assistant measuring the trunk length of a child, late 1930s

Children washing their hands before mealtime, Preschool Laboratories, early 1940s

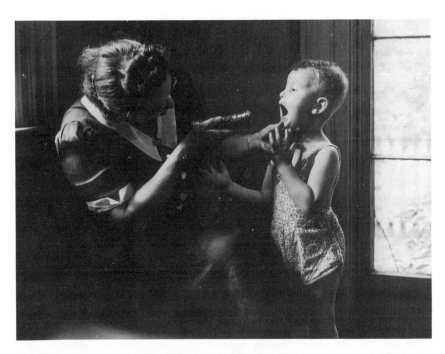

Routine examination, Preschool Laboratories, early 1940s

Organized patriotic pageant, Preschool Laboratories, early 1940s.
Note the flags and drums.

Children enjoying the outdoors after a long winter in the Preschool Laboratories, early or middle 1940s

CHAPTER FIVE

THE SCIENCE OF DEMOCRACY

In Nashville, Tennessee, in October 1937, Lawrence K. Frank keynoted the National Association for Nursery Education's (NANE) convention. Alarmed by the rise of totalitarian dictatorships throughout the world, he insisted that the resulting crisis of democratic civilization reflected difficulties and confusions in child rearing. The central problem was that societies trained their young in accordance with their distinctive values; social authority, that is, was involved. The destructive authority parents visited on their children reflected contemporary authoritarianism. Even in America, perhaps the world's most democratic civilization, too many parents responded to social crisis with harsh discipline and authority. If aggression were inborn in mankind, Frank opined, then freedom and democracy were doomed.

Yet, Frank declared, all was not lost. Perhaps aggression was not innate in mankind. Science could rescue democracy. Child development, as the basic science, and the nursery school, as its social technology, would save democratic civilization. In the nursery school, each child could be treated as an individual rather than as a member of a group—a class, a race, a national group, and so on. Direct intervention to redress shameful problems or asymmetries in the larger whole was indicated. Each child was unique; if the whole of the national population was greater than or even different from the sum of its individual members, each person nevertheless had to be treated individually. In the later 1930s, however, Frank was more skeptical of scientific professionalism than he had been during his glory days at the Laura Spelman Rockefeller Memorial. The "professional urge to standardize, to routinize, to substitute academic training for sympathetic insights into children and to look for uniformities and generalizations that will save thinking, all must be critically re-examined by nursery school educators who are aware of these large social responsibilities."[1]

Indeed, the 1930s were somber times. When he spoke before the NANE delegates, he had been at the Caroline Zachry Foundation of New York for a year. His new appointment permitted him to pursue his interests in funding child development research in an atmosphere more ideologically congenial than the General Education Board (GEB). He had resigned from the GEB, then, to have a freer hand. But for six years in that Depression decade he had run the GEB's program in child development research, and this was a great advantage to his friends and allies in child development such as Stoddard. Frank had turned the program away from traditional social and economic science and argued that the new behavioral sciences offered the best clues for understanding such irrational phenomena as the rise of totalitarianism in Europe and Asia. The key to the puzzle, Frank insisted, lay in child rearing, not in class and caste struggles.[2]

As a man who fancied that he agreed with John Dewey on most issues, Frank spoke for a small minority within the American political and cultural Left. Critical of all forms of group determinism, including Marxian socialism, Frank had no use for such orthodox American liberalism as the social class conflict school represented, for example, by such important intellectuals as Charles Beard and Mary R. Beard in their *Rise of American Civilization* (1927), in which American history was, in the main, reduced to a complex series of struggles between "the people" and "the interests." Frank objected to the group determinism stated or implied in such arguments; it was simply untrue that ineluctable social forces created such predetermined groups and thus shaped human behavior.[3]

Frank argued that these mainstream liberals ultimately derived their deterministic, reductionist, and positivist assumptions from the physical sciences without understanding that natural processes and social life were not the same thing. Human social existence was marked by unpredictability and irregularity, not by order, regularity, and constancy, as was physical nature. In human society individuals mattered; group categories were abstract and unreal. In social life individuals learned through social experiences of various kinds. Society and culture were greater than or different from the sum of experiences of all individuals. But they were not truly explained through recourse to the orthodox or mainstream schemes of the natural sciences, either. What determined human behavior, continued Frank, was not so-called objective social and economic conditions that could be measured via the methods of the exact and physical sciences but rather the mental pictures people carried about in their heads of the events outside themselves. In that sense, there was no such thing as objective reality in human affairs as there was with regard to physical nature—to things rather than to beings. The datum of society and culture was the individual, not the group, whether by group one meant class, race, nativity, sex, or the like, for such were the mere mental inventions of culture and society. All causes of human behavior were psychic. Simpleminded deterministic schemes were of no avail any more than were spurious group designations.[4]

By reconstituting the mental hygiene movement's ideology in ways useful to his purposes, Frank papered over his disagreements with his colleagues at the General Education Board. Mental hygiene's founders applied its doctrines toward clinical assessments of individual psychoses. Frank welded mental hygiene to child development research by insisting that inner mental and emotional life had social and cultural consequences. Thus he turned psychiatry into cultural analysis. He assumed that one could literally put a culture on the psychiatrist's couch and analyze its problems. Armed with this new argument, as he had reinterpreted it, Frank developed a program in adolescent research that the GEB trustees could approve.[5]

Soon the trustees implemented Frank's suggestions for funding. In April 1933, they appropriated an initial $600,000. About a third of these funds supported postdoctoral training and research fellowships in adolescence, awarded through the National Research Council's Committee on Child Development; the remainder supported specific large-scale projects. Within three more years, the trustees appropriated about $2.3 million to numerous institutions for adolescent research. Although some GEB funds went to institutions that the memorial had supported in the 1920s—notably the Iowa station and the Institute for Child Welfare at the University of California, Berkeley— overall, the grants went to different centers for new or continuing work.[6]

Frank knew that the grand ambitions he had held for child development and the reconstruction of American society had when he was at the Laura Spelman Rockefeller Memorial gone unfulfilled. Most researchers with whom he interacted disagreed with him intellectually and merely tolerated his antideterminist, antibehaviorist, and antipositivist views. The field's mainstream was profoundly conservative, at least as compared with Frank and his cohorts. Only a handful of the field's professionals agreed with him; beyond the Iowa station, his allies were a small, scattered bunch. He was both a gadfly and a patron to a profession whose members accepted the funds he offered more often than his ideas.[7]

Nor was this all. The Depression's severe financial exigencies threatened child development's institutional base. Rockefeller philanthropy was supposed to be seed money, creating ventures and then withdrawing as other and more regular (usually governmental) sources of funding took over. Over time, Rockefeller philanthropy could engage in systematic social innovation, going from one set of ventures to another. Obviously, the Depression played havoc with this policy; for example, in the inevitable budget cuts following the end of memorial funding at the host institutions, parent education programs were the most expendable components of all. Frank had set great store by parent education, hoping that it would, as Steven Schlossman has put it, carry the gospel of child development to dramatically improve the skills of millions of parents and thus salvage the American family and social order from the stresses and strains of modernity.[8]

Many developmentalists supported parent education. Whether it would reform society and include direct parental participation, as Frank and his allies hoped, or whether it would serve as a mere conduit of the best information from the professionals to the presumably grateful and quiescent laity—the parents, that is—was the crucial question. In reality, parent education was limited in its appeal chiefly to middle-class white parents with above-average education, so that it was, for all practical purposes, preaching to the converted, thus undermining Frank's grand hopes. The cultural conservatism of the 1930s—the reaffirmation of hearth, home, and family in popular culture and society, for example—combined with the Depression's harsh economic realities to impressively shore up the conservatives' and professionals' dominant positions in the field. This was hardly an auspicious context for Frank's grand dreams of social reconstruction.

There were other problems as well. Many parent education programs were not truly self-sustaining. When these programs collapsed, the one-to-one professional-constituent relations that they had nurtured simply evaporated, or, in other instances, made the relations between the professionals and their constituents highly formalistic. That was even the case at the Iowa station, where the original state law invented parent education as one of the station's three missions; the station had perhaps the most well organized and effective program in the country. When budgets were cut, public outreach—parent education, that is—was the first lamb led to slaughter. At Minnesota, director John E. Anderson saved the institute's parent education program by rounding up support throughout the state in the parent-teacher associations. Yet the surviving operations paled by comparison with those they replaced. The

Berkeley institute squeaked through perilous times; as the last original memorial institute, its funding outlasted the Depression's worst ravages. The Institute of Child Welfare at Teachers College, Columbia, closed permanently in 1936 because the trustees had always refused to support it. The Berkeley institute always had a vigorous, multifaceted research program, whereas the Teachers College institute's great strengths were in training nursery school teachers and promoting parent education; thus public outreach and social application were undermined for the sake of specialized research.[9]

The $818,000 grant that Baldwin had negotiated during his last year as director kept the station's budget insulated from fiscal pressures until the mid-thirties. In 1929, the station's budget totaled about $157,000, of which $116,000, or two-thirds, came from the memorial, and about one-third—$41,000—came from the state. Nine years later, $39,000, or about half, was memorial funds. By 1936, the steady decline in memorial funds was causing serious budget problems. For the next three years it was unclear whether the state would support the expanded activities initiated by the memorial's grants, and to what extent. George Stoddard organized a statewide campaign and lined up a formidable array of political allies, such as the *Des Moines Register* and the powerful liberal wing of the Iowa Republican party, to support the station as expanded. Stoddard slashed his budget as the memorial funds diminished by cutting salaries, including his own, and by closing programs. Before the legislature's dominant rural interests would shoulder the burden, a symbolic public financial sacrifice had to be made. An outside consultant's survey of alleged duplication of programs among the state's three institutions of higher learning did the trick. Having been blessed as nonduplicative by the survey, which it always had been by legislative fiat in the statute that created it in 1917, the station was thus anointed to receive fuller state funding without further political harassment.[10]

Stoddard reorganized the station. Research and publication were always his first priority, and he reduced the faculty ranks. With some reluctance he had concluded that Amy Daniels's nutrition research had become routine, that she was slow to publish, and that her work seemed incongruent with the station's current interests. Initially he had hoped to finesse her retirement. When she tried to protect herself through the influence of a powerful legislator—perhaps the ultimate betrayal in a state university—she had to retire.[11] He reassigned some colleagues, notably Wendell Johnson and C. H. McCloy, to speech and physical education, respectively, to balance his budget. Howard Meredith, who had taken his doctorate with Stoddard, stayed on in physical growth as Baldwin's successor. Stoddard cut the parent education program from three faculty to one research associate professor, Ralph H. Ojemann, and two field-workers, May Pardee Youtz and Afton Smith. Stoddard prized the parent education program no less than Frank, and supported its outreach activities vigorously, notably the Radio Child Study Club and the summer Conference of the Iowa Council on Child Study and Parent Education.[12]

These new activities supplanted the more traditional parent education classes and meetings. They were more cost-effective and illustrated how advantageous were the new mass media in organizing—and socializing—constituencies. The Iowa station had never had crowds hanging on its every word on the subject. In any given year, no more than three thousand Iowans, of about 3 million total, ever enrolled in a radio club course, and no more than a thousand ever attended the summer conference. Most who listened or enrolled were mothers, not fathers. What had changed since the early 1900s in Iowa, but also across the nation, was that now the professionals, not the activists, firmly controlled the field's institutional apparatus and defined most of the issues. Indeed, in many important particulars, the earlier era's activists had disappeared, and consumers of the developmentalists' cultural wares had taken their place; put another way, one cluster of social roles and cultural expectations had been exchanged for another. In place of participants there were now mere audiences, or so the expectations of the experts and the laypersons dictated. Thus, Stoddard's commitment to parent education and to the yeasty individualism that Frank espoused made the Iowa station a remarkable place in the 1930s, because it was the only secure dissenting fiefdom in the realm. That singularity had national significance and meaning.

Like his soulmate Frank, Stoddard championed an enlarged role for his field, for a science of democracy. As director, he was the Iowa Child Welfare Research Station's most dynamic public advocate. Within the university he had important advantages. The station, the department of psychology, the college of education, and the school of medicine had all become nationally prominent in the 1920s, the consequence, more or less, of Carl E. Seashore's often imperious, autocratic leadership; Seashore had always been more powerful than any mere university president. As Seashore's protégé, Stoddard thus had a powerful institutional base in the human sciences from which to elaborate his notions and policies. And thanks to the vigorous parent education program of the 1920s and Stoddard's genuine gift for public relations, the station's reputation among Iowans (and their legislators) was very high in the 1930s and 1940s. Iowans then enthusiastically boosted their state and everything in it, including the station and the university. Stoddard shrewdly cultivated these urges, which ranged from mere smugness to frisky xenophobia, for the station's benefit.

If Stoddard did no original research, he still worked closely with his colleagues on the ideological, theoretical, and methodological aspects of their sometimes spectacular and controversial work. Stoddard was an able theorist, and thus a rara avis among American psychologists, who had contented themselves with normative, positivistic research programs. He did not accumulate data against preconceived taxonomies and classifications; rather, he formulated hypotheses and tested them. And his indeterminist, antibehaviorist philosophy of science and his individualistic ideology defined his intellectual leadership and the research agenda of his colleagues at the station. All that distinguished Stoddard from other such directors were his ideas, not the way in which he imposed them on his coworkers.

Stoddard vigorously challenged the conservative mainstream's ideas before as many audiences across the nation as possible. He had one central theme: democracy and education were integrally related. Only a national system of public nursery schools could safeguard democratic civilization. The nursery schools could be extended downward through the nation's existing public school structures at minimal public expense. He insisted that preschools would provide powerful intellectual and emotional nourishment for very young children. No longer could we continue to deprive our nation's children of a proper diet, adequate medical attention, and, all too often, good home environments. Professionals in child development and education had to take as much care about the social consequences of their work as about its scientific quality. Children and the family were society's fundamental building blocks. They were properly nourished with superlative education from the nursery school to the adult community college and beyond. Only this would prepare them for their roles at work and in the polity. Stoddard worked with Frank in the 1930s to incorporate child development into left-liberal progressive education ideology, and to invent a science of democracy. Thanks to unforeseen events they gained an invaluable ally: Kurt Lewin.[13]

In 1967, two decades after his death, the famous American anthropologist Margaret Mead mulled over the larger import of her alliance with Kurt Lewin to reform American democracy with the tools of social science. They had met just after his appointment at Iowa, at a conference on topological psychology in December 1935 at Bryn Mawr, which Frank had subvened with GEB funds.

On many occasions over the next dozen years they discussed new ideas for cooperative ventures to rally American social science's resources to enhance democracy. She recalled that they believed that social science could be used to make things better, "to move us closer to ways of life which we both valued." Lewin had a particularly generous interpretation of the strengths of American culture, she declared, to which "he brought one of those fresh immigrant visions on which American culture had always depended for redefinition."[14]

Mead had a point. As the Iowa station's international celebrity, Lewin did research at Iowa that implied important alterations of the meaning of American democracy. Indeed, he did the most significant work of his career, in topological psychology, regression and frustration, and group dynamics, while at Iowa. For Lewin, politics, culture, and science were intermingled. He was also a sociopolitical activist, an enthusiastic Zionist, and a left-liberal within the American context. Like Stoddard, he combined his passions for science and social betterment into his life and career.

Born in the Prussian village of Mogilno, in 1890, Kurt Zadek Lewin was the second child of Leopold Lewin, a local shopkeeper, and his wife, Recha. When Kurt was fifteen, the family moved to Berlin, and Kurt attended gymnasium, taking his *Arbitur* in the classics and philosophy in 1909. With the *Arbitur* he could enroll in any university in the Reich. Initially he was interested in medicine, but after study at Freiburg and Heidelburg, he moved to Berlin, then Germany's finest university, where he took up philosophy. He threw himself into a most ambitious field, what Germans know as *vergleichenden Wissenschaftslehre*, or the comparative science of the sciences. In 1914, he was studying philosophy and psychology with Carl Stumpf at Berlin. Lewin quickly volunteered for military service after Germany mobilized in Sarajevo's wake. During the war he was a brave and patriotic officer; he was mustered out as a first lieutenant after being severely wounded on the western front in August 1918. He had finished his doctorate with Stumpf in psychology during breaks in his military service during the war.

Like Stumpf, Lewin had far-ranging interests. Stumpf had already recruited the brilliant trio of Gestalt theorists, Kurt Koffka, Wolfgang Köhler, and Max Wertheimer, to Berlin; Lewin became a younger and less orthodox member of the circle. In the twenties Lewin rapidly rose through Berlin's academic ranks to attain the coveted rank of professor before the decade's end. For a Jew, even in cosmopolitan Berlin, this was unusually rapid mobility, even with his well-regarded publications, including his first foray into the comparative science of the sciences, *Der Begriff Des Genese in Physik, Biologie, und Entwicklungsge-*

schichte (*The Conception of Origin in Physics, Biology, and Developmental Theory*).[15]

Psychology became for him a means of testing larger methodological questions. Lewin agreed with the older Gestaltists that behavior should be interpreted holistically—that the whole was greater than or different from the sum of the parts—but he recoiled from their mysticism. He insisted that psychology should be an autonomous experimental science, independent from philosophy and mysticism on the one hand and biology and positivistic determinism on the other. Lewin believed that theory and practice, or theory and experimentation, were always intertwined.[16]

What mainly interested Lewin were the dynamics of behavior, or, in psychological parlance, the psychology of action, as distinct, for instance, from the psychology of learning that was so pervasive among American psychologists. For Lewin the dynamics of behavior were not to be found in fixed instincts or other original equipment of the species and the individual, but in the conflicts, tensions, and needs that arose in the personality. Like Stoddard, then, Lewin championed psychology purged of all biological reductionism and determinism. One had to locate parts of the personality or total psychical systems of the personality in particular loci or places in the environment—the total Gestalt. As Lewin developed his own notions of Gestalt psychology in the twenties and thirties, he used certain concepts, such as field theory in physics and topological geometry in mathematics. When he transferred them into appropriate psychological categories, he effected the qualitative and geometric representation of psychological forces in particular environments. Lewin's topological psychology represented qualitative relationships and relationships between wholes, parts, and forces, not to mention their vectors, or directions of change and pressure. By *field* Lewin meant an analogy from field theory in physics in which one understood the total situation—thus an endeavor in *vergleichenden Wissenschaftslehre*. Lewin's work was a complete departure from American reductionist and determinist psychobiological formulas, as manifested in mainstream theories of developmental science.[17]

Lewin was interested in psychological action now, in the present, at the current moment. Historical perspectives or psychological behavior in the past interested him little. Put another way, Lewin, unlike most American psychologists, was completely unconcerned with the standard American evolutionary and naturalistic kinds of explanations of behavior, with their appeals to forces in the past, whether natural or cultural in character. He wanted to understand how and why people behaved in the immediate present. Obviously, this approach would challenge traditional mainstream dogmas in child development, which were themselves historical or evolutionary in character. Among those problems he and his students attacked were levels of aspiration, incomplete tasks, and regression and conflict. His articles in *Psychologische Forschung* confirmed his credentials as the rising new star in Gestalt circles in Weimar Germany. Given his interests in psychodynamics, an area dependent, for some inspiration at least, on Freudian theory, it was hardly surprising that Lewin turned to problems in child psychology.

By the late 1920s Lewin was gaining a reputation abroad, especially in the United States. In fall 1929, at the International Congress of Psychology, held at Yale University, he became something of a celebrity. His presentation on the effect of the environment on children as represented in incomplete tasks, delivered *auf Deutsch* and accompanied by a film, created a sensation. With Lewin there was always more than the message; the man was warm, enthusiastic, delightful, and modest, at odds with the postwar American stereotype of the Prussian professor. Even those who could barely grasp words here and there in his talk found Lewin utterly captivating. Thus did his reputation spread among American psychologists.[18]

In 1931 Lewin published two articles in English in the United States. Of particular interest to developmental scientists was Lewin's article in Murchison's *Handbook of Child Psychology* on the child and the child's environment. Here Lewin was primarily interested in the psychodynamics of individual behavior, *individual* not defined as typological category, as most American natural scientists meant it, but as any person without—or, more precisely, before—consideration of classifications of race, nativity, sex, religious affiliation, or the like. Any individual or person, he insisted, existed in a particular life-space, or aggregate of the psychic forces influencing that person's attitudes and behavior. Lewin asked radically different kinds of questions than did his reductionist and behaviorist American colleagues. What were the properties of the individual's life-space? How large was it? What was the balance of positive and negative valences at a given moment? What were the other dynamic properties of the child's psychological environment? Lewin insisted that the power and extent of the fields of force of other people in the child's environment varied greatly, depending on many factors, such as the parents' characters, the number, gender, and kind of children in the family and among the child's associates and peers. Usually a child was not a powerful individual; little of its environment was thus free. Lewin investigated the nonmaterial psychological influences and relationships as systems or networks within a larger context.

From these efforts he tried to build theories that would possess scientific validity and predictability.

The question of traits, which for American psychologists had been a fundamental issue for decades, was thus for Lewin simply not of the same importance. His framework placed American normative, reductionist, trait-oriented interpretations of behavior in a very different context. Lewin's discussion of what he called the child's *level of aspiration* illustrates the point. He argued that this level of aspiration, or pretension to success or failure in a particular activity, was related to that child's abilities or traits, to be sure, but was linked, far more importantly, to the child's psychological environment at the moment he or she performed the act in question. Thus a child—or any person, by extension— might aspire to do something considerably at variance with his or her abilities; either the child or some other force in the environment, such as a peer, a sibling, or a parent, for example, might influence the child's level of aspiration far more than the child's abilities as predicted by standard trait-oriented methods, such as notions of genetic inheritance, mental tests, and the like.[19]

Lewin also addressed the problem of *vergleichenden Wissenschaftslehre*, or the comparative science of the sciences, in a brilliant comparison of the differences between the Aristotelian and Galilean methods of thinking in psychology in an American publication, so that his ideas were more generally accessible. When Lewin insisted that psychology could learn from physics, he did not argue that it should imitate the physical sciences' methods, as his American colleagues traditionally had. Rather he insisted that psychologists should grasp the implications of the Galilean revolution in physics for understanding another autonomous part of nature: human psychology. Aristotelian thinking in psychology, he argued, was valuative in character. Its champions tended to pose matters in abstract opposites, such as black and white, heredity and environment, good and bad. They also assumed that natural data were not unified and homogeneous, and, in consequence, that events obeyed natural laws only if they occurred with a preexisting notion of statistical frequency. Most modern, post-1870 psychology was Aristotelian, not Galilean, in character; its practitioners were obsessed with charting normative characteristics, traits, dichotomies, and behavior, and with divining the average event, trait, characteristic, and the like, all the while ignoring the rare, infrequent, or incidental event.

Galilean thinking in psychology, Lewin insisted, required psychologists to abolish all modes of Aristotelian thinking, such as historical or geographical conceptual tools used in learning theory or in explanations in which place and mind were related; to abandon the use of statistics to derive averages, means, and other fictive results; and to cease inventing meaningless classes of events and imputing essences to natural phenomena, such as a gene for feeblemindedness or an instinct to lust. In the new Galilean psychology there could be no value concepts, no dichotomies. All phenomena of psychology had to be unified in the science, or it was not a genuine science. Nothing could be excluded because it was a rare case. Indeed, it was the average case, not the rare one, that was misleading; historical frequency was simply accidental. Aristotelian thinkers tried to prove the common event true or false, whereas Galileans sought to substantiate the rare event true or false in experiment and in theory—in effect, a much higher and more ambitious level of proof. Ultimately, Galilean thinkers assumed not a static but a dynamic world in continual fluctuation and in which the direction of change was shaped by the nature of the whole that constituted the object and the situation. The contrast between Lewin's way of thinking and that of most developmentalists could not appear more clearly.[20]

Lewin found himself eminently welcome in America. His colleagues here accepted him and did not react to his powerful intellectual challenges to their work. Indeed, they commonly admired his personality and his scientific genius. For the 1932–33 academic year Lewis M. Terman arranged for Lewin to teach at Stanford; Terman was not at all upset by Lewin's unorthodox views. There Lewin had as students many who later became famous in child development, including Roger Barker, John W. Gardner, and Robert R. Sears.

The ascension of Adolf Hitler as chancellor of Germany in 1933 hit Lewin like a thunderbolt. He resigned his professorship at Berlin in May 1933 without other prospects. Terman and other influential American psychologists convinced the freshly constituted Emergency Committee in Aid of Displaced German Scholars to include Lewin as one of the several distinguished German Jewish professors appointed at Cornell University. For the next two years Lewin and his family were in Ithaca; Lewin had a visiting appointment in the College of Home Economics teaching and doing research in child psychology. It was the Cornell experience that introduced him to child psychology; *vergleichenden Wissenschaftslehre* now was a more remote intellectual priority. The Rockefeller Foundation, through Frank's efforts at the GEB, matched Lewin's salary at Cornell with funds from the Emergency Committee.[21] Although Lewin's appointment at Cornell was temporary, he was a great success there. As the university's president put it to the Rockefeller Foundation in March 1935 in requesting a renewal of Lewin's grant to remain, "he has been eminently successful and is winning the high regard of his colleagues. We would be glad to have him here."[22]

But such was not to be. The next several years were unsettling, with no guarantee for Lewin of a permanent post. Once Lewin was in the states, Horace Kallen, the philosopher and advocate of cultural pluralism at the New School for Social Research in New York, took a special interest in finding a permanent appointment for him. Both were ardent Zionists, and the two became close friends. Kallen tried to raise funds for a chair for Lewin at the Hebrew University in Jerusalem, Palestine, throughout 1934.[23]

By the spring of 1935, Lewin's prospects were alarming, for neither Kallen's fund-raising efforts or the Rockefeller Foundation seemed to promise much. George D. Stoddard had followed Lewin's career closely; he saw in Lewin a potentially valuable ally within and without the station. Now he stepped into the picture, offering Lewin a one-year appointment as professor of child psychology. Once Lewin understood that staying at Cornell was impossible, he accepted, but asked Stoddard if he could bring Roger Barker, Tamara Dembo, and Herbert F. Wright as research assistants.

Money was not the problem it might have appeared. Frank too had watched Lewin's American career—and in concert with Stoddard. Now Frank intervened. Lewin had told Stoddard that Frank could commit GEB funds for his current work on frustration and regression in child development, but added that the work could not be done in one year. Stoddard took Lewin's hint. He understood that Lewin's work complemented and strengthened that of the station in vital areas, such as mental measurement and child psychology. There were important parallels between the ideas of Lewin and of Wellman and her associates in mental measurement, for example. Although clearly working in different areas of child development, Lewin and Wellman both assumed that psychology could not be reduced to deterministic biological formulas, that individuals existed, whereas groups were but descriptive and normative categories of questionable explanatory power. Stoddard emphatically agreed. By assuming that experiments could evaluate hypotheses about ongoing psychological processes, these researchers took a large step beyond the normative data gathering that workers in the field had contented themselves with since the late nineteenth century. In early 1936 Stoddard and Frank negotiated a three-year grant from the GEB for Lewin and his students at Iowa.[24]

It was another three years before Lewin had a permanent professorship in America. For the next two years it appeared that he might accept a chair at Jerusalem; as he once told Kallen, he and his family liked Iowa very much, but "something has to be done in Jerusalem, and maybe one should not work for science but for a country in which one is really at home. Therefore, we may, after all, decide to go there." It was not until late 1938 that Lewin could finally decide not to go to Palestine, and not until 1940, after two semesters of teaching at Harvard and the offer of a tenured professorship at Iowa, that Lewin finally decided to remain in Iowa.[25]

In the later thirties Lewin devoted himself to the cause of a truly democratic civilization no less than to his science. He and his family quickly adapted to their new home. He found Iowa a congenial place to be a Jew in America—and a scientist, too. He once wrote Kallen that Iowans were rather liberal toward Jews. Now America, not Europe, was his home and represented his future. He took up American citizenship with typical gusto; he told a New York friend excitedly in early January 1940 that "I am citizen! Hurrah!" Those who associated with Lewin as friends, colleagues, or students remembered him as a warm, generous, delightful, and enthusiastic democrat, more democratic than the Americans themselves, the immigrant who challenged the natives to live up to their own self-professed political and social values.[26]

Lewin's horror at Nazism grew apace in the later 1930s and fueled his commitment to his new country. "I really wonder whether any government in the history [*sic*] has been as shameless" as Hitler's, he mused to a friend in January 1936. Two years later he told Kallen that Hitler got what he wanted with the Munich pact, and "we will have an even more terrible war somewhat later on. In the meantime I think the Jewish situation will be worse." He also worried much about his mother, brother, and sister, who remained in Germany. Three months after the invasion of Poland, Lewin told Kallen there was some chance of getting his sister out; his siblings escaped Hitler's *Festung Europa*, but his mother could not. He gloomily told Kallen just before Christmas 1939 that the Jews were doomed to practical extermination in central Europe, regardless of who won, for an Allied victory would take years, and European Jews would have long since perished at the Nazis' hands.[27]

In his popular essays Lewin contributed to the science of democracy. He always blended science and activism, as did Stoddard and most of his colleagues at the station. As an ardent Zionist, he insisted that Jews positively affirm their Jewishness, regardless of the short-run consequences. Jewish children should be raised to understand their heritage and history, but also to grasp fully the problems they faced in the contemporary world. And sometimes his professional articles were indistinguishable from his activist essays. When he wrote about the general problem of failure and success for a personnel journal, insisting, for example, that anyone's success or failure in work was related to his level of aspiration—or sense of how well he or she would succeed at a particular task—he seemed to be writing about science, not politics. But when he added the observation that the group to which society assigned that person might influence his or her level of aspiration, especially if the group were either prestigious or discriminated against, he demonstrated that for him, the line between science and politics was very thin indeed. And when he wrote an ostensibly popular article on current affairs—the differences between Germany and America—he insisted that Germans and Americans had different national characters as the result of drastic differences in life-space for their nations, clearly one of his scientific notions.[28]

For Lewin, his Jewish, American, and democratic identities were synonymous. He threw himself into Jewish affairs, participating in community activities or facilitating the recruitment at Iowa of Gustave Bergmann, a bright young member of the Vienna circle of logical positivists and Iowa City's other Holocaust refugee during the war years. In these and other ways Lewin affirmed his commitments to Judaism and Americanism. He provided for American Jews an important and powerful Americanization of Jewish ideas. In America he began pronouncing his surname as Levine, in Hebrew, rather than as its German equivalent, Lewin, thus again setting aside his German identity.[29]

Lewin was in great demand as a speaker, thus solidifying his position as a great man. He addressed many professional conferences, ranging from the American Psychological Association, the Progressive Education Society, and the American Association of School Administrators to the National Association for Nursery Education, and spoke at many colleges and universities.[30] A manifestation of his status arose through his orchestration of a series of by-invitation-only conferences on topological psychology, which he organized and persuaded Frank to support with GEB funds. Lewin served as the intellectual guru in residence at these meetings. Happily he sat at the back of the room, egging some on and encouraging those who disagreed with him to develop their ideas spontaneously. The third topological meeting, at Bryn Mawr, was the first that the GEB supported. That meeting was crucial in other respects. Forty-six persons attended, the central business being the reconciliation of Lewin's dynamic theories of personality with those of his major American "competitor," Edward C. Tolman of the University of California, Berkeley. Erik Homberger, known after World War II as Erik Erikson, sketched a general theory of developing child personality as seen by the child analyst in which he incorporated Lewin's and Tolman's theories. As long as Lewin lived, the meetings were highly successful.[31]

Lewin's most productive years were at Iowa. In Berlin he helped reorient Gestalt psychology along experimental and empirical lines, and integrated it into conventional psychological discourse to a far larger extent than did traditional Gestaltists. And he advanced the qualitative study of human mind in ways that were provocative and arresting, as in his rejection of staple Anglo-American psychobiological determinism and positivism. Yet at Berlin he did not attract the caliber of students he was to at Iowa.

The situation at Iowa was very different. His work at Iowa was mature and possessed more catholicity of application and theoretical power; as he might have had it, in Berlin he proclaimed the exciting promises of Galilean psychology, but only in Iowa could he fulfill them. His students there could accomplish more than those at Berlin could. From August 1935, when he arrived at Iowa, he slowly build up a cadre of seventeen associates, clearly as substantial a social science research group as any in the contemporary American academy. Among these associates were six serving as postdoctoral fellows: Roger Barker, Dorwin Cartwright, Tamara Dembo, John R. P. French, Ralph K. White, and Herbert F. Wright; eight won doctorates, including Dan L. Adler, Maurice Farber, Leon Festinger, Jacob Kounin, Ronald Lippitt, Charles E. Meyers, Beatrice Wright, and M. Erik Wright; and six did master's degrees with Lewin, including Alex Bavelas, Sybille Korsch Escalona, Joan Kalhorn, and, again, Ronald Lippitt, Beatrice Wright, and Leon Festinger. Lewin and his associates completed eight books and fifty-five articles for publication; the master himself published four books and twenty-nine articles in these years. This was indeed a highly productive group.

That first fall Lewin and his students started in earnest the project on frustration and regression. Its central idea was simple enough. Lewin had observed that frustration in young children often resulted in regression to a younger and, therefore, less differentiated or mature level of behavior. Regression was akin to development in reverse. For almost all children such behavior was the temporary consequence of frustration. The research went on for the first several years Lewin and his assistants were at Iowa; due to unfortunate circumstances, the study was not published until 1941.[32]

The regression project's theoretical assumptions owed much to Lewin's work in Berlin, for it was a study in the processes of personality in any individual. On that level, it was of a piece with Lewin's work on children published before he came to the states in 1933. Lewin wished to study regression because of its commonality in many situations and its inverse relationship to development itself, an inherently more difficult phenomenon to examine scientifically.

It had been amply shown that, in a state of high tension, the action toward an obstructed goal regressed to a primitive level. Lewin wished to show that such regression also shaped behavior not related to the obstructed goal, or, more simply, that with a sufficiently high level of tension, the individual should regress in all or nearly all behavior. He chose children's free play activity for the experiments, chiefly because the effects of regression in the experiments would be temporary. Yet there were deeper theoretical assumptions Lewin made in choosing playful activity as the cluster of behavior patterns to observe. In constructive play the child demonstrated its level of development. Moreover, Lewin believed that an individual's activity was closely related to his or her whole life-space; in other words, constructiveness was intimately linked to realistic and unrealistic levels of the life-space.

The experimental situation was not complicated. In the 1935–36 academic year Lewin and his associates selected thirty children from the station's preschools as their subjects. The children were placed into three age groups, two to three, three to four, and four to five. The children ranged in mental age between thirty and eighty-two months. Their IQs were correspondingly high, from 100 to 157. In short, they were typical individual pupils at the Iowa station's preschools, and it was in both senses that Lewin and his associates thought of them, without reference to any preexisting racial, religious, economic, or national identities. They placed the children in pleasant, then in frustrating situations to measure their behavior.

They took each child to a large room filled with toys. On the first visit only one-half of the room was visible to the child, and it was filled with ordinary toys. The room's other half, which had many shiny new toys, was hidden by a curtain and bounded by a wire gate that the experimenter could lock or unlock. In the first visit each child played with the ordinary toys as long as he or she wished after having been shown each toy by the experimenter. The experimenter, in concert with another observer out of the child's view, took notes on the child's behavior in another part of the room. After about thirty minutes, the child would be bored with the toys; it took but a gentle reminder or two, at the most, before he or she would leave the room, which suggested that the room represented a secure and happy (if none too thrilling) place to play.

On the child's second visit, the experimenter drew back the curtain, opened the wire gate, and let the child see all the shiny new toys. The experimenter introduced the child to each toy, and then returned to a corner in the room for a few minutes and took notes again. Once the child was thoroughly engrossed in playing with the new toys, the experimenter suddenly locked the wire gate, so that the child could see but not touch the new toys. The experimenter returned to his table to take more notes, leaving the child free to play with the old toys and answering all questions the child asked. But the experimenter remained aloof from the situation in as natural a manner as possible. When the frustration period was as long as the prior free play period, the experimenter asked the child if he or she wished to leave, which was almost always the case. Upon making sure that the child wished to leave this frustrating situation, the experimenter then opened the wire gate and allowed the child to play with the new toys for as long as possible, so as to alleviate any effects of frustration on the child.

Lewin and his associates argued that the experiment confirmed their initial expectations. From the two observers' notes they devised a measure, which they dubbed the mean constructiveness of play in the free play and frustration situations. It showed that twenty-five children regressed in the constructiveness of their play, whereas only five increased the constructiveness of their play during the frustration situation, with the mean regression 4.39 times its standard error—a real difference, in other words. Placed in equivalents for mental age, the mean regression was a whopping 17.3 months, somewhere between a quarter and a third of each child's mental age, depending on the individual. The experiment also demonstrated that during the frustration situation, about half the time was spent in constructive activity, and half was spent in various modes of frustrated behavior, such as attempts to open the gate (barrier behavior), to isolate oneself from the situation (island behavior), or to leave (escape behavior). The mean time for all children in the experiment in such nonconstructive behavior increased from 69.2 seconds in free play to 623.3 seconds in the frustration period. Each child spent some time in nonconstructive behavior, although the individual differences in, for example, barrier or escape behavior varied enormously from child to child. Each child responded in a similar way to a frustrating situation by engaging in nonconstructive behavior, thus illustrating the point that psychology was a natural science whose principles could be predicted from experimental work, but that each individual child was different from the aggregate of children, thus stressing the uniqueness of each individual.

Lewin and his associates concluded from their quantitative analysis of the results that obviously constructive play was directly related to the differentiation of play behavior itself, to the degree of hierarchical organization of play, its originality and general adequacy. And what of frustration and regression? Individual children varied enormously in their modes of regressive behavior. In part this was due to the strength of the frustrating situation. The time spent in barrier and escape behavior, for example, indicated the situation's strength as a frustrating obstacle; it also suggested psychological differences among individuals in these matters. Lewin and his associates also insisted that the degree of regression varied directly for each individual; all regressed somewhat, others a good deal, the range being four to twenty-four months of mental age.

Lewin and his associates then drew some general conclusions. Play was an organized sequence of activities in which the individual's degree of constructive behavior was expressed in the differentiation of the unit of action and the degree of hierarchical organization, so that in highly constructive play a central idea governed a host of subideas, which in turn determined certain actions. Development included such behavior as increases in the variety of behavior, in degree of hierarchical organization of behavior, in extension of the area of activities and interests, and in use of time perspectives for the past, present, and future. Regression was, then, the reverse of development. Thus in the experimental situation, once the frustration period began, the behavior of the children became less and less differentiated—*dedifferentiated* was Lewin's Teutonic term for it—as the individual could no longer assume that his or her life-space would not be interrupted, an assumption that led to more serious consequences. Given ample frustration, the child could not articulate his or her frustration in a manner appropriate to his or her place in the life cycle, and thus fell back upon less and less constructive behavior.

Insofar as Lewin and his students were concerned, then, there was no such thing as an individual child apart from the total situation in which he or she existed. The situation included a psychological past, present, and future that combined with the power of other persons in the situation, constituted a particular force field of psychological imperatives that surrounded the individual child's life-space. This was Galilean psychology with a vengeance; the traditional normative, Aristotelian categories simply made no sense with this new individualistic psychology.[33]

Here, then, was a powerful and original contribution to the science of democracy. Lewin had made an impressive debut in his adopted land as a scientist who would do much to champion and to extend the premises and promises of American democratic civilization. Even as the regression study was published, however, both Lewin's group and his faculty colleagues were bringing forth other and even more dramatic arguments for that science of democracy. These involved fresh and interesting ideas about the individual, the group, and the environment, and the role that each played in the development of the mind.

As stunning as Lewin's work was, for many Americans it may have well been a trifle arcane, as least as a political document. Since the later nineteenth century,

Americans had been fascinated by the question of the relative skills and abilities of particular groups in the social order; herein lay the appeal of the Binet test. It is interesting to note the extent to which, in the wake of the debate over the role of heredity and environment in human nature and conduct in the American natural and social sciences in the 1920s, the champions of the mainstream dogmas of child development would go in later decades to buttress their arguments against the dangers of indeterminism.

One of the most effective statements of mainstream doctrine in child development was that seminal work of Goodenough and Anderson, *Experimental Child Study* (1931). They did not merely make assertions about biological and psychological determinism, such as citing the maturation theory and the notion of the fixed IQ. They also worked out deterministic arguments and measurements of the environment. One was an occupational hierarchy they worked out from the 1920 federal census, known as the Minnesota Occupational Scale, which became a common tool of psychometrics in the interwar years. They divided the scale into eight occupational groups, with the most prestigious occupations in the higher categories and those requiring the least skill and formal education in the lower. This hierarchy of occupations assumed a range of unequal cognitive or mental abilities, so that members of occupations in Group II were superior to all save in Group I, and so on, an assumption that Goodenough and Anderson probably borrowed from their doctoral teachers, Lewis M. Terman and Robert M. Yerkes, who had designed the interpretation of the army mental tests during World War I in a similar fashion.

For understanding the home environment, Goodenough and Anderson had their colleague, sociologist F. Stuart Chapin, work out a rating scale for "living room equipment." Chapin's device was an inventory of material possessions in the living room; he assumed that the living room was the central arena of interaction among family members and, thus, revealed much of the dynamics of social relations: furniture, appliances, and the like were a reasonable measure of the "cultural" (really, class) level of the family. From these hard, material artifacts one could predict to what group a family and its members belonged. Matched with the occupational scale, this inventory gave child development scientists another objective tool for the establishment of group identities for each and every individual in any study they might conduct. There were even objective weights assigned to various devices; Chapin declared that built-in bookshelves received one point, built-in bookcases two, a radio crystal set one point, radios with two or more tubes a point for each tube, books a fifth of a point, and so on.[34]

Here, then, was an environmental determinism to match a hereditarian determinism, a symmetrical, balanced whole that definitely was greater than or different from the sum of its parts. In such a formulation, itself the outcome of the heredity-environment controversy, it was inconceivable that development might be other than predictable and linear, that inheritance and biological factors could be easily dismissed, or that the individual could develop in a way different from the expectations of the group to which he or she belonged. Groups and types and reactions were the stuff of natural and social reality; individuals, indeterminism, and happenstance were not. The interaction of nature and culture made such impossible and, more to the point, unthinkable.

In 1935, one of Goodenough's students, Alice M. Leahy, published a study on the relative contributions of nature and nurture to the making of intelligence. She examined parent-child resemblances in two groups of 194 children each, the one adopted, the other not, living with their adoptive and biological parents, respectively. All children were between the ages of five and fifteen. Leahy used the Minnesota Occupational Scale and the Chapin Scale for Rating Living Room Equipment to standardize the home environments of both groups, so that, she argued, the only difference between the adopted and the natural groups, or the experimental and the control groups, was the factor of inheritance between parent and child. The orphans were selected according to several criteria: all had come from state orphanages and were placed in their adoptive homes at six months or younger; all were white, of Christian and north European ancestry, and resided in communities with a population of a thousand or more, to equalize the impact of community institutions; and all were legally adopted. Their adoptive parents had to be married and "of [the] white race, non-Jewish, north-European extraction." Leahy thus explicitly referred to European nativity groups as "races." In selecting children for the control group, she tried to create "matched pairs" with regard to age, race, sex, and community size with those in the experimental group; the control parents had to match the adoptive parents as well.

Leahy argued that children resembled their natural, not their adoptive, parents. Biology was all. She reached these conclusions by deriving only group measurements—averages, means, medians, and the like. She did not measure or "follow" individual persons or even "matched pairs," a method just coming into vogue then. All calculations led to but one question, namely, whether adoptive children resembled their foster parents more than natural children did their natural parents. Among the group comparisons she calculated were intellectual resemblances and contrasts, including those dealing with home environments and occupational ratings. She found consistently low positive Pearsonian coefficients of correlation (approximately $r = +.20$) between adoptive parents and children, and high positive correlations between natural parents and children (about $r = +.50$). To most of her colleagues this constituted overwhelming evidence of the truth of her thesis. Further demonstration—for example, through genetic analysis—would have been superfluous. She argued additionally that variation in intelligence quotient among groups and individuals was caused by variation in the home environment only to the extent of 4 percent (the square root of the correlation $r = +.20$); that the scores from the Chapin scale proved that home environment did not change IQs on the average by more than three to five points; that the hereditary component in IQ scores caused greater variation than did the environment component, on the order of 80 as compared with 20 percent; and, finally, that environment affected personality more than did inheritance. Here was a powerful determinist orthodoxy within the field of child development, worked out to precise mathematical and statistical results, and possessed of seemingly awesome explanatory power and catholicity of application. It was also culture bound. It universalized certain group expectations of class and ethnicity.[35]

In what was to be their most controversial and celebrated work, Stoddard and his colleagues challenged the psychometricians' dogmas. In the early thirties Stoddard had encouraged Beth Wellman to create a retrospective longitudinal research project on the influence, if any, of the station's preschools and of the university elementary and high schools on their pupils. Thus began Wellman's long efforts to study the environmental influences of the preschool upon intellectual growth among its charges. With Stoddard providing the leadership in devising the experiments and the theoretical formulations, Wellman had established a preliminary finding by the middle thirties. Attending the preschools enabled the pupils to make, on the average, small but significant gains in their IQs. It occurred to no one at Iowa to phrase their results in terms other than group averages, for example, in the measurements of individuals, then or until very much later.

In the later thirties Wellman and her colleagues made bolder claims for their work, and thus challenged the conservative assumptions and work of Anderson, Goodenough, Leahy, and other champions of the mainstream perspective. In a project completed with her doctoral student, Hubert S. Coffey, Wellman sharply questioned the Minnesotans' thesis that "cultural status" as measured by such factors as occupational status and household artifacts had any meaningful relationship to IQ standings. Wellman and Coffey examined the role of cultural status in IQ changes among the 417 children who attended the station's preschools from 1921 to 1934 by using the regular IQ exams, routinely given in the fall and spring to every pupil in attendance. They found no gains in median or mean IQs of preschoolers when they were not in school—from the spring to the fall IQ tests, in other words—but dramatic gains in IQs for individual children in all occupational groups, as measured by the Minnesota Occupational Scale, from one to seventeen IQ points, from the fall to the spring tests, the period when the children were attending the preschools. They also found that the greatest gains in IQ scores came for individual children whose entering IQ scores were the lowest of the preschool pupils.

In retrospect, it is obvious that Wellman and Coffey were discussing two kinds of measurements—those of individuals over time, on the one hand, and of the average performances of groups, on the other. They drew attention to individual scores mostly when discussing the phenomenon of gains in IQ scores, and as a way of solidifying claims they made about gains or no gains in group measurements, such as mean, average, or median IQ scores. Thus they argued that the Iowa preschoolers over time made no gains as a group in terms of paternal occupation, home environment, parental educational level, and the like, but made gains only when attending the preschools from fall to spring. To the extent that there were group gains, they fell within the range of five to seven IQ points, a result clearly within the range of statistical error that most psychometricians considered routine. So far they had given an entirely orthodox answer, a group measurement. Yet every reference they made to change was to individual children over time. They could not distinguish between the two perspectives. Even more importantly, for Wellman and her profession, was the belief that group measurements were the ultimate natural and social reality; individual variations were simply illustrations of that reality. Such a distinction, between measurements of individuals over time and of groups at a point in time, simply did not exist in their profession's discourse or imagination; it was literally inconceivable in that era.

Wellman and Coffey were chiefly interested in the educational and political ramifications of their work. Matters of scientific method and professional discourse evidently interested them little. They came very close to saying that group characterizations of persons, whether biological or cultural, could not be regarded as ironclad and predestined; neither anatomy nor culture (to update Freud) was destiny, but a temporary identity that could be modified extensively in practice. What happened inside the school was far more important than what took place outside, provided that the effects of intervention were early and sufficient.

Furthermore, Wellman and Coffey insisted that there was indeed a leveling result in preschool education, a process of leveling upward rather than downward, so that the children with the poorest prospects fell in stride in fairly short order with their most promising peers in the institution. Here was both a science and a technology of democracy: the preschool. As they put it, the "amount of gain made was contingent upon the intelligence level attained when the child began his preschool career, irrespective of his cultural status." This was, of course, a profoundly subversive message that threatened to undercut the entire American social system of class and caste. Inequality, discrimination, poverty—all these and related phenomena were both unnecessary and subject to remedy.[36]

A year later Wellman argued that attendance at the station's preschools made for greater gains in IQs than otherwise would have been the case. Her technique was to divide pupils who had attended the university elementary and high schools into two groups, those who had attended the preschools and those who had not, and compare them. Again, she represented group measurements as natural and social reality, and individual scores as mere symptoms of such reality. In one part of the study, she was able to track seventy-eight university freshmen, all of whom had attended some of the university's schools, but only twenty-one of whom had attended the station's preschools; in another, she obtained American Council of Education test percentiles on eighty-two high schoolers at the university, of whom only half had attended the preschools. In all instances she reported that the group measurements showed that attendance at the preschool had an important influence on IQ scores later on; acceleration in IQ was, therefore, caused by the preschools. The changes were always lawful, she insisted, and could be explained by reference to the educational environments of individuals in the groups so examined. She noted that it was individuals, not groups, that made the most dramatic gains in IQs, but again she thought of group measurements, not those of individuals, as constituting the ultimate reality. Her methodological radicalism was confined to the observation that better techniques would yield results akin to hers, not that the starting point of all work—the social or natural group—was deeply flawed, if not absolutely useless, for the very good reason that on that deeper level she did not understand fully the implications of her data. She was content to restrict her maverick outlook to the political argument that extreme gains in IQs might be expected under superior conditions of schooling (or preschooling). "In a wider social sense," she concluded, "results such as these may even lead us to the conclusion that, as a race, we are intellectually undernourished." Here Wellman concluded from her studies of the nursery school that attendance at the preschool could and did boost intelligence, and cited group averages for proof.[37]

Stoddard took the Iowa IQ argument, as it was coming to be known in the profession, to as many audiences and constituencies as he could, whether they were professionals or laypersons. In so doing he gave his professional critics, notably Lewis M. Terman and Florence L. Goodenough, plenty to mutter about among themselves, and cluck they did about what they thought were his irresponsible claims. In a speech before the National Education Association in 1938 Stoddard argued that young children were, "within very wide limits, truly plastic material," for intelligence was a dynamic function within a larger unity constantly in a state of fluctuation and change; just as heredity and environ-ment always worked together, so the distinct yet interrelated parts of the larger whole worked together. One could not speak of heredity without environment, and vice versa. Inheritance set very wide limits to development. Constitutional factors mattered, too. Under educationally and intellectually nourishing en-vironments, all children, regardless of their mental levels, experienced gains in mental levels over time. The reverse proposition was just as true, he argued; it was possible, in early childhood, to destroy, under certain kinds of depressing circumstances, whatever promise a child might have for a normal mental life.[38]

And in this way Stoddard telegraphed what was to be his colleagues' most spectacular and controversial punch, on orphans' IQs. What eventually became known in the profession as the Iowa Orphanage Studies began quite by chance. In the early thirties a prominent Iowa couple adopted an orphan from the Iowa Soldiers' Orphans' Home, a state institution located in the Mississippi River town of Davenport, some fifty miles east of Iowa City. In time the parents realized that their child was severely mentally retarded—*feebleminded* was then the term in professional discourse—and threatened a lawsuit against the State Board of Control, which supervised the home.[39] The suit was averted through a settlement. Board officials then asked Stoddard for advice on future policies. He jumped at the chance to expand the station's access to research populations. The board accepted his plan. A clinical and research program would be created. A clinical psychologist jointly appointed at the station and the home would advise orphanage officials on policy matters and, by giving Binet tests to all inmates, recommend appropriate placement. In return, station investigators had a free hand to conduct research there. State law defined the Iowa station's subjects as normal children, and the Board of Control's as subnormal and abnormal children. Stoddard knew this was a real bonanza, for it would enable his colleagues to compare different levels of mental ability against contrasting kinds of environments.[40]

The Board of Control accepted the program. It ruled that as of February 1, 1934, all children admitted to the institution would have, in addition to the usual physical, medical, and dental examinations, a Binet test, the Kuhlmann version for children three and younger, the Stanford version for older children. The program gave prospective foster parents all pertinent information on the children's parental background, mental abilities, physical condition, and general health. It also gave the Board of Control protection against future legal and political problems.

Appointed clinical psychologist was Harold M. Skeels, who had studied with Stoddard and Wellman. He arrived in late January. The Iowa Soldiers' Orphans' Home had a central campus on the town's outskirts. About six hundred children, all orphans, lived there, housed in cottages and segregated by sex and age. Each cottage had an attendant. There was a central building for eating and other communal activities. In addition, there was a power plant and a playground. Uniformly the children came from homes of neglect; social workers had advised the courts to remove the children from their parents after numerous efforts had been made to repair the natural families. Such radical measures resulted from desperate circumstances. Almost all the children were born out of wedlock. The natural parents came from the lowest ranks of society—the children seemed of most unpromising genetic potential. Most clinical psychologists throughout the country assumed that like begat like, and that the children had the same combination of marginal abilities and meager prospects as had their natural parents.

In that era, most professionals in clinical psychology and orphanage work assumed that as any foster child grew older in a state institution (such as the Davenport home) his or her IQ—and other developmental measurements— would approximate those of their natural rather than of any future foster parents. This belief was based, of course, on the concept of group determinism, which dominated American social science then—on the notions of maturation and of the fixed IQ, to be precise. Skeels accepted these notions without question. He thought he would be distinguishing between children with borderline normal IQs, on the one hand, and those whose IQs were definitely below normal, defining the children as feebleminded, in contemporary professional parlance, on the other.

Initially Skeels had no reason to think otherwise. During his first year he gave Binet examinations to seventy-three children as an integral part of the process for their permanent adoption. These children had been placed with their foster parents at the age of six months or less, and their mean age at final adoption was two-and-a-half years. As Skeels read the true parents' case histories, he found the expected patterns of parental incompetence—poor schooling, low occupational skills, sporadic employment, and brushes with the law in some instances. The biological mothers of the seventy-three had, as a group, a mean IQ of 84 points, which was definitely marginal; only 10 percent scored over 100 points, or normal, on the Binet, and 38 percent accumulated fewer than 80 points, which classified them as definitely feebleminded (as the retarded were then labeled). Even though the biological fathers could not be given a Binet test, what was known about them suggested that they too were most unpromising and fit the expected biosocial templates.

What expectations could be entertained for children who fit such biosocial templates? According to orthodoxy, children whose parents had such low occupational and educational levels and who were in state orphanages could be expected to have a mean IQ of 82.5 points, or borderline normal (an IQ of 79.0 and below being feebleminded). Skeels calculated the mean IQ of the seventy-three youngsters he examined—all of them having spent at least two years with foster parents—and arrived at the astounding figure of 115.3 IQ points. This was, of course, a group score. It was a surprise, indeed, a shock; Skeels and his colleagues went over their data several times for errors. The seventy-three children had a mean IQ score that more nearly approximated that of their foster than their natural parents. Although the actual number of children was small, the conclusion was inescapable: environmental influence on very young children was apparently formidable. Or, from the clinician's perspective—and Skeels was a clinician and an incorrigible social reformer—massive intervention with the very young child could make a dramatic difference in his or her abilities and prospects. Given strong, persistent intervention, children from impoverished backgrounds could jump from the social class circumstances of their natural parents to those of their adoptive parents. Skeels became thoroughly committed to social activism. As such, he and the Davenport orphanage became an enormously valuable resource for Stoddard's science of democracy. As Skeels said at the annual June 1936 State Conference on Child Study and Parent Education, tragic errors were being made almost daily in the assignment of children at state institutions; thus far, he had found forty children with normal IQs at the state home for the feebleminded, and two hundred feebleminded children in other state homes.[41]

Now Stoddard and Skeels mapped out a much more ambitious research project for the Davenport home. The project's original purpose was to study the effect of a nursery school on the development of children in a state orphanage, including direct investigations of intelligence, nutrition, social adjustment, social competence, the social dynamics of dominative and integrative behavior, ascendance, and language development. In short, it would examine all aspects of the developmental process, or processes, and test a wide variety of hypotheses in developmental science. The nursery school would be on the campus. It would be an all-day affair, directly borrowing the curriculum of the Iowa station's preschools for the appropriate age groups. There would be no other adjustments in the curriculum. Stoddard and Skeels simply assumed that the Iowa City curriculum and methods were infinitely transportable and could be used with the orphans.

The project's research design included an experimental and a control group of children. Members of both groups would live in the orphanage; the only difference between the experimental and control groups was attendance in the special preschool on the home's campus. Those in the experimental group would attend the preschool all day, five days a week, throughout the calendar year. Those in the control group would not. Thus would hypotheses about the influence of the preschool on the experimental group be tested for the large variety of developmental measures that Skeels—but Stoddard, really—had planned in advance. Stoddard and Skeels used the "matched pair" method in constituting each group, a method then commonly in use because an appropriate conception of a random sample was not available in that era. According to this technique, each child in each group was supposed to have a child in the other who was closely matched in all attributes to him or her. At any given time, there were twenty-one children in each group. This method, of course, assumed that individuals existed only as parts of groups, or, conversely, that the only reality was the group. The mean IQs of the two groups at the project's beginning in the fall of 1934 were close, 82.3 for the preschoolers, 81.2 for the control group. The project's research design seemed to be without major problems. Results could be confidently expected to flow from the project in time.

The nursery school operated all day. The children had to walk but a few steps to attend the preschool. They arrived at 8:30 every weekday morning, had organized activities, lunch, a nap, then more play or activities, and left at 3:30 each afternoon. The head teacher and two assistants quickly discovered that the children required considerable socialization. They differed in almost every way from the normal, middle-class children they were used to instructing in Iowa City. They had short attention spans and exhibited violent behavior in play; they were extremely retarded in language and vocabulary; they were hostile toward adults, and especially adult authority, yet they obviously longed, with desperation, for adult attention. They had no appreciation of stories, music, or art, nor were they interested in, or able to, get along with other children. Uniformly, they reacted to toys by destroying them. The children constituted a profound challenge to the teachers' middle-class assumptions about child behavior.

Nothing in the teachers' middle-class backgrounds and experiences prepared them for the preschool's first year. They were shocked that any children could behave in this manner and found the first six months were an unbelievable challenge. About a quarter of their charges had no control of bladder and bowel functions, and fully another half required constant reminding of them. Perhaps two children could manage their own clothing. Few could wash themselves. None was willing to listen to reasonable arguments for getting along or operating within the preschool's rules. They were defiant, their emotions were out of control, and they reacted violently as a mob to any new situation, no matter how benign.

Almost immediately the teachers thus jettisoned their wonderfully comprehensive curriculum for nice, well-scrubbed, middle-class children. Instead they subjected their charges to rigorous training of habits and cultivation of skills that would later permit environmental stimulation. The teachers strongly encouraged each child to develop a sense of self-consciousness, as well as the notions that he or she could accomplish something, no matter how trivial, and that it was satisfying to be friendly with other persons. Eventually, the children were made to understand that they had to assume certain minimal responsibilities for themselves and for others.

During the project's first year, the teachers kept matters simple. They had no choice, for the pupils were simply not middle class in behavior or attitude. They insisted inflexibly on the completion of two habitual activities, toilet training and cleanliness. They stressed simple situations and materials throughout the curriculum. They wanted to stimulate the children just enough to pave the way for progress in the future; it was essential to get the children up to a middle-class cultural level of conduct and capability. Hence there were only a few excursions off the home's campus the first year. The teachers stressed a slow pace of activities and gave as much attention to socialization as possible.

In the preschool's second year, problems of social adjustment gradually diminished, and, correspondingly, the teachers could introduce the usual curricula and activities from middle-class nursery schools. The children slowly

learned various basic routines of normal living. The teachers could then con-
centrate on helping each child toward emotional, social, and cognitive enrich-
ment. In time, the children learned not to tear a book apart upon being handed
it; they came to understand that books had nice stories and pictures, if only one
were patient and waited for the teacher to read its contents aloud. They learned
too to sit quietly in a group situation and enjoy a story or a puppet show. Slowly
they learned to cooperate with one another in various play situations. Aggression became less common, or, more precisely, more middle class in character
and pattern.

As the once-overwhelming behavior problems diminished, and as some
first-year pupils remained, by chance, and socialized the preschool's new recruits, the teachers found time to teach the pupils more and more of a normal,
middle-class curriculum, including those activities that were deemed effective
for mental stimulation. Progress was slow. It was only in retrospect, particularly
in the second year, that the teachers could begin to see real changes and think
that they were laboring in something approximating a "normal" preschool.
The teachers began to understand the magnitude of their accomplishment,
which was nothing less than the installation of middle-class cultural notions
and behavior patterns in children whom the natural and social sciences said
could not receive such social blessings and advantages. In a sense, the teachers
had accomplished a miracle that they had neither expected nor had been
prepared to produce. During the project's last year, there was a complete
change of teaching staff, and all adults involved understood that because the
Laura Spelman Rockefeller Memorial funds were exhausted, the project would
terminate in June 1937, which it did.

In 1937 Skeels published a progress report on the preschool's first nine
months. He declared that, so far, group measurements of the intelligence of the
experimental and control children showed no changes, up or down. Almost as
an aside, he remarked that any and all differences that emerged between the
two groups rather consistently favored the preschool children. Noting that all
children came from obviously deprived backgrounds, Skeels stated, as apparent
substantiation, that the older a child was in chronological years the lower was
its IQ score, even when compared with his or her younger natural siblings.
Obviously Skeels thought about fitting his data into group measurements; even
his observation of individuals, as in the last point, he oriented toward com-
menting on group, as distinct from individual, phenomena.[42]

It is no exaggeration to say that the project's findings were other than Skeels
and his associates had anticipated. They also became the subject of much

confusion and controversy. This was especially true with the findings regarding measurements of intelligence (IQ). In designing the project, Stoddard and Skeels assumed that preschool attendance would make a large difference in the scores the preschool children achieved—they were the experimental group, the group stimulated by the supposedly crucial variable, the nursery school. Yet the mountain appeared to have yielded the proverbial mouse. The mean gain in IQ points for the preschool children was 4.6 points, precisely the mean loss for the children in the control group. The period covered was twenty months, the longest period of residence for the children studied in the project.

Unfortunately for Stoddard's political purposes, a mean gain of 5 points or less on a mental tests was widely assumed in scientific circles then to be a mere artifact of the testing situation, or the normal variance of an essentially fixed intelligence quotient. At best, Stoddard seemed to have reaped a very small yield for a very large investment; at worst, the results could be (and were to be) interpreted as showing that no institution, whether a preschool or an orphanage, could influence a child's intelligence. The project's main finding—if this were it—could be deployed in support of the notion of the fixed IQ. Environment mattered little or not at all, it could be argued. But it is crucial to understand that so far the project's scientists had used the same *group* measurements as their professional colleagues and critics did. They had not departed from their profession's methods, theories, and discourses at all, save to assert that their colleagues' determinism was wrong; or, put another way, they had shifted the locus of concern from the group to the individual, without really understanding that they had done so.

The most startling discovery that Skeels and his associates made was, on the other hand, a complete surprise, and it was not the result of a controlled experiment. It was not about the children in the experimental group or even about the nursery school. Instead, it was about the children in the control group—and, by extension, the orphanage.

The longer many or even most individual children in the control group remained in the orphanage, the more likely it was that their later IQ scores as individuals would move downward, toward the range of high feeblemindedness, that is, 70 to 79 Binet points, or even lower. And the project's findings with respect to other aspects of development were in close accord with those regarding intelligence. The children in the experimental group and those in the control group gained and lost, as groups, modestly, but the individuals in each group often made dramatic changes over time. Yet the finding with the largest importance was indeed shocking: the orphanage was apparently turning children who were, on average, borderline normal in intelligence into high-grade morons or worse the *longer* they were wards of the state.

Indeed, rapid outplacement was the only relatively safe guarantee of a normal life for any of the orphanage children, preschool or not. The longer they remained in the orphanage, the worse their prospects were. The preschool children stood higher on all developmental measurements than did the control children, but neither approached middle-class norms when adjusted for age. These results were the same in measures, individual and group, in language and vocabulary, retention of general information, social maturity, constructive behavior, and motor control. And there was a bitter irony in the principle of length of time spent in the orphanage. If children, individually and as a group, who remained longest in the preschools suffered the least losses in cognitive development, nevertheless residence in the orphanage, as a general proposition, was a disaster for all children, experimental and control. At best, their lives would be tragically limited, and the most extreme disasters would be avoided only for a fortunate few.[43]

The Davenport project had problems, not the least of which was that it was not a controlled experiment. It was state policy to encourage adoption of as many children as possible; clearly no research project could keep a child from being adopted, even without considering Skeels's startling discovery that the orphanage was wreaking such havoc with its inmates. Thus a constant stream of children selected for the experimental and control groups was leaving the orphanage during the project's duration. Leakage was substantial. Of the fifty-nine children assigned to the experimental group, only thirty-five, or about 60 percent, remained at least six months, the minimum Skeels believed essential to make them legitimate parts of the study. The corresponding figure for the control group was twenty-three children, of a total of fifty-three children, or 43 percent, who remained six or more months. Skeels kept the groups at twenty-one at any given time; six months was the minimum necessary because the full battery of tests, including the all important Binet tests, were given every six months, meaning that for inclusion, the child took one round of tests when admitted to its group, and another after six months. Nor was this all. While Skeels and his colleagues clearly understood that the longer any child remained in the institution, the more its environment would damage the child's chances to avoid developmental disaster and a stunted life, they seemed to grasp this only from a political, not a scientific, point of view; they never seemed to recognize that such reality would be a factor that could not be controlled in their experiment.

The Davenport project reflected the Iowa scientists' fundamental confusions, which, to a considerable degree, their colleagues, and their fellow Americans, for that matter, shared as well. From the standpoint of statistical method, the Iowa scientists used the standard array of group measurements available to them in their profession and discipline—and culture. These measurements assumed that individuals did not exist save as a part of a group, even an experimental or a control group. Indeed, the evidence is overwhelming that, regardless of what they might have said and done with regard to public policy issues, when it came to their scientific and professional roles and to the discourses that they deployed in these roles, they could not conceive of an individual apart from the group to which he or she "belonged."

What the Iowa scientists measured throughout the Davenport project (and the others as well) was group performance. This performance was shown as something more profound than group averages, means, and the like, as important as those were. The practice of creating "matched pairs" was a method that posited the desirability of making an evidentiary baseline of phenomena to be measured by tried-and-true group means after a stipulated period of time had passed. Persuasive evidence that the Iowa scientists could not conceive of an individual existing apart from the group to which it belonged was the casual, incidental manner in which children were replaced in either group by other children who were supposedly matched to another child in the other group. Individuals were distinct, perhaps, but they were also sufficiently like interchangeable parts that they did not disturb the symmetry and intricate interrelations of the larger whole. Practically speaking, the Iowa scientists, no less than their critics, could not conceive of individuals with any distinct identities, characteristics, bumps, dents, or any other singularities that mattered. Thus it was a curious kind of individualism that the Iowa scientists espoused. The group was all. Group membership, therefore, was not a matter of randomness, of individualness, one might say, but was an ironclad aspect of the very structure of the group in question. Simply put, groups were the ultimate stuff of natural and social reality for the Iowa scientists no less than for their colleagues, and for the good reason that their national culture and their professional scientific subculture had taught them that over and over again.

Yet matters were not as simple as that. The Iowa scientists—Stoddard, in particular, but also Skeels, Wellman, and Lewin—also recognized individual behavior as distinct from the group. This was certainly true in the arguments they made on public policy issues. They recognized it with elegance and coherence in Lewin's work on regression, and with clumsiness and inarticulate-ness in the work on mental testing. Even then, however, the individuals in Lewin's studies were just as interchangeable as those in the IQ investigations. That outlook was due partly to the researchers' ultimate assumption that mental events, rather than psychobiological characteristics, caused behavior. But there was more. When Wellman and Skeels referred to dramatic IQ changes, they were discussing individuals—tracking the performance of particular children over various periods of time. That they did not understand the difference as yet between group and individual behavior was clear from the manner in which they discussed and explained such phenomena. In fact, such would be difficult to conceive of so long as they assumed that the whole of reality was symmetrical, for with a symmetrical universe it is difficult to differentiate among parts—or individuals—whereas with an asymmetrical taxonomy of reality it is not. They were not aware that they had launched themselves on a pathway toward the recognition in the human sciences of the profound differences between the measurement and interpretation of individual and group behavior, and, to the extent that there are paths from the past to the present, to the articulation of a profound individualism. But they had, and, if maintained, that course would define what could be regarded as the Iowa station's ultimate contribution to modern social thought.

CHAPTER SIX

INDIVIDUALISM RECONSIDERED

In the 1930s the New Deal created the basis of the modern American national welfare state. Of relief that was addressed to young people and children, clearly some was temporary, like, for example, the Civilian Conservation Corps (CCC), which provided jobs for about 2.5 million young men to work on various government projects, as in road building, forest conservation, and the like, and the National Youth Authority (NYA), which offered educational and vocational training opportunities for about 600,000 college and 1.5 million high school students. These programs assisted categories or groups of young people; not only were women excluded from the CCC, but gender and racial stereotypes usually defined the NYA's options available for young men and women.

The federal government enacted two laws that offered permanent haven to children. Under the Social Security Act (1935), Aid to Dependent Children (ADC) paid federal monies, which the states administered on a matching-fund basis, to mothers with dependent children. Congress restricted eligibility with prescriptive expectations of proper maternal behavior and gave little evidence that the welfare of children per se mattered; rather, the intent of the program was the promotion of good, middle-class family values among the nation's proles. The other federal law was the Fair Labor Standards Act (1938), America's first permanent national child labor law.

This legislation did not single children out as a special category of persons apart from the family, the community, or any other social network in which they functioned and were situated. Children were part of a larger, symmetrical social system. That they received assistance at all resulted from those larger symmetrical relations they had with other elements of the social system. There was no sense of children as individuals apart from society or as victims of the social system who had special needs and, therefore, particular rights that should be addressed.[1]

Historians Barry D. Karl and Stanley N. Katz have argued that much of the New Deal legislation was not intended to be permanent. Indeed, those who fashioned it hoped that the federal government would continue to speak as moral leader for national policy, but not to create, after the fashion of the European states, a national bureaucracy to administer national policy. Rather, Franklin Roosevelt wished to restrict the federal government's role in normal times, as his predecessor, Herbert Hoover, had done, to that of a coordinator of the many distinct yet interrelated agencies, institutions, and interests in the discussion and implementation of national policy, including local and state government, private foundations, the professions, various business interests, and the like. This holistic model of cooperation, with its belief in the merits of intermediate and complex structures for the resolution of conflicts, was typical of the interwar years. It succeeded the binary and conflictual model of the late nineteenth and early twentieth centuries, in which some interests ended on the top of the heap, and most fared less well. And this holistic, symmetrical, balanced model of the alignment of forces to solve public policy programs seemed to apply to policies toward children as well as to any other topic or problem.[2]

In the later 1930s, George Stoddard championed policies in which government would intervene in the social system on behalf of children. More than mere material assistance doled out to various categories of the national population was needed, he argued. Each and every individual's full potentiality would thus be achieved. The invention of a creative, imaginative, and emancipatory school system for all from preschool to working adults would best accomplish this. Education was the ultimate reform. The government as educational system would intervene to improve and uplift the lives of all individuals, regardless of race, religion, national origin, or any other group identity. That philosophy was the full measure of Stoddard's radicalism in the Depression decade.

Stoddard and the Iowa Child Welfare Research Station were gaining national attention from far beyond the tiny professional scientific subculture of child development. In its November 7, 1938, edition, *Time* magazine published an article with the provocative title "I.Q. Control," about the IQ work being done at the station. It was clear from the account that the Iowa work cast grave doubt on the group determinism of their science. *Time* welcomed the

Iowa station's heresies. The major newspaper wire services carried the *Time* story, which simply made the Iowa station's work more noted than before. The next January, Stoddard published an article for the National Conference of Christians and Jews in honor of its latest instrument, National Brotherhood Day. Stoddard argued that American democratic education should stimulate each and every unique child to achieve his or her maximum potentiality, and that his colleagues at the Iowa station were showing how this could be done via the methods and processes of modern science, for example, in the atmospheres and IQ projects. Early intervention in the individual's life cycle could build a better tomorrow. A truly democratic society could be created, composed of individuals who think for themselves and who respect one another as individuals, not who regard others as members of a hierarchy or system of classes and castes—of predetermined groups. In March, Stoddard spoke on a topic entitled "Cultivating the Child's Mind," on the Columbia Broadcasting System's weekly "Adventures in Science" radio program. He insisted that each and every individual could be liberated intellectually and culturally, and that our national educational system was not doing its job, which was to unlock the unique potentialities of every person in the nation.[3]

That June, Stoddard spoke at the University of California, in Berkeley. The pessimists of science and society, he argued, should not be permitted to limit the potentiality of every American citizen. The work at the Iowa Child Welfare Research Station, he insisted, showed that the nation had not even begun to explore the possibilities of human improvement through modern science. There were many distinct yet interrelated factors in any situation, and it served neither science nor society well to be pessimistic, to believe that individuals had no control over their own destinies. After all, much was still unknown about heredity and environment. Was biology responsible for diversity as well as uniformity? Who could say? Stoddard likened the environment to a good pacemaker, which "may step up the tempo, without bunching the competitors." He pointed to Lewin's work, which showed that regression could occur in response to repeated frustration, but that children in other circumstances could be taught to surmount such frustration in a wholesome and constructive manner. Stoddard argued that Lewin and his students were also working on a new kind of research into what factors went into the creation of democratic and autocratic environments in group situations. Such traits could be taught. Heredity and environment were not closed, completed subjects, as his colleagues liked to believe. Researchers at the Iowa station, he insisted, were not fatalistic in their outlook and were humbled by their lack of knowledge about the big questions in the making of human nature and conduct. Pointing to the work of Beth Wellman and Harold Skeels on environment and IQ, Stoddard argued that it remained unclear whether the causes of these remarkable changes in IQs were nature or nurture. Indeed, nature apparently could not be disentangled from nurture, a point of view that echoed the new interactionist, symmetrical model of nature cum nurture that had emanated from the nature-nurture controversy of the 1920s. These matters needed to be considered in new and imaginative ways; the old questions and answers no longer served. He appealed to no less an authority than Alfred Binet in concluding that a child's intelligence and mentality were not fixed but were like a harvest that could be increased by better and better nurturing. Once again did Stoddard tease out the possibilities of child science as his colleagues developed it for the reconstruction of American society and culture. His spectacular claims brought the Iowa station increasingly into the national limelight.[4]

Lewin's embrace of American democracy was rapidly reflected in his work and that of his students. And they did much to carry forward the complex professional discourse on group and individual. In particular did they address the problem of the dynamics and statics of small groups. The first of these projects that Lewin supervised focused on democratic, autocratic, and laissez-faire "atmospheres" in small groups. This work was of theoretical and practical importance, as the first American effort to formulate the psychology of group dynamics from the "inside out," that is, from studying the interactions of individuals within groups and their patterns of behavior as members of groups. Even the work that Lois Jack and her colleagues had done a few years before was but preparatory, albeit not knowingly, to Lewin's researches, for its substantive perspective was the impact of the group on individual behavior, as illustrated in ascendant or submissive behavior. The political message of the regression project was that individuals were made, not born; seemingly automatic maturation processes could be reversed. That of the atmospheres project was that the team was a unit or group of democratic processes, within which each individual had much in common with every other member of the team, so that these distinct individuals were ultimately interchangeable.

In 1939, Ronald Lippitt ended up by chance in Iowa City for graduate work. At his alma mater, Springfield College, in Massachusetts, Lippitt had acquired an interest in the practical aspects of group leadership. When he spoke to Lewin about this as a master's thesis topic, Lewin suddenly became very excited, and right away they began talking about autocratic and democratic styles of group leadership. Lippitt would compare autocratic and democratic leadership of children's groups. He would create democratic and autocratic "atmospheres" and study their group dynamics.[5]

By *atmospheres* Lewin meant something very specific. As no physicist would try to understand the movement of a body without considering the character of the field of gravity in which it was located, he declared, so the psychologist had to find out how to conceive of and to measure quantitatively and qualitatively the general field in which the person was located. That field was the ground on which the person stood. And it determined the group's character, too. The atmosphere, then, was the psychological and emotional field, or, in Lewinesque jargon, the social powerfield, in which the dramatis personae in the experiments would act.

For the democratic and autocratic groups, Lippitt selected two groups of ten- and eleven-year-old children from the fifth and sixth grades of the university elementary schools. None of the ten children so chosen knew one another in advance. Lippitt was group leader. Each group became a club whose goal was to make theatrical masks. The masks would belong to the group as a whole and would be made one at a time by all the members; individual members would not make their own masks. Hence the groups would be teams, not aggregates of individuals. Thirty-minute meetings would be held twice a week for twelve weeks. Four observers took extensive running notes, including quantitative accounts of the social interactions of the children in each group; notations of ascendant, submissive, and objective responses; minute-by-minute analyses of group structure; and a stenographic record of all conversation and a debriefing of Lippitt after each meeting for further data. Lewin and Lippitt wanted a precise quantitative and qualitative record of all behavior in all groups.

For methodological reasons, members in both groups had complete free speech. As autocratic leader, Lippitt determined all policies. He outlined every action that each child was to take during the meetings. He announced goals one at a time, so that the children would always be uncertain about the future. He criticized or praised the children individually. He remained aloof and detached, not emotive or involved. As leader of the democratic group, Lippitt established a totally different atmosphere of involvement, cooperation, and permissiveness. He provided technical assistance, was friendly and encouraging, but he did not instruct the children. He encouraged them to make their own decisions as a group—by voting. He left the division of tasks up to the children. He offered praise only to the group, never to specific individuals. In

Lewinesque language, the leader so dominated the autocratic group's atmosphere that he diminished rather than augmented the members' social power-
fields collectively and individually; he accomplished the reverse with the democratic group.

The children's behavior in the two groups—or teams—contrasted greatly. In
the autocratic group, the boys continually challenged Lippitt's power as leader.
Increasingly, the participants cared only for themselves, not their peers, and
became less and less creative, letting the leader make all the decisions. By the
experiment's end, they had become apathetic toward all group tasks and responsibilities and unpleasant to one another, picking fights and even forcing
the strongest of their number out of the group by making him a scapegoat.
They toadied up to the group leader when he paid them attention, and mocked
him—and the group's objectives—behind his back. In the democratic group,
there was no domineering leader to react against. The boys were congenial with
one another and cheerfully cooperated on various tasks, working together on
common goals and developing mutual respect. Lippitt insisted that by not
permitting the leader in the democratic group the same dominant social powerfield as in the autocratic group, the democratic group developed increased
group cohesion, greater group resiliency and stability, and far more participation in both the creation and the completion of common tasks. The group
leader was friendly, cooperative, and supportive toward the boys. Democracy
brought out the best in human nature, thanks to the "higher unity of the
democratic life with its greater amount of objectivity and cooperativeness of
interpersonal relations."[6]

For his doctoral thesis, Lippitt joined with peers Daniel L. Adler and Ralph
K. White to make the experiment larger and more complex. They studied four
comparable clubs of ten-year-old boys. Again mask making was the clubs'
central task. They created a new group atmosphere—laissez-faire—to compare
with the democratic and autocratic. In it, the group leader offered no information. He only encouraged the boys to do everything for themselves. Each boy
spent some time in each group atmosphere. Lippitt, Adler, and White gathered much more information. The results tallied with those of the first experiment. In one autocratic group, group relations tempestuously degenerated,
members were aggressive toward one another, and scapegoats were created; in
the others, the boys were simply apathetic, presumably as a reaction to the
leader's domination. The democratic groups perked along as before, whereas
the laissez-faire groups experienced comparable levels of morale with the democratic groups but accomplished far less work. Almost all of the boys preferred

the democratic to the autocratic leader, and the laissez-faire leader was somewhat less popular than the democratic one.[7]

Not surprisingly, Lewin interpreted these results as justifying a scientific
theory proving that democracy was superior to autocracy. He confided to
Kallen that "we are doing experiments on autocracy and democracy which are
going along very nicely." Lewin disseminated news about the atmospheres
projects in the later thirties and early forties. He taught at Harvard in the 1939
and 1940 spring semesters; from that convenient perch he spread the word.
Lewin and his students also published articles in professional journals and gave
talks at professional conferences to promote the work.[8]

In the later thirties Harold M. Skeels and his associates mined the orphanage project for several more studies and pushed ahead the discussion on
the individual and the group and on the plasticity of human nature. Two in
particular were to attract attention. The Davenport orphanage project was
profoundly controversial. Its general finding, that morons were made, not
born, had horrific implications for scientists and ordinary, middle-class Americans alike. It suggested that public institutions gratuitously manufactured a
harsh, cruel environment for hapless infants. It also implied that the American
social class and caste structure was anything but natural and inevitable.

In her doctoral dissertation, Marie Skodak probed whether children in state
orphanages could be placed in middle-class homes and adapt culturally and
educationally to the levels of their foster rather than their natural parents.
Orphans in such institutions were almost always the illegitimate offspring of
poor and working-class parents. Skodak's concerns were practical. As an aspir-
ing social worker, she wanted to know whether children of such unpromising
backgrounds could be safely placed in normal, middle-class homes. For her
study she compared a group of 154 children placed in foster homes when they
were under the age of six months with another group placed when they were
older, two-and-a-half to five years of age. She used the Minnesota Occupational Scale to measure the social status, when known, of the birth parents.
Initially the mean IQs of the foster children and of the foster parents showed
no measurable correlation; the longer the children remained with their foster
parents, the more parental and child IQs came to resemble one another, until
the children mirrored the average IQs, as defined by Terman, Goodenough,
and Anderson, of their foster parents' occupational levels. All children tended
to gain in average IQ scores on retesting so long as they remained in a home
environment more favorable than that of the orphanage. But the gains also
depended on the foster environment. Children shunted from one foster home

to another, for example, did not do as well as those placed in a superior home and kept there.

So far, she had discussed only group performance, after the fashion of Terman's group portraits for his genius project. In the spirit of determining who benefited the most from this outplacement, she found that the individual children whose initial IQ scores were among the lowest gained the most IQ points on retesting, and vice versa: those with the highest initial scores made the smallest gains. She concluded that it "was the home rather than the child's family background which . . . sets the limits of his mental development," and if biological inheritance set the limits of intellectual growth, "these limits are extremely broad," for environment could produce changes that might represent a shift from one extreme to another. Insofar as placing orphans was concerned, Skodak insisted that it was necessary only to put children in good homes in which their future development would not be hampered or restricted. If Skodak was aware of the fact that she had shifted the level of discourse from "snapshots" of groups at moments in time to tracking individuals over time, paying attention to individuals apart from the larger group(s) she studied, she betrayed no sign that she had done precisely that. Yet she had.[9]

Skeels published the other study. One of Skeels's responsibilities at the Davenport home was to select out, through intelligence testing, the feebleminded from the normal children, and to dispatch the former to the state home for the feebleminded in the hamlet of Glenwood. By chance, the unusual particulars of the case of two retarded infants thus transferred to the Glenwood institution came to Skeels's attention. The infants had tested at 46 and 35 IQs at ages thirteen and sixteen months, respectively. Because the Glenwood home chronically suffered from a surfeit of trained personnel, the two infants were put on a ward with female inmates ranging from eighteen to fifty years in chronological age, and from five to nine years in mental age.

Six months later, Skeels and several colleagues made a routine visit to check on all the children he had transferred to Glenwood. They were astonished at the obvious improvement in the infants' behavior; they stood up, played with toys, and responded to adults in ways unheard of for children of their supposedly dismal IQs. Skeels was a tenderhearted, conscientious soul. He worried that he had made a ghastly error in classification, and immediately ordered the children to be retested with a special version of the Binet developed for children under the chronological age of three-and-a-half years. The babies, now eighteen and twenty-two months old, tested at 77 and 87 IQ points, a gain of 31 and 52 IQ points, respectively; twenty-one months later, the younger child tested at 95 and the older at 93 IQ points, or additional gains of 18 and of 6 points. Now that these two children tested in the normal range, Skeels ordered their transfer back to the Davenport orphanage. In due course, they were permanently adopted.

Why had this astonishing change occurred? Why did the IQs of these infants rise in such meteoric fashion? Skeels assumed that it was a combination of factors not commonly found on the ward. The babies had received intensive attention from the women. There was an unusually high ratio of adults to children, with the women at a much higher mental level than that of the infants. This situation would not have continued to have such a salubrious effect indefinitely, he argued; at this level of early development, however, it was obviously beneficial. Professionals in the field later told him that this was not an uncommon occurrence, but that they did not discuss it openly for fear of public ridicule or worse. The mentally retarded were not persons to whom much attention was paid by most Americans beyond their cruel stigmatization as "feebleminded."

Skeels always championed the welfare of children, whether they were feebleminded or not. He thought his serendipitous discovery could help other children. This led him to do the second, spin-off study from the Davenport project. He persuaded higher authorities at Glenwood and the Board of Control to let him test his hypothesis about the retarded older women as suitable attendants for children. Probably Skeels saw the possibility of using older inmates constructively, and, more grandly, of making such institutions curative rather than merely custodial, with Glenwood as a model. Then too, this was a way to stretch budgets for schools for the feebleminded, which were usually thin, especially in the Depression and in Iowa.

As Skeels designed the study, all children at the Davenport orphanage classified as feebleminded and under three years of age were transferred to Glenwood, as the law stipulated. There they were placed in wards where they would receive the same kind of attention the two infants had. These thirteen children became the experimental group; they had a mean chronological age of 19.4 months, ranging from 7.1 to 35.9 months in age. Their IQ scores were definitely in the feebleminded category, with their mean at 64.3 and their median at 65.0 points respectively, and a range of 35 to 89 IQ points. Upon their transfer to Glenwood, they were wholly unsuitable for adoption: their retardation was simply too severe. They were compared with a control group of children from the Davenport orphanage who were typical in every standard measurement of "normal" orphanage children and who had never been in the station's preschool. This group's mean chronological age was 16.6 months. Their initial IQ scores were borderline normal to normal, with the mean and median IQ at 86.7 and 90 points, respectively, and the range for all but two between 91 and 103 IQ points. The project continued for better than eighteen months, with several systematic measurements.

The study's results were shocking. The children in the experimental group at Glenwood gained, on the average, 27.5 IQ points. Those in the control group at Davenport, on the other hand, experienced a mean loss of 26.2 IQ points. The institution for the feebleminded apparently cured its specially treated charges of that affliction, whereas the orphanage for normal youngsters seemed a manufactory whose product was mental retardation! Without comment or explanation Skeels and his coauthor, Harold Dye, Glenwood's supervisor, then listed each *individual* by case number and gains or losses in IQ points. Clearly they had gone far enough beyond thinking of their charges merely as members of a group to present their data in a way most unusual for that time. They made next to nothing out of this presentation of data, as if the facts spoke for themselves. Although it is difficult to know what they thought they were doing, the fact that they were mute about what they did is strong presumptive evidence that they "understood" the problem from the same angle of vision as did their contemporaries.

Like Skodak, Skeels drew not a theoretical but a practical message from his adventitiously designed study. He suggested that in cases in which there was no organic disease or physiological deficiency, a retarded young child could, through specific training, be brought up to a normal mental level. Of particular importance were two factors. The child had to be young, no more than three years, most likely. And there had to be an intimate and close relationship between an adult and a child in a stimulating environment.[10]

Stoddard and his colleagues had trouble thinking about the scientific aspects of the group-individual problem, as the above suggests, and far more than when they thought of the problem in political terms, where it seemed a mere question of recommending social intervention rather than grappling with the baffling explanation of how there could be individualism (and asymmetry) within a holistic, symmetrical world; if all were symmetrical and holistic, how could intervention be justified at any particular point in the social system—why at this point and not at that one? This problem seemed extraordinarily difficult for contemporaries. It had a distinct configuration in their professional discourse and appeared in a certain light. And this difficulty was true for all their national colleagues, friends and critics alike.

In 1939 and 1940, for instance, Benjamin R. Simpson, a professor of education at Western Reserve University, attacked Beth Wellman's nursery school
studies. Simpson's main argument was over selection. He insisted that since
children left the study over a period of years, that kind of selection robbed the
study of any statistical validity. It was clear in the exchange between Simpson
and Wellman that she was thinking primarily of large gains in IQs for individuals, not groups, in which case selection was obviously an irrelevant criticism,
whereas Simpson was thinking of the children entirely as members of preexisting groups. That Wellman took Simpson's charge to heart and answered him
by arguing with him on an empirical basis, rather than pointing to its irrelevance for individual measurements, shows that she too thought of the children
as members of groups even when she was referring to their behavior as individuals whose IQ scores were tracked as individuals over time. Wellman had great
difficulty sorting out the implications of group and individual behavior. She
continued to refer to mean gains in IQ points for the children who persisted in
the study from one sample of testing to the next, even though she would insist
in the same breath that if her study were wrong, why did the individual children who were given successive tests have higher IQ scores later in the study?
Obviously there was nothing available in the professional discourse to help
her.[11]

This confusion in discourse, if confusion it was, cropped up again when, in
April 1939, the popular science writer Albert E. Wiggam came to Iowa City to
interview Stoddard, Wellman, and Skeels about both the preschool and orphan children research projects for a possible article in a prominent woman's
magazine. Fortunately, a transcript of their conversations survives. In explaining their IQ work to Wiggam, they began by referring, after the fashion of
their professional colleagues, to changes in group measurements in test scores.
But in almost the same breath, they focused almost entirely on the performances of individual children in the evidence to which they referred and the
events that they discussed. That is, when they explained to Wiggam why IQs
varied up and down so dramatically, they insisted that what made the group
measurements of IQs of their charges rise or fall were the dramatic variations of
particular children. Put another way, they ascribed the causes of group behavior
to that of individuals.

They insisted that the individual, not the group, was the fundamental reality
of nature and society. Groups were aggregates of those complex, symmetrical
entities—individuals. And individuals were dynamic organisms constituted of
many distinct, interrelated, and balanced parts. Thus Skeels argued that culture

was a suit of clothes that the individual could put on or take off, almost at will, a highly convenient assumption for someone like Skeels, who was chiefly interested in promoting child welfare. Wellman told Wiggam that the IQ was not fixed. Individuals could and did experience dramatic changes in IQ in early childhood. Such changes could vary above or below their initial scores by large margins. Nor was there any scientific evidence that the IQ was fixed in any way in the early years of childhood. Indeed, there was no evidence for the claim of many psychometricians that IQs of individual children had a ceiling or—she could have added from the orphanage study—a floor. She spoke entirely about how individuals performed. Stoddard discussed these matters in exactly the same way; when he referred to the environment, he insisted that it was not a monolithic force (as many developmentalists tended to regard it) but a complex unity of many distinct yet symmetrically interrelated forces that influenced different aspects of the life history of each individual in multiple ways.[12]

Their colleagues all believed, to the contrary, that groups, not individuals, were the stuff of reality. An individual could not stand alone, apart from the group to which nature and society had "assigned" him or her. In a very real sense, the Iowa scientists were talking beyond their colleagues. But they were also talking beyond themselves, in the sense that they were virtually inarticulate in presenting to themselves and their colleagues their discoveries on the individual and individual IQ gains and losses. They could, as the discussions they had with Wiggam strongly suggested, discuss these phenomena as phenomena, and they could think of them in terms of their sociopolitical applications, in their utility, that is, for child welfare. The obvious answer for this disparity, that they were inarticulate as scientists, simply will not wash, for they were no less inarticulate about their "discoveries" or more inept as scientists than were the bulk of their colleagues. The problem, rather, seemed to be that they and their contemporaries worked from within the limits of the same conceptual discourse, and the only difference between them was their values and priorities, not their sense of how reality was organized.

For that matter, Skeels, Wellman, and Stoddard were not alone in their profession in calling attention to the phenomenon that they had observed, that the IQs of very young individual children seemed highly sensitive to long-term environmental pressures of either a positive or a negative character. In short, this was no will-o'-the-wisp, no spurious apparition of the time. A handful of colleagues had made the same discovery. Probably the scientist with the most prestige who corroborated the Iowans' position was Jean Walker Macfarlane of the Institute of Child Welfare at the University of California at Berkeley. Her support for the Iowa claims was important precisely because she was an academic scientist in one of the field's top research institutes, and because she had directed one of the institute's—and field's—most heralded longitudinal research projects, the so-called Berkeley Guidance Study, since its initiation in 1928.

Speaking before a crowd estimated at one thousand persons at the National Association for Nursery Education, on October 25, 1939, Macfarlane attacked important elements of the field's conventional wisdom. Like the Iowa scientists, she spoke of tracking individual children and their IQ scores over time. Group averages or other measurements were simply not a part of her language, at least in this talk. She insisted that many children in their early years experienced significant changes in IQs. The IQs of some children fluctuated as much as 100 points. Some children began with low IQs and over time had high ones; others followed the reverse pattern. The IQs of children of preschool years, at least, should not be regarded as constant, she insisted. It was essential for workers in the field to go beyond group measurements, which simply disguised the experiences of individuals, and to study actual persons rather than abstract scientific processes and principles, as most workers in this subspecialty tended to do. She concluded that the causes of these dramatic changes in IQ scores of preschool age and younger children were to be located chiefly, if not entirely, in the social and emotional environment of individual children interacting with other individuals in their families, schools, neighborhoods, and other social contexts, or, in brief, in the mental processes occurring in the minds of individuals and groups, not in natural and social forces.[13]

Macfarlane's defection from the ranks of the mainstream in child science sheds some light on the context and realities of the field then. The Berkeley Guidance Study began as an offshoot of Lawrence K. Frank's enthusiasms. Frank and Macfarlane were close friends; they saw eye to eye on most professional issues. Indeed, Frank had worked with her since the early 1920s to get her university to accept Laura Spelman Rockefeller Memorial funding to start the Institute of Child Welfare under the conditions and with the understandings that he wanted. The project's original purpose was to study a sample of infants for six years to determine if intensive parental nurture and guidance would lessen or eliminate behavioral difficulties, a quintessentially Frankian project. Macfarlane identified a random sample of 248 twenty-one-month-old Berkeley infants, divided them into experimental and control groups, and used intensive parental guidance as the variable test between the groups. Macfarlane and her associates gathered mountains of material on each individual child, following as they did that contemporary notion of the normal child as being a complex, balanced, entity of many distinct yet interrelated parts.

The Guidance Study was always intended to generate data and conclusions for social application, and Macfarlane identified powerfully with that tradition in the field. In that sense, she was not so different in her point of view from Wellman, Stoddard, or Skeels, or most of the Iowa station's staff in those years. The California institute was home to another longitudinal study, the Berkeley Growth Study, begun also in 1928; its director was Nancy Bayley, who had actually taken her doctorate with Carl Seashore at Iowa, and whose thinking on matters of innate IQ was much closer to the traditional view; for whatever reason, Bayley agreed with Seashore. Bayley began with a selected sample of seventy-four infants, chiefly white and middle class in background, born in the city of Berkeley. With no natural terminal point, Bayley's investigation became an open-ended scientific inquiry into all manner of questions about infant and child development. Much of the material had to do with mental development, broadly defined. Unlike her activist colleague Macfarlane, Bayley used group measurements. Even though Macfarlane and Bayley worked closely together on many common assignments and often used similar approaches, there remained in 1939 this crucial difference between them. Macfarlane saw individuals and measured them as such, whereas Bayley perceived groups and regarded them as the stuff of reality. That intellectual difference was to have important consequences.[14]

Others who agreed with the Iowa scientists' position on the IQ were social workers or clinical psychologists whose experiences and exposure to real-life situations were similar to those of Skeels, Wellman, and their associates. H. O. O'Neill, of the prestigious Philadelphia Child Guidance Clinic, found the same kind of wide IQ variance among his young clients, that is, a variance significantly higher on retesting than the five-point difference most professionals in the field expected. Donald Syngg of the Toronto Infants Home and Mental Hygiene Clinic wrestled with the problem of orphan placement from much the same perspective as had Marie Skodak. He too found little intellectual similarity between foster children and their true parents, as did two social workers at the Amherst H. Wilder Child Guidance Clinic in Saint Paul, Minnesota. They recommended early placement in good homes, regardless of the IQs or other traits of the true parents.

In these instances the authors all studied individual children, not groups; they took measurements of the performance of individuals over time, in true longitudinal fashion; and they all disagreed, as Macfarlane, and Stoddard, Wellman, and Skeels had, with that convention of the field, that the IQ was fixed at birth. Not even feeblemindedness in either or both parents was to be feared in the children so long as they were placed very early in life—preferably as neonates or infants. George Speer, another social worker, initially had doubted the Iowa findings on orphanage placement. Indeed, he had written to Wellman that her behavior was irresponsible, for she was encouraging parents to court disaster by adopting hopelessly feebleminded children who would surely issue from any union in which there was at least one feebleminded parent. Wellman dared Speer to replicate the Iowa methods. He did, and found his investigation corroborated the Iowa findings.[15]

Yet most developmental scientists sincerely believed that the question of the IQ's constancy had long been settled, and by methods superior to those the Iowa scientists employed. The reasons for this widespread belief combined technical and cultural factors in various ways, including the resolution of the controversy over heredity and environment in the twenties; the pervasiveness of positivism and determinism in the scientific community; the equally widespread notion throughout the culture that group identity for the individual was coercive and unchangeable; and the pervasive belief that differences of class and caste in American society and culture were created naturally, not as artificial instruments of social and racial oppression.

The Binet test's design contributed to this belief in the IQ's fixity. It was constructed so that of those taking it, half would always pass at some average point, one-fourth would pass at a superior level, and one-fourth would fail, presumably because of stupidity. Thus, almost all investigators found that the mean IQs for groups retested were highly constant, which they and virtually all specialists interpreted as signifying that the IQ was constant for individuals. So compelling and deeply embedded in the culture was the belief that groups, not individuals, constituted the structure of social and natural reality, that it occurred to almost no one, including the Iowa scientists and their allies, that this belief was an artifact of the test's design. When the issue of individual measurements arose in professional discourse, specialists had available plenty of evidence that the IQ was constant: some studies showed the high consistency of IQs of individual children retested from the school years to adulthood; others demonstrated a high intercorrelation of various test scores for the same individuals; and still others suggested that IQ test results correlated closely with other measures of success or failure, including family occupational status and academic success. Scientists had also published various studies in which test scores of persons with varying degrees of familial inheritance, such as parents, cousins, siblings, and twins, were correlated, with the general result that the greater the degree of presumed shared genetic inheritance, the greater the correlation of IQ scores.[16]

Stoddard and his allies thus placed themselves in the uncomfortable position of championing an idea that almost all their scientific contemporaries intuitively knew was nonsensical, in the category of such notions as a flat earth or the divine creation of species. It is very important to grasp the further point that even with support from scholars such as Macfarlane, the Iowa work on IQ was simply not believed because it confounded and contradicted what contemporaries knew to be true. Of course, it did not help that the Iowa position was embraced by social workers and enthusiasts for child welfare; sniffy academic scientists, believing that theirs was a "pure" and "basic" science, were glad to ignore such endorsements as the result of muddled thinking and giddy articulation. The key to understanding the controversy over the Iowa station findings on IQ was not how many, but how few, scientists took any interest whatsoever in the question. The debate took place with only a handful of participants. Others either ignored the controversy or simply cheered on what they regarded as the "right" side, those who opposed the Iowa claims for the wandering IQ.

The annual *Yearbook* of the National Society for the Study of Education (NSSE) provided the framework for the major debate on the Iowa IQ findings. The NSSE was a private, not-for-profit, professional organization in Bloomington, Illinois, founded in 1900 by and for schoolteachers and administrators who wished to sponsor policy research on contemporary educational matters and to address important public issues in education. Starting in 1901, the NSSE published an annual *Yearbook*, one, and sometimes two, large volume crammed with studies on that year's theme. Interest groups within or constituencies without the NSSE usually suggested the *Yearbook*'s theme, which the NSSE's board of directors then ratified. In turn, they selected a *Yearbook* committee, whose half-dozen members divided up the chores for soliciting papers, editing the volume, and planning that year's annual program.

Lewis M. Terman of Stanford University edited the NSSE's twenty-seventh *Yearbook*, published in 1928. Its theme was nature and nurture in the making of intelligence. As might have been expected of a *Yearbook* committee in which Terman, the inventor of the Stanford Binet test, was the key figure, many who contributed studies wanted to discuss the limits, rather than the potentialities, that most children faced in life. Guy M. Whipple, long-time NSSE secretary and prominent advocate of nature over nurture in the making of intelligence, nevertheless wrote in this *Yearbook*, known professionally as the "Terman volume," that no one who read it could "put it away with the conviction that general intelligence is an absolutely fixed, immutable, innate capacity, but neither can one put it away with the conviction that it is readily susceptible to environmental influence." The truth, Whipple insisted, lay "between these two extremes."

In fact, one of Terman's own doctoral students and protégés, Barbara Stoddard Burks, wrote the volume's most representative contribution. She compared foster child and foster parent resemblances, on the one hand, with true parent and true child resemblances, on the other. In her heart a hereditarian, she accepted as a conscientious scientist the new interactionist paradigm that had emanated from the heredity-environment controversy. She argued that mental development occurred only with the interaction of heredity and environment; it was artificial and wrongheaded to attempt to separate them. She stressed that she had selected a socially and ethnically homogeneous population. Given this selection, environment would matter less in her results. She concluded in general that about 17 percent of the variability in intelligence was caused by differences in home environment, and that without such selection as in her study, environment could contribute no more than about 20 percent to the making of intelligence. Inheritance caused the rest.[17]

Thus did an important part of the intellectual consensus for the interwar years take hold in the natural and social sciences. Interestingly enough, the one dissenting member of the 1928 *Yearbook* committee was none other than Bird T. Baldwin. In the last two years of his life, he spent some time, and probably some professional credibility too, attacking the hereditarian and deterministic tone that his *Yearbook* colleagues had taken. He disagreed, not with the interactionist paradigm of nature cum nurture, but with the positivistic and deterministic interpretations that the mainstream in his profession gave it. Baldwin criticized the *Yearbook*'s themes because of an experience in his own family that changed his perspective. When his daughter first entered the station's preschool, she was diagnosed as mentally retarded. He refused to place her in the Glenwood institution. Rather, he enrolled her in the station's preschool, and within a year and a half, she had gained enormously in IQ points, from 84 to 143 points. Baldwin's first wife had died in 1925. Later, he and Beth Wellman fell in love, and they were engaged to be married when he died in 1928. She adopted his children and raised them as if they were her own. Presumably, her stepdaughter's experience suggested much to Wellman and, in time, to her colleagues at the station.[18]

Given Stoddard's prominence in professional educational and scientific circles, it was hardly surprising that various individuals would clamor for the NSSE to publish a "Stoddard volume" to balance the "Terman volume." Precisely what role, if any, Stoddard played in this remains unclear, although he never missed an opportunity to publicize the Iowa point of view. He had allies in such organizations as the National Association for Nursery Education, an organization he helped found, and the John Dewey Society, which he also helped create. Indeed, Stoddard hobnobbed with important New York intellectuals such as William Heard Kilpatrick of Teachers College, among others. In fact, Stoddard had positioned himself to be the national authority on boosting the IQ for left-liberals of the New Deal coalition. In his various public pronouncements in the middle thirties, he had argued, among other things, that racial discrimination was a national disgrace, that the average parent did not know as much about children of preschool age as did the average preschool teacher, that a national system of public nursery schools would rescue much human potentiality that was now wasted in the nation's schools, and that there were as yet no known limits to the IQs of most normal persons.[19]

The NSSE's directors appointed Stoddard chair of a new *Yearbook* committee in February 1937. Stoddard's mandate was to prepare a *Yearbook* that, unlike Terman's, would be more positive and would explore intelligence's possibilities, not its limits. That was not to be so easy a task. Of the seven committee members, only two, Stoddard and Wellman, embraced the indeterminist Iowa position, while a third, Harold E. Jones of the California Institute of Child Welfare, was publicly neutral but probably was a determinist. The committee's other four members, Leonard Carmichael, now president of Tufts, Leta S. Hollingworth of Teachers College, Florence L. Goodenough of the Minnesota Institute of Child Welfare, and Lewis M. Terman, all embraced the field's dominant orthodoxy, and two, Carmichael and Terman, had been major architects of that orthodoxy. In short, Stoddard was outnumbered on his own committee.[20]

Over the next three years, committee members solicited work for the volume. It was immediately apparent that the demand for such investigations far exceeded the supply. Florence Goodenough of the Minnesota Institute of Child Welfare, who was especially close to Terman, solicited papers from former students and colleagues throughout 1938 without much success. One former student begged off, saying that while she was "very much interested in your research battle with Beth Wellman" and was eager to see what materials could be gathered, she had no resources or time for a new study at her university. "I'm sorry you will not be able to locate some dope for the Yearbook," Goodenough replied. "I am very anxious to secure as much data as possible for if there is some magic educational process by which morons can be made into geniuses I'd like to have the recipie." She concluded tartly that "if there isn't, prevailing rumors ought to be quashed as completely as possible."[21]

Indeed, Goodenough and Terman kept in close postal contact for the next several years on all matters relating to the volume, including recruiting papers favorable to their point of view. As the time grew closer for the final conference and the volume's publication, they orchestrated a strong campaign against Stoddard and the Iowa argument. Of the two, Terman was the more vitriolic and mean spirited. He believed that Stoddard and Wellman dishonestly manufactured evidence. Goodenough was the more charitable. She assumed only that they had deluded themselves. Their position was irresponsible and had to be quashed, Goodenough argued to friends and colleagues, for serious tragedies would occur otherwise when unwary parents adopted children who turned out to be feebleminded because of their poor ancestry. Goodenough and Terman lined up Hollingworth, who agreed with them anyway. By the fall of 1939, Goodenough, with Terman's blessing, had been able to recruit more authors who agreed with their point of view for the *Yearbook* than Stoddard had. Stacking the volume against the opposition was something that simply did not occur to Stoddard, Wellman, Skeels, or any of their associates. Yet Terman and Goodenough could think of little else with *Yearbook* preparations. As Goodenough put it to her friend Dr. Amanda Herring, a member of the Minnesota State Board of Control, in May 1939, "far from changing over to the Iowa point of view, I am in the process of collecting lots of data from here and elsewhere which seem calculated to set the Iowa people up a very high chimney."[22]

Not all whom Goodenough contacted agreed to join in the crusade against the Iowa scientists. Terman wrote Arnold Gesell at Yale for a contribution; it eventually came, but Gesell was not interested in stirring up the ruckus that Terman apparently wanted. Terman wrote his former student, Barbara Stoddard Burks, who had been such a major player in Terman's NSSE *Yearbook*, for another contribution. Now a research associate at the Carnegie Institution of Washington's Department of Genetics, a world-famous laboratory at Cold Spring Harbor, New York, Burks agreed with Terman that it would be unfortunate if the 1928 *Yearbook* were overturned "through some dramatic and highly publicized . . . but . . . provisional findings on young orphanage children and foster children"; the Iowa scientists had pushed their "interesting" argument too far, too fast on the basis of insufficient evidence. But she had nothing underway that was appropriate for the volume; nor was she any more interested in what seemed in beating a dead horse than was Gesell—or the vast majority of scientists in child development, for that matter. They were not at all alarmed by the Iowa work, which seemed more a tempest in a teapot than anything else.[23]

By summer 1939 Terman had his knives out for the Iowa scientists. At the seventy-seventh annual convention of the National Education Association meeting in San Francisco that July, Terman had set up a symposium on the forthcoming NSSE *Yearbook*, in which Stoddard could participate for but ten of the allotted sixty minutes and would be given no chance for rebuttal. Terman flailed Stoddard and his coworkers in the harshest possible tone. Terman insisted, for example, that either the Iowa findings with regard to the influence of the preschools on later academic performance were right, and that was the most important scientific discovery in the last thousand years, or they were a fraud. Terman attacked the methods of the Iowa scientists as unscientific and lacking rigor. Terman was especially angry about the Iowa studies of the feebleminded. He ridiculed the Skeels and Dye study as improbable and ridiculous; he derided with great sarcasm their claim that "moron nursemaids" could teach other "morons" to become mentally normal. It was quite obvious from the text of his remarks, and from other evidence, that Terman believed in the universality and fairness of his test and was indignant at any suggestion that it could not measure the IQs of all social castes and classes in the national population.[24]

That fall, Goodenough and Terman again attacked the Iowa scientists' credibility. They knew that they were possessed of the highest truth and that it was their sacred duty to battle the Iowans' naïveté and fraud. Yet in many respects they spoke chiefly to themselves. Not too many of their scientific colleagues across the country shared their alarm or anger; indifference, not involvement, was the attitude that most developmentalists took. Terman was asked to represent his views in an upcoming symposium on intelligence at the American Association for the Advancement of Science. He declined on grounds of his age and the prospect of a tedious train ride to Columbus, Ohio. He and Goodenough then went to considerable trouble to find an appropriate candidate, who turned out to be a fifth-to-seventh choice whom Goodenough had to tutor in the issues, and who clearly agreed to do the chore because he revered his mentor, Terman. At the same time, Goodenough kept feeding Terman rumors, passed along by former graduate students, of the Iowa faculty's methodological ineptitude in matters statistical, thus providing further proof, if such were needed, that Stoddard and his associates were nothing less than misguided fools doing scientific hackwork. When Goodenough was invited to give a talk on the IQ—and ultimately on the Iowa findings—at Columbia University that fall, Terman advised her to be none too polite, for the stakes were too high for civility. She obeyed.[25]

The Iowans' critics stepped up the pace of their attacks that fall. John E. Anderson, the Minnesota institute's director, published a statistical critique of the Iowa preschool and orphanage studies. His article mattered, for it summarized for the defenders of the reigning orthodoxy of the fixed IQ many of the statistical arguments against the Iowa findings available in the field's professional discourse. Taking his cue from the argument of Nancy Bayley and others at the California institute that IQ measurements of infants and young children might not be reliable predictors of later scores, Anderson insisted that reliable IQ measures came later rather than earlier in the developmental sequence. This position was precisely the reverse of the Iowa studies; Wellman and Skeels used early tests as the starting point for evaluation of IQ growth. Since the initial tests were most likely invalid, the validity of subsequent retests that the Iowa studies had used was undermined. He conceded that tests for preschool age children were more likely to be accurate than those for infants, but these instruments missed much. In effect, Anderson insisted that Stoddard and his associates did not understand the developmental sequence. Put more simply, Anderson took the orthodox maturation theory as the basis of his statistical critique. Since he believed that theory to be absolutely true and beyond refute, it followed that the Iowans' results were statistically invalid and substantively incorrect.[26]

Goodenough cheered her chief, Anderson, on and joined the fray with several articles and her Columbia talk that fall. She argued that the Iowa studies were irresponsible, for they legitimated false hopes that retarded children could be trained to be normal. Such tragedies must be avoided, she declared, cataloging the several claims the Iowa scientists made: the nursery school could boost true or innate intelligence; feebleminded children could be made normal by superior homes or even by "moron nursemaids in an institution for the feebleminded"; and normal children could be made into morons by an unstimulating environment. Goodenough declared that the Iowa IQ research depended on several questionable assumptions, including the predictive unreliability of intelligence tests for children under the age of three, the tests' vulnerability to statistical regression from errors in measurement and test administration, and the dangers of selection of samples that would spoil the results.

Goodenough made methodological, not substantive, criticisms beyond pointing to earlier studies by others. She dismissed the Iowa scientists' claims about wide variation in individual IQs as the phenomenon in group IQ testing in which problems in test administration produced errors in individual scores. Whether she would have grasped that they were talking about the behavior of individuals, not the measurement of groups, if they had been more clear on the point themselves remains impossible to say, of course; but the widespread disinterest in Macfarlane's clear—and widely disseminated—distinction between group and individual phenomena in the profession is strong evidence indeed for the near-inconceivable character of the Iowa scientists' argument for that age. So, for that matter, was their inability to make the distinction themselves. Nor can it be said that Goodenough or any other critic of the Iowa IQ work was less than well versed and highly competent in contemporary statistics and mental measurement. And it is highly suggestive that psycho-metricians had not developed formulas and methods for the purpose of tracking individuals over time but only for taking group measurements at specific points in time. It is difficult to escape the conclusion that matters were far more profound, and functioned on a deeper level, than the mere actions and happenstances of particular scientists.

Just before the NSSE's annual meeting in Saint Louis, where the Stoddard volume would be discussed, Goodenough told Terman that surely the *Yearbook* studies had left the Iowa scientists "without even a wooden leg to stand on." But the "amazing thing," she confided, was that their friends in Iowa City had still learned nothing and continued to talk in the old way, without understanding the meaning of statistical regression, let alone the huge inconsistencies in their arguments and assumptions. But no matter, she told Terman, with more prescience than either could have imagined; already, "I think," their work "is going the way of ESP and I strongly suspect that within a couple of years from now the whole matter will have passed into the same limbo of lost memories."[27]

The *Yearbook*, published in February 1940 in two husky volumes, provided the major arena for the controversy over the Iowa IQ research. As such, it was a highly complex artifact of its time. Most contributors upheld the traditional view that the IQ was fixed and that maturation was predetermined. And that majority interpreted studies done since the Terman volume, whether theirs or someone else's, as substantiating these mainstream theses. Yet the evidence adduced by numerous contributors did not necessarily contradict the Iowans' findings on IQ with regard to nursery school children or orphans nor did it sustain the conclusions and interpretations that the Iowans' critics themselves offered. Data and their interpretation, in other words, were not always synchronized.

In the first volume various experts reviewed work done since the Terman volume and offered opinions but no new evidence. In the main, the station's critics dominated the field and made the obvious points of developmental orthodoxy. John Anderson again insisted that the Iowa scientists, misunderstanding the developmental sequence, used invalid test scores of infants. Goodenough and Terman reiterated their statistical criticisms, which applied to errors in group statistics, not to the measurement of individuals. They were also outraged at the Iowa scientists' suggestion that the feebleminded could be made normal; Terman's anger was especially vitriolic, as if Stoddard and his colleagues had suggested that social class and caste lines were other than permanent and natural. Leonard Carmichael corroborated in detail Anderson's argument that the Iowa scientists misunderstood the developmental sequence because physiological maturation took place for more than a year before psychological maturation began, thus making the testing of infant IQs problematic in the extreme. Leta S. Hollingworth reviewed recent literature on groups of children of different racial backgrounds and on the mentally normal or subnormal, which, she said, proved that the IQ was innate and fixed. And so it went. No new insights or perspectives appeared about groups and individuals.

In the second volume, thirty-eight contributors wrote about twenty-six research projects, or summaries thereof, of which all but four were integrated into the *Yearbook*'s intellectual themes. Apart from Wellman's defense of her nursery school investigations, nine other studies of nursery schools appeared. The authors of eight of the nine declared themselves opposed to Wellman's findings, insisting that their research undercut hers; so far, the score was eight against and two for the Iowa position. The authors of all seven longitudinal studies were unsympathetic toward the Iowa findings in varying degrees, and the authors of six studies of adopted children were deeply divided.

Evidently, Terman and Goodenough had succeeded in their campaign against the Iowa scientists in the *Yearbook*. Stoddard and his colleagues knew their views mustered scant support among their coprofessionals. Stoddard responded by asking whether anyone who followed their procedures obtained results similar to theirs. He answered his own rhetorical question affirmatively. And he was right. Take the example of the nursery school investigations done for the volume. Elizabeth K. Starkweather and Katherine E. Roberts, of the Merrill-Palmer Institute in Detroit, Michigan, combed their institution's nursery school records to ascertain if the children had gained in IQs from the time of entrance to later periods while still in attendance. They copied Wellman's techniques and found similar results, with the 210 children whose records they could use experiencing, as a group, a mean gain of 5.5 IQ points while in nursery school. They also concluded that these gains seemed authentic; the children maintained them after leaving nursery school. And in a fashion similar to Wellman's original studies, they made nothing of the performances of individuals. Group measurements seemed all important. Nothing else made sense to them.

The eight other nursery school studies described, in each case in which the authors actually reported gains or losses in group IQs, gains on retesting from fall to spring. In that sense the authors replicated Wellman's methods fairly closely. And they did find gains in mean IQs. Thus nursery school studies at Western Reserve University showed a 2.63 point boost, at Rhode Island College of Education a 1.8 point difference, at Utah State College a 3.3 point gain, and at the California Institute of Child Welfare nursery schools a 14.3 point gain in IQ over two years. Even Florence L. Goodenough had to report a mean gain of 4.6 IQ points in her study of the Minnesota Institute of Child Welfare's nursery school, although she worked very hard to discount it as the mere artifact of selection. Harold E. Jones of the Berkeley institute was more open-minded than the other contributors, but he doubted the Iowa claims for the nursery schools, even after having found dramatic confirmation of them. The others, such as Goodenough, simply denied that the gains were important or signified anything at all. Grand theory in developmental science simply had too powerful a hold on these scientists for them to shake their disbelief in the Iowa findings.

And so it went with the longitudinal investigations. Arnold Gesell contributed to the *Yearbook* after all. He reiterated his support for the maturation theory in his report on thirty children, now in their teens, whose development he claimed to have followed in the last decade. He argued that it was possible to predict from the child's development at age two all aspects of growth, including mental growth. Leta S. Hollingworth and two colleagues reported on an investigation of 112 dull-normal children exposed to a specially enriched curriculum for three years. The children ranged in age from five-and-a-half to twelve years. Finding the mean gain to be 1.11 IQ points, they dismissed it as inconsequential, even though they admitted that there were extreme variations in the IQs of some individuals and that half gained and half lost IQ points in the period of the investigation. The children were not of preschool age, but the authors nevertheless insisted that the study undermined Wellman's work by showing that special schools were no substitute for good brains. Several other authors of longitudinal investigations failed to replicate one or more of the methods the Iowa scientists used, yet insisted that their studies overturned the Iowa results.

The Iowa scientists won some support. The authors of the other three longitudinal studies raised significant questions about the maturation theory and the notion of the fixed IQ. Nancy Bayley of the Institute of Child Welfare at Berkeley contributed two articles from the Berkeley Growth Study. Unlike her colleague Jean Walker Macfarlane, Bayley did not repudiate either the fixed IQ thesis or the maturation theory. She argued from her data that there was relatively little variation from one test to another for the group, that test consistency and predictability increased with age, and that early tests did not correlate well with later ones—standard arguments for orthodoxy in the field. But Bayley supported the Iowa research to the extent of noting, for those scientists concerned with the growth of individual children, that a quarter of the children changed 10 or more IQ points on retesting, and an equal number changed 17 or more IQ points over three years. Different children had their own distinctive growth spurts. Not all was linear and progressive.

In her second essay, Bayley reviewed the statistical correlations between mental test scores and other variables—measurements of health, size, and bodily proportions, skeletal maturity, socioeconomic status, and attendance at nursery school—to explain the wide variations of individual mental growth. Bayley concluded each child developed according to his or her individualized inherent characteristics, and thus came about as close to saying that individuals, not groups, were the stuff of natural and social reality without consciously repudiating the mainstream's orthodoxy of group determinism. She warned against making facile judgments. In fact, she was not entirely satisfied with either the mainstream arguments or those of the Iowa scientists. Bayley's institute colleague Marjorie Honzik summarized the Berkeley Guidance Study's findings by noting the many individual differences in growth curves of all individuals, thus agreeing with Bayley. Another longitudinal investigation, done at Teachers College, attempted to probe whether IQs gained over time, but the children were enrolled in the elementary grades, not a preschool, and, in any instance, the results were mixed. Hence it cannot be said that no one could replicate the findings that the Iowa scientists had made. The question was a matter of interpretation, not empirical discovery (or intellectual fraud) per se.

The Iowa research won the most support among the contributors who conducted investigations of adoptive children placed in foster homes in which parents' backgrounds were superior to those of the biological parents. Not surprisingly, those who criticized the Iowa orphanage studies were academics, not clinical psychologists or social workers with long-term experience working in eleemosynary institutions, and, conversely, those clinical psychologists who followed the Iowa methods, sometimes skeptically at first, essentially corroborated the findings of Skeels and Skodak.

In the volume's conclusion, Skeels, Wellman, and Stoddard vigorously defended their positions. Skeels insisted that such statistical artifacts as regression and selection could not explain the large gains or losses that he had reported in his work at the orphanage and with the so-called moron maidens. When Goodenough or others insisted that the biological parents of the adopted children must have had something approximating a normal background, Skeels insisted that these critics simply did not understand the social realities of rural Iowa, in which, for example, a tenth-grade education meant virtually nothing with automatic promotion in Iowa one-room schools, and so on. Skeels insisted that intelligence was more responsive to environmental influences than had been commonly acknowledged before. In particular was the home environment crucial, he continued. It was essential that parents take care in providing sufficient mental stimulation for their children. Wellman too decried the artificiality of the statistical arguments that Goodenough, Terman, and others had used against her studies. Indeed she challenged them to stop arguing from their armchairs and to study children in real life. Stoddard dismissed the arguments of such contributors as Anderson, Terman, and Goodenough. He also pointed out that the Iowa findings did not stand alone, as their critics had charged. There was plenty of support for the Iowa research in the present volume, he insisted, pointing to the preschool studies in which gains in IQ points were actually reported, and in several other studies, such as the longitudinal ones at California. It is notable that the Iowans did not make the point that they observed wide variations in IQ gains in individuals upon retesting, nor did they present their data as anything other than group measurements.[28]

After the NSSE's meeting that February in Saint Louis, Stoddard went on the offensive. He had fun, to be sure. He pointed out that others besides the staff at Iowa had reported gains in IQs for nursery school children from spring to fall. Helen Thompson Woolley had made that claim as early as 1925, and, he continued, in the 1940 *Yearbook*, all who bothered to ascertain whether there were group gains or losses in median IQs found them. In more than a few studies, there was good evidence that individual children varied enormously in IQ scores over time. Obviously, Stoddard now understood the difference between group measurements at a specific point in time and measurements of individuals over time. So did Skeels, Wellman, and the others. Apparently the distinction became clear to them in the wake of the controversy over the NSSE *Yearbook*. Their new studies eventually contained this distinction. But as the above analysis of the *Yearbook* suggests, that distinction, and all its implications, had yet to persuade the majority of their colleagues, let alone find them a niche in their science's professional discourse.[29]

Soon the controversy was over. Statistician Quinn McNemar of Stanford, one of Terman's protégés, delivered the final blow. McNemar focused on what he called the gross statistical flaws of the Iowa studies. In thirty densely written and intensely argued pages, McNemar took them apart with a running commentary on their sloppy techniques and, at best, naive statistical assumptions; he accused the Iowa scientists of a multitude of statistical errors, including regression toward the mean on retesting, selection of a population, and inflated *N*s, or the practice of counting the same individuals more than once in the retesting sequences. And McNemar angrily dismissed the argument that the feebleminded young child could be made normal in a normal environment, and a normal child could be driven to feeblemindedness in a subnormal milieu. Evidently, McNemar took it for granted that the IQ was fixed in the individual. His statistical criticisms made a lot of sense to contemporaries. According to much subsequent oral history testimony, it was the charges that the Iowa work was statistically inept or worse that caused most developmentalists to dismiss it entirely.[30]

Thus passed the high-water mark of Stoddard's decade-long campaign to reorient the nation's schools so as to reconstruct American society. It cannot be said that the Iowa studies made unique empirical discoveries. Others had found wide variation in IQs among very young children, including Jean Walker Macfarlane at Berkeley, many *Yearbook* contributors, and some social workers, at least one of whom who had been skeptical initially. As for arguments and evidence of the influence of an impoverishing environment on the mental development of young children, numerous respectable workers in the field, such as Mandel Sherman of the University of Chicago and Otto Klineberg of Columbia University, had published important studies in the thirties whose conclusions agreed, at least in broad outline, with those of the Skodak and Skeels studies.[31]

Yet we have seen repeatedly that these dissenting messages made little or no sense to contemporaries, and that, more often than not, most of the dissenters themselves were decidedly unclear about what they had observed. More was involved than met the eye. Child development had just taken shape as a scientific discipline in the early thirties. As such, it played a vital, if not necessarily well understood, role in the intellectual and scientific life of the day. It was especially crucial in the interwar years to the articulation and elaboration of human evolutionary theory, in its biological and its cultural aspects. The first important step in this reorientation of human evolutionary theory was the heredity-environment controversy of the 1920s, the result of which was a new nature cum nurture paradigm, which became the basis for discussions of the causes of evolution and variation—for, in short, macroevolutionary theoretical issues. The second crucial step was the crystallization of the field of child development, for that science was to serve as the basis for the articulation of microevolutionary theoretical issues, that is, the evolution *and* development of individuals, of particular subpopulations, and of groups more generally. What appeared at first glance to be no more than a kind of updated embryology of intellect and character (in terms of the jargon of classical evolutionary theory) was actually more important than that.[32]

Child development was of undeniable importance to human evolutionary theory because it purported to explain how and why organisms, especially humans but any species, developed from conception to maturity. In addition to its powerful scientific implications, child development mattered enormously to social policy, for it had much to say about the development of particular groups in the national population. By positing group determinism, and spinning out the notions of the fixed IQ and of predetermined maturation, mainstream developmentalists articulated a profoundly conservative vision of the American national population. Herein was the crucial importance of the Iowa orphanage studies from the standpoint of social class and caste in middle-class American culture. If it could be demonstrated that so-called morons were made, not born, then other fundamental questions could be raised about the evaluation of particular groups in the population.

Ultimately, child development was more than a mere part of human evolutionary theory. It was also a part of the tacit social and cultural understandings that knit together the social order, and, as such, it had explosive implications for the distribution of status, power, wealth, and justice in society. If the Iowans and their allies were really right about the kind of individualism in nature and society that they advocated, then the social network of groups and their relative positions to one another could be regarded as cruel, arbitrary, and oppressive. Some contemporaries of Terman's dismissed his intense anger at the Iowa "moron studies" as the result of an old man's silly crotchets. Perhaps so. Or perhaps Terman knew only too well the implications of the Iowa work. Certainly there was a sense of outrage in his critiques and his private correspondence, indicating that somehow Stoddard and his colleagues had crossed some line that they should not have, that they had betrayed their science, their profession, and their social class. From this historical distance, we can only speculate about such matters.

Lewin's work escaped the firestorm of criticism that the Iowa IQ studies had received. At first this appears odd. After all, Lewin supported the work fully. It would be difficult to imagine a more searching philosophical and methodological criticism of psychometrics à la the mainstream than Lewin's proposals for Galilean psychology. Stoddard and Lewin in particular were quite articulate in calling for the emancipation of psychology from contemporary biology's reductionist, determinist, and positivist assumptions. It was only when psychology could deal with the psychological level of discourse, free of the dead hand of physics, biology, chemistry, and the like, they argued, that there would be a true psychological science.

But on balance Lewin's treatment at the hands of his American colleagues was not so peculiar. It is easy, but erroneous, to ascribe this to Lewin's great personal charm, his stunning brilliance, and the enormous sympathy he had among American psychologists for being a refugee from Hitler's Nazi barbarism. Such personal factors mattered, doubtless, but they were not fundamental. Stoddard too was highly intelligent and well liked personally in many quarters. Lewin's work on groups and individuals, as in the democratic atmospheres and the regression projects, appeared to have different implications from that of Wellman and Skeels on IQ variance, and appeared less threatening to the body politic than did theirs. And the very ahistoricity of Lewin's topological psychology helped such hard-nosed determinists as Goodenough and Gesell to accept his work; to the mainstream thinkers in the field, time was the crucial dimension. By staying entirely in the immediate present, Lewin did not price his theories out of the professional market. And his political nostrums as represented in the democratic atmospheres projects flattered American cultural and social values. About his only opponents, and they tended to mutter among themselves about Lewin, were such devotees of classic behaviorist learning theory as Clark Hull of Yale, who was not interested in behavior that could not be explained with rigid, biologically oriented stimulus-response formulas.[33]

It did not help Skeels and Wellman with regard to their views on the IQ that the vast majority of their colleagues were indifferent to the issue, believing that it had long since been settled and any controversy had been recently (and rightly) quashed by Goodenough and McNemar. In such a context, in which only a handful participated in the debate and most did not care, it was all too easy for Goodenough and Terman to prevail. Some workers continued to mine the vein that Wellman and Skeels had opened, including Wellman herself throughout the 1940s. Even though she continued to develop an increasingly intricate and differentiated notion of the environment and its influences on mental development, it was all for naught. Few among academic researchers in child development cared about Wellman's work—or anyone else's who took up that line of argument. The only constituencies for the IQ arguments of the Iowa scientists were clinical psychologists and social workers, who were by definition occupants of a lower caste in the professional hierarchy insofar as the academicians of the field were concerned. In a very real sense, one could see the outline of the old split between the advocates of child welfare and child development in that debate.[34]

The group-individual problem with regard to the Iowa psychometric studies flared up once more. In 1944, Wellman and a graduate student published a reassessment of the original data on IQ losses and gains in the Davenport project, in which they reiterated its original conclusions, that the children in the control group lost IQ points and those in the experimental group barely avoided the same fate. The 1940s were a transitional time for the use of statistics in the social and behavioral sciences. Increasingly, scientists used inferential, not descriptive, statistics. Inferential statistics could discern whether a result yielded by descriptive statistics was significant or merely due to chance, whereas a descriptive statistic merely gave a result. The Iowa scientists, like most of their national colleagues then, often used inferential statistics as if they were descriptive statistics; it was as if they were pinning a medal on a specific product of statistical calculation, as in their naive use of the critical ratio when assessing changes in IQ scores.[35]

The next year Quinn McNemar of Stanford published a short critique of this study. He had reanalyzed the raw data from the preschools and the orphanages that Beth Wellman had provided him in the *Yearbook* controversy. He argued that the Iowa scientists should use inferential, not descriptive, statistics to assess their data. In his brief note, he used covariance, or analysis of similarity and dissimilarity of Pearsonian coefficients of correlation over time. He argued that long-term residence in the orphanage did not produce substantial IQ losses, nor did the preschool tend to counteract the orphanage's damaging environment. To prove his point that there were neither important gains nor losses, McNemar then analyzed the correlations of the test scores of the children in the control and experimental groups in the Davenport study. He did find that there were plausible correlations to substantiate the gains in IQs when he used covariance to reanalyze the correlations among repeated IQ scores of the experimental group, but dismissed them with the more standard objection that one could not tell whether these were due to the preschool experience or to increased rapport between examiner and examinee. Then he turned to the question of IQ losses. Here he worked very hard to deny these phenomena by discussing the IQ losses of the several clusters or aggregates of control children. Thus there were eight children in the Davenport control group with 839 or more days of residence who were largely responsible for the huge IQ losses, as reflected in the large negative correlation of IQ scores of $-.40$, whereas there were thirty-six other control children with up to 686 days of residence who experienced the "trivial" loss of $-.04$. He interpreted these "facts" (he did not think of them as processed data but as real events), and other "facts" about other clusters of children in the study, as overturning the Davenport study's general themes. Revealingly, McNemar ended his argument with discussions of individual cases to buttress his thesis.[36]

McNemar won the day in the scientific profession. Most scientists were impressed by his seemingly proficient use of covariance. And there the matter rested until it was reopened in the 1960s. Most national colleagues, already well prepared to think that only group measurements mattered, concluded that the Iowa station's scientists, whatever their contributions might have been in other areas, were a bit amiss in the field of psychometrics. The most charitable reaction among many was that the Iowa scientists were deluded by their sentimental politics and naive understanding of statistics. And, indeed, the station's research program in psychometrics went into decline, with only Beth Wellman running it. She died in 1952 after a long and ghastly battle with cancer.

But matters were more complex than they appeared. With hindsight we can gain a rather different understanding than contemporaries could attain. What the Davenport study and McNemar's critique showed was something that no one could grasp (or, perhaps, wanted to admit) then: that such institutions had different kinds of inmates, those who had normal intelligence and those who had below-normal intelligence, and that the orphanage's cultural milieu pushed all children whose intelligence was still developing toward the lowest common denominator. In other words, not all groups were the same, and not all individuals were interchangeable—there were glaring differences among the institution's inmates.

The Iowa scientists tried to say all this with their qualitative discussions in the original monograph of the condition of the children in the orphanage. But they had neither the statistical expertise nor methods to show what they had found, and, in truth, no such instruments were then available. All they could do was make the observation that relatively normal individuals were experiencing developmental disaster, and others belonged in an institution for the retarded. They could not explain their horrifying discovery within the parameters of their professional discourse, or, indeed, in any public discourse then available to them.

In fact, there was no good way to represent, with the statistical tools then available, what Skeels and his associates had found at the Davenport orphanage. Covariance, for example, is a method used to measure the likeness of individuals over time, but it assumes that the individuals do not interact and that the differences among them at the initial point of measurement are zero—both highly fallacious assumptions in the case at hand. The case that McNemar and his supporters had against the Iowa scientists had some strengths, to be sure. Selection, or the adopting out of the more intelligent individual children from the groups, skewed the results; that was a valid criticism. The Iowa scientists were indeed naive and ill-informed about many aspects of statistics, and they made mistakes. McNemar made serious mistakes as well. For example, he and his allies regarded a Binet scale as one would a temperature gauge, so that a child with an IQ of, say, 60 points, was assumed to be half as bright as a child with an IQ of 120 points. We know today that assumption is absurd. Indeed, it was perhaps the unspoken or even unrealized assumption of most mainstream testers and developmentalists that the function of group measurements—averages, means, modes, Gaussian distributions, and the like—was to finesse that very point. With group measurements, if one case did not prove one's point, another one would—or so the reasoning most likely went. McNemar's note, and his resorting to individual cases to prove his thesis, simply validated the Iowa scientists' most important discovery, that there were disparate, radically different clusters of individual children within the orphanage, some already with circumscribed lives, others whose lives were clearly at risk.[37]

CHAPTER SEVEN

THE PERILS OF PROFESSIONALISM

By the early forties there were signs
aplenty that the nation's mood had become more nationalistic and conservative
since the yeastier days of the twenties and of New Deal reformism. Throughout the 1930s the New Deal delivered relatively little for the improvement of
the lives of ordinary children. And the congressional elections of 1938 marked
the point at which opponents of FDR's New Deal programs gained control of
the House and Senate. As historian LeRoy Ashby noted in a review of the
welfare of American children in the 1930s and 1940s, "Children and youth
were not only absent from much of the national agenda . . . but they were also
largely hidden from public view except as symbols and abstractions."[1]

Symptomatic of the troubled times for the welfare of America's children was
the 1940 White House Conference on Child Health and Protection. Held
every decade since Theodore Roosevelt's presidency, the White House Conferences represented a technique of symbolic politics characteristic of the new
American national culture that had gelled in the later nineteenth century.
Involved was the creation of an institution—an agency, a commission, or the
like—whose purpose was to address itself to a particular social problem and to
propose solutions for it, leaving implementation of solutions up to the Congress, or, if the dogma of separation of powers required it, to lesser governmental
and public bodies. Such institutional structures and arrangements guaranteed
that public discussion would flow through the federal government while nevertheless placing ultimate practical responsibility for change with the concerned
constituencies themselves. Often, this provided a safety valve for public discon-
tent at minimal cost in terms of expansion of the central government itself.

The White House Conferences gathered together concerned citizens and professional experts alike for a few days of discussions and recommendations for action. Sometimes a concrete product resulted, such as the federal Children's Bureau, which Congress created in 1912 to gather information on child health and protection for possible legislation, or the federal Year of the Child, whose purpose was to legitimate those outside the federal government to take action on behalf of children. Clearly the White House Conference with the most ambitious apparatus was that held in 1930 under Herbert Hoover's sponsorship. Hoover was famous, of course, for his concern for children. The conference he authorized seemed designed to further his reputation of interest in child welfare. It also was a manifestation of the style of national political problem solving of that era of which he was so representative a champion. The conference gathered a large number of participants. Experts wrote all manner of reports for action on a multitude of social problems. The 1930 conference was then organized to implement Hoover's notions of federalism, in which the federal government became the sounding board and moral authority for action on social problems that alliances of citizens, experts, and local public and private institutions would then address and resolve. Perhaps not surprisingly, there were few concrete results.[2]

The 1940 conference was a far less ambitious affair. Preoccupied as the Roosevelt administration was with the complicated domestic and foreign policy issues and a reelection campaign, it promised little and delivered less to the conferees. The conference's theme, "Children in a Democracy," was quintessential New Deal wordsmithing, crafted with a practiced eye toward maximum public consumption. The conference's final report could be regarded as one of the most advanced public statements yet by any American public body on issues of child health, protection, and welfare. In a complex mixture of essays, chapters, and position papers, conference participants discussed in multiple ways a host of serious problems, including racial oppression and discrimination, poverty, women's issues, social services, unemployment, disparities in regional wealth and resources, among many others. Here was a long list of issues that the left-liberal members of the New Deal coalition believed so crucial to address. And in most instances, unlike the Hoover conferees, the Rooseveltians outdid their master with long, donnish pieces in which they presented solutions to social problems that, half a century later, have remained mostly proposals.

The conference's theme was vintage contemporary left-liberalism with some genuflections to that decade's fashionable celebrations of hearth and homeland. The family was to be the incubator of democracy. It was the primary social institution that taught such values as self-reliance, cooperation, and democracy. Economic democracy was, of course, fundamental to all other kinds of democracy, whether political, religious, racial, or cultural. Economic problems still threatened the nation's social fabric. They created poverty, poor education, inadequate housing, health, and other public services. Once all Americans could enjoy the benefits of a fully prosperous modern industrial democracy, the conferees insisted, social problems such as racial and religious discrimination would end. Indeed, in the articles addressed to the problems of discrimination on the basis of class and caste, most contributors insisted on a politics of individualism, in which each and every individual in the nation was given equal opportunity without regard to race, religion, or national origins—the credo of the left-liberal elements of the New Deal coalition and certainly that of such figures as George D. Stoddard and his allies within the field of child development. Little resulted from the 1940s conference save an airing of what passed for fairly progressive political proposals for that era.[3]

Child development as a field had changed since the early twenties. Then there were but a handful of organizations devoted to research on children, notably the Iowa station itself, the Merrill-Palmer School in Detroit, and Arnold Gesell's psycho-clinic in the Yale medical school. The child welfare mentality still dominated the field and defined the issues. By the late twenties, thanks to Rockefeller largess, there were numerous research organizations, such as those at Iowa, Minnesota, and California, in child development, as well as other such enterprises within universities, such as the Harvard Growth Study and Stanford's genius project with Terman. From the Commonwealth Fund and other sources, the mental hygiene movement helped spawn the child guidance movement in the same decade. The field was becoming both an academic profession and, to a lesser extent, a scientific discipline.

In the thirties the number of programs in child development grew at such universities as Michigan and Chicago. The child guidance movement, like that of child development, expanded to fill its niches in the national market for such services, essentially as a network of private child-helping institutions to serve clients and constituencies not inclined to use public institutions. Both child development and child guidance became professional scientific subcultures, with centers for research and training, access to resources for research and public outreach, professional organizations and journals, and the like. They also had developed professional ideologies to address thorny issues of their relations with their patrons, clients, and research populations, not to mention with policy institutions, whether governmental or eleemosynary in character.

Furthermore, by the early forties each field had developed a body of thought—a discipline, more precisely—with its own distinctive controlling assumptions, methods, fundamental principles, research traditions, and paradigms. Each had social and political implications that were profoundly conservative. In child development, as we have seen, the central notion was the parallelism of physical, physiological, and psychobiological maturation in the individual. In child guidance, theorists and care givers alike insisted that it was important to redirect or channel the patient's impulses into socially approved patterns of behavior.[4]

In sum, child science was settling in as an established science and profession in the American scientific and academic system. Researchers were coming into the field who were just as interested in the child as an object of scientific research as others were in the child's well-being. And, as the debate over the Iowa IQ studies suggested, among the professionals, the researchers outnumbered the activists by a very large ratio. It was not true that no professional could be an activist, but increasingly few were. As for the kind of lay activism that characterized the women's child welfare movement of the early 1900s and 1910s, it had not so much dissipated as had been redirected into new channels. In particular did the experts reach their constituents through the mass media, particularly magazines such as *Parents Magazine* or *Better Homes and Gardens*, various syndicated advice columns in the newspapers, and the books by experts on child rearing and development.

Probably the child scientist with the greatest public audience in the later thirties and early forties was Arnold L. Gesell, the field's most prolific popularizer. He wrote wondrously clear books about the child. As might have been expected from one of the major architects of the maturation theory, Gesell told his readers that growth was a ceaseless process from birth to death, a succession of distinct periods in the life cycle.

As a specialist in infancy and early childhood, Gesell offered a detailed portrait of infant maturation at, for example, four, sixteen, twenty-eight, forty, fifty-two, and eighty weeks, at which times behavior traits of a typical child appeared or, in other cases, progressed, all in proper sequence. He synthesized the work of Watson, Coghill, Carmichael, and others into a behavioristic morphology, in which form dictated function. Clearly the infant constituted a whole that was greater than or different from the sum of its parts, and the parts were themselves interrelated yet discrete as well. Gesell insisted over and over again in his popular pieces that the child was an individual and should be considered as such. By this he meant only that each child possessed a moral individuality, not unlike the moral equality that the nation's founding fathers had approved in the Declaration of Independence. In practice, like every other mainstream developmental scientist, Gesell dealt with group categories and measurements, his term for group being the slightly anachronistic notion of type: in it, he retained many elements of pre-1920s typological thinking (as about species) in the biological sciences. In both his popular and technical works, Gesell forthrightly advanced the maturation theory with its conservative implications. He explained both mental and physical development according to the maturation theory.[5]

These were times for battening down the hatches. New departures in science and social policy seemed but remote possibilities. Even Lawrence K. Frank, for two decades the single most influential foundation official in the field of child development, had had his wings clipped. In October 1936, he left the General Education Board and, therefore, the world of Rockefeller philanthropy and any position of large influence in the field. Parent education had by the forties become upstaged by the mass media. In any event, the field's first casualty occurred around the country whenever developmentalists had to balance their institutional budgets.

But there was more. The Second World War itself wreaked havoc with the profession. The massive mobilization of more than fifteen million adult Americans plucked from developmental science's various institutional bases a large fraction of specialists for war duties. Relatively few saw combat, but many were distracted from the field, part- or full-time. At least one contemporary believed that wartime mobilization reduced the critical mass of professionals below what might be considered the minimum standard to keep the field functional as a scientific profession. Emblematic of that problem was the failure of the field's professional organization, the Society for Research in Child Development, to meet between 1940 and 1946; furthermore, memberships lapsed, the society's treasury became bare, and its three journals experienced severe difficulties making ends meet and getting issues out. In a word, the field was contracting for reasons within and without the science and profession.[6]

And, indeed, more conservative times seemed in store even for the Iowa Child Welfare Research Station. In mid-October 1941, a discouraged Kurt Lewin wrote his good friend Horace Kallen, of the New School for Social Research, that the "news with me is that Dr. Stoddard goes to New York [State] as Commissioner of Education. You will find him an excellent man, progressive, liberal, and realistic." But "for the Child Welfare Station it is awful. We cannot get as good a man again and I really don't know what I shall do," he concluded glumly. Stoddard's new post was a bully pulpit indeed for this warrior for the liberal wing of the Democratic party and the progressive education movement. As commissioner of education for the entire state of New York, he supervised an annual budget of $120 million and the entire school system of the nation's largest state, from private preschools to the state's colleges and universities. And, in a sense, it was the perfect appointment for Stoddard, for his powers and responsibilities were to advise, to lead, and to inspire, rather than to administer institutions. Lewin had reason to be unhappy. Stoddard was a rarity among the field's leaders, a liberal activist with the scientific credentials to direct the Iowa Child Welfare Research Station; who would the university administration appoint to replace him? Lewin in particular fretted that a mere specialist would succeed Stoddard, and the Iowa station would never be the same again. In that judgment he was absolutely right: the station's history changed course. But its intellectual singularity had not yet run its course.[7]

The man appointed to replace Stoddard was Robert R. Sears, who arrived in the fall of 1942. Thirty-three years old then, Sears won his position in the fashion common in the times. Mark A. May, director of Yale's Institute of Human Relations, recommended Sears to Stoddard. He told Stoddard that Sears was a good researcher, an excellent teacher, and a man blessed with public relations skills. Stoddard was impressed by Sears, and doubtless he prevailed upon the new university president, Virgil M. Hancher, to appoint him. In any event, Hancher had just appointed another Yale product whom May had recommended for the chairmanship of the psychology department, Kenneth W. Spence, and he was favorably disposed toward May's evaluations. In this way were major university appointments often or even usually made then.[8]

Born in 1908 in Palo Alto, California, the son of Jessie Brundage Sears, a professor of education at Stanford University, Sears's early interests were literary, not scientific. Indeed, as an adolescent he had more than a nodding acquaintance with the young John Steinbeck; Sears always admired Steinbeck's ability to portray human emotions via literary means. Sears majored in English until he was a senior at Stanford, when he switched to psychology as a field more in tune with his interest in understanding human emotions. Quickly he came to Terman's attention, then head of Stanford's psychology department, probably because he was a participant in the genius project. Terman persuaded Sears to take his doctorate in psychology at Yale, which he did in 1932; he worked with Clark L. Hull.

Hull was an arch-behaviorist who equated his role in psychology with that of Newton in physics. He was interested chiefly in working out rigid stimulus-response behavioral learning theories, a bundle of ideas with obvious affinities with the then-crystallizing maturation theory in developmental science. Like the developmentalists, Hull and his behaviorist disciples were holists who insisted that the organism was an entity that was greater than or different from the sum of its parts; like them as well, Hullians were determinists who, in assuming that all actions were interrelated yet distinct, believed in their balance, symmetry, and predictability. As reductionists, they were interested in predicting the smallest possible units of behavior. Above all, Hull wanted to create a science of conditioning and learning that would enable him to predict behavior at all levels.[9]

Sears found Hull's focus on experiments with laboratory rats too rigid and unrelated to the real world of human emotions for his taste. Sears was a holist like Hull, in that he viewed reality as a system of systems of distinct yet interrelated elements. Yet Sears thought Hull's work artificial, unreal, too academic, and boring, pedantic, pettifogging, and trivial. It did not deal with the real world of actual human beings. It was the man's message, not the man, that Sears found wanting. In his first position, at the University of Illinois, Sears taught abnormal psychology, which exposed him to Sigmund Freud's psychodynamic notions of human emotions. Here were real-life actions, such large-scale emotions and behavior sequences as projection, frustration, displacement, and aggression, among others. Sears wanted to subject these Freudian mechanisms to precise measurement and experimentation. He sought answers to such questions as whether people in the real world repressed their feelings, projected their inadequacies on others, or became aggressive toward others because of their inner frustrations. He had serious reservations about Freudian method; Freud was too mentalistic, too much of a clinician, and not enough of an experimenter, among Sears's other objections. Sears had a strong interest in psychological theory, just as Stoddard and Lewin had. Indeed, Sears had known Lewin since the great man taught at Stanford in the early thirties.[10]

Thus Sears found his intellectual identity as a psychologist. He soon became a theorist in the new field of personality studies, attempting to use those elements of Freudian psychodynamic theory that could be verified through the most rigorous experimental methods. Soon Sears was putting Freudian ideas to the acid test of experimentation. In addition to his widely cited paper on hypnosis, he published articles on projection and repression while still at Illinois. His experiment with projection illuminated his approach. He tested Freud's theory that individuals without insight into themselves typically projected those unpleasant wishes not compatible with their personas upon others.

Using rating scales, college fraternity members answered with regard to themselves and others for such traits as stinginess, disorderliness, and obstinacy, Sears found that his experiment worked out perfectly. Those fraternity members who lacked insight into themselves characteristically projected their failings onto others. Indeed, Sears was so proud of his results that he wrote Sigmund Freud about them. Freud never responded.[11]

Following a wholesale reorganization of the Institute of Human Relations at Yale in 1936, and the appointment of Mark A. May as the new director, Sears left Illinois for Yale. He was delighted. Here was the chance to work with Hull as a colleague, for Hull was clearly the institute's intellectual leader. Despite his earlier reservations, Sears thought Hull thoroughly capable of creating a unified social science, the mandate that the Rockefeller Foundation had given the institute. Initially, all went well, and in Hull's seminar, discussions centered for some time on Young Turk Sears's notions of creating a behavioristic basis for Freudian psychodynamics and, through that, for a rigorous experimental science of the human personality. Within a couple of years, however, Hull and Sears drifted apart. Sears discovered that the flaws he had found earlier in Hull's work reappeared in his new learning theory. It was too simple, too rigid, too removed from the real world of people, and it was deterministic. And Sears did not share the orthodox behaviorist's group determinism, an inheritance from Watson, Coghill, and Carmichael. Sears wanted to create a holistic stimulus-response dynamic experimental psychology from which could be derived scientific principles about how and why people loved, hated, competed, shared, became frustrated, and responded in other such large units of behavior. Sears began working on a behavioristic approach to human personality theory as a field of experimental research, not as what he would have contemptuously regarded as armchair guesswork. In an early study, he and a colleague tested the hypothesis that the strength of the instigation to aggression varied directly with the amount of interference with the frustrated goal-response. They correlated lynchings in the American South with the ups and downs of the nation's business cycle. There were other such projects as well.[12]

Sears's major work before coming to Iowa was *Frustration and Aggression* (1939), a team effort with six colleagues at the Yale Institute. Hull was interested only in a deterministic learning theory, in which one posited the circumstances under which the organism exhibited behavior in response to new situations. The institute's Young Turks, including Sears, found this too narrow. They wanted to develop action theory, in which behavior of any sort is explained. Kurt Lewin and George Stoddard were developing action theory and action research at the Iowa Child Welfare Research Station at the same time, but they were using it as a basis for stimulating desirable social change; the mere explanation of behavior no longer sufficed for them. For Sears and his colleagues at the Yale institute, tellingly, action research and action theory instead served the academic purpose of accounting for action in the present. And they believed Sigmund Freud to be, for that day, the outstanding action theorist available to them because of his complex theories of psychodynamics. Thus communal interest in action theory at the institute was inspired by Freud, who had developed the most elaborate theory of the relations between frustration and aggression, and from John Dollard, a social anthropologist at the institute whose *Caste and Class in a Southern Town* (1935) applied Freudian notions of frustration and aggression to race relations in the American South.

After a year and a half of intensive discussions and experiments, Sears and his colleagues wrote *Frustration and Aggression* (1939), with Sears as the senior editor and writer. The book was an elaborate contribution to action theory and purported to explain the dynamics of individual psychology. Its basic hypothesis was that aggression always resulted from frustration. After discussing definitions and principles, Sears and his colleagues applied their hypothesis to such topics as socialization, crime, and adolescence. Sears and his colleagues were not rigid determinists and behaviorists; they freely admitted the role of contingency in human affairs. Their stimulus-response formulations were always cast in terms of if-then propositions, taking full measure of the complexities of culture and society. They were not biological reductionists. As almost all scientists interested in the matter would have said, the expression of the emotions in the individual is always dependent on an almost infinite number of complex, interactive variables.[13]

Frustration and Aggression was the first statement of the school of social learning in dynamic social psychology. According to John Dollard and Neal E. Miller, who published an important statement in 1941, imitation was a cultural, not an instinctive, process. For evidence, they discussed the ways in which children learned in society. Their approach was thoroughly appropriate in an age in which scientists believed that the cultural and the natural were interdependent variables. If natural scientists had to take account of society and culture, they argued, so social scientists had to understand the psychobiological mechanisms that enabled the individual to participate in the social order. Dollard and Miller proposed a synthesis of individual and group behavior theory that embraced the biological and cultural aspects of human nature and conduct—the culture and personality continuum (and dichotomy) that the anthropologist Alfred L. Kroeber first suggested in 1917.[14]

This was the intellectual baggage that Sears brought with him to Iowa. He was as committed as were Stoddard and Lewin to the construction of theories of human nature and conduct that were, from Sears's own perspective, not reducible to deterministic psychodynamics, after the fashion of their colleagues in developmental science. Above all, Sears did not accept the fatalistic notion of the meaning of group identity for the individual that was so dominant in the field of child development then. But he shared the notion, common to that age, that individuals, if distinct, were nevertheless interchangeable. In several senses, he was a thoroughly appropriate replacement for Stoddard. All three— Stoddard, Lewin, and Sears—wanted to demonstrate in their work and that of their associates that psychological and mental phenomena existed as a fact in nature and society and were not reducible to some other level of discourse and function. On scientific matters, the differences between Sears on the one hand, and Lewin and Stoddard on the other, were more apparent than real. Yet Sears differed from Stoddard and Lewin in one important respect. He did not so much disagree with their political views then as assume that science existed for science's sake; he was a thoroughly professional scientist with no particular political agenda. Put another way, he took a minimalist view of action research and action theory; science existed to solve scientific problems, not to make the world into a better place. And that was to make a crucial difference in the history of the Iowa Child Welfare Research Station, even with all the fruitful and creative work Lewin, Sears, and their colleagues did on individual and group psychology in the 1940s.[15]

Sears soon discovered that there were problems aplenty at the Iowa station. The faculty, so illustrious in the field in which he was now preparing himself, was not a cohesive intellectual community. Indeed, morale was low; faculty tended to work in their own little spheres with their graduate students. He regarded Lewin as the most important researcher there, and was taken aback that Lewin had long since finished his work with children. During Sears's first year he spent much time reading up on the literature of child development, engaging in public relations work by giving radio talks and speeches before various women's groups, holding first-ever staff meetings, attempting to interest his colleagues in group projects to break down their mutual isolation, and evaluating the faculty and graduate students in an effort to assess the station's future.[16]

A year after he arrived Sears submitted to President Hancher the plan for reorganizing the station that the president had requested upon his arrival. Sears recommended that the Iowa station's research programs be narrowed in focus, consolidating what was once a general research organization into one that was far more specialized. No longer should the Iowa Child Welfare Research Station be the pioneer, defining the whole field and investigating in all its various subareas. It should specialize in a limited program and do it well. Not surprisingly, the focus he chose reflected his interests, what he termed interpersonal relations, or all relations between two or more people with various attitudes and emotional states. The station's research and teaching program would stress the development of character and personality in children, children's group organization and dynamics, and the social anthropology of childhood and preschool education, all of which were distinct yet interrelated parts of that larger balanced, symmetrical whole of interpersonal relations.

Sears insisted that interpersonal relations depended on the development of traits in childhood that began at birth and ended before adulthood. His definition of the field was sufficiently broad to encompass his interests in character and personality, or the dynamics of individual development, and those of Lewin in group dynamics. Thus Sears proposed an updating of Kroeber's culture-personality dichotomy of the 1910s for the 1940s—his own age—in which culture and personality would represent a continuum of separate but interactive levels of reality, as if oil and water could mix in harmony. Furthermore, his formulation represented a different way of resolving the puzzle of the meaning of group identity for the individual, for it did not assume any more than Boasian anthropological theory did that group identity was necessarily a permanent stain on the individual. Rather his idea was predicated on a less freighted cluster of methodological assumptions, the gist of which was that behavior of individuals qua individuals differed from that of individuals when they belonged to or participated in the behavior of a group.

The station's first priority in research, Sears said, was personality and social development of young children. The field was of immediate contemporary relevance. He counted himself, Lewin, Ruth Updegraff, Beth Wellman, and, as an unsalaried research associate, his wife, Pauline Sears, as constituting the core of such a program. Only Harvard could rival Iowa in this field; Harvard specialized in the adult personality, whereas Iowa had the lead in both child personality and social development and groups. Thus the Iowa Child Welfare Research Station would be unique; its staff could focus their talents and energies on problems not undertaken anywhere else in the world. The research thus accomplished would be of great theoretical and practical significance. Two new faculty were required to complete the program. A clinical psychologist should be appointed to work on problems of individual personality in systematic experimental fashion, in coordinated interdisciplinary projects but never on episodic individual cases, as clinical psychologists usually did by the nature of their employment. The other appointment would be in child anthropology—a new field.

Child anthropology was, for Sears, a crucial specialization. He insisted that no matter what the child's inherited traits were, his social milieu was an important determinant of his conduct. The institutions, customs, social forces, and stimuli that surrounded an individual helped provoke and shape conduct, and it was through the learning process that the individual's behavior became habitual. Traditionally, investigators had gathered normative data on the child's natural capacities and how a boy or girl learned on the basis of his or her abilities. Few, if any, investigators had discovered "the properties of the social milieu in which the child lives and from which the forces come which give quality or direction to his behavior," Sears insisted. The work of child anthropology fell into those large questions centering on the continuities of child *and* adult societies. In child societies, little was known about how an individual advanced from one age grouping to another, how these structures were maintained, or even how social differentiations of class and caste functioned within the age groups. In adult societies, researchers had yet to begin investigating such large questions as the nature and source of adult standards of child conduct and the child's role as understood by persons of different ages, let alone different social levels of class and caste. It would not be until the war's end, unfortunately, that the handful of persons trained in the field would be available. In the meantime, current faculty would have to work closely with graduate students, as Lewin was doing with such splendid results.

And what of the other research programs at the station? Sears marked the fields of parent education and infant development for elimination if current tenured faculty were to leave, as these projects seemed less urgent. On the other hand, he believed that the station's programs in physical growth and intellectual development were excellent, and the university had a major investment in each; these should be placed on a maintenance basis. Thus Sears planned to make the Iowa station a more specialized and professionalized organization than it had been before.[17]

Sears did not want to diminish the Iowa station's activities in disseminating information to the public or in exhibiting concern for the welfare of Iowa's— and the nation's—children. He recognized these vital roles that the station's staff had fulfilled throughout its history. And he fully supported the work of Lewin, Stoddard, Wellman, and Skeels in both its political and scientific character, even though he was no social activist. Sears himself was more interested in research on motivation than on intelligence or cognition, in large part because he thought it an exciting new area that promised to go beyond what he regarded as the dull-as-dishwater normative research that was so pervasive in the social sciences, especially in child development. He thought that the IQ work that Stoddard, Skeels, and Wellman sponsored had considerable theoretical power. It was not mere normative fact grubbing, but good experimental work leading to important hypotheses about mental development.[18]

Because as director, Sears had enormous power within the university, he could implement those parts of his ideas over which he had direct control. The immediate effect of Sears's reforms was to develop fully the area of social psychology within the station's research programs. For the next several years, social psychology had the highest national and international visibility among the station's various research programs. Sears and Lewin became the station's star professors, with Sears promoting the interactive social psychology of the individual, and Lewin the symmetrical psychological dynamics of group behavior. By contrast, work in other research areas went into relative eclipse. Sears saw no reason to revive the station's nutrition program. With Stoddard's resignation and Skeels's induction into military service, only Beth Wellman represented the station's program in intellectual and cognitive development, or mental testing. She published work on the various complexities of factors in the environment, but few specialists listened to her; such was the extent of the damage that the controversy with Terman and Goodenough had done to her reputation and, for that matter, to the station itself in the field of mental testing. Howard Meredith continued to publish meticulous studies of physical growth. But that remained a small field within child development; in any event, his pieces seemed increasingly only dry-as-dust reports of measurements, missing the occasional criticism or theoretical point contained in his earlier pieces. Most staff appointed in the halcyon days of the Laura Spelman Rockefeller Memorial grants in the thirties had left Iowa City, or, in other instances, had transferred to other departments within the university. Nor did Sears nurture parent education or infant development. Sears got what he asked for the station, a narrower focus and more specialization—and less social activism.

Decades later Sears remembered that when he arrived, only Lewin and his students seemed at all vital or creative. Generally speaking, faculty and graduate students appeared dispirited and isolated intellectually from one another; there seemed no larger intellectual community or sense of a common goal.

Sears had a point. American universities, like most institutions in the social order, then were organized in a rigid, complex, hierarchical fashion. Thus, the station's director had much power to influence those whom he administered. Sears was uncomfortable with the deference that his colleagues paid him. He was also disappointed with the station's graduate students, most of whom as alumni had not fulfilled whatever promise they might have had as scientific researchers. Research assistants seemed selected "for docility and ability to follow directions than for promise as self-motivated scientists of high caliber," and students did "not appear to have learned how to continue under their own steam." This was a damning indictment. Little wonder Sears felt free to re-orient the station's intellectual focus—and standards.[19]

Both Baldwin and Stoddard had used their office's prerogatives to establish an intellectual identity for the Iowa station. Baldwin had been the dominant figure in his time, doing most of the research and publishing and deciding what research projects would be carried out. Stoddard exerted a different style of leadership, that of the orchestra conductor rather than the bureau chief. He worked hard to establish the station's priorities in research and advocacy, and it is not difficult to see his intellectual influence as guru, as he asked provocative questions and spurred on his colleagues in virtually every area of research save that which Lewin and his students did. Baldwin did most of the station's research, whereas Stoddard did little research but guided most of that which his colleagues did. Stoddard believed that he and Lewin were the station's theoreticians.

As Stoddard became increasingly involved in the controversy over the IQ studies and its aftermath, however, the intellectual cohesion that he helped impart to his colleagues slowly dissipated; increasingly in his public actions he became a one-man band, preoccupied with the issues of IQ inconstancy and nursery school education. By the time Sears came to Iowa, the generalized intellectual community that Stoddard had built no longer existed. And Sears's new policies precluded any possibility of its revival. Suddenly the station's distinction apparently depended on a particular specialization and two key professors.

It was no small irony that Sears and Lewin, now the brightest stars in the Iowa station's firmament, identified less in their careers with the science of child development than did their colleagues at the station or, for that matter, anywhere else in the field of child development. Sears turned himself into a child psychologist after being appointed director, whereas Lewin left the field entirely, shifting his research interests from children to the group dynamics of adults after he completed the atmospheres project with Lippitt and other students. This constellation of expertise and interests provided some genuine possibilities for fresh and exciting work, in offering suggestions for combining research on personality and culture in the same cooperative projects, and for examining childhood from the perspectives of adults and of children. Neither Sears nor Lewin was afraid to try new methods. And both were more inter-disciplinary than many of their colleagues in child development, whether at Iowa or elsewhere. These foci also blurred the distinction between psychology and child development as distinct sciences, which in turn created other prob-lems for the station.

From the standpoint of the reigning orthodoxy in child development, and that in traditional psychology as well, Lewin and Sears were mavericks indeed. Neither betrayed the slightest interest in upholding child development's two main maxims, the fixed IQ and the maturation theory. Indeed, they considered these notions the result of boring, unimaginative positivist reasoning, what Sears contemptuously referred to then and decades later as "Dustbowl empiri-cism." They were after ideas that were considerably fresher and more creative—and more open-ended. Unlike most American psychologists, Lewin was inter-ested in theories of action—that is, the explanation of performance at a given time, usually the immediate present. And again, unlike most American psy-chologists, and like a good German Gestaltist, Lewin believed that all psycho-logical phenomena were mental events. He wanted to know what perceptual occurrences made people act the way they did at a specific point in time. Orthodox behaviorists, whose numbers among American psychologists were legion, found much to criticize in Lewin's general orientation, including his antireductionism and antideterminism, his refusal to use series of linear events to explain behavior, his geometric rather than statistical approach, and his insistence that, as he put it to Clark Hull in 1943, psychologists ignored at their peril the fact that they were studying living, breathing organisms who had real mental experiences.[20]

Hull corresponded regularly with Kenneth W. Spence, a protégé of Hull's who was now chair of Iowa's psychology department. They constantly groused to one another about what they thought was Lewin's duplicity in claiming to be both a behaviorist and a mentalist. Spence in particular took umbrage at Lewin's views. Like his mentor Hull, Spence believed in the complete separa-tion of facts and values and, hence, of science and social activism; Spence believed it was his responsibility to be a scientist, not a social crusader. That hardly jibed with Lewin's notions of action research, the point of which was to do the kind of scientific research that would improve the moral quality of human behavior. Nor was this all; Spence and Lewin disagreed over the value of atomism versus holism and mechanistic versus experiential models. Yet ultimately, both accepted the taxonomy of reality of their age. What Spence (and Hull) did not like in Lewin's holism was its ahistoricity and its "mentalism," not its sense of the whole as greater than or different from the sum of the parts. Spence and Lewin also agreed that psychology was best viewed from within a Galilean framework, a world of facts and data, not metaphysics. For Spence this meant use of the empirical laws of conditioning, and for Lewin it meant his ahistorical topological social psychology.[21]

Sears did not agree with the extreme views of his former mentor or his present colleague. But so powerful was the behaviorist mentality as a professional ideology among psychologists then that Sears sincerely believed at that time that he used stimulus and response variables, such as frustration, that were not perceptual concepts in his own work, and that this differentiated him from Lewin, who used such mentalistic conceptions as regression. Late in life, Sears realized his error.[22]

In fact, Lewin and Sears had complementary intellectual approaches, preferences, and views. They were mutually interested in explaining the dynamics of human emotions and other psychological states. Each studied perceptual concepts or events, the difference being that Sears deployed learning theory, or accounting for changes in the potentiality for action, which created a time dimension, whereas Lewin was interested in action theory, which focused on the immediate present. Both successfully used experimental designs from the natural sciences in which one could test as many variables and hypotheses as practical in a given experiment. That approach, too, was a departure from psychology's past, in which investigators conducted experiments on ongoing events after the fashion of natural history rather than of modern experimental physical science, in which the intervention of the investigator and the rearrangement of the natural processes for the convenience and preference of the investigator were crucial. Above all, their common interest in psychodynamics, and in rehabilitating Freudian psychoanalysis for use in contemporary experimental psychology, placed them outside the mainstream of developmental science.

Lewin was always thinking up new projects in action research. In 1939 alone he came up with two, the one academic, the other activist. The first involved cooperation between the Iowa station and Chicago's Institute for Psychoanalysis, in which specialists in Lewinite topological psychology from the station and in psychiatry at the institute would be trained in the other's methods at the opposite institutes for a year. The goal was to mix and meld the methods and perspectives of each field to the mutual benefit of both. The project was funded, but the results were meager for a variety of reasons, including methodological difficulties.[23]

The second project was infinitely more ambitious. Officials of the Chicago Park District contacted Lewin about adapting his research on group atmospheres to train recreation leaders to be more effective. Chicago was a completely segregated city; the district maintained more than fifty recreation centers, each for specific ethnic neighborhoods. Lewin jumped at the opportunity. Here was action research on the largest possible scale. He saw in it the potentiality of going far beyond the limited sphere of the small groups of children he had studied so far. The project would permit the extension of his research from small laboratory settings to large groups in everyday life. He submitted a proposal that permitted ongoing investigation and training of group leaders on three levels: the formal community, selected groups of individuals, and individuals themselves. His hope was to test for a host of variables and to use an interdisciplinary team of specialists in education, recreation leadership, psychiatry, sociology, cultural anthropology, and child psychology. Thus, Lewin wished to assemble an interdisciplinary whole of various partners, each distinct yet interrelated, who could transcend disciplinary boundaries in the social sciences. The proposal was large in scope and vague in description. The sticking point was funding. Lewin attempted to win support from the Rockefeller Foundation's program in the social sciences, but the foundation's external referee, a thoroughgoing behaviorist, nixed the idea as too impractical and woolly-headed.[24]

Lewin had better luck with less grandiose schemes. Several involved the extension, in one way or another, of the atmospheres project he had conducted with Lippitt into new areas. By chance, one of Lewin's graduate students, Alex Bavelas, suggested to Lewin that group leaders followed a script, as it were, in their work; Lewin immediately realized that meant that group leaders could be trained. In the terminology of the Lippitt project, it should be possible to train persons to be democratic leaders even if they had autocratic leadership styles in other social contexts. Lewin and Bavelas soon persuaded Works Progress Authority officials in Des Moines, Iowa, to allow them to experiment with training democratic leaders at a recreation camp in the summer of 1941, with the full cooperation of the Des Moines Jewish Community Center. Lewin and Bavelas selected six particularly unsatisfactory—autocratic, in Lewinesque terms—recreation leaders, three in a control group, three in an experimental group, the latter to be changed if possible to be democratic leaders à la Lippitt's mask clubs through three weeks' intensive training. Careful observations of all group behavior were made, including quantitative and qualitative measurements. The results were an almost exact replication of the democratic and autocratic atmospheres of the original Lippitt mask clubs, with the focus this time on the interrelations of the leaders with the dynamics of their respective groups rather than on the members and their group dynamics. The ultimate result was to enhance morale among leaders and pupils alike, to encourage more participation by the group members, to define democracy and respect for authority in terms of participation by group members, and to redefine group leadership in terms of close identification of the leader's values with those of the group. As Lewin told his friend Horace Kallen that fall, they had succeeded in retraining flawed recreation leaders into "top democratic leaders within three weeks." Initially, Kallen was excited by the prospects of training an entire nation of democratic leaders, a giddying prospect indeed for a man of Kallen's left-liberal political views. Lewin warned that the going must be slow, as it was a complicated business.[25]

In what was probably his most important wartime assignment, Lewin investigated further the functioning of democratic styles of leadership within the dynamics of small groups. In late 1940 the National Research Council (NRC) established a Committee on Food Habits, ostensibly to discuss ways to organize food production and consumption to assist in national defense. Among the committee's members in 1941 was George D. Stoddard, who made sure that his colleagues discussed problems of malnutrition among the nation's poor as well as questions of war and peace. The committee was reorganized in late 1941 with a new chair, new committee members, and an executive secretary, Margaret Mead, the famous American Museum of Natural History anthropologist and champion of left-liberalism from within the New Deal coalition. The committee now had the mandate from the NRC to organize research projects that would suggest ways to persuade American consumers to alter their dietary habits to meet the needs of national defense, "of getting people to wish what they need." In other words, here was action research again, getting people to change their behavior for the common good. The reorganized committee met the day before the Japanese attack on Pearl Harbor; by the time Mead took up her duties that January in Washington, the nation was at war.[26]

Mead soon recruited her good friend Lewin. Eventually, Lewin and his associates worked on seven distinct projects for the committee. The common thread among all of the projects was not merely to encourage people to change their behavior for the better. It was to get them to think like a team, with the same goals and values, while still believing that they were individuals freely consenting to take on this common task rather than conforming to an authoritarian personality. In short, it was the age's classic sense of the relations between the group and the individual: each individual was distinct, all were interrelated with all others, and all were interchangeable with one another.[27]

Among the more interesting of these projects was an experiment in audience persuasion that Lewin designed, in which he and his coworkers devised contrasting means of persuading upper-, middle-, and lower-class housewives from nearby Cedar Rapids and representatives of the city's two "ethnic" groups, Americans of Czech background and black Americans, to pass up such prestigious, well-liked, and expensive meats as prime rib or steaks for organ meats such as kidney, brain, and liver. Housewives from these various social groups were exposed to two contrasting situations. In the first situation, a nutrition expert lectured wives for thirty minutes on the economic and nutritional reasons for switching to the organ meats; the housewives could not participate, save to express their preferences after the lecture. In the second, the same nutrition expert lectured the housewives for about seven minutes. Then Alex Bavelas took charge as the group discussion leader who encouraged participation as a democratic leader and who tried to persuade them to change to the new meats. His techniques came from earlier experiments, including his own. Unlike the nutrition expert, Bavelas appealed to their patriotism, indeed, their incipient team spirit. Allowing them to participate fostered the sense among the housewives that they were in control of the situation, that, in short, they were a team of individuals united in common goals and purposes, one individual just as good and valuable as the other. The second situation produced a startling change in habits, whereas the first did not. Simply put, the members of the second group became a democratic team, and those in the first did not.[28]

Lewin also involved himself more directly in politics as a scientist. In 1942, for example, he served as president of the Society for the Psychological Study of Social Issues (SPSSI), an organization that socially conscious younger psychologists had recently set up to promote psychological research on pressing social problems and disseminate the results of this action research to policymakers and interested citizens. As with other action research projects, Lewin's intent was to do research on what made people act better, not merely what made them behave. During his presidency, he directed SPSSI's efforts to the problem of civilian morale. And morale was crucial to the problem of team spirit, the democratic group, and what Professor William S. Graebner has called the problem of democratic social engineering in modern America. How can authority and democracy be "engineered" to function together in human situations? That was the question. Creating morale for the common cause was clearly an important technique. In the resulting publication, various contributors rode no single hobby horse. But in different ways, they drew sharp contrasts between the team spirit of American democracy and conformist Axis totalitarianism. In their political views the contributors were staunch individualists who criticized the use of racial, religious, ethnic, and class stereotypes, as, for example, when the young Harvard psychologist Gordon Allport, a close friend of Lewin's, insisted that true democracy involved "sincere regard for the individual" and resulted "in the growth of human personality."[29]

Lewin discussed morale from the standpoint of the terrible situation for Europe's Jews, who faced mass destruction. He argued that Jews must think of themselves positively; they must not accept the hideously negative notions of anti-Semites. The solution to the world's problems was to further the democratic dogma, Lewin believed. Democracy meant diversity, "the right of individuals or groups to be different." What the world sorely needed was a fully articulated experimental science of group dynamics. Such a science would address the problems of leadership, leadership training, ideology, culture, group morale, cooperation, production, discipline, and organization—in short, all phases of group life. Group decisions provided a context in which the individual cooperated as a member of the group—or, in this instance, the team—independently of his or her personal inclinations. In a democracy, democratic leadership involved establishing a proper democratic atmosphere in the group.[30]

Nor did this exhaust Lewin's contributions to contemporary political and social issues. Three former students, Charles Hendry, Ronald Lippitt, and Alex Bavelas, became involved, with Lewin's ultimate supervision, in retraining leaders in the Boy Scouts of America. The project was based on the assumption that the advance of democracy, in America or in any other country in the world, required the retraining of leaders at all levels in the techniques of democratic group dynamics. Lewin had been involved for many years in working out problems of worker morale in various business establishments; in the 1940s he worked directly for the Harwood Corporation, which his friend Alfred J. Marrow owned, helping to devise schemes to raise worker productivity and morale through group dynamics. In 1944, in the wake of such recent events as the race riots in Harlem and Detroit and the zoot-suit riots in Los Angeles, the American Jewish Congress established the Commission on Community Interrelations (CCI), the congress's research arm, with Lewin as director. Again, Lewin was committed to action research. It was probably fortunate for him that he was an optimist. Aware that engineering democracy had ethical problems of its own, he nevertheless believed that group manipulation could be avoided, insisting that group management could be done by and for the American people. Science could thus promote democracy and the freedom of the individual, and the group was no threat to that freedom.[31]

During their years together at Iowa, Lewin and Sears worked closely together on matters of mutual interest, such as training graduate students. Sears was as committed to liberal notions as was Lewin, but for Sears, science, not politics, was the great passion of his life. He fulfilled his public responsibilities as the station's director, and he worked very hard on a military research project for the U.S. Office of Scientific Research and Development. But he was never the political theorist that either Stoddard or Lewin was. He devoted his free research time during the war to developing a behavioral science of personality. An important contribution to that field was the short book he wrote for the prestigious Social Science Research Council, *Survey of Objective Studies of Psychoanalytic Concepts* (1943). This seminal work led to the blossoming of the field of personality research in the 1940s and 1950s. In it Sears scoured the research literature to ascertain what key psychoanalytic concepts were supportable, in whole or in part, by high-grade experimental work, and to recommend appropriate research methods. Sears believed that psychoanalysis was bad science, even though Freud, in his view, had spun out some powerful and interesting suggestions for a sophisticated dynamic theory of personality.

Sears plucked Freud's work out of its late nineteenth-century historical context and upgraded and modernized it for his own age. He reported that the idea of infant sexuality was sound, but there was no proof, as Freud had insisted, that it was innate. Sears was inclined to think it was socially learned, through imitation and other postnatal experiences, as social learning theorists would have it, but there was no experimental evidence either way. Freud's concepts of fixation and regression were fine, but his notions of regression and learning were simply too primitive to be useful. Sears's third general conclusion was that the laboratory work on regression and projection so far was relatively unproductive. He concluded that a rigorous behavioral science of personality was possible. It should be based on concepts of growth, learning, and social milieu—virtually a literal reiteration of Dollard and Miller's social learning theory. And there were three possible kinds of research methods, that could be used singly or in some combination, depending on the issues to be tackled: longitudinal studies of the same persons over time, to see how personality traits developed; studies of object fixations, or habits, to follow the influence of learning on motivation; and cross-cultural comparative studies to understand the importance of the social milieu.[32]

The professional reaction to Sears's book was highly favorable. Sales of the first printing were quickly exhausted. Sears became a sought-after figure in the field, a man whose advice was earnestly solicited in many quarters. And he went ahead with his own research. By November 1943 he wrote John Dollard that he had several graduate students hard at work on behavioral studies of personality development. In a variety of public forums in the early to middle forties, Sears proclaimed the promises of this new field of research. Lewin and his students made important contributions, too. Dorwin Cartwright, for example, published a highly sophisticated and brilliant study of the time it took an organism to respond to a stimulus, and Leon Festinger constructed a mathematical derivation of an exact test for means of samples from exponential populations. Both solved complex and tricky problems in psychology dealing with the amount of time it took an organism to make a decision and the way to measure the frequency of cultural or institutional behavior that took place chiefly at the cultural norm. These were important contributions to the mathematization of topological psychology.[33]

In *Authority and Frustration* (1944) Lewin and four associates went beyond earlier topological discussions and extended their work to include the aspects of authority of group structure and the frustrations related to it. After an opening methodological statement in which Lewin attacked all forms of reductionism and determinism in psychology, including the notions of the fixed IQ and predetermined development, his colleagues discussed their empirical findings. Charles E. Meyers insisted that positive persuasion, including anticipating group members' problems with acceptance of authority and allowing them to adjust to authority, was the most effective and constructive means of managing group members to be as restrained as possible in their ideas and actions. Joan Kalhorn found profound differences in cultural values between pietistic Mennonite and secular, property-oriented non-Mennonite children. In a study of criminals in prison, Maurice Farber extended Lewin's insight that time perspective and goals were always interrelated. Prisoners' behavior was dominated by the overpowering desire to get out as soon as possible. Hence, indeterminant sentencing made sense, Farber argued, so long as expert knowledge was used in a case-by-case basis. In a complex and inventive experiment involving two groups of college students who reacted to an apparent emergency situation, one group organized before, the other not, John R. P. French found that the previously organized group behaved as if it had an existence of its own apart from the notions of its individual members, whereas the other group's members acted as individuals in response to the situation. In these ways were Lewin and his coworkers expanding their knowledge of group dynamics—of how they were structured, how they acquired an identity of their own, and how they influenced the behavior and perceptions of their members.[34]

By 1944 Lewin was becoming restless in Iowa City. For almost five years he had done no important work on children, nor had any of his students. Furthermore, Lewin was a metropolitan person and a Jew; living in a city with only a few thousand other citizens, almost none of them Jewish, probably became less and less satisfying; the midwestern small-town cultural milieu was probably less than fulfilling to this cosmopolite. By the latter half of 1944 he was working in Washington, D.C., as a consultant to the federal government, and was involved in serious negotiations with the University of California and the Massachusetts Institute of Technology. The MIT offer came first; he resigned from the Iowa station. Suddenly the Iowa Child Welfare Research Station was deprived of one of its most prestigious and accomplished faculty and, more importantly, of its most celebrated and determined advocate of action research in the behavioral sciences. MIT established a Research Center for Group Dynamics for him and his coworkers. All went well until his sudden death from a heart attack in February 1947. The MIT Center did not survive him.[35]

"I loved him dearly," said Sears, remembering Lewin some four decades after he left the Iowa Child Welfare Research Station. "He was a wonderful guy and more fun to be with than you could possibly imagine." Sears was genuinely sorry to see Lewin go, but he knew very well that Lewin had long since left the field of child development and that his resignation made it possible for the station to find a social psychologist more interested in children than Lewin had been. Sears could not recruit more faculty for the war's duration. His graduate students would have to shoulder a heavier burden in the kind of cooperative research that Sears thought appropriate than would otherwise have been the case.

Yet the Iowa station was undergoing a silent intellectual transformation with Lewin's departure and death. True enough, Sears had schooled himself in the principles and procedures of child development research. But he did so from within the intellectual world of traditional psychology, even though Sears himself was an avant-garde psychologist in many respects. The intellectual and ideological baggage of child development and child welfare, especially that which focused on the improvement of the lives of children, was not a part of Sears's point of view as a developmental scientist. He had not fought the old battles that Baldwin, Stoddard, Skeels, and Wellman had, even though he agreed with many of their ideas. It was hardly a surprise that the work that began to come from the Iowa station was, quite simply, child psychology, and that it was in many respects the kind of work that any psychologist could have done. The yeastier days of interdisciplinary scholarship, of united advocacy, and, in the case of Lewin and his allies, of action research were gone—none of these fields was a part of Sears's experience or intellectual identity. In other words, the distinctions between child development and developmental psychology as intellectual and scientific constructs were, for Sears, relatively narrow, whereas for someone like Stoddard, child development, while related scientifically to child psychology, was also a political and cultural construct about making the world a better place. Even among those developmentalists—the mainstream, that is—who rejected that call for social intervention, the issue of social intervention was a major element of their intellectual and ideological identity. For Sears and, increasingly, for the Iowa Child Welfare Research Station, such issues were unimportant to the main job at hand: scientific research and interpretation of said results. Sears himself drew a line between his generation of psychologists and developmentalists, who wanted to use theory to explain behavior, and the generation they succeeded, who conducted normative research that he considered dry-as-dust. What might also be said is that the normative research he dismissed, when analyzed carefully, contained all sorts of assumptions about how the world of children should be or should have been, whether we reflect on Lewis M. Terman's version of the Binet test, the maturation theory, or any other element of the now "mature" science of child development.[36]

In a public address in 1945 at the university, Sears sketched out a new research agenda, which illustrated its distance from the old issues of child welfare. He insisted that the new methods of research in child development were observational sampling of behavior, cross-cultural comparison, and projective techniques, in which subjects projected their feelings in ways that could be observed or measured, such as doll play or Rorschach tests. Yet Sears and his students had little success with the Rorschach tests, which Sears seemed to regard as instruments that were too blunt for fine analysis. More promising was doll play, a technique that psychiatrist Melanie Klein pioneered in the 1930s, in which the child would act out, with dolls representing real persons in his or her life, various hostilities and other patterns of behavior. After all, preschool age children were too inarticulate and inexperienced to be able to offer verbal testimony about their innermost feelings about events.[37]

In short order, Sears directed several students in their work with doll play with the children from the station's preschool. He made sure that each made a methodological contribution and that all followed the most rigorous experimental procedures that could be devised. In an initial feasibility study, George Bach showed that normal children displayed intensively aggressive fantasies, that individual children differed enormously in their play, and that there were enormous differences in stereotypical behavior between boys and girls. In a project in which she tested two variables, the effect of length of play and of realistic play materials, Ruth Phillips again corroborated the diagnostic value of doll play; Elizabeth Robinson also concluded that the dolls were useful indications of the child's innermost thoughts. Margaret Pintler's investigation underscored a different point, that doll play had to constitute a structured situation before children would react. She also argued that aggression increased over time in doll play. The general conclusion that Sears drew from all of these studies was that doll play verified the essential tenets of social learning theory as applied to children.[38]

The next step that Sears took in the construction of personality theory was to design experiments to test the importance of interactions between individuals. This contrasted sharply with orthodox behaviorist stimulus-response notions that focused on learning sequences in organisms. In an early study of mother-child interaction, Sears and a student opened up the whole area of mother-child interactions, thus leading to the first fruits of the investigation of interpersonal relations that Sears had called for in his report to the university administration a couple of years before. Sears and his students developed these themes in a variety of ways. From the additional research and experiments of Pintler and Phillips on sex or gender differences in behavior, done under Sears's supervision, Sears argued that a sex typing process took place very early in life through social learning. This had important implications, he continued. Clinical observations had to take this into account. And there was obviously much room for investigating the cultural factors that presumably caused such sex differentiation by age three or four in most individuals. Sears and his students also probed the role and importance of the father in the interpersonal relations that constituted the family, again using doll play as the major technique. Boys were more aggressive when their fathers were home than when they were not, and the reverse was true for girls, save their responses were less vigorous than those of the boys. There were definite sex differences in behavior between boys and girls. Fathers contributed much to the sex typing of their sons, causing more frustration and, therefore, more aggression the longer they were in the home.[39]

Sears wanted to develop a more sophisticated general theory of personality. In early 1944 he invited himself to lunch in New York with Alan Gregg, program director for medicine of the Rockefeller Foundation. Gregg was impressed. He noted in his official diary that Sears struck him as an able young man on the way up who wanted to meld psychology and psychiatry. In the fall of 1945, Sears's former Yale colleague, Carl I. Hovland, now working as a consultant for the Rockefeller Foundation, asked Sears what fresh ideas he was working on—an open invitation to submit a proposal. That spring Sears did. He wanted to probe the interrelations between parents and children, or the interdependent problems of social learning in the cultural milieu in which parents and children lived. He wanted an interdisciplinary research team of a child psychologist, a social psychologist, a social anthropologist who was knowledgeable about children, and another social anthropologist who understood adult societies. He had already persuaded the university administration to support the project to the tune of $133,000 over the next five years, and he wanted another $52,000 from the foundation. It took foundation officials another year to commit to Sears's project. Meanwhile Sears had already appointed two new faculty for the project, Vincent Nowlis to replace Lewin in social psychology in 1945, and John Whiting in 1947 as a specialist in child anthropology.[40]

Together with Pauline S. Sears, who took the place of the adult anthropologist, Robert Sears, Nowlis, and Whiting made up the team of principal investigators. They collected most of the data in the 1947–48 academic year. The project, in its final design, focused on the interactions of mothers and their children. Sears outlined the project's theoretical framework within the context of social learning theory. The mother had specific motives, chiefly nurturance and pain avoidance, that made her receptive to the child's signals for help and compliance. The child rapidly learned to behave in ways that would send signals to the mother, either of the aggressive or the dependent and attention-getting variety. These varied widely among individuals and were the products of particular experiences in personality and culture. The next step in the developmental process was the transformation of these instrumental action systems, as Sears dubbed them, into acquired drive systems. Thus aggressive and dependent actions gradually became the goals for the socially learned and acquired drives of aggression and dependency. Punishment and frustration clearly determined the strength of both drives.

Sears and his associates used forty children, almost equally split between boys and girls, together with their mothers. They taped a three-hour interview with each mother; in addition they used direct observation of units of behavior, doll play, and teachers' ratings in the preschool laboratories, all to measure the children's behavior. Once the laborious process of transcribing the interviews was completed, team workers then placed the raw data into predetermined categories. Then they rated the information on scales related to such phenomena as severity of early and current frustration, extent of each mother's nurturing, and the mothers' relative punitiveness toward their children. From the standpoints of content and method, this was a new departure in the field. No one had ever studied parent-child interactions from this complex theoretical framework of antecedent-consequent dynamic drive theories before, and the research methods were as original as they were demanding to manage.[41]

In the final study, published in 1953, several years after he had left the Iowa station, Sears and his associates discussed their results in terms of several general conclusions. First, they argued, the character and quantity of frustration and punishment the child experienced were major determinants of both dependent and aggressive drives. Second, there were radical differences between boys and girls in the social learning processes by which aggressive and dependent drives developed within them. Most likely these were the result of their interactions with their mothers. And, after the child's first year, there were deep and pervasive differences in the ways mothers treated sons and daughters.

Here, then, was a landmark study in the field that did not replicate the standard principles, hypotheses, or agendas of orthodox child development as a science—or scientific ideology. Like Lewin's work in group dynamics, it combined the most up-to-date psychodynamic theories then available with complicated and, for the time, rigorous experimental techniques and methods. Neither the work of Lewin or Sears nor that of their respective associates and coworkers looked to the past of their science. Neither used the field's now-traditional intellectual traditions of determinism, positivism, and reductionism. By dissipating the mainstream notion of the meaning of group identity for the individual, those at the Iowa station associated with Lewin and Sears had looked to a new science of child and human development, a science whose practitioners would describe the development of autonomous, asymmetrical, and unique individuals—a science that was not quite born.[42]

Yet matters cannot be so facilely described. More was involved. It is one thing for work in a particular present to resemble something in a past now over or a future not yet realized. It is something entirely different (and highly improbable, to say the least) for specific historical artifacts to exist outside the age in which they existed. Lewin and Sears may have divested the old child development and child welfare research of many of its connotations, for example, with their notions of the individual and the group. But their notion of the individual resembled in all its architectural or design characteristics that of their contemporaries, for such individuals were commonly thought to be distinct yet interrelated and interchangeable. Only by embracing this blueprint of the individual could one preserve the larger blueprint of symmetrical, interdependent holism that was a part of that age's sense of the order of things. Hence Lewin and Sears remained intellectually contemporary; their ideas did not, in any profound *historical* way, anticipate the future.

And there was a crucial difference between the work of Lewin and his associates and Sears and his students on group dynamics, one that was to cast a shadow on the field's future history. Lewin thought of an individual in a variety of ways, but always in his action research as a person whose free will could be persuaded to improve his or her moral behavior. There were, in short, given philosophical, political, and moral connotations and dimensions to the individual as Lewin and his coworkers thought of the problem. Sears, on the other hand, separated the world of facts from the world of values, not unlike his mentor Hull had. The individuals in all the work that Sears directed at the Iowa station were thus devoid of political content, meaning, or even symbolism. They were merely experimental subjects, and there was no particular reason for the projects in which they were involved to be located at the Iowa Child Welfare Research Station, or any other child development institute, save for the obvious point that these were experiments about child psychology.

If Sears was no political activist, after the fashion of Stoddard and Lewin, nevertheless he did play the role of statesmen in his field. He had high standards as a scientist and little love for ideas in the field without scientific support. An opportunity to lecture on oral habits in a pediatrics class at the University of Kansas Medical School in 1947 led Sears to launch an experiment to ascertain whether the sucking drive was innate, as orthodox Freudian theory said it was. As the project continued, Sears approached Lawrence K. Frank at the Caroline Zachry Institute of New York, to use his influence to obtain research funds from *Parents Magazine* (as the Iowa station was entitled to under agreements Frank had made in the late twenties). Frank happily complied, but, ever confident that he understood the field better than the professionals, gratuitously told Sears to read an early paper of Erik Erikson's on the matter, and added that he hoped Sears would not use the frustration-aggression formula, which "is misleading and inadequate." Sears tartly responded that Erikson's work had little data, which at that time was his harshest condemnation. And Erikson's stress on internal factors to the exclusion of the external and their interrelations was specious, he told Frank. Perhaps characteristically, Sears concluded that Freud was wrong on the sucking drive; it was completely learned. There was nothing innate about it.[43]

Sears told a friend in 1947 that Leonard Carmichael's reissue of the old Murchison manual showed how intellectually sterile the field was, how obsessed were most specialists with dry-as-dust facts. Only the chapters that Margaret Mead and Kurt Lewin had written had any theoretical flair whatsoever; if he was not overly impressed with their theoretical positions, nevertheless "their two chapters were the bright spots in the book so far as I am concerned." Sears was concerned with other professional issues as well. For example, he took a high profile with the American Psychological Association's mandate in arguing for the upgrading of training and certification for clinical psychologists, so that laypersons would obtain better treatment. While he was director at the Iowa station, he also spoke frequently throughout the state on the importance of the mental hygiene movement's ideas to the health of contemporary society. Sears was offended by popularizers who misled parents with scientifically unsound advice, of whom, he argued, John B. Watson was such a flagrant example. Watson's rigid stimulus-response formulas and his antimentalism offended Sears. Watson had many imitators today, he insisted, scientists and journalists alike.[44]

The immediate postwar years found both the Society for Research in Child Development (SRCD) and the Committee on Child Development (CCD) of the National Research Council moribund institutions. In a word, the field was stale, if not dead, intellectually. In 1946 Sears was one of a handful of specialists who took charge of the SRCD's revival as a scholarly organization and publisher for the field. Within two years it was functioning, the debts for the journals had been paid off, and the field as a national professional subculture of professionals was coming alive after its long hiatus. The CCD had, of course, served as the SRCD's creator, but the CCD's effectiveness declined as its long-term chair, Robert S. Woodworth, who had served since the twenties, could not devote sufficient attention to it; in any event, no one could be found to replace him during the war. After suitable reorganization, Sears became Woodworth's successor. As committee chair, Sears continued to reinvigorate the SRCD and its journals. He also won the mandate from the CCD's reorganization to seek major federal funding for a child development research institute, to be either a free-standing organization or to be incorporated into the new federal institutes of health.[45]

The campaign for a national child research institute proved to be Sears's last important contribution as director of the Iowa Child Welfare Research Station to the field of child development, although he did not know that when he began. Nor, for that matter, did he know that he had walked into a complicated, if not precisely Byzantine, situation. In the summer of 1948, at the behest of George Hecht, the publisher of *Parents Magazine*, Sears accepted the chairmanship of one of Hecht's inventions, the American Parents Committee. The committee's stated purpose was to lobby for vastly increased federal funds for child research. It appeared to Sears from his experience with the CCD that the Truman administration was highly sympathetic to an enlarged federal role for research on children. The question was which entity of the federal government would get the money and the right to administer it. As the federal government's only agency devoted to children, the Children's Bureau was interested. Many of Sears's scientific peers were somewhat skeptical of the Children's Bureau as the appropriate authority for funding original investigation, as distinct from the social scientific cum advocacy research the bureau's staffers had done for generations, which was part of its legislative mandate. Presumably they would have preferred a different institutional locus for funding.

Sears had no proprietary interest in the funds coming to the CCD as such. He simply wanted more money for people in the field because he believed it essential to the nation's welfare. As he told his close friend J. McVicker Hunt in December 1948, the field's crying need was to have more imaginative researchers such as Hunt well situated in first-class universities, with ample research funds, to train the next generation of researchers. "Iowa is the only institution in the country that is training any significant number of people in this field," he told Hunt. "Last year was a big year for us; we turned out two Ph.D.s. We will get one through this year," he concluded, saying that if all the money went into pathology, and nothing into cure and prevention, the results for the country at large would be disastrous, thus echoing from a perspective entirely different from hers, one of Cora Hillis's major themes.[46]

In actuality, the Children's Bureau presented no particular difficulties for Sears. Indeed, his relations with key bureau officials, for example, Martha May Eliot, were good. The fly in the ointment was George Hecht himself, at least from the perspective of Sears and those who agreed with him. As a newcomer to child development, Sears was initially unaware of Hecht's relations with many of the field's professionals. As publisher of *Parents*, Hecht had accepted substantial funds from the Laura Spelman Rockefeller Memorial to make the magazine succeed, Lawrence K. Frank's rationale being that the four major research centers, Iowa, Yale, Minnesota, and Berkeley, would receive dividends from the stock the memorial purchased in their name that they would in turn use for research. Hecht simply refused to declare a dividend, even though his magazine was enormously successful. Precisely why Hecht organized the lobbying campaign for federal funds for child research can only be imagined. He wanted full control of the entire lobbying campaign, however, and the right to dictate the bill's final outline. In August, Sears wrote his friend Lewis M. Terman that everything with Hecht seemed all right. By November, all he could say to Martha May Eliot after an evening session with Hecht was "Mercy, what a man!" His friend J. McVicker Hunt told him the week before that Eliot was worried about the bill's chances; she did not trust Hecht and looked to Sears "as savior." Sears responded that the committee "has me hanging on the ropes," but that he told Hecht he was going ahead to establish a larger committee independent of Hecht's, which Sears and many other professionals believed would attract sponsors who were more generous in their support. After some back and forth, Sears and Hunt finally decided in early 1949 to allow Hecht to try and fail, with the hopes that a better campaign could be organized in two or three years.[47]

When Sears announced his resignation at Iowa in January 1949, to take a new appointment at Harvard's Graduate School of Education, he did not stop working for the enactment of the child research bill, even though he was less than cheered by the thought of having to cooperate with Hecht. He worked at a furious pace for the rest of the academic year, writing politicians and scientists alike, conferring with government officials and people in the field, and trying, too, to keep scientists disgruntled with Hecht behind the bill. There were rumors that the Truman administration wanted its own version of the legislation, and that the Bureau of the Budget wanted no more national scientific research institutes. By March, Sears had rewritten the bill for the third and final time, and it was introduced into the Congress; if passed, it would provide $7.5 million a year for research grants and administrative costs.[48]

Three months later the bill was dead. Child development specialists did not have a powerful enough lobby or an array of powerful constituencies to overcome the particular difficulties they faced in the political process to obtain passage of the measure. After all, they were not doctors, atomic scientists, or even chemists. As practitioners of a small scientific field and self-proclaimed guardians of the nation's children, their possibilities for success in national politics were circumscribed indeed.

But that was not the end of the tale. Within the National Institute of Mental Health, colleagues in psychiatry and clinical psychology who sat on major policy panels included child development within their purview. Within an astonishingly short period of time, specialists in child development found their prescribed niche in the new postwar federal system of patronage for scientific research and training. The practical benefits for workers in the field were not inconsiderable.

But the symbolic meaning appears, at least in retrospect, to have had a larger significance, for by incorporating child development under the rubric of the established National Institutes of Health, child development was no longer a field apart from the rest of the nation's scientific community. It was now a normal and accepted specialization, without special constituencies or interests, as it had had from its origins in the teens and twenties.[49]

This symbolic domestication of the field of child development within the world of American science and academe also brought a parallel normalization of the Iowa Child Welfare Research Station. Since the twenties, its intellectual primacy had disappeared as competing institutes and programs emerged in the field. With the resignations of Lewin and Sears, its intellectual singularity in its own age was now problematic, imperiled by the benisons of scientific professionalism, such as they were.

In early March 1949, Clark Hull wrote his protégé, Kenneth W. Spence, head of the University of Iowa's psychology department, for his confidential impressions about Sears's resignation. "I have always been sorry that you didn't write me about him before you took him on at Iowa," Hull said, "though apparently he didn't turn out to be quite as bad as I had feared he would." Hull could not hide his distaste for the heterodoxy that Lewin in particular but Sears as well had exhibited in their work at the Iowa station. Any doctrines not congruent with Hullian stimulus-response learning theory were just so much poppycock. And Spence agreed, emphatically. "With both Lewin and Sears gone," Hull concluded, "you ought to be relatively happy." Spence was. He now had the opportunity, as the university's senior psychologist, to influence the Iowa Child Welfare Research Station as never before, especially with university president Hancher, who continued the university's tradition, broken only by President Jessup, of weak and ineffectual presidents.[50]

Spence did not wait for Hull's letter to act. A month before, he had initiated a process that led, assuredly with his approval, to a review of the Child Welfare Research Station, using Sears's resignation as the rationale. Initially Spence complained that standards for graduate training were lower in the station than in his department. In the ensuing ruckus he had stirred up—he had casually suggested as a remedy that the station's right to engage in graduate teaching be eliminated—the university president appointed a review committee. Station faculty reported on their teaching, research, and service, that holy trinity of the modern American university. The review committee concluded its business that summer. Their recommendations pleased Spence, for they placed him and his department in a very strong position vis-à-vis the station. The station was to return to its initial general research focus on the psychological, sociological, physical, and physiological aspects of children, thus making the station something other than a direct competitor with the psychology department. Indeed, Spence's department was allowed to have a narrow focus so as to have an outstanding program with limited resources. The station would with enormous difficulty be nationally competitive, let alone excellent, in its field, especially given the Iowa taxpayers' notorious parsimony and reverence for mediocrity. Teaching and research would go on in tandem with the appropriate departments on campus. And the station would be limited to child development. It could not duplicate work done in other departments. Obviously, Spence had won an enormous victory.[51]

In the 1950s and early 1960s the Iowa station maintained its reputation as a leading institute in its field. There were good reasons for this. Sears's successor as director, Boyd McCandless, had taken his doctorate at the station in Stoddard's day and made important efforts to rehabilitate the station's reputation in the general area of intelligence and learning. Good students continued to be attracted to graduate study at the station; a significant number have become leading figures in the field since. To the 1950s, it was the Iowa station's faculty, not its graduates, who had great distinction in the field. From the 1950s on, that equation was reversed. And, for that matter, the quantity of graduates was impressive too; of the 151 doctorates the station granted between 1917 and 1967, 53, or about one-third, were awarded after Sears's departure to 1967. Faculty productivity did not suffer in these decades, with 291 research publications, or slightly less than a quarter of the total between 1917 and 1967, appearing in those years. Yet there were complexities that the above does not suggest. The station's research foci were concentrated in two areas, learning and motivation, and child somatology; one-third and one-fifth, respectively, of the total research publications were generated in these areas. The work in child somatology was clearly the result of Howard Meredith's relentless productivity. That on learning and motivation did not come from Beth Wellman, who died in 1952, or even from McCandless, who shared some of her notions about science and politics, but rather from a group of faculty and students who patterned their work with children after that of Spence and, ultimately, Clark Hull, on rat learning. Increasingly, the work of the staff at the Iowa Child Welfare Research Station, revealingly renamed in 1964 the Institute of Child Behavior and Development, was based on one model of learning derived from a rigid, positivist, behaviorist theory. The leader of this new group was Charles Spiker, certainly a child psychologist of rigor, intelligence, and energy—and a particular point of view. In effect, Spence had won.[52]

The Iowa Child Welfare Research Station's intellectual singularity as an institution and intellectual community had thus come to an end, although, as shall be seen presently, the ideas that the Iowa scientists had generated had an eerie resonance in contemporary, or postmodern, America after World War II. The Institute of Child Behavior and Development did not survive a decade in its new identity. In 1974, the Iowa State Board of Regents, the university's trustees, accepted the recommendations of a new review committee to close the institute as an organization devoted to teaching, research, and dissemination of information about the normal child, to parcel out the tenured faculty to various cognate departments, and to make the institute into a clearinghouse for the university community on the matter of children, especially children at risk. The funds for research were to come from the shares of stock in *Parents Magazine* that Frank had purchased for the station on behalf of the Laura Spelman Rockefeller Memorial so that the station's staff would have ample funds for research on children. A small irony was thus involved in the institute's denouement. Inasmuch as it was possible for men and women affiliated with the University of Iowa in the mid-1970s to respond to Cora B. Hillis's pleas to do research first and foremost on children who needed protection—"children at risk," as our own age would have it—they did so. Presumably, she would have been pleased.[53]

TOWARD HEAD START

During the 1974 Christmas holidays, Louvenia Palmer and her husband, a warehouseman in New Haven, Connecticut, cleaned out the junk room in their home, painted it bright yellow and turned it into a playroom for their three children. "I learned that having a place like this for them to go to is important," she declared some six months later in a newspaper interview. "Even the color makes a difference" in giving the children self-esteem, social competency, and a leg up on their middle-class peers in school, she insisted. Palmer learned these lessons in a course in early childhood education she took at a Head Start center in her local community. She enrolled in the course because some of her friends and neighbors told her that her family met the economic guidelines of Head Start, and she wanted to give her children the best boost in life that she could.[1]

Nine-and-a-half years before Mr. and Mrs. Palmer cleaned out their junk room, the federal government initiated a most remarkable venture in social engineering, Project Head Start. Acting under the broad authority of the Economic Opportunity Act of 1964, and considerable political pressure, the Office of Economic Opportunity (OEO) became the focal point through which this interesting and unprecedented social experiment served, during that summer, some 561,359 children in 11,068 centers. Head Start took shape as the result of certain developments in the late 1950s and early 1960s. Head Start was not merely an early childhood education program. It sought to address a variety of concerns about children living in "pockets of poverty," including their cognitive skills, their health, their nutrition, the quality of life in their families and communities, and the relations of their parents and other important adults in the community to the centers of power in the larger society. From this point of view, some children were disadvantaged and others were not; there was no such thing as a level playing field for all comers, and life was not fair. The point of Head Start, in the minds of its most ardent champions, was to make a difference by bringing all children up to an imaginary starting line by the time they entered school, so that they could all compete in a fair contest.[2]

Central to the roots of Head Start, then, was an important shift in American culture in the 1950s and early 1960s. Children had been viewed previously as integral parts of families, with the attention of public policy, such as it was, directed toward the family as a symmetrical whole constituted of distinct yet interrelated parts. The new perspective included only unique individual parts and no integrated whole, which translated into a view that depicted children as individuals, some radically more disadvantaged than others—a situation out of balance, proportion, and justice, an asymmetrical, imbalanced, and peculiar context setting the tone. Increasingly, policymakers for children and the family viewed the situation with alarm, for they saw underprivileged children as individuals who were disadvantaged by the overwhelming social forces of the time, such as poverty, racism, poor education, and the like. Such children were widely believed to be at serious risk as individuals and in need of proper attention and services if they were to grow up to be law-abiding, contributing members of society. The conclusion was obvious: active intervention in the present was necessary to redress the problems of the past and the present, and to guarantee the future. This was precisely what Harold M. Skeels or George D. Stoddard or Kurt Lewin or any of their like-minded colleagues tried to say in a different age in America's cultural history.[3]

Issues of power and equity were involved in this new perspective in which at-risk children were perceived as individuals caught up in an oppressive social system as well. Michael Harrington, for example, published *The Other America: Poverty in the United States* (1962), in which he laid bare the impoverishment of so many Americans in the midst of an allegedly "affluent society." Harrington joined with a growing list of social critics in the 1950s and 1960s who charged, from different (and sometimes conflicting) perspectives, that the social system was oppressing most Americans, whether poor or not. The list included William H. Whyte, whose trenchant *Organization Man* (1956) decried the all-powerful organization that stifled creativity and individuality; Sloan Wilson, whose *Man in the Gray Flannel Suit* (1955) criticized the monolithic conformity of corporate capitalism; and the beat generation's intellectuals and writers, who argued that the system sought to obliterate free expression.

Even the structures and processes of popular culture had altered from the holistic symmetry of the interwar years to the asymmetrical individualism or individuation of the post-1950s era, for example, with the emergence of rock-and-roll music and the disappearance of the big bands of the 1940s; the replacement of such singing groups as the homogeneous Mills Brothers by distinctive individuals called the Beatles; and the shift from modernism to postmodernism in the arts. Furthermore, there appeared to be good reason to view children as individuals more than as members of larger social entities, such as families, neighborhoods, communities, or other groups. As James B. Gilbert has pointed out, the immediate postwar national campaign to abolish juvenile delinquency, as pushed by various governmental agencies, private interests, and social critics, had dissipated by the early 1960s, and was replaced by an overwhelming concern for and interest in "youth" as a distinct period in the life cycle of the individual, as a social unit within the society, and as a group with money to spend and its own interests in popular culture and consumer goods. What went out the window as well with the decline of the juvenile delinquency problem was the sense that children were potential threats to society. Rather the new wisdom seemed to be that those who were at risk could be saved provided there was the proper kind of intervention.[4]

And intervention in the individual's life cycle became the rallying cry for the new wisdom on what to do about children at risk in 1950s and 1960s America. By the late 1950s, evidence was accumulating in some social- and natural-science circles that pointed to a reassessment of the mainstream dogmas of developmental science, the maturation hypothesis, and the notion of the fixed IQ. In 1961, child psychologist J. McVicker Hunt published a seminal book, *Intelligence and Experience*. In that now-classic account, Hunt reviewed the scientific literature on early childhood development. Of particular interest was his dissection of the evidence for and against the maturation theory and the idea of the fixed IQ, together with a lengthy discussion of the work of the Swiss child psychologist Jean Piaget.

Without discounting the importance of biological inheritance, Hunt concluded that experience directly shaped and influenced the way in which the human brain developed. In other words, development was neither automatic nor predetermined. Organized structures existed as a part of the genetic endowment of species and even of families (depending on what was being discussed). Experience was not a straight-line process with no deviation whatsoever. There were multiple, although not infinite, possibilities in any given situation. The same held true, charged Hunt, for the proposition that the IQ was fixed from birth. He pointed to a growing body of evidence from the work of developmental scientists from the late 1940s on that these two main theses of "classic" developmental science were in serious error.[5]

Hunt had always mixed advocacy and research in his career. If Hunt advocated the stimulative importance of the child's environment and insisted on the mother's importance, it was another scientist, Benjamin Bloom, who went even further than Hunt. Bloom collected and analyzed data from longitudinal research projects all over the world in his *Stability and Change in Human Characteristics* (1964). He insisted that, among other things, half of the variation possible in mental powers was determined by age four. Thus he justified direct intervention in the lives of young children who would be at risk—whose development, in short, would be forever impaired by external social circumstances and events.

Bloom based his startling claim on the observation that the IQ score of a four-year-old could predict half of the variation in that person's IQ score when fully mature. Unfortunately, Bloom and others did not immediately recognize that by deploying the same arguments and logic, one could conclude that because the average of the natural parents' IQ could predict half of the range of variation of their offspring's adult IQ, half of that person's IQ happened before he or she was born—presumably not a point any sensible person, scientist or not, would wish to embrace.[6]

Hunt and Bloom worked in a particular temporal context. As Ellen Condliffe Lagemann makes clear in a most useful book, the 1950s and 1960s were a time of unusual ferment in American education and in what she calls the politics of knowledge. In the 1950s a group of conservative educational critics came to the fore, including University of Illinois historian Arthur E. Bestor, Jr., Admiral Hyman Rickover, of the U.S. Navy, and Harvard chemist and educational spokesman James B. Conant. Although their messages varied, they commonly argued that American education was in peril because it lacked its traditional standards of precision, excellence, and rigor. All manner of things were not interdependent and interactive, they insisted. There were priorities. Some parts of the larger whole were crucial for national survival; others were unimportant or even deleterious. In such a perspective, the whole was less important than this element or that, one priority or two over several others that could be imagined. Discrimination among the parts—the individuals—was essential.

On a less sweeping level, other educational reformers in the 1950s and 1960s insisted that there should be distinctions between the various levels of instruction, as well as exact special knowledge and a strong academic orientation in the schools. The new mathematics was pushed at first by a group of mathematicians at the University of Illinois who wanted to make students think through problems rather than learn through mere rote work; psychologist Jerome Bruner of Harvard's Center for Cognitive Studies insisted on the importance of thinking in education.

Fundamental to these proposals for changing American education and, therefore, American culture and society, were the actions of several foundations, especially the Carnegie Corporation, now under the leadership of John W. Gardner, who had won his doctorate at the Institute of Child Welfare at Berkeley in the 1930s and taken up working with foundations after World War II. In particular did Gardner, through the Carnegie Corporation's leadership and resources, promote educational reform. Among those scholars whose work he supported was J. McVicker Hunt himself. What Gardner realized, of course, was that the private foundations would never have the resources, or the moral authority with the American public, to reform American education. And the experience of philanthropic work in the interwar years was that pilot projects, no matter how enticing and imaginative to their potential supporters, remained largely that—interesting ideas. Vast sums of money and national leadership responsible to the masses of voters—these were the instruments necessary for the renewal of American society and culture through a new American education that took account of the many disparities, inequities, and special circumstances of the land. And such leadership and money could come only from the federal government, united by popular support, a sufficiently large system that would heal all wounds, overcome all opposition, and remake society—all, of course, for the better. Gardner had two such redistributionist projects for the federal government, one for a national program of early childhood education, the other for federal assistance to established school districts for the special needs of disadvantaged, at-risk children. Such a spin on the ball got around the practical political problem of federal aid to parochial schools and constitutional issues of church-state relations. Whether Gardner knew it or not, he was helping shift the responsibility for the solution of public policy problems from that holistic mechanism of many distinct elements and agencies—federal, state, local, eleemosynary, professional, and for-profit institutions—to the one and one alone: the federal government. This radical departure in the history of American public policy deserves infinitely more discussion and analysis than is possible here.[7]

At least one of the Iowa scientists, Harold M. Skeels, was also active in the late 1950s and early 1960s. After being mustered out of service at the end of World War II, he went to work for the federal government as a clinical psychologist. By the late 1950s he was at the Community Research and Services Branch of the National Institute of Mental Health. In 1959 he decided to do a final follow-up of the twenty-five "morons" whom he and Harold S. Dye had studied in the late 1930s. Skeels and Dye had tried to show that babies transferred from the Davenport orphanage to the Glenwood Home for the Feebleminded and given caring attention by older inmates who were also feebleminded attained over a period of many months a mental level more nearly normal than retarded. Skeels had to squeeze the work into the already busy schedule demanded by his federal position.

Skeels published his study under the austere title *Adult Status of Children with Contrasting Early Life Experiences: A Follow-Up Study*, in 1966. Over a period of several years, and on his own time, Skeels tracked down every individual in the experimental and control groups for that study. The thirteen in the experimental group, who had been nurtured by the Glenwood institution's "moron nursemaids" as very young infants, went on to have normal lives at social, economic, scholastic, and cultural levels to be expected of their adoptive parents. The twelve selected from the Davenport orphanage who remained in the orphanage led lives of a totally different character. In other words, early life experiences seemed to set the limits and possibilities of adult status.

Thus Skeels confirmed Hunt's and Bloom's arguments as they had legitimated his. Central to Skeels's method was to consider each individual as a distinct case in his or her own right. And he based all of his conclusions upon the facts that could be ascertained, two decades after the original study was published, about those twenty-five adults. As he pointed out in his conclusion, the individuals in each group had kept their differing patterns of development into adulthood. All in the experimental group were self-supporting adults, and "none was a ward of any institution, public or private." In contrast were the fates of the members of the control group: one died in adolescence in a state institution for the mentally retarded; four were still wards of institutions; one was in a mental hospital; and the other three were in institutions for the mentally retarded. In education, occupational levels, and virtually every other objective measure of individual attainment, the contrast was striking. Even in matters of the heart and family was there a difference. Only two of the twelve in the control group had married: one had serious problems of abnormality; the other had four apparently normal children. In the experimental group, all but two had married: nine had a total of twenty-eight children, whose IQs ranged from 86 to 125, with a median and a mean IQ of 104, and none of the children had the slightest evidence of abnormality.[8]

Skeels's study was published in developmental science's important monograph series. His professional peers quickly accepted his results, even in instances in which the scientists in question had doubted the Iowa work of the 1930s and 1940s. It was quite obvious that in the 1960s, unlike a generation ago, that there was a professional, not to mention a lay, discourse in which the Iowa work could be understood and evaluated on its own terms. Put another way, the notion of the meaning of group identity for the individual that had been so pervasive in the profession of child development and in American culture, save chiefly at Iowa, in the 1930s and 1940s had dissipated and been replaced by a different sense of the order of things. This change helped stimulate a sense of the meaning of group identity in which the individual could be thought of as a person whose group membership was no fatalistic identity, and whose membership in a particular group could be questioned, if for no other reason than the individual's perceived distinctiveness, idiosyncrasy, and asymmetry.

The federal government's Head Start program had its own origins in the 1950s and, especially, the 1960s, and in no direct or causal sense did the work of the Iowa scientists lead to it. It is interesting to note, however, that as President Lyndon B. Johnson's secretary of health, education, and welfare, John W. Gardner, formerly of the Carnegie Corporation, was able to champion his two pet projects, a federal program in early childhood education, or Head Start, and federal assistance to school districts on behalf of disadvantaged children, or the Elementary and Secondary Education Act of 1965. Thus had the torch been passed within the world of public policy. Meanwhile, within the world of developmental science, the new views that Hunt and Bloom represented in the developmental sciences led to the establishment of a number of small-scale experimental early intervention programs by almost a dozen investigators in the early 1960s. At first, and for some time, these scientists were not aware of one another's work. Each study was founded independently of all others; in many crucial respects, they were different from one another and thus not comparable.

Yet more than science was involved. By happenstance what was to become Head Start, including most of its social science rationale, became a part of President Johnson's War on Poverty in the middle 1960s. The War on Poverty was politically unpopular among local administrators around the country because it promised to bypass them and empower ordinary, and needy, citizens in targeted communities. R. Sargent Shriver, OEO's director, devised a program in compensatory education for poor children of preschool age that was based on his own interrogations of social scientists and his notions of what was useful for the War on Poverty. Most specialists told Shriver he should have a pilot program, with but a few thousand students, to evaluate results; there were not enough teachers for a mass program, in any event. But Shriver, encouraged by President Johnson, thought solely in terms of a massive program involving perhaps a million pupils for Head Start's first summer tryout.[9]

The program probably deflected criticism of other aspects of the War on Poverty, but it also became controversial itself. So-called compensatory education had always had its critics within the field of child development, as the experience of the Iowa scientists in the 1930s and 1940s suggested. In the middle and late 1960s there was a rising chorus of critics, ranging from Arthur Jensen, who insisted that at least 80 percent of IQ was inherited and that there were persistent gaps between blacks and whites in average IQ scores, regardless of which study was examined, to conservative columnist Russell Kirk, who stoutly insisted that one could not make a silk purse out of a sow's ear.[10]

Head Start nevertheless survived these and other criticisms. Perhaps the most damning criticism leveled against Head Start came from the so-called Westinghouse Learning Corporation study, published in 1969, which suggested that the intellectual gains of preschool compensatory education evaporated after a few years in elementary school. It was perhaps on the basis of this study that the Nixon administration, not anxious to follow in the ideological footsteps of its predecessor, scaled back Head Start's funding. Yet the program was too popular with Americans, liberal or conservative, to kill, for both could imagine how giving a toddler a bit of a boost would prove one's pet social theories. And the program had never been intended to be merely academic in character. Its ultimate agenda included the full range of the child's development, meaning health, nutrition, social competence, and all other aspects of normal, healthy, child development.

By the mid-1970s, Head Start seemed to have made a niche for itself in the national political system. After the first summer, it became a year-round program to assist children from poor families to become ready for school in all respects so that they could compete on a level of equality with their middle-class peers. In 1975, Head Start operated out of 9,400 centers, dispensed grants to 2,200 groups or agencies to run such centers, and enrolled approximately

350,000 children at an annual cost of $392 million. Eighty percent of those children attended their Head Start programs on a full-year basis. During the Reagan administration, Head Start suffered serious cutbacks, but bounced back to a close approximation of its high-water mark of enrollees by 1990, at an annual cost of $2 billion. Inasmuch as any social action program with a large constituency from the 1960s may still be said to be alive and functional in the 1990s, besides such sacrosanct programs as Social Security and Medicare, it is probably Head Start, which even has its own federal bureau. Whether that is symptomatic of Head Start's political vitality or entombment, only time will tell.[11]

There were signs in the early 1980s, however, that developmental scientists had finally put closure on the issues that the Iowa IQ studies—among others in their time—had raised as scientific issues. In 1982, Irving Lazar and Richard Darlington, together with a dozen other colleagues in developmental science, published a massive study that constituted a landmark of a sort, a collaborative study in which the long-term effects of early childhood education on children from low-income families was evaluated. In 1976, twelve developmentalists who had long-term experiments in early childhood education for poor children agreed to pool their data. In most instances, these scientists had begun their studies before the OEO founded Head Start in 1965. All had begun their work independently of one another. After combining those elements of their raw data that could be placed into a larger, unified study, they conducted a coordinated follow-up of the original subjects, who ranged in age in 1976 from nine to nineteen years old. Two new investigators joined the project to serve as overall supervisors for data collection and analysis. Not all data collected in the various studies was pooled, because not all of it was relevant to the new project's general concerns or comparable to data collected in other studies.

Lazar and his colleagues asked two simple questions of the raw data so merged: Did early childhood programs have long-term effects? And were different subgroups of the children influenced differently by these programs? In methodological terms, the investigators appeared capable of surmounting several potentially thorny problems, including how to handle data gathered in undeniably different problems; whether early education, regardless of how it was done, could be said to influence children as a general proposition; and whether there had been too much attrition for the studies to provide a reasonable and empirical set of answers to the questions posed. The overall answer was *yes* to the first question and *no* to the second. Early education mattered to children from low-income backgrounds, and importantly so.

Lazar and his colleagues declared that early education programs had long-lasting effects in four respects—competence in school; the full articulation of development; the attitudes and values that children had; and a beneficial impact on the families. In every case there were experimental and control groups established, defined, and tracked. The differences between the experimental and the control children were in each of these four areas palpable and real, the investigators argued. No investigator made the careless claims that George Stoddard occasionally had in the later thirties, when he seemed to imply that a silk purse could be made out of a sow's ear, or, for that matter, that R. Sargent Shriver and other liberal political figures of the 1960s often uttered on the political hustings. Early education program graduates were less likely than the controls to be assigned to special education classes or to be retained in grade. Program graduates outperformed their controls on the Stanford-Binet intelligence test for several years after the program had ended; they had pride in their accomplishments based on their notions of their own merits and work; their families were more ambitious for and supportive of their children. There were no significant or important differences among low-income children in these effects by gender, race, or other factors. In a very real sense, these results provided a kind of posthumous legitimation of some of the Iowa station's most controversial work.[12]

The Iowa Child Welfare Research Station did become, in the interwar era, an important center for new and interesting ideas about the nature of human nature. In the philosophical and moral, but not the historical, sense, these ideas have influenced scientists, activists, and ordinary citizens alike in our own time, including ideas about the complexities of group and individual development and the dynamics of small groups and of democratic group leadership—what one sophisticated historian has called "democratic social engineering." Since World War II, there have been two basic theoretical alternatives to Hullian (and Skinnerian) learning theory, both pioneered at the Iowa station: Lewin's small group dynamics and Sears's social learning theory. In that sense, a humdrum location was nevertheless the setting for new and interesting ideas that perhaps were somewhat ahead of their time.[13]

The ability to anticipate future ideas is most likely a gift, even an accident, probably not comprehensible in most instances to those who do so. We should understand, however, that there are always differences between the meanings of notions and beliefs in different ages. Quite literally Americans acted and thought as if reality was constituted in very different ways in the two eras—the interwar versus the postwar periods. Thus Harold M. Skeels, Beth Wellman, and George Stoddard acted and thought from a very different view of the world, and intended a different agenda, when they "anticipated" Head Start than have Head Start's most important champions. More likely than not, Kurt Lewin meant something very different by democratic group leadership from the often vulgar techniques that democratic social engineers have developed in our own time. It would seem, in short, that technical knowledge—like any other kind of knowledge, popular, religious, social, political, and the like—is a very specific product of the age in which it waxes and wanes, and is not in any important or meaningful sense an artifact that is timeless. What appear to be the same words and actions in one age may exist in another, but it would seem sounder to assume that there are many distinct pasts in the past—each distinct from every other—than to believe that there is one continuous past, stretching back from our own present to the most remote beginnings, and that movement from that point to our own time is either progress or decline. The idea of progress, like that of decline, would appear to involve a preset bundle of commitments through which the historiographer gazes at the past. Were the Iowa scientists a "failure" or a "success"? Whatever any reader may wish to think about that question, it may be fairly doubted that it is one that can be answered with the methods and outlook of high-grade historical scholarship. The pasts that constitute the past meant many things to their own contemporaries, and they will mean many other things to us today. For us to be able to grasp, however imperfectly, the meanings of a given age to its contemporaries is the ultimate—and daunting—challenge of the historian.

NOTE ON PRIMARY SOURCES

For this study, manuscript collections were obviously indispensable; these materials were especially rich for the period to the 1930s. The Archives of the University of Iowa, in the University Libraries, was the place to begin. For the Iowa station's inner history, I used the University of Iowa Presidential Correspondence, in literally hundreds of boxes, which were highly useful inasmuch as during the period I wrote about, the presidents were deeply involved in the affairs of each unit of the university, including the station; fortunately, after 1917 there was a central file for each unit and individual that had correspondence with the university presidents. The Iowa Child Welfare Research Station Records were very useful for understanding the campaign for the station and the station's early years; they constituted forty linear feet of boxes. Unfortunately, the collections of other faculty associated with the station were not particularly useful, or even preserved, including those of George D. Stoddard, Charles H. McCloy, and Wendell Johnson. Much correspondence and all data files have not been preserved. The Faculty Vertical Files, or personnel files on individual faculty members, and the records of the station's successor, the Institute of Child Behavior and Development, were helpful. The Cora Bussey Hillis Papers at the State Historical Society of Iowa, also in Iowa City, constitute a small collection of great utility for understanding this complex and remarkable person and the people, events, and movements around her. In addition, there are large numbers of Hillis letters in the records of the Iowa Child Welfare Research Station.

A major repository for the history of child development is the Rockefeller Archive Center in North Tarrytown, New York. Especially crucial for my work were the massive files of the Laura Spelman Rockefeller Memorial, but useful also were the records of the General Education Board, the Spelman Fund, and, upon occasion, the Rockefeller Foundation. I found that the records of the Carnegie Corporation and especially of the Commonwealth Fund, also at the Rockefeller Archive Center, were helpful, too. Lawrence K. Frank's papers as a Rockefeller officer are in the appropriate collections at the Rockefeller Archive Center, and there are twenty-six boxes of Lawrence K. Frank papers at the History of Medicine Division of the National Library of Medicine, Bethesda, Maryland. These collections were indispensable. Other manuscript collections at the National Library of Medicine that I examined included the papers of Wayne Dennis, Helen Thompson, Milton J. E. Senn, and Julius Richmond (the first director of Head Start) and the records of the Society for Research in Child Development and the Child Research Council of Denver.

There are also papers of those who were at the Iowa station or involved in its history located at the Archives of the History of American Psychology, University of Akron, Akron, Ohio, including those of Kurt Lewin and Kenneth W. Spence, especially Spence's correspondence with Clark L. Hull. Also useful were the papers of Lewis M. Terman and Robert R. Sears at the Stanford University Archives, Stanford, California. I also found some correspondence to and from Robert R. Sears in the Robert M. Yerkes Papers at the Sterling Library of Yale University, New Haven, Connecticut. Also helpful were the Florence L. Goodenough Papers at the University of Minnesota Archives, Minneapolis, Minnesota.

Quite revealing were the records of particular child welfare and parent education centers, including those of the Institute of Child Welfare, Teachers College, Columbia University; the Institute of Child Welfare, University of Minnesota, Twin Cities; and the Institute of Human Development (known before the 1960s as the Institute of Child Welfare), University of California, Berkeley; all located in their respective university archives. The Ada Hart Arlitt Papers in the University of Cincinnati archives, Cincinnati, Ohio, shed much light on parent education.

Also helpful in a more general sense were the papers of child development scientists, including those of G. Stanley Hall, Clark University Archives, Worcester, Massachusetts; William E. Blatz and Edward A. Bott, University of Toronto Library, Toronto, Canada; Arnold L. Gesell, Manuscripts Division, Library of Congress, Washington, D.C.; Henry H. Goddard, Archives of the History of American Psychology, University of Akron, Akron, Ohio; J. McVicker Hunt, University of Illinois Archives, Urbana-Champaign, Illinois;

Margaret Mead, Manuscripts Division, Library of Congress, Washington, D.C.; and the Horace M. Kallen Papers, which contain much Kurt Lewin correspondence, Institute for Jewish Research of New York. In addition, there were several other helpful smaller collections, such as the records of the Committee on Food Habits at the archives of the National Academy of Sciences, Washington, D.C.; and the papers of Ellen Swallow Richards at the American Home Economics Association, also in Washington, D.C. For more information on archival materials in child development, see Hamilton Cravens and Lind Heath Curry, "History of Child Development: Primary Source Materials. First Compilation of Abstracts," in *Child Development Abstracts and Bibliography* 58 (1984): 123–41.

The largest collection of oral histories for the child development and child guidance movements (nearly 190) were conducted by Milton J. E. Senn, for which there are transcripts at the National Library of Medicine in Bethesda, Maryland; a microfilm edition of them was available. Probably useful for most scholars is Senn's distillation, *Insights on the Child Development Movement in the United States* (Chicago: University of Chicago Press, 1975). Very useful is Flora M. Rhind's five-volume oral history memoir, conducted by the Oral History Research Office of Columbia University; Rhind worked within Rockefeller philanthropy from the 1920s to the 1950s. Useful too is the oral history interview of Lois Stolz by Ruby Takananshi, at the National Library of Medicine. Interviews of associates of Kurt Lewin and Henry H. Goddard at the Archives of the History of American Psychology at the University of Akron are helpful, as are interviews of Carl Seashore and of Ruth Updegraff at the University of Iowa Archives. I interviewed Robert R. Sears about his career up to his departure from Iowa; there are copies of the transcripts at the university archives at the University of Iowa and Stanford University. Those interested in Sears's career after Iowa will find interviews with him and his wife in the Senn collection, plus an additional interview with Sears concerning his career at Stanford.

Indispensable were the several thousand scientific articles and books published in the field to the 1960s. Crucial also is Charles C. Spiker, comp., *The Institute of Child Behavior and Development: Fifty Years of Research, 1917–1967* (Iowa City: University of Iowa, 1967), a bibliography of the station's publications. For bibliographical leads to the literature of child science, I began with a list of persons and institutions in the field that was generated for the archival preservation project of the Society for Research in Child Development, with which I was associated for several years; I then followed these leads through standard bibliographical sources and the field's journals. Especially useful was Carl Murchison, ed., *A Handbook of Child Psychology* (Worcester, Mass.: Clark University Press, 1931) and subsequent editions.

I also read newspapers and magazines. Before the 1920s I used, in appropriate time periods, the *Des Moines Register* and the *Des Moines Tribune*, which covered state news, especially political news, in considerable depth. For news stories from the 1920s to the 1950s, I depended heavily on a massive scrapbook of press clippings in the university archives.

NOTES

ABBREVIATIONS

AJDC	*American Journal of Diseases of Children*
AJP	*American Journal of Psychology*
AG	Arnold Gesell Papers, Manuscript Division, Library of Congress, Washington, D.C.
CBH	Cora Bussey Hillis Papers, State Historical Society of Iowa, Iowa City, Iowa
CD	*Child Development*
CE	*Childhood Education*
CW	Iowa Child Welfare Research Station Papers, University of Iowa Archives, Iowa City, Iowa
DI	*Daily Iowan*
DMR	*Des Moines Register*
DMT	*Des Moines Tribune*
ESJ	*Elementary School Journal*
FLG	Florence L. Goodenough Papers, University of Minnesota Archives, Minneapolis, Minnesota
GEB	General Education Board Papers Rockefeller Archive Center, North Tarrytown, New York
HMK	Horace M. Kallen Papers, Yivo Institute, New York, New York
ICBD	Institute of Child Behavior and Development Papers, University of Iowa Archives, Iowa City, Iowa (faculty initials after symbol indicate a specific file, e.g., ICBD:KL means Kurt Lewin's file in these records)
ICPC	*Iowa City Press-Citizen*
IP	Papers of the Presidents of the University of Iowa, University of Iowa Archives, Iowa City, Iowa
JASP	*Journal of Abnormal and Social Psychology*
JCP	*Journal of Comparative Psychology*
JConP	*Journal of Consulting Psychology*

JEP	*Journal of Educational Psychology*
JER	*Journal of Educational Research*
JEE	*Journal of Experimental Education*
JExpP	*Journal of Experimental Psychology*
JGP	*Journal of Genetic Psychology*
JHE	*Journal of Home Economics*
JJR	*Journal of Juvenile Research*
JN	*Journal of Nutrition*
JP	*Journal of Pediatrics*
JPsy	*Journal of Psychology*
JSP	*Journal of Social Psychology*
KL	Kurt Lewin Papers, Archives of the History of American Psychology, University of Akron, Akron, Ohio
LSRM	Laura Spelman Rockefeller Memorial Papers, Rockefeller Archive Center, North Tarrytown, New York
LKF	Lawrence K. Frank Papers, History of Medicine Division, National Library of Medicine, Bethesda, Maryland
LMT	Lewis M. Terman Papers, Stanford University Archives, Stanford, California
PB	*Psychological Bulletin*
PR	*Psychological Review*
PSJGP	*Pedagogical Seminary and Journal of Genetic Psychology*
PIAS	*Proceedings of the Iowa Academy of Sciences*
PSEBM	*Proceedings of the Society for Experimental Biology and Medicine*
RER	*Review of Educational Research*
RRS	Robert R. Sears Papers, Stanford University Archives, Stanford, California
RF	Rockefeller Foundation Papers Rockefeller Archive Center, North Tarrytown, New York
SF	Spelman Fund Papers, Rockefeller Archive Center, North Tarrytown, New York
SOHI	Milton J. E. Senn Oral History Interviews in Child Development and Child Guidance, History of Medicine Division, National Library of Medicine, Bethesda, Maryland
SS	*School and Society*
UISCW/UISSCW	*University of Iowa Studies, Studies in Child Welfare*
VF	Faculty Vertical Files, University of Iowa Archives, Iowa City, Iowa (faculty personnel files, matched with initials of faculty member, e.g., VF:KL means Kurt Lewin vertical file)

PREFACE

1. Bernard Wishy, *The Child and the Republic: The Dawn of Modern American Child Nurture* (Philadelphia: University of Pennsylvania Press, 1968), vii–x.

2. Hamilton Cravens, *The Triumph of Evolution: The Heredity-Environment Controversy, 1900–1941* (1978; reprint, Baltimore, Md.: Johns Hopkins University Press, 1988).

3. See Alan I Marcus, *Quest for Legitimacy: Farmers, Colleges, and Experiment Stations, 1870–1890* (Ames: Iowa State University Press, 1985); Marcus, *Plague of Strangers: Social*

Groups and the Origins of City Services in Cincinnati (Columbus: Ohio State University Press, 1991); William S. Graebner, *The Engineering of Consent: Democratic Social Engineering in America* (Madison: University of Wisconsin Press, 1987); and my "History of the Social Sciences," in Sally G. Kohlstedt and Margaret W. Rossiter, eds., *Historical Writing on American Science: Problems and Prospects* (Baltimore, Md.: Johns Hopkins University Press, 1986), 183–207. For a different perspective, see Dorothy Ross, *The Origins of American Social Science* (New York: Cambridge University Press, 1991).

4. Joseph M. Hawes, *The Children's Rights Movement: A History of Advocacy and Protection* (Boston: Twayne, 1991), 96–122.

5. Edward B. Fiske, "Head Start: Ten Years Old and Planning Experiments," *New York Times*, June 8, 1975, sec. 1, p. 40.

INTRODUCTION

1. Ellen Key, *The Century of the Child* (New York: G. P. Putnam's Sons, 1909), 243; the German edition, of which many more were printed than of the original Swedish edition and which is the basis for all subsequent translations, is *Das Jahrhundert Des Kindes*, studien von Ellen Key; autorisierte übertragung von Francis Mario (Berlin: S. Fischer, 1905). The official biography is Louise Nystrom-Hamilton, *Ellen Key: Her Life and Her Work*, trans. A. E. B. Fries (New York: G. P. Putnam's Sons, 1913).

2. W. E. B. Du Bois, *The Philadelphia Negro; A Social Study* (Cambridge, Mass.: Harvard University Press, 1899). For a perceptive analysis of this work, see Zane L. Miller, "Racism and the City: The Young Du Bois and the Role of Place in Social Theory, 1893–1901," *American Studies* 30, no. 2 (Fall 1989): 89–102. See also Ellen Church Semple, *The Influence of Geographical Factors in American History* (New York: Henry Holt, 1903); Jane Addams, *Twenty Years at Hull House* (New York: Macmillan, 1910); and Allen F. Davis, *American Heroine: The Life and Legend of Jane Addams* (New York: Oxford University Press, 1973), the standard biography; Hamilton Cravens, "Establishing the Science of Nutrition at the USDA: Ellen Swallow Richards and Her Allies," *Agricultural History* 64 (Spring 1990): 122–33.

3. Robyn Muncy, *Creating A Female Dominion in American Reform, 1890–1935* (New York: Oxford University Press, 1990). On the rise of female careers, see, for example, Eleanor Flexner, *Century of Struggle: The Women's Rights Movement in America* (Cambridge, Mass.: Harvard University Press, 1959); William O'Neill, *When Everyone Was Brave: A History of Feminism in America* (Chicago: Quadrangle, 1969); Carl N. Degler, *At Odds: Women and the Family from the Revolution to the Present* (New York: Oxford University Press, 1980); Margaret W. Rossiter, *Women Scientists in America: Struggles and Strategies to 1940* (Baltimore, Md.: Johns Hopkins University Press, 1982); Sara M. Evans, *Born For Liberty: A History of Women in America* (New York: Free Press, 1983); Mary Ryan, *Womanhood in America: From Colonial Times to the Present*, 3d ed. (New York: Franklin Watts, 1983); Pnina Abir-Am and Dorinda Outram, eds., *Uneasy Careers and Intimate Lives: Women in Science, 1789–1979* (New Brunswick, N.J.: Rutgers University Press, 1987).

4. On child-saving and progressive education, see, for example, Grace Abbott, ed., *The Child and the State*, 2 vols. (Chicago: University of Chicago Press, 1938); Mimi Abramovitz, *Regulating the Lives of Women: Social Policy from Colonial Times to the Present* (Boston: South End Press, 1988); LeRoy Ashby, *Saving the Waifs: Reformers and Dependent Children, 1890–1917* (Philadelphia: Temple University Press, 1984); John Bodnar,

"Schooling and the Slavic-American Family, 1900–1940," in Bernard Weiss, ed., *American Education and the European Immigrant* (Urbana: University of Illinois Press, 1982), 78–95; Paul Boyer, *Urban Masses and Moral Order in America, 1890–1920* (Cambridge, Mass.: Harvard University Press, 1978); Robert H. Bremner, *From the Depths: The Discovery of Poverty in the United States* (New York: New York University Press, 1956); Dominic Cavallo, *Muscles and Morals: Organized Playgrounds and Urban Reform, 1880–1920* (Philadelphia: University of Pennsylvania Press, 1980); Ronald D. Cohen and Raymond A. Mohl, *The Paradox of Progressive Education: The Gary Plan and Urban Schooling* (Port Washington, N.Y.: Kennikat Press, 1979); Lawrence A. Cremin, *The Transformation of the School: Progressivism in American Education, 1876–1955* (New York: Alfred A. Knopf, 1962); Jeremy P. Felt, *Hostages of Fortune: Child Labor Reform in New York State* (Syracuse, N.Y.: Syracuse University Press, 1965); Linda Gordon, ed., *Women, the State, and Welfare* (Madison: University of Wisconsin Press, 1990); Patricia A. Graham, *Community and Class in American Education, 1865–1918* (New York: Alfred A. Knopf, 1974); Louis R. Harlan, *Separate and Unequal: Public School Campaigns and Racism in the Southern Seaboard States, 1901–1915* (Chapel Hill: University of North Carolina Press, 1958); Joseph M. Hawes, *Children in Urban Society: Juvenile Delinquency in Nineteenth Century America* (New York: Oxford University Press, 1971); Jack M. Holl, *Juvenile Reform in the Progressive Era: William R. George and the Junior Republic Movement* (Ithaca, N.Y.: Cornell University Press, 1971); Edward Krug, *The Shaping of the American High School, 1880–1920* (New York: Macmillan, 1964); Charles Larsen, *The Good Fight: The Life and Times of Ben B. Lindsey* (Chicago: Quadrangle, 1972); Marvin Lazerson, *Origins of the Urban School: Public Opinion in Massachusetts, 1870–1915* (Cambridge, Mass.: MIT Press, 1971); Roy Lubove, *The Professional Altruist: The Emergence of Social Work as a Career, 1880–1930* (Cambridge, Mass.: Harvard University Press, 1965); David Macleod, *Building Character in the American Boy: The Boy Scouts, YMCA, and Their Forerunners, 1870–1920* (Madison: University of Wisconsin Press, 1983); Robert M. Mennel, *Thorns and Thistles: Juvenile Delinquents in the United States, 1825–1940* (Hanover, N.H.: University Press of New England, 1973); Judy Jolley Mohraz, *The Separate Problem: Case Studies of Black Education in the North, 1900–1930* (Westport, Conn.: Greenwood Press, 1979); Anthony Platt, *The Child Savers: The Invention of Delinquency* (Chicago: University of Chicago Press, 1969); Dorothy Ross, *G. Stanley Hall: The Psychologist as Prophet* (Chicago: University of Chicago Press, 1972); Steven L. Schlossman, *Love and the American Delinquent: The Theory and Practice of "Progressive" Juvenile Justice, 1825–1920* (Chicago: University of Chicago Press, 1977); Schlossman and Ronald D. Cohen, "The Music Man in Gary: Willis Brown and Child-Saving in the Progressive Era," *Societas* 7 (Winter 1977): 1–17; Susan Tiffin, *In Whose Best Interest? Child Welfare Reform in the Progressive Era* (Westport, Conn.: Greenwood Press, 1982); Louise Tilly and Patricia Gurin, eds., *Women, Change, and Politics* (New York: Russell Sage Foundation, 1990); Walter Trattner, *Crusade for the Children: A History of the National Child Labor Committee and Child Labor Reform in America* (Chicago: Quadrangle, 1970); Paul Violas, *The Training of the Urban Working Class: A History of Twentieth Century American Education* (Chicago: Rand, McNalley, 1978).

5. Mennel, *Thorns and Thistles*, and Schlossman, *Love and the American Delinquent*, ably cover the juvenile court and its problems; Platt, *The Child-Savers*, is a less scholarly and more polemical work.

6. Tiffin, *In Whose Best Interest?*; Muncy, *Creating A Female Dominion In American Reform*; and Emma Octavia Lundberg, *Unto the Least of These: Social Services for Children* (New York: Appleton Century Crofts, 1948), 113–402.

CHAPTER ONE

1. National Congress of Parents and Teachers, *The Parent-Teacher Organization: Its Origins and Development* (Chicago: National Congress of Parents and Teachers, 1944), 138–78.

2. Hazel Hillis, *The First Fifty Years: Iowa Congress of Parents and Teachers, 1900–1950* (n.p., n.d.), 9–15. See also *Washington Post*, Mar. 31, 1899; *Des Moines Capitol*, Apr. 14, 1899.

3. H. Hillis, *The First Fifty Years*, 9–10; "Guide to the Cora Bussey Hillis Papers" and the "scrapbook materials" (clippings, certificates, etc.), Box 2, Folder 1, CBH; "Hillis Memorial Issue," *Iowa Bulletin* 4 (Sept. 1924); Ginalie Swaim, "Cora Bussey Hillis: Woman of Vision," *Palimpsest* 60 (1979): 162–77.

4. H. E. Krantz to Cora B. Hillis, Jan. 25, 1899, CBH.

5. As cited in H. Hillis, *The First Fifty Years*, 12–13.

6. Ibid., 10–15; "Iowa Wants the Congress," *Washington Post*, Mar. 31, 1899; "Not a Baby Convention," *Des Moines Capitol*, Apr. 14, 1899, Box 2, Folder 12, CBH; Dorothy Ross, *G. Stanley Hall: The Psychologist as Prophet* (Chicago: University of Chicago Press, 1972), 287, 363.

7. "Not a Baby Convention"; reprinted in H. Hillis, *The First Fifty Years*, 14.

8. "The Congress of Mothers' Work," *Iowa State Register*, Sept. 24, 1899; "Women Much Interested," Sept. 6, 1899; "Talked Mothers' Congress"; "The Congress of Mothers"; Talks at the Valley"; "Of Interest to Women"; "Business Men Wanted," April 20, 1900 [1899?]; "Mother's Clubs Organize," Feb. 20, 1900. See also H. Hillis, *The First Fifty Years*, 16–24, Box 2, Folder 1, CBH.

9. Cora B. Hillis speech, May 15, 1900, "Madam President, Ladies and Gentlemen of the Fourth National Congress of Mothers," Box 1, CBH.

10. H. Hillis, *The First Fifty Years*, 28–30. See also these clippings: "No Suffrage for the Congress"; "Mrs. Birney Calls to Order the Opening Session of the Mothers' Congress"; "Iowa Mothers Form a Congress"; "Went Away Much Pleased," Box 2, Folder 1, CBH. Excerpts from the constitution and bylaws of the Iowa Congress are reprinted in "The Congress of Mothers," *Suggestions* 1 (Mar. 1901): 3, Box 2, Folder 2, CBH; "Reasons for Uniting with the National Congress of Mothers," *Suggestions* 1 (May 1901): 2–3, Box 2, Folder 2, CBH. Many clippings in Box 2, Folder 2, CBH further illustrate Hillis's ideas.

11. Mrs. Frederic Schoff to Cora B. Hillis, Jan. 11, 1902, Box 1, CBH. *First Iowa State Congress of Mothers* (n.p., 1902); "National Congress of Mothers to Be Held Here Again Jan. 18–22"; "Mothers' Congress Now Open"; "Mothers' Congress Is Anxious to Have Some Important Legislation"; all in Box 2, Folder 2, CBH; Judge Richard S. Tuthill to Hillis, Dec. 1, 1903, Jan. 10, 1904; Jane Addams to Hillis, May 22, 1903; Schoff to Hillis, Jan. 11, 1904; Benjamin B. Lindsey to Hillis, Jan. 11, 1904; Lindsey to Albert B. Cummins, Feb. 2, 1904; Cummins to C. C. Powell, Feb. 19, 1904; all in Box 1, CBH; H. Hillis, *The First Fifty Years*, 42–47. On the juvenile court law's passage, see "A Juvenile Court Law Is Demanded," *DMR*, Dec. 11, 1903; "Looks Bright for Juvenile Court," *Des Moines Capitol*, Mar. 11, 1904; "Judge Lindsey Will Speak," "Garst upon Juvenile Bill," "Separate Courts for Children," "One Boy in Five Gets into Jail," "Juvenile Court Gets Big Impetus," *DMR*, Mar. 11, 1904; "Judge Lindsey's Way of Dealing with His Boys"; all in Box 2, Folder 2, CBH. See also G. W. Burnham to Hillis, Mar. 15, 1904; Mrs. J. T. Bowen to Hillis, Feb. 24, 1905; Lindsey to Hillis, Apr. 10, 1905, May 18, 1906; all in Box 1, CBH. Hillis to Lindsey, Nov. [?], 1904; Lindsey to Hillis, July 2, 1904; Benjamin B. Lindsey Papers, Library of

Congress, Washington, D.C. (hereafter cited as Lindsey Papers). See also Ralph Mills Sayre, "Albert Baird Cummins and the Progressive Movement in Iowa," Ph.D. diss., Columbia University, 1958.

12. Cora B. Hillis to Benjamin B. Lindsey, Feb. 7, 1908, Lindsey Papers.

13. Cora B. Hillis to Thomas H. MacBride, Oct. 27, 1914, IP.

14. Quotes in Cora B. Hillis to George E. MacLean, Feb. 24, 1908, IP. See also MacLean to Hillis, Feb. 13, 1908, Mar. 1, 1909; Hillis to MacLean, Feb. 24, 1908; MacLean to Carl E. Seashore, June 2, 1909; all in IP.

15. My interpretation, based on Sayre, "Albert Baird Cummins and the Progressive Movement in Iowa," and on articles appearing in the *Des Moines Register and Leader* and the *Des Moines Capitol*, especially during the biennial legislative sessions, 1909–17. See also note 23.

16. Carl N. Degler, *At Odds: Women and the Family in America from the Revolution to the Present* (New York: Oxford University Press, 1980), 298–361, gives perceptive analyses of these phenomena. See also H. Hillis, *The First Fifty Years*, 48–52.

17. J. L. Pickard, "Historical Sketch of the State University of Iowa," *Annals of Iowa* 4 (Apr. 1899): 21–33; Clarence Ray Aurner, *History of Education in Iowa*, 4 vols. (Iowa City: State Historical Society of Iowa, 1916), vol. 4; George T. W. Patrick, "Founding the Psychological Laboratory at the State University of Iowa: An Historical Sketch," *Iowa State Journal of History and Politics* 34 (1932): 404–16; see also Stow Persons, *The University of Iowa in the Twentieth Century: An Institutional History* (Iowa City: University of Iowa Press, 1990), 65–66, 127–28. Evaluative and comparative data from the catalogs of both institutions and the annual *Report of the United States Commissioner of Education* (Washington, D.C.: Government Printing Office, 1880–1920) every five years between 1880 and 1920; Cora B. Hillis to Carl Seashore, Dec. 2, 8, 11, 13, 1913; Seashore to Hillis, Dec. 2, 5, 10, 11, 18, 1913; all in CW.

18. Julia Lathrop to Cora B. Hillis, Nov. 22, 1912; Thomas H. Smith to Hillis, Apr. 26, 1912; both in CBH; "Notes Re Cora Bussey Hillis, interview with Dean [Carl E.] Seashore, September 20, 1943," CW.

19. See Carl E. Seashore, *Pioneering in Psychology* (Iowa City: University of Iowa Press, 1942).

20. "Memorandum on Child Welfare Station after Conference with President MacBride, November 14, 1914," IP. Carl E. Seashore to Cora B. Hillis, Nov. 28, 1914, CW. "Minutes of the Meeting of the Committee on the Child Welfare Station . . . December 7th, 1914 . . . ," attached to Seashore to Hillis, Dec. 8, 1914; Hillis to Seashore, Dec. 11, 1914; IP. Florence B. Sherbon to Seashore, Dec. 15, 1914; Seashore to Hillis, Dec. 19, 1914; Hillis to Seashore, Dec. 24, 1914; Seashore to Hillis, Dec. 24, 1914; Hillis to Florence B. Sherbon, Dec. 25, 1914; "Minutes of Conference Held December 23, 1914," and "Minutes of Child Welfare Committee Meeting Held December 22, 1914," CW.

21. See correspondence between Cora B. Hillis and Carl Seashore, Dec. 1914, CW. Mrs. Rose S. Clark to Thomas H. MacBride, Dec. 2, 1914; MacBride to Clark, Dec. 15, 1914; Florence B. Sherbon to Seashore, Dec. 15, 1914; Hillis to Sherbon, Dec. 25, 1914; Seashore to Sherbon, Dec. 26, 1914; Seashore to Florence Richardson, Dec. 26, 1914; Sherbon to Hillis, Dec. 26, 1914; Richardson to Seashore, Dec. 19, 1914; Clark to Sherbon, Dec. 31, 1914; all in CW; Hillis to MacBride, Dec. 27, 31, 1914; Mrs. L. D. Carhart to MacBride, Dec. 28, 1914; both in IP.

22. *DMR*, Jan. 6, 1915.

23. See Leland Sage, *A History of Iowa* (Ames: Iowa State University Press, 1974), 148–

216; Sayre, "Albert Baird Cummins and the Progressive Movement in Iowa"; E. Daniel Potts, "The Progressive Profile in Iowa," *Mid-America* 47 (1965): 257–68; Potts, "A Comparative Study of the Leadership of Republican Factions in Iowa, 1904–1914," M.A. thesis, University of Iowa, 1956; William M. Bowers, "The Fruits of Iowa Progressivism, 1900–1915," *Iowa Journal of History and Politics* 57 (1959): 34–60; Fleming Fraker, Jr., "The Beginnings of the Progressive Movement in Iowa," *Annals of Iowa* 35 (1961): 578–93. See also Ruth A. Gallagher, *Legal and Political Status of Women in Iowa: An Historical Account of the Rights of Women in Iowa from 1838 to 1918* (Iowa City: State Historical Society of Iowa, 1918), 172–221; Mrs. W. H. Snider, comp. and ed., *Iowa Federation of Women's Clubs: Yearbook, 1915–1916* (Davenport, Iowa: n.p., 1915), 28–104, has a directory of all women's clubs affiliated with the IFWC that lists location, date founded, current number of members, and club purpose; on women's organizations in their "natural" settings, see Eleanor Flexner, *Century of Struggle: The Woman's Rights Movement in the United States* (1959; reprint, New York: Antheneum, 1970), 179–92; see also Jennie Croly, *The History of the Woman's Club Movement in America* (New York: n.p., 1912), 451–79; and Mary I. Wood, *History of the General Federation of Woman's Clubs for the First Twenty-Two Years of Its Organization* (New York: n.p., 1912), 29–30. See also *DMR*, Jan. 3, 4, 5, 7, 10, 11, 12, 16, 18, 20; Carl E. Seashore, "The Conservative Psychologist," *DMR*, Jan. 12, 1915; Cora B. Hillis, "Looking to the Children," *DMR*, Jan. 15, 1915; Hillis to Seashore, "Monday noon," [Dec. 1914 or Jan. 1915], Younkers' Bros. restroom letterhead, 4 pages, Jan. 1, 1915; Dr. Florence B. Sherbon to Seashore, Jan. 1, 1915; Seashore to Hillis, Jan. 2, 7, 1915; Seashore to Sherbon, Jan. 2, 1915; Seashore to Florence Richardson, Jan. 2, 1915; Seashore to Mary T. Watts, Jan. 9, 1915; all in CW. Thomas H. MacBride to Hillis, Jan. 4, 1915, IP. Hillis and Seashore wrote numerous letters in January 1915 to various individuals to support the bill; located in CW, there are too many to be cited here.

24. *DMR*, Feb. 11, 20, 22, 25, 1915. The struggle over suffrage can be followed in *DMR*, Jan. 26, Feb. 13, 24, 1915. The temperance fight can be followed in *DMR*, Jan. 8, 11, 12, 14, 16, 20, Feb. 9, 10, 11, 12, 13, 14, 15, 17, 18, 19, 21, 24, Mar. 1, 2, 11, 1915. The conflict over the highway commission can be followed in *DMR*, Jan. 3, 4, 5, 8, 10, Feb. 24, Mar. 21, Apr. 4, 1915. The legislative battle over the station can be followed in *DMR*, Feb. 6, 8, 9, 11, Mar. 25, 29, Apr. 10, 12, 15, 17, 18, 20, 1915. See also Will O. Coast to Thomas H. MacBride, Mar. 6, 1915; MacBride to Frederick Larrabee, Mar. 6, 13, 1915; all in IP. Seashore to H. C. Ring, Feb. 12, 1915; Hillis to Seashore, Feb. 12, 1915; Seashore to Hillis, Feb. 15, 1915; Seashore to Coast, Feb. 15, 1915; Hillis to Seashore, Feb. 17, 1915; all in CW. *DMR*, Apr. 14, 16, 1915; Hillis to Seashore, Apr. 19, 1915; in CW; *DMR*, Mar. 14, 15, Apr. 13, 15, 1915; Hillis to Seashore, Mar. 16, 17, 19, 23, Apr. 13, 15, 19, 1915; Seashore to Hillis, Mar. 15, 18, 22, 30, Apr. 2, 5, 15, 1915; all in CW.

25. *DMR*, Apr. 12, 28, May 19, 20, 21, 22, 1915. See also Snider, *Iowa Federation of Women's Clubs Yearbook, 1915–1916*, 133. Cora B. Hillis to Carl E. Seashore, Apr. 30, May 15, June 4, 1915; Seashore to Hillis, May 6, June 9, 1915; "Copy of Resolution Passed May 20th 1915—at Child Welfare Conference, Iowa City"; Hillis to Florence B. Sherbon, June 3, 1915; all in CW. Hillis to Thomas H. MacBride, June 3, 1915; MacBride to Hillis, June 11, 1915; both in IP. Seashore to Hillis, June 23, 1915, CBH. Hillis to Seashore, July 13, 1915, Sept. 11, 1916, CW. On Jessup as president and his attitude toward the research station and similar issues, see Persons, *The University of Iowa*, 66–69.

26. Gallagher, *Legal and Political Status of Women in Iowa*, 219–20; Thomas G. Ryan, "Male Opponents and Supporters of Woman's Suffrage: Iowa in 1916," *Annals of Iowa* 45 (1981): 537–50; Cora B. Hillis to Carl E. Seashore, May 27, 1916, CW. E. T. Meredith to

Hillis, Oct. 20, 1916; W. L. Harding to Hillis, Oct. 23, 1915; both in CBH; Hillis to Seashore, Sept. 11, 24, Oct. 7, 17, Dec. 4, 8, 16, 30, 1916, Jan. 31, 1917, CW.

27. *DMR*, Jan. 4, 5, 6, 10, 13, 14, 26, 1917; "Letter Sent to Farmers' Institutes," by Mrs. Hillis, early January 1917, CW; *DMR*, Mar. 12, 13, 14, 16, 17, 18, 23, 24, 28, Apr. 2, 1917.

28. *DMR*, Feb. 19, 25, Mar. 3, 7, 20, 22, 30, Apr. 1, 2, 10, 18, 1917. Cora B. Hillis to Carl E. Seashore, Jan. 27, 31, Feb. 7, 1914; Mrs. C. W. Carhart to Seashore, Jan. 29, 1917; Seashore to Hillis, Feb. 7, 1917; Hillis to Seashore, Jan. 23, 27, 31, Feb. 7, Mar. 1, Apr. 2, 1917; *DMR*, Mar. 10, 11, 1917; Hillis to William L. Harding, Feb. 16, 1917; all in CBH. Hillis to Seashore, Jan. 19, 23, Mar. 1, 1915, CW; *DMR*, Feb. 14, Apr. 15, 1917.

29. *DMR*, Apr. 7, 12, 13, 22, 24, 1917.

30. Hamilton Cravens, "Child-Saving in the Age of Professionalism, 1915–1930," in Joseph M. Hawes and M. Roy Hiner, eds., *American Childhood: A Research Guide and Historical Handbook* (Westport, Conn.: Greenwood Press, 1985), 415–88.

31. William James, *The Principles of Psychology*, 2 vols. (New York: Henry Holt, 1890); Hamilton Cravens and John C. Burnham, "Psychology and Evolutionary Naturalism in American Thought, 1890–1940," *American Quarterly* 23 (1971): 635–57; Cravens, *The Triumph of Evolution: The Heredity-Environment Controversy, 1900–1941* (1978; reprint, Baltimore, Md.: Johns Hopkins University Press, 1988), 56–88.

32. Edwin A. Kirkpatrick, *Fundamentals of Child Study: A Discussion of Instincts and Other Factors in Human Development with Its Practical Applications* (New York: Macmillan, 1914).

33. *The Work and Words of the National Congress of Mothers: First Annual Session, 1897* (New York: D. Appleton, 1897).

34. Ross, *G. Stanley Hall*, 279–308.

35. Ibid.; G. Stanley Hall, *Adolescence: Its Psychology, Anthropology, Sociology, Sex, Crime, Religion and Education*, 2 vols. (New York: D. Appleton, 1904).

36. Lewis M. Terman, "A Study in Precocity and Prematuration," *AJP* 16 (1905): 145–83, quote at 182.

37. Lewis M. Terman, "Genius and Stupidity: A Study of Some of the Intellectual Processes of Seven 'Bright' and Seven 'Stupid' Boys," *PSJGP* 13 (1905): 303–73, quote at 309.

38. Henry H. Goddard, "Heredity of Feeble-Mindedness," *Proceedings of the American Philosophical Society* 51 (1912): 173–77.

39. Henry Pickering Bowditch, *The Growth of Children: 8th Annual Report* (Boston: Massachusetts Board of Health, 1875), 273–323; Bowditch, *Growth of Children: 10th Annual Report* (Boston: Massachusetts Board of Health, 1879), 33–62.

40. Franz Boas and Clark Wissler, "Statistics of Growth," in U.S. Bureau of Education, *Annual Report of the Commissioner* (Washington, D.C.: Government Printing Office, 1904), 24–132; Boas, *Changes in Bodily Form of Descendants of Immigrants: Partial Report on the Results of an Anthropological Investigation for the United States Immigration Commission*, Senate Document no. 208, 61st Cong., 2d sess. (Washington, D.C.: Government Printing Office, 1911).

41. John Higham, *Strangers in the Land: Patterns of American Nativism, 1860–1925* (New Brunswick, N.J.: Rutgers University Press, 1955), 125; George W. Stocking, Jr., *Race, Culture and Evolution: Essays on the History of Anthropology* (New York: Free Press, 1968), 163–94.

42. See Kurt Danziger, *Constructing the Subject: Historical Origins of Psychological Research* (New York: Cambridge University Press, 1990), and on mental testing, 107–13. On Binet, see A. Binet and T. Simon, "Sur la nécessité d'établir un diagnostic scientifique des états

inférieurs de l'intelligence," *L'Année psychologique* 11 (1905): 163–90; Binet and Simon, "Méthodes nouvelles pour le diagnostic du niveau intellectuel des anormaux," *L'Année psychologique* 11 (1905): 191–244; Binet and Simon, "Le developpment de l'intelligence chez les enfants," *L'Année psychologique* 14 (1908): 1–94; an excellent biography of Binet is Theta H. Wolf, *Alfred Binet* (Chicago: University of Chicago Press, 1973). For Goddard's and Terman's "adaptations," see Henry H. Goddard, "A Measuring Scale of Intelligence," *Training School* 6 (1910): 146–54; Goddard, "Four Hundred Feeble-Minded Children Classified by the Binet Method," *PSJGP* 17 (1910): 388–97; Goddard, "Two Thousand Normal Children Measured by the Binet Measuring Scale of Intelligence," *PSJGP* 18 (1911): 232–59; Lewis M. Terman, "The Binet-Simon Scale For Measuring Intelligence," *Psychological Clinic* 5 (1911): 199–206; Terman et al., *The Stanford Revision and Extension of the Binet-Simon Scale for Measuring Intelligence* (Baltimore, Md.: Warwick and York, 1917); Robert M. Yerkes, ed., *Psychological Examining in the United States Army*, Memoirs of the National Academy of Sciences, vol. 15 (Washington: Government Printing Office, 1921); Cravens, *The Triumph of Evolution*, 78–86.

43. See Hamilton Cravens, "Establishing the Science of Nutrition at the U.S. Department of Agriculture: Ellen Swallow Richards and Her Allies," *Agricultural History* 64 (Spring 1990): 122–33; I am indebted to Alan I Marcus for helpful discussions of the history of nutrition. See also Harvey Levenstein, "The New England Kitchen and the Origins of Modern American Food Habits," *American Quarterly* 32 (1980): 369–86.

44. E. V. McCollum, *The Newer Knowledge of Nutrition: The Use of Food for the Preservation of Vitality and Health*, 2d ed. (New York: Macmillan, 1923). See also Harvey Levenstein, *Revolution at the Table: The Transformation of the American Diet* (New York: Oxford University Press, 1988).

45. William McDougall, *An Introduction to Social Psychology* (London: Methuen, 1908).

46. Cravens, *The Triumph of Evolution*, 71–78.

47. Arnold L. Gesell and Beatrice Chandler Gesell, *The Normal Child and Primary Education* (Boston: Ginn and Company, 1912), quotes at vii, viii, and 61.

48. Cravens, *The Triumph of Evolution*, 71–78; Cravens, "Child-Saving in the Age of Professionalism," 415–22.

49. Bird T. Baldwin, "The Normal Child: Its Physical Growth and Mental Development," *Popular Science Monthly* 85 (1914): 559–67, quotes at 559 and 566.

50. Roswell C. McCrea, *The Humane Movement: A Descriptive Survey* (New York: Columbia University Press, 1910).

51. Susan Tiffin, *In Whose Best Interest? Child Welfare Reform in the Progressive Era* (Westport, Conn.: Greenwood Press, 1982), 48–57, but see also Ronald D. Cohen, "Child-Saving and Progressivism, 1885–1915," in Hawes and Hiner, *American Childhood*, 273–309; Emma Octavia Lundberg, *Unto the Least of These: Social Services for Children* (New York: Appleton-Century-Crofts, 1947); and Robyn Muncy, *Creating a Female Dominion in American Reform, 1890–1935* (New York: Oxford University Press, 1991), a helpful and suggestive book, especially on the connections between the separate spheres and male and female professionalism.

52. Rudolph R. Reeder, *How Two Hundred Children Live and Learn* (New York: Lloyd Adams Noble, 1917).

53. Jack M. Holl, *Juvenile Reform in the Progressive Era: William R. George and the Junior Republic Movement* (Ithaca, N.Y.: Cornell University Press, 1971).

54. Tiffin, *In Whose Best Interest?*, 88–214.

55. William Healy and Augusta F. Bronner, "The Child Guidance Clinic: Birth and

Growth of an Idea," in Lawson G. Lowrey and Victoria Sloane, eds., *Orthopsychiatry, 1923–1948: Retrospect and Prospect* (New York: American Orthopsychiatric Association, 1948), 14–49.

56. Henry H. Goddard to G. Stanley Hall, Nov. 11, 1899, October 19, 1901, G. Stanley Hall Papers, Clark University Archives, Worcester, Massachusetts.

57. Henry H. Goddard, "Anniversary Address," in Edgar A. Doll, ed., *Twenty-Five Years: A Memorial Volume in Commemoration of the Twenty-Fifth Anniversary of the Vineland Laboratory, 1906–1931* (Vineland, N.J.: Training School at Vineland, Department of Research, 1932), 55–57; "New Jersey Association for the Study of Children and Youth . . . March 31, 1900 . . . Program . . . ," Folder 5, Box M37, Henry H. Goddard Papers, Archives of the History of American Psychology, University of Akron Library, Akron, Ohio (hereafter cited as Goddard Papers).

58. On Vineland's history, see Bird T. Baldwin, "The Psychology of Mental Deficiency," *Popular Science Monthly* 79 (1911): 82–93; Lucy Chamberlain, "The Spirit of Vineland," *Training School Bulletin* 19 (1922–23): 113–20; Doll, *Twenty-Five Years*; Joseph B. Byers, *The Village of Happiness: The Story of the Training School* (Vineland, N.J.: Smith Printing House, 1934), 1–90.

59. Henry H. Goddard to J. [*sic*] S. Woodward and Members of the Board of Trustees of the Carnegie Institution of Washington, June 1, 1908, Folder AA2, Box M33, Goddard Papers.

60. Henry H. Goddard to Charles B. Davenport, Mar. 15, May 5, 27, July 18, 26, 31, Oct. 1, 18, 25, Nov. 21, Dec. 9, 1909; Davenport to Goddard, Mar. 18, Apr. 19, May 7, 24, July 9, 21, 24, 28, Aug. 5, 14, Sept. 7, Oct. 2, 26, Nov. 26, 1909, Henry H. Goddard File, Charles B. Davenport Papers, Library of the American Philosophical Society, Philadelphia, Pennsylvania.

61. Henry H. Goddard, "The Binet and Simon Tests of Intellectual Capacity," *Training School* 5 (1908): 3–9; Goddard, "The Grading of Backward Children," *Training School* 5 (1908): 12–14.

62. Henry H. Goddard, "Heredity of Feeble-Mindedness," *American Breeders' Magazine* 1 (1910): 165–78; Goddard, "Four Hundred Feeble-Minded Children," 388–97; Goddard, "Two Thousand Normal Children Measured by the Binet Measuring Scale of Intelligence," *PSJGP* 18 (1911): 232–59.

63. Henry H. Goddard, "The Institution for Mentally Defective Children: An Unusual Opportunity for Scientific Research," *Training School* 7 (1910): 275–77.

64. Goddard, "Four Hundred Feeble-Minded Children," 388–97.

65. See, for example, Henry H. Goddard and Helen F. Hill, "Delinquent Girls Tested by the Binet Scale," *Training School* 8 (1911): 50–56.

66. Henry H. Goddard, *The Kallikak Family: A Study in the Heredity of Feeble-Mindedness* (New York: Macmillan, 1912); Goddard, *The Criminal Imbecile: An Analysis of Three Remarkable Murder Cases* (New York: Macmillan, 1915).

67. Cora B. Hillis to Carl E. Seashore, Sept. 11, 1916, CW. Walter A. Jessup to Lewis M. Terman, May 29, June 4, 11, 13, 16, 18, 1917; Terman to Jessup, May [n.d.], May 31, June [n.d.], June 17, 1917; Lotus D. Coffman to Jessup, May 3; Seashore to Jessup, June 2, 17, 18, July 2, 11; Arthur J. Todd to Jessup, June 29; Jessup to Todd, July 3; all in IP. Seashore to Hillis, June 19, 1917, CW. Jessup to Bird T. Baldwin, July 17, Aug. 2, 13; Baldwin to Jessup, July 22, 30, Aug. 6; Seashore to Baldwin, Aug. 13; Jessup to Seashore, July 26, 1917; all in IP. Seashore to Hillis, Aug. 13, 1917, CW.

68. Baldwin, "The Normal Child," 559–67; Baldwin, *The Physical Growth of Children*

From Birth to Maturity, UISCW, vol. 1, no. 1 (Iowa City: University of Iowa, 1920); Baldwin, "The Psychology of Mental Deficiency," 82–93; Baldwin, "The Learning of Delinquent Adolescent Girls as Shown by a Substitution Test," *JEP* 4 (1913): 317–22; Baldwin to Robert M. Yerkes, Feb. 8, 1915, Feb. 24, 1916, Bird T. Baldwin Author File, Robert M. Yerkes Papers, Sterling Library, Yale University Libraries, New Haven, Connecticut.

69. Bird T. Baldwin to Walter Jessup, Sept. 29, 1917, Jan. 28, 1918; Baldwin to Amy L. Daniels, Mar. 22, 1918; Daniels to Baldwin, Mar. 27, 1918; Jessup to D. D. Murphy, Apr. 6, 1918, p. 4; "Minutes of the Meeting of the Council of the Station, Mar. 26, 1918"; "Minutes of the Advisory Council Iowa Child Welfare Research Station, Monday, April 22, 1918"; all in CBH. Baldwin to Jessup, Nov. [?], 1917, p. 5; Baldwin to Clyde L. King, Nov. 10, 1917; King to Jessup, Nov. 24, 1917, Jan. 4, 1918; Baldwin to Jessup, Jan. 4, 15, 1918; all in IP.

70. Cora B. Hillis to Bird T. Baldwin, Nov. 7, 1914; Baldwin to Hillis, Nov. 14, 1917; both in CBH.

71. "Minutes of the Meeting of the Advisory Council of the Iowa Child Welfare Research Station, Old Dental Building, Thursday, February 28, 1918"; Bird T. Baldwin, "Memorandum for President Jessup and Dean Seashore," Feb. 25, 1918; Baldwin, "Report of the Iowa Child Welfare Research Station," Mar. 11, 1918, pp. 8–10; Ellsworth Faris, "Suggestions on Organization to County Chairmen," n.d. [but filed with above material]; "Tentative Schedule of the Iowa Child Welfare Research Station for Children's Year"; "Comment on Specific Items" and "Tentative Information Schedule for Children's Year, Prepared by the Iowa Child Welfare Research Station," n.d. or signature [but filed with Faris memorandum of Apr. 17, 1918, above]; all in IP.

72. Bird T. Baldwin to Walter A. Jessup, n.d. [probably Nov. 1917], and attached "Available Child Welfare Lectures," IP.

73. Bird T. Baldwin to Ellsworth Faris, Feb. 13, 1918; Baldwin, "Memorandum for President Jessup and Dean Seashore"; Baldwin to Walter A. Jessup, Mar. 6, 1918; Jessup to Baldwin, Apr. 4, 1918; Baldwin, "Report of the Iowa Child Welfare Research Station, Submitted to the President of the State University of Iowa, March 11, 1918"; all in IP. Carl E. Seashore to Cora B. Hillis, Apr. 17, 1918; Seashore to Hillis, June 26, 1918; both in CBH. Hillis to Jessup, Sept. 10, 1918; Jessup to Hillis, Sept. 20, 1918; both in IP. Hillis to President Woodrow Wilson, Oct. 12, 1918, CBH. Seashore to Hillis, Oct. 29, 1918; Ellsworth Faris to Hillis, Nov. 16, 1918; both in CBH. Faris, "To the Members of the Advisory Council of the Iowa Child Welfare Research Station," Apr. 15, 1919, IP.

74. Cora B. Hillis to Carl E. Seashore, Jan. 6, 1919; Seashore to Hillis, Aug. 28, 1919; both in CW. Faris, "To the Members of the Advisory Council of the Iowa Child Welfare Research Station"; Bird T. Baldwin, "Memorandum for President Jessup," Oct. 23, 1919; all in IP. Baldwin to Hillis, Nov. 14, 1919, CW. Ida B. Wise Smith to Baldwin, Nov. 16, 1919, IP. The full details may be found in Ohio Historical Society/Michigan Historical Collections, *Report of the Forty-Sixth Annual Convention of the National Woman's Christian Temperance Union, Held at . . . St. Louis, Missouri, November 15–20, 1919* (Woman's Christian Temperance Union Microfilm Series), Roll 9, Frames 2314, pp. 322, 335–37, 340.

75. Carl E. Seashore to Walter A. Jessup, July 1, 1918, titled "Plan for the Cooperation of the National Woman's Christian Temperance Union with the Iowa Child Welfare Research Station of the State University of Iowa," Mar. 20, 1920, IP; on eugenics, see Cravens, *The Triumph of Evolution,* 157–90; Cravens, "Oaks and Cacti," *Reviews in American History* 14 (1986): 104–9.

76. Anne E. Jackson to Marcella Hotz, Mar. 11, 1920; Bird T. Baldwin to Walter A. Jessup, Oct. 5, 1920; Baldwin to Cora B. Hillis, Apr. 27, 1920; Baldwin to Jessup, memorandum, June 30, 1920; all in IP.

77. Bird T. Baldwin to Walter A. Jessup, Aug. 16, Sept. 25, 1920; Baldwin, "Report to the Members of the Advisory Council," May 24, 1921; all in IP. Baldwin to Cora B. Hillis, Sept. 2, 1920, CBH.

CHAPTER TWO

1. On child welfare, see the citations in note 4, Introduction.

2. Merle Curti and Roderick Nash, *Philanthropy in the Shaping of American Higher Education* (New Brunswick, N.J.: Rutgers University Press, 1965), 212–15. See also Raymond B. Fosdick, *The Story of The Rockefeller Foundation* (New York: Harper and Row, 1952); or his *Adventure in Giving: The Story of the General Education Board* (New York: Harper and Row, 1962); especially good is Ellen Condliffe Lagemann, *The Politics of Knowledge: The Carnegie Corporation, Philanthropy, and Public Policy* (Middletown, Conn.: Wesleyan University Press, 1989). See also Robert E. Kohler, *Partners in Science: Foundations and Natural Scientists, 1900–1945* (Chicago: University of Chicago Press, 1991).

3. Barry D. Karl and Stanley N. Katz, "The American Philanthropic Foundation and the Public Sphere," *Minerva* 19 (1981): 236–70; Lagemann, *The Politics of Knowledge*; Hamilton Cravens, "Child-Saving in Modern America, 1870s–1990s," in Roberta Wollons, ed., *Children at Risk in Modern America: History, Concepts and Policy* (Albany: State University of New York Press, 1992), 3–31.

4. Carl E. Seashore to Cora B. Hillis, May 13, 1919, CBH.

5. Carl E. Seashore to Cora B. Hillis, Sept. 18, 1920, CBH.

6. Bird T. Baldwin, "Memorandum, President Jessup," Sept. 30, 1920, IP. See also Baldwin to Bishop J. C. Hartzell, Sept. 15, 1920, and attached "Conservation of 'Young America': A War Necessity," by Cora B. Hillis, CBH.

7. Walter A. Jessup to Bird T. Baldwin, Oct. 23, 1920, IP.

8. Bird T. Baldwin to Cora B. Hillis, Nov. 2, 1920, CBH; Hillis to George E. Vincent, Nov. 15, 1920, Series 3, Subseries 5, Box 40, Folder "State University of Iowa," LSRM.

9. W. S. Richardson to Bird T. Baldwin, Dec. 16, 1920, Series 3, Subseries 5, Box 40, Folder "State University of Iowa," LSRM.

10. George E. Vincent to W. S. Richardson, Mar. 24, 1921, ibid.

11. Carl E. Seashore to Cora B. Hillis, May 14, 1921, CW.

12. Bird T. Baldwin to Cora B. Hillis, Apr. 2, 1921, CW. A copy of the original plan, "Memorandum on the Need for Expansion of the Iowa Child Welfare Research Station," is attached to Hillis to George E. Vincent, Nov. 15, 1920, Series 3, Subseries 5, Box 40, Folder "State University of Iowa," LSRM.

13. Bird T. Baldwin, "Report to the Members of the Advisory Council," May 24, 1921, IP.

14. Quote in Bird T. Baldwin to Walter A. Jessup, Feb. 16, 1922, IP; Baldwin to Jessup, "Memorandum in Regard to Miss Quin's Visit," Feb. 15, 1922, IP.

15. Quote in Bird T. Baldwin to Cora B. Hillis, Apr. 12, 1923, CBH; see also Baldwin to Walter A. Jessup, Mar. 20 1922, IP.

16. Bird T. Baldwin to W. S. Richardson, Jan. 18, 1922, Series 3, Subseries 5, Box 40, Folder "State University of Iowa," LSRM.

17. Bird T. Baldwin, "Report to the Members of the Advisory Council," May 24, 1921, IP.

18. William L. Bowers, *The Country Life Movement in America, 1900–1920* (Port Washington, N.Y.: Kennikat Publishers, 1974). See also Henry D. Shapiro, *Appalachia on Our Mind: The Southern Mountains and Mountaineers in the American Consciousness* (Chapel Hill: University of North Carolina Press, 1978).

19. Hamilton Cravens, *The Triumph of Evolution: The Heredity-Environment Controversy, 1900–1941* (1978; reprint, Baltimore, Md.: Johns Hopkins University Press, 1988), 49, 131–33, 149; Julius Weinberg, *Edward Alsworth Ross and the Sociology of Progressivism* (Madison: University of Wisconsin Press, 1972), 191–202; Edward Alsworth Ross, *The Old World in the New* (New York: Century Company, 1914).

20. Hornell Hart, *Selective Migration as a Factor in Child Welfare in the United States, with Special Reference to Iowa, UISSCW,* vol. 1, no. 7 (Iowa City: University of Iowa, 1921), 1–137.

21. Walter A. Jessup to Beardsley Ruml, July 21, 1922, IP.

22. Bird T. Baldwin to Walter A. Jessup, Nov. 22, 1922, IP.

23. Bird T. Baldwin to Walter A. Jessup, Mar. 9, 1923, and attached "Investigation of the Rural Child in Iowa," IP.

24. Laura Spelman Rockefeller Memorial, *Report of the Laura Spelman Rockefeller Memorial* (New York, 1923), 12–19.

25. Lawrence K. Frank to Milton J. E. Senn, Jan. 10, 1966, p. 2; Frank, Interview no. 22; both in SOHI.

26. Biographical information on Frank can be found in Milton J. E. Senn, *Insights on the Child Development Movement in the United States*, Monographs of the Society for Research in Child Development, vol. 40, no. 161 (Chicago: University of Chicago Press, 1975), 11–24; Steven L. Schlossman, "Philosophy and the Gospel of Child Development," *History of Education Quarterly* 21 (Fall 1981): 275–99; Robert R. Sears, *Your Ancients Revisited: A History of Child Development* (Chicago: University of Chicago Press, 1975), 19–20.

27. Joyce Antler, *Lucy Sprague Mitchell: The Making of a Modern American Woman* (New Haven, Conn.: Yale University Press, 1987).

28. See, for example, Lawrence K. Frank, "Two Tasks of Education," *School and Society* 15 (June 17, 1922): 655–59.

29. Lawrence K. Frank, untitled memorandum, Oct. 22, 1922, pp. 9, 10, Series 2, Subseries 3, Box 3, Folder "Policy LSRM," SF. See also Beardsley Ruml to Raymond B. Fosdick, Sept. 5, 1922, Series 2, Box 2, Folder "Policy 1921–1929," LSRM.

30. Lawrence K. Frank, untitled memorandum, Oct. 22, 1922, pp. 10–36.

31. Laura Spelman Rockefeller Memorial, *Report for 1923* (New York, 1924), 7.

32. Ibid., 11; Lawrence K. Frank, "Child Study and Parent Education," Oct. 1924, 2–6, Series 3, Subseries 5, Box 31, Folder "Policy LSRM," LSRM.

33. Frank, "Child Study and Parent Education."

34. Lawrence K. Frank, "Memorandum: Child Study and Parent Training," May 23, 1924, Series 3, Subseries 5, Box 31, Folder "Policy LSRM," LSRM.

35. Frank, "Child Study and Parent Training," Oct. 1924, ibid.

36. See, for example, Cora B. Hillis to Walter A. Jessup, Feb. 1, 1923; Jessup to Hillis, Feb. 3, 1923; Hillis to Jessup, Feb. 4, 1923; all in IP.

37. James B. Weaver to Walter A. Jessup, Jan. 17, Feb. 5, May 26, 1924; Bird T. Baldwin, "Child Development in Iowa: Abstract of Address Given for the Board of Control, March 11, 1924"; both in IP.

38. "Parent Training Centers in Iowa," *Daily Iowan,* Apr. 20, 1924; *Iowa Alumnus,* May 5, 1924; *Mason City Gazette,* July 1, 1924; *New York Times,* June 27, 1924; *Sigourney News,*

Oct. 30, 1924; *Sigourney Review*, Nov. 19, 1924. Bird T. Baldwin to Walter A. Jessup, Dec. 25, 1923; Jessup to Baldwin, Apr. 15, 1924; [Baldwin], "Budget for Child Training Groups, Laura Spelman Rockefeller Memorial and Iowa Child Welfare Research Station, 1924–1925," Jan. 29, 1924; Baldwin, "Memorandum to President Jessup, Subject: Child Training Groups," Jan. 29, 1924; Jessup to Baldwin, Apr. 15, 1924; all in IP. This development can also be followed in Series 3, Subseries 5, Box 40, Folder "State University of Iowa," LSRM.

39. Bird T. Baldwin, "Memorandum to the Laura Spelman Rockefeller Memorial, Subject: Training for Parenthood," May 12, 1924; Baldwin, "Memorandum to Laura Spelman Rockefeller Memorial (1st draft), Subject: A Special Laboratory and Courses in the Training for Parenthood," May 24, 1924; Baldwin, "Memorandum to the Laura Spelman Rockefeller Memorial, Re: Child Development and Parent Training Centers," Dec. 11, 1924; all in IP.

40. Beardsley Ruml to Bird T. Baldwin, Dec. 20, 1924; Lawrence K. Frank to Baldwin, Jan. 12, 1925; both in Series 3, Subseries 5, Box 40, Folder "State University of Iowa," LSRM.

41. Bird T. Baldwin to Lawrence K. Frank, Jan. 20, 31, 1925, and attached Baldwin, "Memorandum to the Laura Spelman Rockefeller Memorial, Subject: Laboratory of Child Development and Parent Training," Jan. 29, 1925, ibid.

42. This can be followed in Series 3, Subseries 5, Box 32, Folder "Iowa State College," and Box 40, Folder "State University of Iowa," LSRM; Lawrence K. Frank to Bird T. Baldwin, Mar. 23, 1925, IP.

43. Bird T. Baldwin to Lawrence K. Frank, Mar. 27, 1925, and attached "Proposed Annual Budget (Five Year Program), State University of Iowa, Child Welfare Research Station and Extension Work," Mar. 27, 1925; Frank to Baldwin, Mar. 31, 1925; Baldwin, "Memorandum to the Laura Spelman Rockefeller Memorial," Apr. 2, 1925; Frank to Baldwin, Apr. 20, 1925; all in Series 3, Subseries 5, Box 40, Folder "State University of Iowa," LSRM. Baldwin to Walter A. Jessup, Apr. 12, 1925; Arthur Woods to Jessup, Apr. 14, 1925; Jessup to Woods, May 6, 1925; all in IP.

44. Anna E. Richardson to Lawrence K. Frank, Apr. 3, 1925 and attached "Recommended Development in Child Care and Training at Iowa State College," Apr. 3, 1925; Arthur Woods to Raymond Pearson, Apr. 14, 1925; all in Series 3, Subseries 5, Box 32, Folder "Iowa State College," LSRM.

45. W. R. Boyd, W. H. Gemmill, and J. W. Bowditch, "The Iowa Child Welfare Research Station: A Coordinating Center," Apr. 15, 1925, CW.

46. "Report of Committee of Representatives from Three State Institutions on Child Development and Parent Training Work," Apr. 21, 1925, CW. Bird T. Baldwin to Homer H. Seerley, Nov. 14, 1925; Seerley to Baldwin, Nov. 24, 1925; Baldwin to Walter A. Jessup, Nov. 27, 1925; all in IP. See also the letters in Series 3, Subseries 5, Box 32, Folder "Iowa State Teachers College," LSRM.

47. "Report of Committee of Representatives from Three State Institutions on Child Development and Parent Training Work." Bird T. Baldwin to Lawrence K. Frank, May 11, 1925, Series 3, Subseries 5, Box 40, Folder "State University of Iowa," LSRM. See also correspondence between Richardson, Baldwin, and Frank in 1925 in Series 3, Subseries 5, Box 32, Folder "Iowa State College," LSRM. See also Baldwin to Frank, July 4, 1925, Series 3, Subseries 5, Box 40, Folder "State University of Iowa," LSRM.

48. "Report of Committee of Representatives from Three State Institutions on Child Development and Parent Training Work"; "Conference," Dec. 12, 1925; "It Is Recommended," n.d. [early Feb.] 1926; both in CW. Bird T. Baldwin to Homer H. Seerley, Nov.

14, 1925; Seerley to Baldwin, Nov. 24, 1925; Baldwin to Walter A. Jessup, Nov. 27, 1925; all in IP. See also Series 3, Subseries 5, Box 32, Folder "Iowa State Teachers College," LSRM.

49. "Conference of Representatives of State Organizations and Educational Institutions in Iowa Having Programs in Child Study and Parent Education," Sept. 24, 1926; Ruth Haefner to Lawrence K. Frank, Dec. 28, 1926, and attached two pages; both in Series 3, Subseries 5, Box 40, Folder "State University of Iowa," LSRM. "State Conference, Iowa City, November 1 and 2, 1926"; "Tuesday, November 2, 1926"; both in CW. *DMR*, Nov. 12, 1926.

50. *Oskaloosa Daily Herald*, Feb. 15, 1926.

51. *DI*, June 14, July 2, 1925.

52. On the 1927 conference alone, see, for example, *DI*, Mar. 2, June 10, 19, 26, 1927; *DMR*, June 10, 1927.

53. See, for example, Richard Wightman Fox and T. J. J. Lears, eds., *The Culture of Consumption: Critical Essays in American History, 1880–1980* (New York: Pantheon, 1981); Eric Barnouw, *The Tower of Babel* (New York: Oxford University Press, 1966); D. J. Czitrom, *Media and the American Mind: From Morse to McLuhan* (Chapel Hill: University of North Carolina Press, 1982); and Susan J. Douglas, *Inventing American Broadcasting, 1899–1922* (Baltimore, Md.: Johns Hopkins University Press, 1987).

54. [Anna E. Richardson], "Child Care and Parental Education, Home Economics Division, Iowa State College, Ames, Iowa, February 5, 1926," Series 3, Subseries 5, Box 32, Folder "Iowa State College," LSRM; *DMR*, July 11, 1926.

55. See May Pardee Youtz to Bird T. Baldwin, Apr. 15, 1927; Ruth Haefner, "Brief Report on the Status of Child Study and Parent Education in Council Bluffs," Feb. 21, 1927; Haefner, "Report of Child Study and Parent Education Program At Sioux City," Feb. 21, 1927; "Child Study and Parent Education in Iowa, State University of Iowa, Field Laboratories, Council Bluffs City Schools, 1925–1926," vol. 4, pt. 2, July 1, 1926; "Child Study and Parent Education in Iowa, Iowa Child Welfare Research Station, Coordinating Center, State University of Iowa, Iowa City, Iowa, in Vol. I, July 1, 1926"; Iowa Child Welfare Research Station, "Annual Report, 1927–1928," 57–157; all in CW. See also "University of Iowa: Extracts from Report of the Work in Child Development and Parent Education of the Iowa Child Welfare Research Station. Submitted by Dr. Bird T. Baldwin, October, 1927," Series 3, Subseries 5, Box 40, Folder "State University of Iowa," LSRM.

56. These complex negotiations can be followed in the massive correspondence of 1927–28 in Series 3, Subseries 5, Box 40, Folder "State University of Iowa," LSRM.

57. Bird T. Baldwin to Beardsley Ruml, Feb. 11, 1928; Baldwin to J. W. Studebaker, Feb. 11, 1928; Studebaker to Baldwin, Feb. 23, 1928; Ruml to Walter A. Jessup, Mar. 3, 1928; Studebaker to Ruml, Oct. 22, 1928; all in ibid. Raymond H. Hughes to Ruml, Jan. 13, 1928; [Marian A. Knight], "Progress Report: Iowa State College of Agriculture and Mechanic Arts," Feb. 18, 1929; [Knight], "Iowa State College of Agriculture and Mechanic Arts Progress Report," Dec. 8, 1931, Folder "Iowa State College"; [Knight], "Progress Report: Iowa State Teachers College," Feb. 18, 1929; [Knight], "Progress Report: Iowa State Teachers College," Nov. 19, 1929; all in ibid., Box 32, Folder "Iowa State Teachers College."

58. Laura Spelman Rockefeller Memorial, *Report for 1924* (New York: n.p., 1924), 7–11; idem, *Report for 1925* (New York, 1926), 8–13; idem, *Report for 1926* (New York, 1927), 7–12; idem, *Report for 1927 and 1928* (New York, 1929), 7–14.

59. Lawrence K. Frank, memorandum of interview with Dean [J. E.] Russell, Feb. 18, 1924; Frank, "Memorandum, Institute of Child Research," Feb. 21, 1924"; Frank, "In-

stitute of Child Life," Mar. 29, 1924; all in Series 3, Subseries 5, Box 42, Folder "Teachers College," LSRM.

60. James E. Russell to the Laura Spelman Rockefeller Memorial, Apr. 3, 1924, ibid.

61. Lawrence K. Frank, "Memorandum, Child Life Projects," Apr. 5, 1924; Beardsley Ruml to James E. Russell, May 28, 1924; ibid.

62. Otis W. Caldwell to Lawrence K. Frank, May 29, 1925, and attached "Educational Clinic, Institute of Child Welfare Research, Teachers' College, Columbia University," by Bess V. Cunningham; Frank's displeasure is expressed in an attached note, n.d., to Ruml; all ibid.

63. Lois Meek Stolz, Interview no. 71, p. 21, SOHI. Lawrence K. Frank to Helen T. Woolley, Feb. 2, 1927; Raymond B. Fosdick to Beardsley Ruml, Mar. 15, 1927; both in Series 3, Subseries 5, Box 42, Folder "Teachers College," LSRM.

64. Lawrence K. Frank, memorandum of interview with Teachers' College and Trustees of Hope Farm, Feb. 15, 1926; Rudolf C. Bertheau, memorandum of interview with Mark A. May and Hugh Hartshorne, Apr. 1, 1926; Rudolf C. Bertheau, memorandum of interview with Mabel Carney, June 15, 1927; all in Series 3, Subseries 5, Box 42, Folder "Teachers College," LSRM.

65. Lawrence K. Frank, memorandum of interview with Dean [James E.] Russell, June 15, 1926, ibid.

66. J. E. Russell to Lawrence K. Frank, May 6, 1926; Frank, memorandum of interview with Mrs. Helen Woolley, Dec. 13, 1926; Frank, memorandum of interview with Dean [J. E.] Russell, Jan. 13, 1927; all ibid.

67. Herbert R. Stolz, Interview no. 71, pp. 21, 29–32, SOHI.

68. James Rowland Angell to Beardsley Ruml, Oct. 10, 1922; Ruml to Angell, Feb. 8, 1924; both in Series 3, Subseries 5, Box 79, Folder "Yale University," LSRM.

69. These negotiations can be followed in ibid. See also Robert M. Yerkes, "The Scientific Way" (typescript autobiography), 251–57, Robert M. Yerkes Papers, Sterling Library, Yale University Libraries, New Haven, Connecticut (hereafter cited as Yerkes Papers).

70. Yerkes, "The Scientific Way," 255; William Greulich, Interview no. 24, pp. 3–8; Mary Cover Jones, Interview no. 35, pp. 9, 23; Myrtle McGraw, Interview no. 48, p. 3; Lois B. Murphy and Gardner Murphy, Interview no. 51, pp. 9–11; Judith Schoellkopf, Interview no. 62, p. 47; all in SOHI.

71. Lawrence K. Frank, memorandum of interview with Arnold Gesell, Jan. 20, 1925, Series 3, Subseries 5, Box 47, Folder "Yale Institute of Psychology–Child Research, 1923–1934," LSRM.

72. Yerkes, "The Scientific Way," 256.

73. Ibid., 251–57.

74. See the correspondence between Frank and Gesell, 1926–28, in Series 3, Subseries 5, Box 47, Folder "Yale University," LSRM; Roswell P. Angier to Beardsley Ruml, July 9, 1926, and attached "Report of the Chairman on the Work of the Institute of Psychology, Yale University, for 1925–1926" (typescript), ibid., Box 79, Folder "Yale University."

75. Willard Olson, Interview no. 52, p. 1; Lawrence K. Frank, Interview no. 22, recording by Frank, p. 4; both in SOHI.

76. Lawrence K. Frank, "University of Minnesota," Oct. 6, 1924, Series 3, Subseries 5, Box 45, Folder "University of Minnesota," LSRM; Yerkes, "The Scientific Way," 205–6.

77. Lotus D. Coffman to the Laura Spelman Rockefeller Memorial, Feb. 6, 1925, and attached "The Proposal of the University of Minnesota for the Establishment of an Institute of Child Welfare" and "Report of the Committee on the Institute of Child Welfare at the

University of Minnesota," Series 3, Subseries 5, Box 45, Folder "University of Minnesota," LSRM.

78. Lawrence K. Frank to Lotus D. Coffman, Feb. 9, 1925, ibid.

79. Lawrence K. Frank, "The University of Minnesota," Feb. 18, 1925; Frank, memorandum of interview with L. D. Coffman, Feb. 27, 1925; "Revised Proposal for an Institute of Child Welfare, answering the questions raised by Mr. Lawrence K. Frank, March 6, 1925"; and all attached documents; all ibid.

80. Lawrence K. Frank to Dean F. J. Kelly, Apr. 23, 1925; Kelly to Frank, Apr. 25, 1925; Frank, "Memorandum," to Dr. G[uy] S[tanton] Ford, May 5, 1925; Kelly to Frank, June 9, 1925; all ibid.

81. See, for example, Marian R. Yarrow, Interview no. 79, p. 6; Dale Harris, Interview no. 26, pp. 2–4; Willard Olson, Interview no. 52, pp. 1–2; Edith Boyd, Interview no. 10, pp. 20–30, 42–55; Myrtle McGraw, Interview no. 48, p. 2; all in SOHI.

82. John E. Anderson to Dorothea Davis, Apr. 13, 1927, and all attached documents, Series 3, Subseries 5, Box 45, Folder "University of Minnesota," LSRM.

83. *Mercury Herald*, May 10, 1923, Oakland, California, clipping; Lawrence K. Frank, memorandum of interview with faculty and officers, University of California, Berkeley, Mar. 6–12, 1925; ibid., Box 43, Folder "University of California I.C.W."

84. Jean Walker to Lawrence K. Frank, Oct. 23, 1924; Frank to Walker, Oct. 29, 1924; ibid. See also Mary Cover Jones, Interview no. 35, p. 607; Jean Walker Macfarlane, Interview no. 45, pp. 2–4; both in SOHI.

85. Lawrence K. Frank to Charles B. Lipman, June 1, 1925, Series 3, Subseries 5, Box 43, Folder "University of California I.C.W.," LSRM.

86. Richard A. Bolt to Lawrence K. Frank, July 21, 1925, and attached memo; Frank to Bolt, July 28, 1925; Warner Brown to Frank, Aug. 26, 1925; Frank to Brown, Sept. 10, 1925; all ibid.

87. George M. Stratton to Lawrence K. Frank, Feb. 2, 1926; Frank to Stratton, Feb. 3, 1926; Stratton to Frank, Mar. 1, 1926, and attached; Charles B. Lipman to Stratton, Feb. 18, 1926; all ibid. W. W. Kemp to Edna W. Bailey, Feb. 11, 1926, and attached "Report of Subcommittee Appointed by Dean Lipman to Draft a Tentative Proposal for the Establishment of an Institute for Child Welfare at the University of California" (typescript), n.d., Folder F, Archives of the Institute of Human Development (formerly Institute of Child Welfare), Tolman Hall, University of California, Berkeley.

88. Lawrence K. Frank, memorandum of interview with William C. Wood, Ethel Richardson, Grace C. Stanley, Mar. 17–20, 1925; Stanley to Frank, Apr. 21, 1925, and enclosed "Purpose of Day Nursery Training School for Parenthood," n.d.; Frank, memorandum of interview with Will C. Wood, Nov. 2, 1925; Frank, memorandum of interview with Miss Ethel Richardson, Mar. 29, 1926, and attached "Set-up of Proposed Parent Education Program of California," May 24, 1926; "Department of Education—State of California," May 24, 1926; Beardsley Ruml to Will C. Wood, June 4, 1926; all in Series 3, Subseries 5, Box 27, Folder "California Department of Education," LSRM.

89. Lawrence K. Frank and Dorothea Davis, memorandum of interview with Edna Bailey, Dec. 16, 1926; Frank, Davis, and Beardsley Ruml, memorandum of interview with Herbert Stolz, May 25, 1925; ibid. W. W. Campbell, "A Tentative Proposal for an Institute of Child Welfare at the University of California," Feb. 1, 1927; Frank to Campbell, Mar. 1, 19, 1927; Campbell to Ruml, Apr. 22, 1927; Frank to Campbell, Apr. 28, 1927; Ruml to Campbell, May 31, 1927; Ethel Richardson to Frank, Apr. 7, 1927; Frank to Richardson, Apr. 15, 1927; Frank to Campbell, Mar. 19, 1927; C. A. Kofoid to Frank, Apr. 2, 1927;

Frank to Kofoid, Apr. 7, 1927; Campbell to Frank, Apr. 22, 1927; Kofoid to Frank, Apr. 25, 1927; Campbell to Laura Spelman Rockefeller Memorial, June 3, 1927; all ibid., Box 43, Folder "University of California I.C.W." Mary Cover Jones, Interview no. 35, p. 8; Dale Harris, Interview no. 26, pp. 14–15; and Jean Walker Macfarlane, Interview no. 45, pp. 20–21; all in SOHI.

90. Harold E. Jones to Lawrence K. Frank, Sept. 22, 1927, Sept. 28, 1928; Herbert R. Stolz to Frank, Nov. 7, 1928, and attached document; Stolz to Marian A. Knight, Oct. 28, 1929, and attached document; all in Series 3, Subseries 5, Box 43, Folder "University of California I.C.W.," LSRM. Harold E. Jones submitted annual reports of research, as, for example, Jones, "University of California, Institute of Child Welfare," Research Bulletin no. 1, Mar. 1, 1928 (mimeograph), Archives of the University of California, Berkeley.

91. Nancy Bayley, "Research in Child Development: A Longitudinal Perspective," *Merrill-Palmer Quarterly of Behavior and Development* 11 (1965): 183–208, quote on p. 191; Bayley, Interview no. 8, pp. 1–12, SOHI.

92. Jean Walker Macfarlane, Interview no. 45, p. 4, SOHI; Mary Cover Jones, "A Report on Three Growth Studies at the University of California," *Gerontologist* 7 (1967): 49–54.

93. Mary Cover Jones, Interview no. 35, pp. 6–14, 16–21; Jean Walker Macfarlane, Interview no. 26, pp. 14–15; Nancy Bayley, Interview no. 8, p. 25; Lois M. Stolz, Interview no. 71, pp. 29–32; all in SOHI.

94. These developments can be followed in Series 3, Subseries 5, Box 46, Folder "University of Nebraska," Folder "University of Montana," and Box 42, Folder "Swarthmore College," LSRM.

95. Frank's negotiations can be followed in ibid., Box 33, Folder "Merrill-Palmer Institute, 1923–1930."

96. See, for example, "Report by the President of Mills College to the Spelman Fund of New York Concerning Appropriation No. 40," Aug. 15, 1931; Marian A. Knight, "Progress Report Mills College," Sept. 10, 1931; ibid., Folder "Mills College, 1926–1934."

97. These negotiations can be followed in Box 31, Folder "Cornell University"; Box 38, Folder "Regents of the University of the State of New York"; and Box 26, Folder "Albany Board of Education and Albany State Teachers College, 1930–1936"; all ibid.

98. Pauline Park Knapp, Interview no. 38, p. 5, SOHI; these negotiations can be followed in Series 3, Subseries 5, Box 44, Folder "University of Georgia, 1924–1935," and Folder "University of Cincinnati," LSRM.

99. [Bird T. Baldwin], "History: 1920–1926, The Committee on Child Development of the Division of Anthropology and Psychology of the National Research Council," n.d., in Papers of the Committee on Child Development, Folder "Committee on Child Development: Activities; Summary 1926," Division of Anthropology and Psychology, National Research Council Archives, National Academy of Sciences, Washington, D.C.

100. These complex developments can be followed in Series 3, Subseries 5, Box 30, Folder "National Research Council Committee on Child Development, 1924–1930," LSRM. See also Alice Boardman Smuts, "The National Research Council Committee on Child Development and the Founding of the Society for Research in Child Development, 1925–1933," in Smuts and John W. Hagen, eds., *History and Research in Child Development*, Monographs of the Society for Research in Child Development, vol. 50, nos. 4–5 (Chicago: University of Chicago Press, 1986), 108–25.

101. Steven Schlossman, "Perils of Popularization: The Founding of *Parents' Magazine*," in Smuts and Hagen, *History and Research in Child Development*, 65–77.

102. Laura Spelman Rockefeller Memorial, *Report for 1927 and 1928*. On the reorganization of Rockefeller philanthropy, see Kohler, *Partners in Science*, 233–62.

CHAPTER THREE

1. *Mason City Gazette and Times*, Mar. 10, 1923.
2. See, for example, *Union-Signal*, Jan. 11, 1923; *Dallas News*, Feb. 10, 1923; *DMR*, July 22, 1923; Bird T. Baldwin, "Prohibition: A Protector of Childhood," *Union-Signal*, Aug. 16, 1923, 4, 12; *Oakland Tribune*, Oct. 23, 1923; *New York Post*, Dec. 31, 1923; *DI*, Jan. 1, 1924; *Sioux City Tribune*, Nov. 13, 1924; *Clinton Advance*, Nov. 14, 1924.
3. Dorothy E. Bradbury, "A Review of the Published Writings of Bird Thomas Baldwin," *PB* 28 (1931): 257–68; Marion Hossfeld, "Bibliography of the Published Writings of Bird Thomas Baldwin," ibid., 269–76. Baldwin's major publication before coming to Iowa was *Physical Growth and School Progress: A Study in Experimental Education*, U.S. Bureau of Education Bulletin no. 10, whole no. 581 (Washington, D.C.: Government Printing Office, 1914).
4. Bird T. Baldwin, "Report of the Iowa Child Welfare Research Station Submitted to the President of the State University of Iowa," Mar. 11, 1918; Ellsworth Faris, "The Iowa Child Welfare Research Station" (typescript), Aug. [?], 1918; Baldwin to President Jessup, Nov. [?], 1917 (typescript); all in IP. "Graduate Course: Offered for 1917–18 (Second Semester) by the Iowa Child Welfare Research Station . . . the Normal Child—Professor B. T. Baldwin" [Jan. (?), 1918], CW; Baldwin, *The Physical Growth of Children from Birth to Maturity*, UISSCW, vol. 1, no. 1 (Iowa City: University of Iowa, 1920), 320–402; Baldwin to Cora B. Hillis, Sept. 8, 1919, CBH. Baldwin, "Memorandum to President Jessup: The Psychological, Sociological, and Nutritional Examination of So-Called Normal Children by the Child Welfare Research Station," Sept. 15, 1919; and Baldwin, "Principles Governing the Scope of Work and Policy of the Iowa Child Welfare Research Station," Apr. 30, 1919; both in IP.
5. Bird T. Baldwin to Walter A. Jessup (typescript), Nov. [?], 1918, IP.
6. Bird T. Baldwin to Walter A. Jessup, Nov. 9, 1917, IP. Ellsworth Faris, "Suggestions on Organization to County Chairmen," Apr. 17, 1918; Faris, "To the County Chairmen," Apr. 17, 1918; "Saving a Regiment of Babies," n.d. [1918]; "Suggestions for Publicity," n.d.; [Baldwin], "Tentative Schedule of the Iowa Child Welfare Research Station for Children's Year," n.d. [1918]; [Baldwin], "Comment on Specific Items," n.d. [1918]; [Baldwin], "Notes on Proposed Schedule for Children's Year," n.d. [1918]; [Baldwin], "Tentative Information Schedule for Children's Year Prepared by the Iowa Child Welfare Research Station," n.d. [1918]; Dr. Leanna Means, "The Children's Year. April 6, 1918–April 6, 1919. To Save the Lives of 100,000 Children in U.S.," n.d. [1918]; all in CW. Baldwin, "Memorandum," n.d. [1918]; Faris, "Annual Report of the Iowa Child Welfare Research Station, State University of Iowa" (typescript), n.d. [July or August 1918]; Faris, "The Iowa Child Welfare Research Station"; all in IP.
7. Bird T. Baldwin, *Physical Growth of School Children*, Extension Bulletin no. 59 (Iowa City: University of Iowa Press, n.d. [1917]).
8. Rosemary Loughlin to Walter A. Jessup, Aug. 15, 1919, IP.
9. Ellsworth Faris, "To the Members of the Advisory Council of the Iowa Child Welfare Research Station," Apr. 15, 1919, ibid.
10. Bird T. Baldwin to Cora B. Hillis, Sept. 8, 1919, CBH; Baldwin to Walter A. Jessup, Aug. 25, 30, 1919, IP.

11. Bird T. Baldwin to Walter A. Jessup, Sept. 15, 1919, IP.

12. See Daniel J. Kevles, *In the Name of Eugenics: Genetics and the Uses of Human Heredity* (New York: Knopf, 1985), chaps. 4–7; see also my "Oaks and Cacti," *Reviews in American History* 14 (1986): 104–9.

13. Anna A. Gordon, "Plan for the Cooperation of the National Woman's Christian Temperance Union with the Iowa Child Welfare Research Station of the State University of Iowa," Mar. 2, 1920, attached to Bird T. Baldwin to Walter A. Jessup, Mar. 10, 1920; see also Baldwin, "Memorandum for President Jessup," Oct. 23, 1919; both in IP. Baldwin to Cora B. Hillis, Nov. 14, 1919, CW. Ida Wise Smith to Baldwin, Nov. 16, 1919, IP. Baldwin to Hillis, Nov. 14, 1919; Baldwin to Hillis, Nov. 19, 1919; both in CBH. Smith to Baldwin, Nov. 25, 1919, IP. Baldwin to Hillis, Sept. 2, 19, 1920, CBH.

14. Bird T. Baldwin, *Administration and Scope of the Iowa Child Welfare Research Station*, University of Iowa Series, *Aims and Progress of Research*, n.s. 33, July 1920, vol. 1, no. 10 (Iowa City: University of Iowa, 1920), quote on 15.

15. Bird T. Baldwin, "Memorandum, President Jessup," Sept. 30, 1919, IP.

16. Bird T. Baldwin to Cora B. Hillis, Jan. 18, 1921, CBH. See also Baldwin, "Memorandum, President Jessup," Jan. 27, 1921; Lorle I. Stecher, "Memorandum, President Jessup," Mar. 7, 1921; both in CW. Baldwin, "Memorandum, President Jessup," May 4, 11, 1921, IP. Baldwin to Cora B. Hillis, May 12, 19, 1921, CW. Baldwin, "Report to Members of the Advisory Council," May 24, 1919, IP. Baldwin to Hillis, June 2, July 2, 1921; Hillis to Baldwin, Sept. 1, 1921; Baldwin to Hillis, Sept. 13, 1921; all in CBH.

17. *DI*, Sept. 23, Oct. 21, 1921.

18. Ibid., Jan. 19, 1922. On the preschool as an institution, see Bird T. Baldwin and Lorle I. Stecher, *The Psychology of the Preschool Child* (New York: D. Appleton and Company, 1925), 16–25, 180–200.

19. See Baldwin and Stecher, *The Psychology of the Preschool Child*, 201–54.

20. Elizabeth A. Perkins, "Visit to the Child Welfare Research Station at Iowa State University," *Union-Signal*, Oct. 27, 1921, Jan. 1, 1922; see also *New York Sun*, Mar. 1, 1922, and *Union-Signal*, Jan. 11, 1923; *DI*, Oct. 1, 1921; *ICPC*, Oct. 1, 1921; *DMR*, Oct. 1, 1921; *Union-Signal*, Oct. 13, 1921, Oct. 12, 1922, Aug. 30, 1923, Sept. 11, 1924; Bird T. Baldwin, "Prohibition: A Protector of Childhood," *Union-Signal*, Aug. 16, 1923, 4, 12; Perkins, "Saving the Baby," *Union-Signal*, Jan. 29, 1920, 6. See also *ICPC*, Apr. 29, 1920. A very different conception of what *eugenics* meant in American culture has been described by historians of the organized American eugenics movement, most recently by Kevles, *In the Name of Eugenics*. Obviously, *eugenics* meant different things to different groups of people.

21. *Waterloo Courier*, Oct. 16, 1920.

22. See, for example, *Philadelphia Record*, Jan. 25, 1920; *Dearborn Independent*, July 23, 1921; *Sioux City Journal*, Dec. 11, 1921; *ICPC*, Feb. 8, 1922; Bird T. Baldwin, "The Scientific Prediction of the Physical Growth of Children," in *Eugenics in Race and State*, vol. 2 of *Scientific Papers of the Second International Congress of Eugenics* (Baltimore, Md.: Williams and Wilkins, 1923), 25–29. See also Baldwin, "New Standards of Physical Growth and Their Use in Nutrition Classes," *National Education Association Addresses and Proceedings* 59 (1921): 391–92; Baldwin, *Scale for Measuring Height* (Iowa City: Iowa Child Welfare Research Station, n.d. [1922, 1923, or 1924]); Baldwin, "Increments of Growth for Different Types of Children with Special Reference to Height, Weight, and Breathing Capacity Development," *National Tuberculosis Association Transactions* 8 (1922): 600–613.

23. Baldwin, *The Physical Growth of Children from Birth to Maturity*.

24. Bird T. Baldwin and L. I. Stecher, *Mental Growth Curve of Normal and Superior*

Children Studied by Means of Consecutive Intelligence Examinations, UISSCW, vol. 2, no. 1 (Iowa City: University of Iowa, 1922); Baldwin and Stecher, "The Fluctuations of the I.Q. of Normal and Superior Children at Successive Examinations," *PB* 18 (1921): 99–100; Baldwin and Stecher, "Additional Data from Consecutive Stanford-Binet Tests," *JEP* 13 (1922): 556–60; Baldwin, "The Relation between Mental and Physical Growth," *JEP* 13 (1922): 193–203.

25. Bird T. Baldwin, "Memorandum to President Jessup," Jan. 10, 1923, IP; see also *Cleveland Plain Dealer*, Jan. 7, 1923; Baldwin, "The Capacity of the Child for Education," *American Association of School Administrators Yearbook, Department of Superintendence, National Education Association, Second Yearbook* (Washington, D.C.: National Education Association, 1924), 15–29. On Cleveland, see Baldwin, "Making Health of Mind and Body the Basis of School Promotion," *Woman's City Club of Cleveland Bulletin* 8, no. 1 (Apr. 14, 1923); *Cleveland Plain Dealer*, June 11, 1923; *New York Post*, Dec. 31, 1923; *Rochester Herald*, Apr. 23 [?], 1924; *Rochester Democrat*, Apr. 24, 1924; *Fort Dodge Messenger*, Oct. 19, 1923.

26. Bird T. Baldwin, "Anthropometric Measurements," in *Mental and Physical Traits of a Thousand Gifted Children*, vol. 1 of Lewis M. Terman, *Genetic Studies of Genius* (Stanford, Calif.: Stanford University Press, 1925), 135–71. See also Baldwin to Walter A. Jessup, Apr. 2, 1923, IP; Baldwin to Terman, June 7, 1923, LMT; *Stanford Daily*, Apr. 3, 1923; *Union-Signal*, Apr. 5, 1923; *Waterloo Evening Courier*, July 14, 1923; *Sacramento Daily World*, Oct. 26, 1923; *Oakland Tribune*, Oct. 23, 1923.

27. Baldwin, "The Capacity of the Child for Education," 16.

28. *Waterloo Evening Courier*, Mar. 12, 1924; *DI*, Jan. 29, Feb. 28, Mar. 29, Apr. 4, 1924; *Rochester Herald*, Apr. 23 [?], 1924; *Rochester Democrat*, Apr. 24, 1924; *South Bend Tribune*, Aug. 25, 1924; *Sioux City Tribune*, Nov. 13, 26, 1924; *Tulsa Tribune*, Nov. 11, 1924; *Clinton Advance*, Dec. 9, 1924; *Wilmington Every Evening*, Dec. 31, 1924, Jan. 2, 1925; *New Haven Register*, Jan. 5, 1925.

29. Bird T. Baldwin, "Bridging the Gap between Our Knowledge of Child Nature and the Training of Children," in M. V. O'Shea, ed., *The Child: His Nature and Needs. A Survey of Present-Day Knowledge Concerning Child Nature and the Promotion of the Well-Being and Education of the Young* (New York: Childrens Foundation, 1924), 13–30.

30. See Alan I Marcus and Howard P. Segal, *Technology in America: A Brief History* (San Diego, Calif.: Harcourt, Brace, Jovanovich, 1989), 257–310.

31. Amy L. Daniels and Nelle I. McClurg, "Influence of High Temperatures and Dilute Alkalies on the Antineuritic Properties of Foods," *Journal of Biological Chemistry* 37 (1919): 201–13.

32. Albert Byfield, Amy L. Daniels, and Rosemary Loughlin, "The Antineuritic and Growth Stimulating Properties of Orange Juice," *AJDC* 19 (1920): 349–58.

33. Amy L. Daniels and Rosemary Loughlin, "A Deficiency in Heat-Treated Milks," *Journal of Biological Chemistry* 44 (1920): 381–97; Daniels and Loughlin, "Note on the Fat-Soluble Growth-Promoting Substance in Lard and Cotton-Seed Oil," *Journal of Biological Chemistry* 42 (1920): 359–62; Daniels, "Can Yeast Be Used as a Source of the Antineuritic Vitamin in Infant Feeding?" *AJDC* 23 (1922): 41–50.

34. See, for example, Amy L. Daniels and Genevieve Stearns, "The Effect of Heat Treatment of Milk Feedings in Mineral Metabolism of Infants," *Journal of Biological Chemistry* 61 (1924): 225–40; Daniels and Mary K. Hutton, "Fertility of the White Rat on Purified Rations," *PSEBM* 23 (1925–26): 225–27; Daniels and Stearns, "The Nitrogen and Mineral Balances in Infants Receiving Cow's and Goat's Milk," *AJDC* 30 (1925): 359–

66; Daniels and Lilah Brooks, "Further Evidence of Destruction of Vitamin B in Evaporated Milk," *PSEBM* 25 (1927–28): 161–63; Daniels and Hutton, "Mineral Deficiencies of Milk as Shown by Growth and Fertility of White Rats," *Journal of Biological Chemistry* 63 (1925): 143–56.

35. Amy L. Daniels, "Malnutrition in Iowa Rural Schools," *Nation's Health* 4 (1922): 319–20; Daniels, *Diet for the School Child*, University of Iowa Extension Bulletin no. 57 (Iowa City: University of Iowa, 1919); Daniels, *Feeding the Baby*, ibid., no. 65; Daniels, *The School Lunch*, ibid., no. 70; Daniels, *Child Feeding Schedule*, ibid., no. 193. Albert H. Byfield and Daniels, "The Role of Parental Nutrition in the Causation of Rickets," pt. 1, *Journal of the American Medical Association* 81 (1923): 360–62. Also helpful is E. V. McCollum, *The Newer Knowledge of Nutrition*, 2d ed. (1918; reprint, New York: Macmillan, 1922), esp. pp. 1–122, which is historically oriented. See also my "Establishing the Science of Nutrition at the USDA: Ellen Swallow Richards and Her Allies," *Agricultural History* 64 (Spring 1990): 122–33; and Harvey Levenstein, *Revolution at the Table: The Transformation of the American Diet* (New York: Oxford University Press, 1988), 72–98.

36. Frank E. Horack, *Child Legislation in Iowa*, UISSCW, vol. 1, no. 6 (Iowa City: University of Iowa, 1921); A. Ione Bliss, *Iowa Child Welfare Legislation Measured by the Federal Children's Bureau Standards*, UISSCW, vol. 2, no. 3 (Iowa City: University of Iowa, 1922).

37. Sara M. Stinchfield, *A Preliminary Study in Corrective Speech*, UISSCW, vol. 1, no. 3 (Iowa City: University of Iowa, 1920).

38. Clara H. Town, *Analytic Study of a Group of Five- and Six-Year-Old Children*, UISSCW, vol. 1, no. 4 (Iowa City: University of Iowa, 1920).

39. Phineas W. Whiting, "Heredity in Wasps: A Study of Heredity in a Parthenogenetic Aspect. The Parasitic Wasp, Hadrobracon," *Journal of Heredity* 12 (1921): 262–66; Whiting, "Rearing Meal Moths and Parasitic Wasps for Experimental Purposes," *Journal of Heredity* 12 (1921): 255–61; Whiting, "Heredity in the Honey-Bee," *Journal of Heredity* 13 (1922): 3–8; Whiting, "Further Points in the Relation of Cytology and Genetics," *Journal of Heredity* 14 (1923): 116–18; Whiting, "The Analysis of Genetic Differences through Haploid Parthenogenesis," in *Eugenics, Genetics and the Family*, vol. 1 of *Scientific Papers of the Second International Congress of Eugenics* (Baltimore, Md.: Williams and Wilkins, 1923), 102–5; Whiting, "Three Different Types of Genetic Sterility in the Parasitic Wasps, Hadrobracon," *PIAS* 31 (1924): 406; Whiting, *A Study of Hereditary and Environmental Factors Determining a Variable Character: Defective and Freak Venation in the Parasitic Wasp Hadrobracon Inglandis (Ashm.)*, UISSCW, vol. 3, no. 1 (Iowa City: University of Iowa, 1924). See also *DI*, Oct. 23, 1921, Oct. 17, 1922, Nov. 4, 1922, Apr. 3, 1924; *DMR*, Nov. 12, 1922; *ICPC*, Mar. 28, 1924. For a discussion of changes in genetics as a science and profession, see Hamilton Cravens, *The Triumph of Evolution: The Heredity-Environment Controversy, 1900–1941* (1978; reprint, Baltimore, Md.: Johns Hopkins University Press, 1988), chap. 5; and Garland E. Allen, *Life Science in the Twentieth Century* (New York: Wiley and Sons, 1975).

40. Hornell N. Hart, *Selective Immigration as a Factor in Child Welfare in the United States with Special Reference to Iowa*, UISSCW, vol. 1, no. 7 (Iowa City: University of Iowa, 1921); Hart, *Differential Fecundity in Iowa*, UISSCW, vol. 2, no. 2 (Iowa City: University of Iowa, 1922); Hart, "Science and Sociology," *American Journal of Sociology* 27 (1921–22): 364–83; Hart, "What Is a Social Problem?" *American Journal of Sociology* 29 (1924): 345–52; Hart, "A Socialization Test," *Survey* 47 (1921–22): 249; Hart, "Research Possibilities with a Socialization Test," *Journal of Applied Sociology* 7 (1922–23): 163–66; Hart, "Mongolian

Amentia and the Ages of the Mothers at the Births of Aments," *Journal of the American Statistical Association* 18 (1923): 900–903; Hart, "Occupational Differential Fecundity," *Scientific Monthly* 19 (1924): 527–32; Hart, "Correlation between Intelligence Quotients of Siblings," *School and Society* 20 (1924): 382; Hart, "The Slowing Up of Growth in Mental Test Ability," *School and Society* 20 (1924): 523–74; Hart, "School Progress and Mental Test Ability," *School and Society* 21 (1925): 181–82; Hart, *A Test of Social Attitudes and Interests, UISSCW*, vol. 2, no. 4 (Iowa City: University of Iowa, 1923); on Hart's views and activities, see also *Cedar Rapids Gazette*, June 8, 1920; *DMR*, Feb. 3, 1921; *Le Mars Semi-Weekly Sentinel*, Feb. 8, 1921; *ICPC*, Mar. 12, 1921; *DMR*, Sept. 27, 1922; *ICPC*, Sept. 28, 1922; *Iowa City Daily Republican*, Sept. 27, 1922; *DI*, Feb. 13, 1923; Elizabeth A. Perkins, "Prohibition Promotes Welfare of Child," *Union-Signal*, Mar. 3, 1924.

41. Margaret W. Rossiter, *Women Scientists in America: Strategies and Struggles to 1940* (Baltimore, Md.: Johns Hopkins University Press, 1982).

42. Oral History Interview with Ruth Updegraff, Feb. 3 and 10, 1977, Iowa City, Iowa, by James Beilman, for the University of Iowa Libraries, pp. 1–2, 4–5, 7–8; original in University of Iowa Libraries, Iowa City.

43. Ruth Updegraff, "A Preliminary Study of the Nature of Finality in Melody," *PIAS* 33 (1926): 279–82.

44. Oral History Interview with Ruth Updegraff, p. 4.

45. Hamilton Cravens, interview with Robert R. Sears, June 2, 1984, pp. 67–69, Stanford University Archives, Stanford, California, and University of Iowa Archives, Iowa City, Iowa.

46. Allen, *Life Science in the Twentieth Century*, 73–147.

47. Cravens, *The Triumph of Evolution*.

48. Hamilton Cravens, "Child-Saving in the Age of Professionalism, 1915–1930," in Joseph M. Hawes and N. Ray Hiner, eds., *American Childhood: A Research Guide and Historical Handbook* (Westport, Conn.: Greenwood Press, 1985), 453–60; Roy Lubove, *The Professional Altruist: The Emergence of Social Work as a Career* (Cambridge, Mass.: Harvard University Press, 1965); Margo Horn, "The Moral Message of Child Guidance, 1925–1945," *Journal of Social History* 18 (Fall 1984): 25–36; Horn, *Before It's Too Late: The Child Guidance Movement in the United States, 1922–1945* (Philadelphia: Temple University Press, 1989).

49. Hamilton Cravens, "Applied Science and Public Policy: The Ohio Bureau of Juvenile Research and the Problem of Juvenile Delinquency, 1913–1930," in Michael M. Sokal, ed., *Psychological Testing and American Society, 1890–1930* (New Brunswick, N.J.: Rutgers University Press, 1987), 158–94.

50. John B. Watson, *Behavior: An Introduction to Comparative Psychology* (New York: Henry Holt and Company, 1914); Watson, *Psychology from the Standpoint of a Behaviorist* (Philadelphia: J. B. Lippincott and Company, 1919); Watson and Rosalie Raynor, "Conditioned Emotional Reactions," *JExpP* 3 (1920): 1–14; Ben Harris, "Whatever Happened to Little Albert?" *American Psychologist* 34 (1979): 151–60; and my "Behaviorism Revisited: Developmental Science, the Maturation Theory, and the Biological Basis of the Human Mind, 1920s–1950s," in Keith R. Benson, Ronald Rainger, and Jane Maienschein, eds., *The American Expansion of Biology* (New Brunswick, N.J.: Rutgers University Press, 1991), 133–63.

51. Leonard Carmichael, "Heredity and Environment: Are They Antithetical?" *JASP* 20 (1925): 245–60.

52. Leonard Carmichael, "The Development of Behavior in Vertebrates Experimentally

Removed from Influence of External Stimulation," *PR* 33 (1926): 51–58; Carmichael, "A Further Study of the Development of Behavior in Vertebrates Experimentally Removed from the Influence of External Stimuli," *PR* 34 (1927): 34–47; Carmichael, "A Further Experimental Study of the Development of Behavior," *PR* 35 (1928): 253–60.

53. G. E. Coghill, *Anatomy and the Problem of Behavior* (Cambridge: Cambridge University Press, 1929); see also Coghill, "The Genetic Interrelation of Instinctive Behavior and Reflexes," *PR* 37 (1930): 264–66.

54. On the pecking instinct, see Charles Bird, "The Relative Importance of a Maturation and Habit in the Development of an Instinct," *PSJGP* 32 (1925): 68–91; Bird, "The Effect of Maturation upon the Pecking Instinct of Chicks," *PSJGP* 33 (1926): 212–33; Bird, "Maturation and Practice: Their Effects upon the Feeding Reactions of Chicks," *JCP* 16 (1932): 343–66; Wendell Cruze, "Maturation and Learning in Chicks," *JCP* 19 (1935): 371–409; Cruze, "Maturity and Learning Ability," *Psychological Monographs* 50, no. 5 (1938): 49–65. For Leonard Carmichael's later work, see Carmichael, "An Experimental Study in the Prenatal Guinea-Pig of the Origin and Development of Reflexes and Patterns of Behavior in Relation to the Stimulation of Specific Receptor Areas during the Period of Active Fetal Life," *Genetic Psychology Monographs* 16 (1934): 337–497; Carmichael, "A Re-Evaluation of the Concepts of Maturation and Learning as Applied to the Early Development of Behavior," *PR* 43 (1936): 450–70.

55. Arnold L. Gesell, "Maturation and Infant Behavior Pattern," *PR* 36 (1929): 307–19, quotes at 307 and 318; Gesell, *The Mental Growth of the Preschool Child* (New York: Macmillan, 1925); Gesell, *Infancy and Human Growth* (New York: Macmillan, 1928).

56. Arnold Gesell and Helen Thompson, "Learning and Growth: An Experimental Study of the Method of Co-Twin Control," *Genetic Psychology Monographs* 6 (1929): 1–124.

57. See, for example, Arthur I. Gates and Grace A. Taylor, "An Experimental Study of the Nature of Improvement Resulting from Practice in a Mental Function," *JEP* 16 (1925): 583–92; Gates and Taylor, "An Experimental Study of the Nature of Improvement Resulting from Practice in a Motor Function," *JEP* 17 (1926): 226–36; Florence L. Goodenough and C. R. Brian, "Certain Factors Underlying the Acquisition of Motor Skills by Preschool Children," *JExpP* 12 (1929): 127–55; Josephine Hilgard, "The Effect of Early and Delayed Practice on Memory and Motor Performances Studied by the Method of Co-Twin Control," *Genetic Psychology Monographs* 14 (1933): 493–567; Hilgard, "Learning and Maturation in Preschool Children," *PSJGP* 41 (1932): 36–56; J. A. Hicks, "The Acquisition of Motor Skill in Young Children," *CD* 1 (1930): 90–105; Hicks and E. W. Ralph, "The Effects of Practice in Tracing the Porteus Diamond Maze," *CD* 2 (1931): 156–58; Mary Shirley, "A Motor Sequence Favors the Maturation Theory," *PB* 27 (1931): 204–5; A. J. Jersild and S. F. Bernstock, "The Influence of Training on the Vocal Ability of Three-Year-Old Children," *CD* 2 (1931): 272–91; Jersild, *Training and Growth in the Development of Children* (New York: Columbia University, Teachers College, Bureau of Publications, 1932).

58. On the idea of innate IQ, see my *Triumph of Evolution*, 56–86; and Sokal, *Psychological Testing and American Society*.

59. Lewis M. Terman, "Mental Growth and the I.Q.," *JEP* 12 (1921): 325–41, 401–7, quote at 325.

60. Lewis M. Terman, "The Psychological Determinist: Or Democracy and the I.Q.," *JER* 6 (1922): 57–62, quotes at 62. See also Terman, "The Use of Intelligence Tests in the Grading of School Children," *JER* 1 (1920): 20–32; Terman and Ethel D. Whitmire, "Age and Grade Norms for the National Intelligence Tests, Scales A and B," *JER* 3 (1921): 124–

32; Terman, "The Possibilities and Limitations of Training," *JER* 10 (1924): 335–43; Terman, "The Mental Test as a Psychological Method," *PR* 31 (1924): 93–117; Terman, "Educational Psychology," in Edward M. East, ed., *Biology in Human Affairs* (New York: McGraw-Hill, 1931), 94–122.

61. Lewis M. Terman and Jessie M. Chase, "The Psychology, Biology and Pedagogy of Genius," *PB* 17 (1920): 397–409; Terman and Jessie C. Fenton, "Preliminary Report on a Gifted Juvenile Author," *Journal of Applied Psychology* 5 (1921): 163–78; Terman, "A New Approach to the Study of Genius," *PR* 29 (1922): 310–18; Terman, "Adventures in Stupidity: A Partial Analysis of the Intellectual Inferiority of a College Student," *Scientific Monthly* 14 (1922): 24–40; Terman, "Talent and Genius in Children," in V. F. Calverton and Samuel D. Schmalhausen, eds., *The New Generation: The Intimate Problems of Modern Parents and Children* (New York: Macaulay Company, 1932), 405–23.

62. Lewis M. Terman, *Genetic Studies of Genius* (Stanford, Calif.: Stanford University Press, 1925–30): vol. 1, Terman and Barbara S. Burks, *Mental and Physical Traits of a Thousand Gifted Children*; vol. 2, Catherine M. Cox, *The Early Mental Traits of Three Hundred Geniuses*; vol. 3, Terman, Burks, and D. W. Jensen, *The Promise of Youth: Follow-Up Studies of a Thousand Gifted Children*.

63. Helen T. Woolley, "The Validity of Standards of Mental Measurement in Young Childhood," *School and Society* 2 (1925): 476–82.

64. H. E. Barrett and Helen L. Koch, "The Effect of Nursery-School Training upon the Mental Test Performance of a Group of Orphanage Children," *PSJGP* 37 (1930): 102–22; Rowena Ropin, "A Comparative Study of the Development of Infants in an Institution with Those in Homes of Low Socio-Economic Status," *PB* 30 (1933): 680–81.

65. John E. Anderson, "Report: Institute of Child Welfare, University of Minnesota, 1925–1926" (typescript), n.d., subsection, "A Report on Psychological Investigations of Institute of Child Welfare, 1925–1926," Project 8, p. 2, University of Minnesota Institute of Child Welfare Papers, University of Minnesota Archives, Minneapolis, Minnesota. See also Florence L. Goodenough, "A Preliminary Report on the Effects of Nursery School Training upon the Intelligence Test Scores of Young Children," in Guy M. Whipple, ed., *National Society for the Study of Education, Twenty-Seventh Yearbook*, pt. 1, *Nature and Nurture: Their Influence upon Intelligence* (Bloomington, Ill.: Public School Publishing Company, 1928), 361–69.

66. See my "Recent Controversy in Human Development: A Historical View," *Human Development* 30 (1987): 325–35.

67. Florence L. Goodenough and John E. Anderson, *Experimental Child Study* (New York: Century Company, 1931), quotes at 25.

68. Truman Lee Kelley, *Crossroads in the Minds of Man: A Study of Differentiable Mental Abilities* (Stanford, Calif.: Stanford University Press, 1928).

69. Robert L. Thorndike, "The Effect of the Interval between Test and Retest on the Constancy of the I.Q.," *JEP* 24 (1933): 543–49. See also Thorndike, "Constancy of the I.Q.," *PB* 37 (1940): 167–86.

70. Nancy Bayley, "Mental Growth during the First Three Years: A Developmental Study of Sixty-One Children by Repeated Tests," *Genetic Psychology Monographs* 14 (1933): 1–92. See also Bayley and Harold E. Jones, "Environmental Correlates of Mental and Motor Development: A Cumulative Study from Infancy to Six Years," *CD* 8 (1937): 329–41; Marjorie Honzik, "The Constancy of Mental-Test Performance During the Preschool Period," *PSJGP* 52 (1938): 285–302.

71. Committee on Child Development, Division of Anthropology and Psychology, National Research Council, *Conference on Research in Child Development, Gramatan Hotel,*

Bronxville, New York, October 23 to 25, 1925 (Washington, D.C.: National Research Council, 1925); idem, *Second Conference on Research in Child Development* (Washington, D.C.; National Research Council, 1927); idem., *Third Conference on Research in Child Development, University of Toronto, Toronto, Canada, May 2–4, 1929* (Washington, D.C.: National Research Council, 1929); idem., *Fourth Conference on Research in Child Development, The University of Chicago, Chicago, Illinois, June 22–24, 1933* (Washington, D.C.: National Research Council, 1933).

72. Carl Murchison, ed., *A Handbook of Child Psychology* (Worcester, Mass.: Clark University Press, 1931); 2d ed. (1933).

73. Baldwin and Stecher, *The Psychology of the Preschool Child.*

74. See, for example, Lovisa Wagoner, *The Constructive Ability of Young Children, UISSCW*, vol. 3, no. 2 (Iowa City: University of Iowa, 1925), 1–56; Julia A. Kirkwood, *The Learning Process in Young Children, UISSCW*, vol. 3, no. 6 (Iowa City: University of Iowa, 1926), 1–107; Madora E. Smith, *An Investigation of the Development of the Sentence and the Extent of Vocabulary in Young Children, UISSCW*, vol. 3, no. 5 (Iowa City: University of Iowa, 1926), 1–93; Beth L. Wellman, *The Development of Motor Coordination in Young Children: An Experimental Study in the Control of Hand and Arm Movements, UISSCW*, vol. 3, no. 4 (Iowa City: University of Iowa, 1926), 1–93; Leslie Ray Marston, *The Emotions of Young Children, UISSCW*, vol. 3, no. 3 (Iowa City: University of Iowa, 1925), 1–99; Otis T. Caldwell and Wellman, "Characteristics of School Leaders," *JER* 14 (1926): 1–13; Esther Van Cleve, "A Rating Scale for the Study of Social Behavior in Young Children," *PIAS* 34 (1927): 313–14; Eva Leah Hulson, "A Preliminary Study of the Tempos Used by Preschool Children in the Three Rhythms—Walking, Running, and Jumping," *PIAS* 34 (1927): 312–13; Ruth Updegraff, "The Influence of the Size of the Retinal Image and of Perspective Upon Visual Perception of Distance: A Comparative Study," *PIAS* 34 (1927): 311–12; Wellman, "Significant Factors in the Motor Coordination of Young Children," *PB* 25 (1928): 178–79.

75. *Journal of the Minnesota Education Association*, Jan. 1926; *Ohio State Journal*, Mar. 4, 1926; *Columbus Dispatch*, Mar. 2, 1925; *Philadelphia Evening Public Ledger*, July 1, 1926; *DI*, Nov. 30, 1926; *Dallas News*, Mar. 3, 1927; Bird T. Baldwin, "Is It Heredity and Environment or Capacity and Training?" in *Southern California Society for Mental Hygiene, Modern Parenthood: Proceedings of the Southern California Conference Held at Los Angeles, California, December 15th, 16th, 17th, and 18th, 1926* (Los Angeles: Wolfer Printing Company, n.d. [1927?]), 89–103; *Los Angeles Daily Times*, Dec. 17, 1926; *Los Angeles Evening Herald*, Dec. 23, 1926; *Los Angeles Evening Express*, Dec. 23, 1926; Baldwin, "A Study of the Preschool Age—Abstract," *Proceedings of the National Educational Association* 64 (1926): 145–46; Baldwin, "An Experiment in Child Study and Parent Education," in Richard O. Beard, ed., *Parent Education, Northwest Conference on Child Health and Parent Education* (Minneapolis: University of Minnesota Press, 1927), 173–80.

76. Bird T. Baldwin, "Heredity and Environment—Or Capacity and Training?" *JEP* 19 (1928): 405–9; on that National Society for the Study of Education Yearbook, see Cravens, *The Triumph of Evolution*, 257–60; Baldwin, "Child Development," *Canadian Nurse* 25 (1929): 607–11.

77. See, for example, Bird T. Baldwin to Lawrence K. Frank, May 24, 1924; Baldwin to Beardsley Ruml, Apr. 2, 1924, and attached "The Rural Child in Iowa, Excerpts from a Progress Report, January to March, 1924, for the Laura Spelman Rockefeller Memorial, New York City" (typescript); all in Series 3, Subseries 5, Box 40, Folder "State University of Iowa," LSRM.

78. Bird T. Baldwin, Eva Abigail Fillmore, and Lora Hadley, *Farm Children: An Investigation of Rural Child Life in Selected Areas of Iowa* (New York: D. Appleton and Company, 1930).

79. See Robyn Muncy, *Creating a Female Dominion in American Reform, 1890–1935* (New York: Oxford University Press, 1991); Nancy Cott, *The Grounding of Modern Feminism* (New Haven, Conn.: Yale University Press, 1987); Hawes and Hiner, *American Childhood*, has several useful essays; see also Hawes, *The Children's Rights Movement: A History of Advocacy and Protection* (Boston: Twayne, 1991), 66–79. Emma Octavia Lundberg, *Unto the Least of These: Social Services for Children* (New York: Appleton-Century-Crofts, 1947).

CHAPTER FOUR

1. "Telephone conversation from Prest. [*sic*] [Walter A.] Jessup to Beardsley Ruml. N.Y. [*sic*] City, May 14, 1928 A.M.," IP.

2. *DI*, July 14, 1928; Frank N. Freeman to Walter A. Jessup, May 24, 1928, IP.

3. Mrs. S. E. Lincoln to Beardsley Ruml, Nov. 12, 1928; Lincoln to Lawrence K. Frank, Nov. 12, 1928; Ruml to Lincoln, Nov. 22, 1928; Frank to Lincoln, Nov. 23, 1928; all in Series 3, Subseries 5, Box 40, Folder "State University of Iowa," LSRM.

4. *DI*, July 11, 1929.

5. See "Financial Exhibits, Iowa Child Welfare Research Station, University of Iowa, 1923–1933," Exhibit A, Table 2, p. 2, attached to George D. Stoddard to W. W. Brierley, Feb. 28, 1934, IP.

6. Iowa Child Welfare Research Station Budget, July 25, 1920; Iowa Child Welfare Research Station Budget, May 19, 1934; both in IP.

7. My calculations for all statements drawn from Charles C. Spiker, comp., *The Institute of Child Behavior and Development: Fifty Years of Research, 1917–1967* (Iowa City: University of Iowa, 1967), a bibliography of the publications of the station and its successor, the institute.

8. Typical of developmentalists' view that nutrition was not within their purview is Carl Murchison, ed., *A Handbook of Child Psychology*, 2d ed. (Worcester, Mass.: Clark University Press, 1933), ix.

9. Amy L. Daniels, Dorothy Jordan, and Mary K. Hutton, "The Development of the Suckling Young of Milk-Fed Rats," *JN* 2 (1929): 19–29; Daniels, Mate L. Griddings, and Jordan, "The Effect of Heat on the Antineuritic Vitamin of Milk," *JN* 1 (1929): 455–66; Daniels, Hutton, and Catherine Marks, "Relation of Food Consumption of Milk-Fed Rats to the Growth of the Suckling Young," *PSEBM* 27 (1930): 759–60; Daniels and Ruth Bennett White, "Vitamin F in Relation to the Development of the Thyroid and Thymus of Suckling Young," *PSEBM* 27 (1930): 760–61; Daniels and White, "Influence on Development of Suckling Young of Addition of Certain Amino Acids to Diet of Mother during Lactation," *PSEBM* 27 (1930): 761–62; Daniels and Ivy Burright, "Heart Weights of Normal and Anemic Animals," *PSEBM* 30 (1933): 857–58; Daniels and Gladys J. Everson, "The Relations of Manganese to Congenital Debility," *JN* 9 (1935): 191–203.

10. Amy L. Daniels, Mary K. Hutton, Genevieve Stearns, and Lucea M. Hejinian, "The Relations of Rate of Growth in Infants to Diet," *AJDC* 37 (1929): 1177–86; Daniels, Stearns, and Hutton, "Calcium and Phosphorous Metabolism in Artificially Fed Infants," pt. 1, "Influence of Cod Liver Oil and Irradiated Milk," *AJDC* 37 (1929): 296–310; Daniels and Hejinian, "Growth in Infants from the Standpoint of Physical Measurements and

Nitrogen Metabolism," pt. 1, "Creatinine," *AJDC* 37 (1929): 1128–34; Daniels and Hejinian, "Growth of Infants from the Standpoint of Physical Measurements and of Nitrogen
Metabolism," pt. 2, "Creatine," *AJDC* 38 (1929): 499–506; Jennie Rowntree, "A Study of
the Absorption and Retention of Vitamin A in Young Children," *JN* 3 (1930): 265–87;
Rowntree, "The Effect of the Use of Mineral Oil upon the Absorption of Vitamin A," *JN* 3
(1931): 345–51; Daniels, Hutton, Elizabeth Knott, Gladys J. Everson, and Olive Wright,
"Relation of Milk Ingestion to Calcium Metabolism in Children," *PSEBM* 30 (1933):
1062–63; Daniels, Hutton, Knott, Everson, and Wright, "Relation of Ingestion of Milk to
Calcium Metabolism in Children," *AJDC* 47 (1934): 499–512; Everson and Daniels, "A
Study of Manganese Retentions in Children," *JN* 8 (1934): 497–502; Daniels and Wright,
"Iron and Copper Retentions in Young Children," *JN* 8 (1934): 125–38; Daniels and
Everson, "A Study of Anorexia in Preschool Children," *JHE* 27 (1935): 43–49; Daniels et
al., "A Study of the Protein Needs of Preschool Children," *JN* 9 (1935): 91–107.

   11. Amy L. Daniels, "Nutrition and Health, Discussion Group I. Introduction, Amy L.
Daniels, Chairman," in *Fourth Conference of the National Association for Nursery Education,
Philadelphia, Pennsylvania, November 12–14, 1931* (Boston: National Association for Nur-
sery Education, 1931), 16–17.

   12. Helen Garside, "Physical Traits of Young Children," *AJDC* 38 (1929): 541–46;
Grace Clark, "A Method of Computing the Cross-Section of the Chest for Children at
Seven, Eight and Nine Years," *Human Biology* 2 (1930): 539–46; S. I. Pyle and Charles L.
Drain, "Some Conditions in the Dentition of Preschool Children," *CD* 2 (1931): 147–52;
Pyle, "Physical Traits of Iowa Infants," *AJDC* 42 (1931): 1137–43; June F. Constantine, "A
Slide Rule for Calculating Ages," *CD* 2 (1931): 143–46; Constantine, "Methods of Cal-
culating Ages Including a Newly Devised Slide Rule," *JER* 26 (1932–33): 132–35.

   13. Howard V. Meredith and George D. Stoddard, "Physical Growth from Birth to
Maturity," *RER* 6 (1936): 54–84, 140–44, quote at 83; Meredith, "The Reliability of
Anthropometric Measurements Taken on Eight- and Nine-Year-Old White Males," *CD* 7
(1936): 262–72; Meredith, *Physical Growth of White Children: A Review of American Research prior to 1900*, Monographs of the Society for Research in Child Development, vol. 1,
no. 2 (Chicago: University of Chicago Press, 1936).

   14. Howard V. Meredith, *The Rhythm of Physical Growth: A Study of Eighteen An-
thropometric Measurements on Iowa City White Males Ranging in Age between Birth and
Eighteen Years*, UISSCW, vol. 2, no. 3 (Iowa City: University of Iowa, 1935); Bernice
Boynton, *The Physical Growth of Girls: A Study of the Rhythm of Physical Growth from
Anthropometric Measurements on Girls between Birth and Eighteen Years*, UISSCW, vol. 12,
no. 4 (Iowa City: University of Iowa, 1936).

   15. Howard V. Meredith and Virginia B. Knott, "Changes in Bodily Proportions during
Infancy and the Preschool Years," pt. 1, "The Thoracic Index," *CD* 8 (1937): 173–90.

   16. Ibid., pt. 2, "Width of Hips in Relation to Shoulder Width, Chest Width, Stem
Length, and Leg Length," *CD* 8 (1937): 311–27.

   17. Ibid., pt. 3, "The Skelic Index," *CD* 9 (1938): 49–62; *DI*, Jan. 22, 1936.

   18. Howard V. Meredith, "An Empirical Concept of Physical Growth," *CD* 9 (1938):
161–67.

   19. Howard V. Meredith, "Length of Head and Neck, Trunk, and Lower Extremities on
Iowa City Children Aged Seven to Seventeen Years," *CD* 10 (1939): 129–44; Meredith,
"Stature and Weight of Private School Children in Two Successive Decades," *American
Journal of Physical Anthropology* 28 (1941): 1–40; Elizabeth J. Martens and Meredith, "Ill-
ness History and Physical Growth," *AJDC* 64 (1942): 618–30; Fairye C. Wise and Mer-

edith, "The Physical Growth of Alabama White Girls Attending WPA Preschools," *CD* 13 (1942): 165–74; Meredith, "Comments on 'The Varieties of Human Physique,'" *CD* 11 (1940): 301–9; Meredith, "Stature of Massachusetts Children of North European and Italian Ancestry," *American Journal of Physical Anthropology* 24 (1939): 301–46; Meredith, review of *Predicting the Child's Development*, by Walter F. Dearborn and J. W. M. Rothney, *PB* 39 (1942): 245–49; Janet E. Redfield and Meredith, "Changes in the Stature and Sitting Height of Preschool Children in Relation to Rest in the Recumbent Position and Activity Following Rest," *CD* 9 (1938): 293–302; Meredith and Addison V. Brown, "Growth in Body-Weight during the First Ten Days of Postnatal Life," *Human Biology* 11 (1939): 24–77; Meredith and Jack L. Goodman, "A Comparison of Routine Hospital Records of Birth Stature with Measurements of Birth Stature Obtained for Longitudinal Research," *CD* 12 (1941): 175–81; Meredith, "Reporting Dental Research," pt. 1, "The Tabular Method," *Journal of Dental Education* 5 (1940): 75–85. See also Meredith, "Physical Growth from Birth to Maturity," *RER* 9 (1939): 47–79, 125–33; Meredith, "Technics of Research in Physical Growth and Anthropometry," *RER* 9 (1939): 80–90, 133–34.

20. Charles H. McCloy, *Appraising Physical Status: The Selection of Instruments, UISSCW*, vol. 12, no. 2 (Iowa City: University of Iowa, 1936).

21. Eleanor Metheny, "The Variability of the Percentage Index of Build as Applied to the Prediction of Normal Weight," *Human Biology* 11 (1939): 473–84; Charles H. McCloy, Metheny, and Virginia B. Knott, "A Comparison of the Thurstane Method of Multiple Factors with the Hotelling Method of Principal Components," *Psychometrics* 3 (1938): 61–67.

22. Everett L. Marshall, "A Multiple Factor Study of Eighteen Anthropometric Measurements of Iowa City Boys Aged Nine Days to Six Years," *JEE* 5 (1936): 212–28; Marshall, "A Comparison of Four Current Methods of Estimating Physical Status," *CD* 8 (1937): 89–92; Marshall, "The Objectivity of Anthropometric Measurements Taken on Eight- and Nine-Year-Old White Males," *CD* 8 (1937): 249–56. See also Marshall, "A Review of American Research on Seasonal Variations in Stature and Body Weight," *JP* 10 (1937): 819–37; Eleanor Metheny, *Breathing Capacity and Grip Strength of Preschool Children, UISSCW*, vol. 18, no. 2 (Iowa City: University of Iowa, 1940); Virginia Bergstresser Knott, *Physical Measurements of Young Children, UISSCW*, vol. 18, no. 3 (Iowa City: University of Iowa, 1941).

23. Albert Paul Weiss and Orvis C. Irwin, "A Note on Mass Activity in Newborn Infants," *PSJGP* 38 (1930): 20–30. Irwin, "The Amount and Nature of Activities of Newborn Infants under Constant External Stimulating Conditions during the First Ten Days of Life," *Genetic Psychology Monographs* 8 (1930): 1–92.

24. Orvis C. Irwin, "A Cold Light for Photographing Infant Reactions with the High-Speed Motion Picture Camera," *CD* 2 (1931): 153–55; Irwin, "Motility in Newborn Infants," *PIAS* 39 (1932): 243; Irwin, "The Amount of Motility of Seventy-Three Newborn Infants," *JCP* 14 (1932): 415–28; Irwin, "The Distribution of the Amount of Motility in Young Infants between Two Nursing Periods," *JCP* 14 (1932): 429–45; Irwin, "The Relation of Body Motility in Young Infants to Some Physical Traits," *JEE* 1 (1932–33): 140–43; Irwin, "Motility in Young Infants," *AJDC*, 45 (1933): 531–37. See also *DI*, Feb. 26, 1932; *DMT*, May 22, 1932.

25. Orvis C. Irwin, "The Latent Time of the Body Startle in Infants," *CD* 4 (1933): 104–7; Irwin, "Infant Responses to Vertical Movements," *CD* 4 (1933): 167–69.

26. LaBerta A. Weiss, "Differential Variations in the Activity of Newborn Infants," *PB* 30 (1933): 680; Weiss, "Differential Reactions of Newborn Infants to Different Degrees of Light and Sound Intensity," *PB* 30 (1933): 582.

27. T. W. Richards, "The Relationship between Bodily and Gastric Activity of Newborn Infants," *Human Biology* 8 (1936): 368–86; Richards, "The Importance of Hunger in the Bodily Activity of the Neonate," *PB* 33 (1936): 817–35.

28. Esther Stubbs and Orvis C. Irwin, "Laterality of Limb Movements of Four Newborn Infants," *CD* 4 (1933): 358–59; Irwin, "Proxi-Modistal Differentiation in Young Organisms," *PR* 40 (1933): 467–77; T. W. Richards and Irwin, "The Pressure Factor in Eliciting Plantar Responses," *PB* 31 (1934): 746–47; Lillian Sophia Kelting, "An Investigation of the Feeding, Sleeping, Crying, and Social Behavior of Infants," *JEE* 3 (1934): 97–106; Richards, "Stimulus-Response Factors in Infantile Plantar Phenomena," *PIAS* 41 (1934): 269–70; Stubbs and Irwin, "A Note on Reaction Times in Infants," *CD* 6 (1936): 291–92; M. A. Wenger and Irwin, "Variations in Electrical Resistance of the Skin in Newborn Infants," *PIAS* 41 (1935): 167–68.

29. Marion A. Wenger, "An Investigation of Conditional Responses in Human Infants," *PB* 32 (1935): 691.

30. Orvis C. Irwin, "The Organismic Hypothesis and Differentiation of Behavior," pts. 1–3, *PR* 39 (1932): 128–46, 189–207, 387–93; Irwin, "Dennis on Mass Activity: A Reply," *PR* 40 (1932): 215–19.

31. Leonard Carmichael, "Origin and Prenatal Growth of Behavior," in Murchison, *A Handbook of Child Psychology*, 134–35.

32. Orvis C. Irwin, "Toward a Theory of Conditioning," *PR* 46 (1939): 425–44.

33. Orvis C. Irwin, "Research on Speech Sounds for the First Six Months of Life," *PB* 38 (1941): 277–85; Irwin and Thayer Curry, "Vowel Elements in the Crying Vocalization of Infants under Ten Days of Age," *CD* 12 (1941): 99–109; Irwin and Han Piao Chen, "A Reliability Study of Speech Sounds Observed in the Crying of Newborn Infants," *CD* 12 (1941): 351–56; Irwin, "The Developmental Status of Speech Sounds of Ten Feeble-Minded Children," *CD* 13 (1942): 29–39; Irwin, "The Profile as a Visual Device for Indicating Central Tendencies on Speech Data," *CD* 12 (1941): 111–20; Irwin, "Can Infants Have IQ's," *PR* 49 (1942): 69–79. See also these other challenges to mainstream maturation theory: Ruth Wildenberg Kantrow, "Conditioned Feeding Responses in Young Infants and Concomitant Behavior Changes," *PB* 33 (1936): 749–50; Janet E. Redfield, "A Preliminary Report of Dark Adaptation in Young Infants," *CD* 8 (1937): 263–69; Josephine M. Smith, "Reply to Peiper," *CD* 8 (1937): 301–4.

34. James Allen Hicks, *The Acquisition of Motor Skill in Young Children: An Experimental Study of the Effects of Practice on Throwing at a Moving Target, UISSCW*, vol. 4, no. 5 (Iowa City: University of Iowa, 1930); Hicks, "The Acquisition of Motor Skill in Young Children," pts. 1 and 2, *CD* 1 (1930): 90–105, 292–97; Hicks and Dorothy W. Ralph, "Brief Reports: The Effects of Practice in Tracing the Porteus Diamond Maze," *CD* 2 (1931): 156–58.

35. Ruth Updegraff, "Preferential Handedness in Young Children," *JEE* 1 (1932–33): 134–39; Updegraff, "Correspondence between Handedness and Eyedness in Young Children," *PSJGP* 42 (1933): 490–92.

36. See, for example, Hjalmar Fletcher Scoe, *Bladder Control in Infancy and Early Childhood, UISSCW*, vol. 5, no. 4 (Iowa City: University of Iowa, 1933); Marion A. Wenger, "Path-Selection Behavior of Young Children in Body-Mazes," *JEE* 2 (1933–34): 197–236; Herman N. Stuart, "A Study of Sensori-Motor and Conceptual Thinking in Children between the Ages of Nine and Eighteen," *JEE* 4 (1935–36): 147–53; Mary B. Hill, "Experimental Procedures in the Study of the Process of Word Discrimination in Reading," *JER* 29 (1936): 473–82; Hill, "A Study of the Process of Word Discrimination in Individuals Beginning to Read," *JER* 29 (1936): 487–500.

37. Carra Lou McCaskill and Beth L. Wellman, "A Study of Common Motor Achievements at the Preschool Ages," *CD* 9 (1938): 141–50.

38. Lois Z. Smith, "An Experimental Investigation of Young Children's Interest and Expressive Behavior Responses to Single Statements, Verbal Repetition, and Ideational Repetition of Content in Animal Stories," *CD* 1 (1930): 232–47; Genevieve L. Harter, "Overt Trial and Error in the Problem Solving of Preschool Children," *PSJGP* 38 (1930): 361–72; Smith and Dorothy E. Bradbury, "How Do Young Children Respond to Animal Stories Containing Single Statements, Verbal Repetition, and Ideational Repetition of Content?" *CE* 7 (1930–31): 18–22.

39. Beth L. Wellman, Ida Mae Case, Ida Gaarder Mengert, and Dorothy E. Bradbury, *Speech Sounds of Young Children, UISSCW*, vol. 5, no. 2 (Iowa City: University of Iowa, 1931).

40. Madora E. Smith, "The Preschool Child's Use of Criticism," *CD* 3 (1932): 137–41; Olive J. Grigsby, "An Experimental Study of the Development of Concepts of Relationship in Pre-School Children as Evidenced by Their Expressive Ability," *JEE* 1 (1932–33): 144–62; Smith, "Grammatical Errors in the Speech of Preschool Children," *CD* 4 (1933): 183–90; Smith, "The Influence of Age, Sex, and Situation on the Frequency, Form, and Function of Questions Asked by Preschool Children," *CD* 4 (1933): 201–13.

41. Esther Van Cleave Berne, *An Investigation of the Wants of Seven Children, UISSCW*, vol. 4, no. 2 (Iowa City: University of Iowa, 1930).

42. Eva Leah Hulson, "An Analysis of the Free Play of Ten Four-Year-Old Children through Consecutive Observations," *JJR* 14 (1930): 188–208; Hulson, "Block Constructions of Four-Year-Old Children," *JJR* 14 (1930): 209–22; Hulson and Helen L. Reich, "Blocks and the Four-Year-Old," *CE* 8 (1931–32): 66–68; Ruth Updegraff and Edithe K. Herbst, "An Experimental Study of the Social Behavior Stimulated in Young Children by Certain Play Materials," *PSJGP* 42 (1933): 372–91; Updegraff and Herbst, "Stimulation of Social Behavior in Young Children by Certain Play Materials," *CE* 10 (1933): 360–63.

43. Ida Gaarder Mengert, "A Preliminary Study of the Reactions of Two-Year-Old Children to Each Other When Paired in a Semi-Controlled Situation," *PSJGP* 39 (1931): 393–98.

44. Wendell Johnson, *The Influence of Stuttering on the Personality, UISSCW*, vol. 5, no. 5 (Iowa City: University of Iowa, 1932), quote at 135.

45. Lee Edward Travis and Wendell Johnson, "Stuttering and the Concept of Handedness," PR 41 (1934): 534–62; Johnson and Lucile Drake, "Changes in Handedness Associated with Onset or Disappearance of Stuttering: Sixteen Cases," *JEE* 4 (1935–36): 112–32; Robert Milisen and Johnson, "A Comparative Study of Stutterers, Former Stutterers, and Normal Speakers Whose Handedness Has Been Changed," *Archives of Speech* 1 (1936): 61–86; Max Davis Steer and Johnson, "An Objective Study of the Relationship between Psychological Factors and the Severity of Stuttering," *JASP* 31 (1936): 36–46; Johnson and Darlene Duke, "The Dextrality Quotient of Fifty Six-Year-Olds with Regard to Hand Usage," *JEP* 28 (1937): 346–54; Johnson and Enod House, "Certain Laterality Characteristics of Children with Articulatory Disorders," *ESJ* 38 (1937–38): 52–58; Johnson, "Research Needs in Speech Pathology," *Journal of Exceptional Children* 4 (1938): 33–36; Johnson, "The Role of Evaluation in Stuttering Behavior," *Journal of Speech Disorders* 3 (1938): 85–89.

46. Harold M. Williams, "An Approach to the Study of Social Behavior in Children," *PIAS* 41 (1934): 271–73.

47. Lois M. Jack, Elizabeth Moore Manwell, Ida Gaarder Mengert, Esther Van Cleave

Berne, Helen Garside Kelly, LaBerta A. Weiss, and Agnes Fairlie Ricketts, *Behavior of the Preschool Child, UISSCW,* vol. 9, no. 3 (Iowa City: University of Iowa, 1934), 9–65.

48. Evaline Fales, "A Rating Scale of the Vigorousness of Play Activities of Preschool Children," *CD* 8 (1937): 15–46; Fales, "A Comparison of the Vigorousness of Play Activities of Preschool Boys and Girls," *CD* 8 (1937): 144–56; LaBerta A. Hattwick, "Sex Differences in Behavior of Nursery School Children," *CD* 8 (1937): 343–55.

49. Florence L. Goodenough and John E. Anderson, *Experimental Child Study* (New York: Century Company, 1931); Ruth Updegraff, "Recent Approaches to the Study of the Preschool Child," pts. 1 and 2, *JConP* 2 (1938): 159–61, 187–89; pt. 3, ibid. 3 (1939): 34–46.

50. Harold H. Anderson, "The Role of Environment in Child Conduct," *State of Iowa Bulletin of State Institutions* 36 (1934): 67–80, quote at 73. See also Anderson, "An Experimental Study of the Dominative and Integrative Behavior in Children of Preschool Age," *Journal of Social Psychology* 8 (1937): 335–45; Anderson, "Research in Mental Hygiene," *CE* 7 (1930–31): 423–27; Anderson, "What Are Behavior Problems?" in *Fourth Conference of the National Association for Nursery Education, Philadelphia, Pennsylvania, November 12–14, 1931* (Boston: National Association for Nursery Education, 1931), 80–86; Anderson, "Mental Hygiene Department," *Iowa Parent-Teacher* 11, no. 6 (1931): 12; Anderson, "Mental Hygiene," *Iowa Parent-Teacher* 12, no. 3 (1932): 9, 31; George D. Stoddard and Anderson, "A Mental Hygiene Program for Every Child," *Better Homes and Gardens* 10 (Jan. 1933): 23, 38–39; Stoddard and Anderson, "How the Public School Can Function in a Great Mental-Health Program," *Better Homes and Gardens* 10 (Feb. 1933): 36, 67–69; Anderson, "Which Shall It Be—Character Education or Mental Hygiene?" *High School Teacher* 9 (1933): 102; Anderson, *Behavior Problems of the Normal Child,* University of Iowa Extension Bulletin no. 307 (Iowa City: University of Iowa, 1933); Anderson, "Dealing with Behavior Problems in the Nursery School," *CE* 9 (1933): 340–44; Anderson, "Home-School Cooperation at the Iowa Child Welfare Research Station," in Alida Visscher Shinn, ed., *Home and School Cooperation in Nursery School, Kindergarten, Primary* (Washington, D.C.: Association for Childhood Education, 1934), 22–23; Anderson, "Character Education or Mental Hygiene—What Shall It Be?" *Mental Hygiene* 18 (1934): 254–62; Anderson, "Mental Hygiene Department: An Open Letter to Local Presidents," *Iowa Parent-Teacher* 16, no. 5 (1936): 5, 16.

51. Elizabeth Skelding Moore, *The Development of Mental Health in a Group of Young Children: An Analysis of Factors in Purposeful Activity, UISSCW,* vol. 4, no. 6 (Iowa City: University of Iowa, 1931).

52. Newell C. Kephart and H. Max Houtchens, "The Effect of the Stimulus Word Used upon Scores in the Association-Motor Test," *AJP* 94 (1937): 393–99.

53. H. T. Woolley, "The Validity of Standards of Mental Measurement in Young Childhood," *SS* 21 (1925): 476–82; H. E. Barrett and Helen L. Koch, "The Effect of Nursery-School Training upon the Mental Test Performance of a Group of Orphanage Children," *JGP* 37 (1930): 102–22. On IQ constancy, and the literature of developmental science more generally, see Joseph McVicker Hunt, *Intelligence and Experience* (New York: Ronald Press, 1961).

54. Beth L. Wellman, "The Experimental Psychology of the Preschool Child," *PIAS* 35 (1928): 299–300.

55. Beth L. Wellman, "Needed Developments in the Psychological Measurements of Preschool Children," *Fourth Conference of the National Association for Nursery Education, Philadelphia, Pennsylvania, November 12–14, 1931* (Boston: National Association for Nursery Education, 1931), 113–15.

56. Beth L. Wellman, "Some New Bases for Interpretations of the IQ," *PSJGP* 41 (1932): 116–26; Wellman, "The Effect of Preschool Attendance upon the IQ," *JEE* 1 (1932–33): 48–69, quote at 69. See also *Cedar Rapids Gazette*, Dec. 31, 1931.

57. Beth L. Wellman, "Growth in Intelligence under Differing School Environments," *JEE* 3 (1934–35): 59–83. See Robert B. Westbrooke, *John Dewey and American Democracy* (Ithaca, N.Y.: Cornell University Press, 1991), a brilliant work.

58. Dorothy E. Bradbury and Esther Leech Skeels, "An Analysis of the Literature Dealing with Nursery Education," *CD* 6 (1935): 227.

59. *DI*, Aug. 26, 1932.

60. George D. Stoddard, "Extending the Schools Downward," *Educational Administration and Supervision* 15 (1929): 581–92; Stoddard, "Some Current Ideas in Nursery Education," *SS* 35 (1932): 277–80; Stoddard, "A Survey of Nursery School Costs," *JER* 26 (1932–33): 354–59.

61. George D. Stoddard, "What Shall Be the Function of the National Association For Nursery Education?" *Proceedings of the Fifth Conference of the National Association for Nursery Education, Toronto, Ontario, October 26–28, 1933* (Boston: National Association for Nursery Education, 1933), 6–7.

62. See, for example, Lawrence K. Frank, memorandum of interview with Harry Hopkins [and others], Oct. 23, 1933; Frank, "Federal Relief Administration," Oct. 26, 1933; George F. Zook to Superintendents of Public Instruction, Nov. 23, 1933, and attached; John D. Rockefeller, Jr., to Edmund E. Day, Nov. 28, 1933, and attached; Frank, memorandum of interview with Zook and Miss Bess Goodykoontz, Dec. 15, 1933; W. W. Brierley to Goodykoontz, Feb. 8, 1934; Zook to Day, Dec. 22, 1933; Zook, Memorandum no. 1, "To All Administrators of Emergency Educational Programs: Cooperation of Private Agencies and Individuals," Jan. 2, 1934; Goodykoontz to Brierley, Feb. 3, 1934; "To the Members of the General Education Board," June 7, 1934; "To the Members of the General Education Board," Oct. 11, 1934; "General Education Board, Officers Conference, November 22, 1934"; all in Folder 3950, Box 378, Series 940, GEB.

63. *DI*, Nov. 5, 1933, Jan. 13, 19, 1934.

64. George D. Stoddard, "Nursery Schools in the Emergency Program," *SS* 40 (1934): 148–49, quote at 149.

65. See, for example, George D. Stoddard to I. Keith Tyler, June 30, 1937, VF:RHO.

66. Alice C. Brill and May P. Youtz, *Your Child and His Parents: A Textbook for Child Study Groups* (New York: D. Appleton and Company, 1932).

67. Perry Holaday and George D. Stoddard, *Getting Ideas from the Movies* (New York: Macmillan, 1933).

68. Ralph H. Ojemann, "An Investigation of the Iowa Radio Child Study Program," *JHE* 26 (1934): 24–25; *DI*, Dec. 4, 1932, Feb. 14, Nov. 27, 1934, Feb. 1, May 9, Aug. 29, 1935; *ICPC*, Jan. 7, 13, 1933; *DMR*, Jan. 14, 1934. See also Ojemann, "The Significance of Valid Child Development Principles for Parent Education," *Parent Education* 1 (1934): 17–20; Ojemann, "Construction of a Curriculum in Parent Education," in *The Reading Ability of Parents and Factors Associated with Reading Difficulties of Parents Education Materials*, UISSCW, vol. 8, no. 1 (Iowa City: University of Iowa, 1934); Ojemann, *Generalizations Relating to Child Development Involved in Intelligent Parental Guidance*, UISSCW, vol. 10, no. 1 (Iowa City: University of Iowa, 1935); Ojemann, *The Measurement of Attitude toward Self-Reliance*, UISSCW, vol. 10, no. 2 (Iowa City: University of Iowa, 1935). See also Ojemann, "Seven Years of Child Study by Radio: An Application of a Policy for Educational Broadcasting," *SS* 50 (1939): 353–57.

CHAPTER FIVE

1. Lawrence K. Frank, "The Fundamental Needs of the Child," *Proceedings of the Seventh Congress, National Association for Nursery Education, Nashville, Tennessee, October 20–23, 1937* (Detroit, Mich.: National Association for Nursery Education, 1937), 7–23, quotes at 23.

2. Interview no. 6, pp. 243–85, Interview no. 7, pp. 276–79, 286–330, in *The Reminiscences of Flora M. Rhind*, Columbia University Oral History Research Office, New York, 1970; copy at Rockefeller Archive Center, North Tarrytown, New York (hereafter cited as *Rhind Reminiscences*). David H. Stevens to Lawrence K. Frank, Apr. 22, 1931; Frank, untitled memorandum (typescript), May 1931; Frank, "Possible Board Action in Present Emergency," 1932; all in Folder 1900, Box 200, Series 1, Subseries 2, GEB. Frank, "Tentative Draft for the Survey Report," Sept. 1, 1932; Edmund E. Day, "Survey Objectives (Statement Supplementary to that of L:K:F: submitted by E.E.D., September 9, 1932)," Folder 3776, Box 365, ibid.

3. The best work yet on John Dewey is Robert B. Westbrooke, *John Dewey and American Democracy* (Ithaca, N.Y.: Cornell University Press, 1991).

4. Lawrence K. Frank, "The Principle of Disorder and Incongruity in Human Affairs," Feb. 8, 1932, Folder 3776, Box 365, Series 1, Subseries 3, GEB.

5. Lawrence K. Frank, "Mental Health," 1932; Frank, "Memorandum on the Relations of School Authorities to Municipal Government," May 1934; Frank, "Human Behavior," 1933; Frank, "Human Resources," 1935; Frank, "Program for the Field of Personality Investigation," n.d.; all in Folder 1900, Box 200, Series 1, Subseries 2, GEB. Frank, "Memorandum on Section III of the Survey," June 10, 1932; Frank to Trevor B. Arnett, Sept. 9, 1932; Arnett to Frank, Sept. 15, 1932; Frank, "Study of Means for Individual Development," Dec. 12, 1932; Frank, untitled memorandum (typescript), Mar. 10, 1931; Frank, "Tentative Draft for the Survey Report," Sept. 1, 1932; Frank, "Varieties of Child Research," July 8, 1932; Frank, "Parent Education in the U.S.," June 29, 1932; Frank, "Education for Individual Development," n.d.; all in Folder 3776, Box 365, Series 1, Subseries 3, GEB. See also Folder "GEB Surveys and Correspondence, 1931–1933," Box 7, LKF. Frank, "Memorandum on the Construction of a Program in the Field of Mental Health," 1931; Frank, "Suggestions for Follow-Up of White House Conference (1930)," prepared in 1931 for Follow-Up Committee; Frank, "Child Research," July 8, 1932; all in Folder "Memoes 1930s" Box 12, LKF.

6. Lawrence K. Frank, "Child Study Program," n.d.; Frank, "Child Study Annual Report 1935–1936," July 17, 1936; both in Folder "Memoes 1930s," Box 12, LKF; see also Raymond B. Fosdick, *Adventure in Giving: The Story of the General Education Board* (New York: Harper and Row, 1962); Interview no. 6, pp. 257–59, in *Rhind Reminiscences*.

7. See, for example, the correspondence between Frank and these individuals in Folder "Jean Walker Macfarlane, 1926–1939," Box 9; Folder "Harold E. Jones, 1930–1941," Box 8; and Folder "Herbert R. Stolz, 1930–1939," Box 11; all in LKF.

8. Steven L. Schlossman, "Philanthropy and the Gospel of Child Development," *History of Education Quarterly* 21 (Fall 1981): 275–99.

9. The above comments are based upon my research in the files of the various institutes and programs in child study and parent education in LSRM and GEB.

10. George D. Stoddard to Walter A. Jessup, May 1, 1933, and attached "Memorandum to Mr. Jessup—May 1, 1933"; Stoddard, memo, May 1, 1933, and attached "A Request to the Spelman Fund for a Change in the Provisions of the Grant"; "Financial Exhibits, Iowa

Child Welfare Research Station, University of Iowa, 1923–1933," n.d. [1934]; Stoddard, "Notes on Reorganization and Support of Station Activities, 1934–1935 and 1935–1936," Apr. 5, 1934; Stoddard, "Iowa Child Welfare Research Station," Aug. 17, 1934; Stoddard to Jessup, May 29, 1934; Stoddard, "Memorandum to Mr. Cobb, September 13, 1934," and attached "Financial Needs of the Iowa Child Welfare Research Station for the Biennium Beginning July 1, 1935," Sept. 13, 1934; Stoddard to President E. A. Gilmore, Jan. 8, 1936, and attached "Memorandum on Child Welfare Station Finances," Jan. 8, 1936; Stoddard to Gilmore, Mar. 4, 1936, and attached page; Gilmore to Catherine Hill Taylor, Mar. 6, 1936; Taylor to Gilmore, Mar. 10, 1936; Constance Murdoch to Gilmore, Mar. 27, 1936; Stoddard to Mrs. M. P. Summers, Mar. 29, 1937; Stoddard to Mrs. Charles F. Pye, Apr. 1, 1937; Stoddard, memorandum to Gilmore, Mar. 29, 1937, and attached Gilmore to Mrs. Dorothy Houghton, Apr. 3, 1937; Gilmore to Stoddard, May 3, 1937; all in IP. Stoddard to Miss Anna Blauvet, May 31, 1933, and attached "A Request to the Spelman Fund for a Change in the Provisions of the Grant"; Blauvet to Stoddard, June 15, 1933; Taylor to Stoddard, July 18, 1933, and attached "Officers' Action—Extension of Period of Appropriation—State University of Iowa—Work in Child Study and Parent Education," July 14, 1933; Gilmore to Blauvet, Jan. 7, 1935; Taylor to Gilmore, Jan. 11, 1935; Gilmore to Taylor, Mar. 6, 1936; Taylor to Gilmore, Mar. 10, 1936; Taylor to Mrs. Norma S. Thompson, Mar. 18, 1936; Murdoch to Gilmore, Mar. 27, 1936, and enclosed "Officers' Action—Extension of Period of Appropriation—State University of Iowa—Work in Child Study and Parent Education," Mar. 25, 1936; all in Series 3, Subseries 5, Box 41, Folder "State University of Iowa, 1930–1940," LSRM. *DI*, June 18, 1935, June 18, 21, Nov. 22, Dec. 9, 1936, Mar. 5, 25, Apr. 7, 27, 1937; *DMR*, July 5, Oct. 4, Dec. 9, 1936, Mar. 25, Apr. 8, 13, 21, 23, Oct. 19, 1937; *ICPC*, July 9, 1936. "Iowa State House Journal Thursday, Feb. 16, 1939, House Concurrent Resolution 11" (copy); Virgil M. Hancher to W. Earl Hall, Dec. 30, 1940; "Iowa State Board of Education: Action Regarding Retrenchments and Economies" (typescript), n.d. [1940]; all in IP. *DMT*, Dec. 28, 1939.

11. The correspondence in VF:ALD does not really clarify why Amy Daniels had so much difficulty at the university, merely that she did.

12. George D. Stoddard, "Notes on Reorganization of Station Activities, 1934–1935 and 1935–1936" (typescript), n.d. [1936]; Stoddard, "Notes on Reorganization and Support of Station Activities, 1934–1935 and 1935–1936," Apr. 5, 1934; both in IP. [Stoddard], "Memorandum on Parent Education Activities, Iowa Child Welfare Research Station," Aug. 18, 1936; [Stoddard], "Parent Education," attached to "Positions of Station Graduates," May 1, 1936; [Stoddard] "Revised Location of Parent Education Groups in Iowa under Parent Education Division of the Iowa Child Welfare Research Station, 1934–1935," n.d. [1936]; [Stoddard], "Needs of the Iowa Child Welfare Research Station for the Biennium, 1939–1941," Oct. 10, 1938; Stoddard, "Memorandum to President Gilmore Concerning Budgetary Changes, Iowa Child Welfare Research Station over a Ten-Year Period," Oct. 3, 1939; Stoddard, "Memorandum to President Gilmore Concerning Budgetary Economies in Child Welfare," Nov. 22, 1939; all in CW.

13. See, for example, George D. Stoddard, "The Nursery School as an Economic Enterprise," *SS* 43 (1936): 49–51; Stoddard, "Editorial Comment: Guidance for Leadership," *CE* 14 (1937–38): 291–92; Stoddard, "Shackling Concepts in Nursery Education," *SS* 50 (1939): 737–40; Stoddard, "Child Development—A New Approach to Education," *SS* 49 (1939): 33–38; Stoddard, "Skill in Straight Thinking," *Nation's Schools* 27 (1941): 60–62.

14. Margaret Mead, evaluation of Kurt Lewin, May 8, 1967, p. 1, Folder 1, Box M944, KL.

15. See, for example, Kurt Lewin, "Filmaufnehmen über Trieb-und-Affektausserungen psychopathischer Kinder (vergleichen mit Normalen und Schwachsinnigen)," *Zeitschrift Für Kinderforschung* 32 (1926): 414–48; Lewin, "Gestalttheorie und Kinderpsychologie," *Wernende Zeitalter* 10 (1929): 544–50; Lewin, *Der Begriff Der Genese In Physik, Biologie, Und Entwickslungsgeschichte* (Berlin: Verlag GmBH, 1922).

16. For biographical information on Lewin, see Albert J. Marrow, *The Practical Theorist: The Life of Kurt Lewin* (New York: Basic Books, 1969); Donald K. Adams, "Lewin, Kurt," Folder 88, Box 88, Donald K. Adams Papers, Archives of the History of American Psychology, University of Akron Libraries, Akron, Ohio; Herbert A. Strauss and Werner Roeder, eds., *International Biographical Dictionary of Central European Emigres, 1933–1945* (New York, London, and Paris: K. G. Sauer, 1983), vol. 2, pt. 2, 720–21, s.v. "Lewin, Kurt Zadek"; "Lewin, Kurt, Psychologie 9.9. 1890 Mogilno [Prov. Posen] 12.2.1947 Washington (USA)," in *Neuere Deutsche Biographie*, Herausgegeben von der Historischer Kommission Bei Der Bayerischen Akademie Der Wissenschaften, Vierzehnter Band, *Laverrenz-Locher-Freuler* (Berlin: Duncker und Humblot, 1985), 413–15.

17. See Kurt Lewin, *Principles of Topological Psychology* (New York: McGraw-Hill, 1936); and Lewin, *The Conceptual Representation and Measurement of Psychological Forces, Contributions in Psychological Theory*, vol. 1 (1938), 1–247.

18. Kurt Lewin, "Die Auswirkung von Umweltkraften," *Proceedings of the Ninth International Congress of Psychology, 1929* (New Haven, Conn.: Yale University Press, 1929), 286–88.

19. Kurt Lewin, "Environmental Forces in Child Behavior and Development," in Carl Murchison, ed., *A Handbook of Child Psychology* (Worcester, Mass.: Clark University Press, 1931), 94–127.

20. Kurt Lewin, "The Conflict between Aristotelean and Galileian Modes of Thought in Contemporary Psychology," *Journal of General Psychology* 5 (1931): 141–77.

21. See, for example, Kurt Koffka to Horace M. Kallen, May 5, 1933, Folder 762, HMK. C. E. Ladd, R. M. Ogden, and F. K. Richmeyer to President Livingston Farrand, June 20, 1933; Farrand to the Rockefeller Foundation, July 20, 1933; Alan Gregg to Farrand, July 26, 1935; Farrand to Fred M. Stein, Sept. 23, 1933, Sept. 18, 1934; all in Emergency Committee in Aid of Displaced German Scholars, Records, Cornell University Archives, Ithaca, New York.

22. Livingston Farrand to Edward R. Murrow, Mar. 25, 1935; Murrow to Farrand, Mar. 29, 1935; both in Emergency Committee in Aid of Displaced German Scholars, Records, Cornell University Archives, Ithaca, New York.

23. Horace M. Kallen to Kurt Lewin, May 7, 1934; Kallen to Chancellor Judah L. Magnes, May 7, 1934; Kallen to Lewin, May 22, 1934; Kallen to Harold Riegelman, Nov. 11, 1934; Kallen to Richard Gottheil, Nov. 17, 1934; Kallen to Lewin, Nov. 27, 1934; Kallen to Franz Boas, Dec. 10, 1934; Kallen to Edward Lee Thorndike, Dec. 18, 1934; all in Folder 762, HMK; Kallen to Lewin, Oct. 28, 1935, Folder 763, ibid.

24. See correspondence of George D. Stoddard, Kurt Lewin, and Lawrence K. Frank, 1935–36, in VF:KL. See also W. W. Brierley to Gilmore, Apr. 22, 1936, IP. See also Frank to Lewin, Jan. 11, Apr. 15, 1936; Lewin to Frank, Apr. 13, 27, 1936; all in Folder "Kurt Lewin," Box 8, LKF. See also Stoddard to Dr. Stephen Duggan, Mar. 4, 11, 1935; Frank to Stoddard, Mar. 6, 1935 (two letters); Lewin to Frank, Mar. 15, 1935; Frank to Lewin, Mar. 18, 1935; Stoddard to Lewin, Mar. 21, 1935; Frank, memorandum of interview, Mar. 29, 1935; all in Folder 3884, Box 372, Series 1, Subseries 3, GEB.

25. Quote in Kurt Lewin to Horace M. Kallen, Mar. 16, 1936, Folder 766, HMK.

Lawrence K. Frank to Lewin, Jan. 27, 1937; Lewin to Frank, Jan. 23, Mar. 27, 1937; Lewin to Frank, Jan. 7, Mar. 15, May 8, 1939; Frank to Lewin, Jan. 23, Mar. 27, 1937; Frank to Lewin, Feb. 21, 1939; all in Folder "Kurt Lewin," Box 8, LKF. See also George D. Stoddard to Lewin, May 4, May 12, June 1 (two letters), 1939, VF:KL. See also Robert J. Havighurst, memorandum of interview with Stoddard, Oct. 17, 1938; Stoddard to Havighurst, Oct. 24, 1938; Havighurst to Stoddard, Oct. 31, 1938; Stoddard to Havighurst, Mar. 4, 1939; Stoddard to Arthur G. Askey, May 16, 1939; General Education Board #39026, "I-2950 State University of Iowa—Iowa Child Welfare Research Station," June 5, 1939; W. W. Brierley to Stoddard, June 8, 1939; all in Folder 3885, Box 372, Series 1, Subseries 3, GEB. See also Stoddard to President E. A. Gilmore, Mar. 7, 1940, IP. See also Lewin to Donald K. Adams, May 23, 1939; Adams to Lewin, May 29, 1939; both in Donald K. Adams Papers, Archives of the History of American Psychology, University of Akron Libraries, Akron, Ohio.

26. Kurt Lewin to Alfred J. Marrow, Jan. 5, 1940, Folder 55, Box M948, KL. On his associates' memories of Lewin in this vein, see, for example, the evaluations of Lewin recorded in 1967, in Folder 1, Box M944, KL; see also interview with Robert R. Sears, by Hamilton Cravens, Mar. 12, 1985, pp. 11–25, Stanford University Archives, Stanford, California, and University of Iowa Archives, Iowa City, Iowa.

27. Kurt Lewin to Monette Marrow, Jan. 7, 1936, Folder 51, Box M948, KL. Lewin to Horace M. Kallen, Mar. 9, 1940, Folder 672, HMK. Lewin to Kallen, Sept. 30, 1938, Dec. 1, 1939, Folder 766, HMK. Lewin to Kallen, Nov. 4, 1940; Kallen to Lewin, Nov. 8, 1940; Lewin to Kallen, Feb. 15, 1940; all in Folder 767, HMK. Kallen to Lewin, Dec. 15, 1938, Folder 648, HMK.

28. Kurt Lewin, "Psycho-Sociological Problems of a Minority Group," *Character and Personality* 3 (1935): 175–87; Lewin, "Psychology of Success and Failure," *Occupations* 14 (1935): 926–30; Lewin, "Some Social Psychological Differences between the United States and Germany," *Character and Personality* 4 (1936); 265–93; Lewin, "Bringing Up the (Jewish) Child," *Menorah Journal* 28 (1940): 297–305; Lewin, "Personal Adjustment and Group Belongingness," *Jewish Social Service Quarterly* 17 (1941): 362–66; Lewin, "Self-Hatred among Jews," *Contemporary Jewish Record* 4 (1941): 219–32; Lewin, "Democracy and the School," *Understanding the Child* 10 (1941): 1–7; Lewin, "Changes in Social Sensitivity in Child and Adult," *CE* 19 (1942): 53–57; Lewin, "Cultural Reconstruction," *JASP* 38 (1943): 166–73; Lewin, "The Special Case of Germany," *Public Opinion Quarterly* 7 (1943): 555–66.

29. *DI*, May 16, July 11, 1936, Dec. 18, 1937, Feb. 22, Dec. 21, 1938, Feb. 19, 1939, Jan. 6, 1940, Apr. 16, 1941. Gertrud Lewin to Mr. and Mrs. Alfred Marrow, Nov. 30, 1935, Folder 51, Box M948, KL. Kurt Lewin to Horace M. Kallen, Feb. 7, 1938, Folder 766, HMK. Lewin to Kallen, Oct. 11, 1941, Folder 767; both in HMK. Lewin to George D. Stoddard, Mar. 11, 14, 1939, VF:KL.

30. *DI*, July 7, 1936, Apr. 15, Dec. 9, 1937, Feb. 22, 24, May 6, Sept. 10, 1938, Jan. 7, 1939, Feb. 18, 1942; Kurt Lewin to George D. Stoddard, May 27, June 1, 1939, VF:KL.

31. Kurt Lewin to Lawrence K. Frank, Nov. 21, 1935; Frank to Lewin, Nov. 25, 1935; "G.E.B. 35-083, December 10, 1935, I-2823. Conference on Research Problems in Child Growth and Development"; Frank, memo to W. W. Brierley, Dec. 11, 1935; Lewin to Frank, Dec. 12, 19, 1935; Frank to Dr. Donald MacKinnon, Dec. 20, 1935; MacKinnon to Frank, Dec. 20, 1935; Frank, memorandum of interview, Conference on Topological Psychology at Bryn Mawr, December 29–31, 1935; Lewin to Frank, Jan. 13, 1936; all in Folder 3875, Box 371, Series 1, Subseries 3, GEB. See also Horace M. Kallen to Lewin,

Oct. 23, 1936; Lewin to Kallen, Nov. 7, 1936; both in Folder 766, HMK. Lewin to Kallen, Dec. 13, 1937; Lewin to Kallen, Dec. 19, 1940; Kallen to Lewin, Feb. 9, 1943; all in Folder 767, HMK. *DI*, Jan. 22, 1937, Feb. 22, 1938.

32. *DI*, Jan. 22, 1937, May 6, 1938; *Time*, Mar. 6, 1939; Kurt Lewin to Horace M. Kallen, Nov. 7, 1936, Folder 766, HMK. See also Roger Barker, evaluation of Lewin, Folder 1, Box M944, KL.

33. Roger Barker, Tamara Dembo, and Kurt Lewin, *Frustration and Regression: An Experiment with Young Children*, Studies in Topological and Vector Psychology II, UISSCW, vol. 18, no. 1 (Iowa City: University of Iowa Press, 1941). See also *DI*, Jan. 22, 1937, May 6, 1938; *Time*, Mar. 3, 1939.

34. Florence L. Goodenough and John E. Anderson, *Experimental Child Study* (New York: Century Company, 1931), 505–15.

35. Alice M. Leahy, "Nature-Nurture and Intelligence," *Genetic Psychology Monographs* 17, no. 4 (1935): 235–309.

36. Hubert S. Coffey and Beth L. Wellman, "The Role of Cultural Status in Intelligence Changes of Preschool Children," *JEE* 5 (1936–37): 191–202, quote at 202.

37. Beth L. Wellman, "Mental Growth from Preschool to College," *JEE* 6 (1937–38): 127–38, quote at 138. See also Wellman, "Guiding Mental Development," *CE* 15 (1938–39): 108–12; Wellman, "Our Changing Concept of Intelligence," *JConP* 2 (1938): 97–107.

38. George D. Stoddard, "Our Children: Their Intelligence," *Proceedings and Addresses, National Education Association* 76 (1938): 61–62.

39. I am grateful to Dr. Marie Skodak Crissey for discussing certain aspects of the orphanage studies with me.

40. See, for example, George D. Stoddard, "Notes on Reorganization and Support of Station Activities, 1934–35 and 1935–36," Apr. 5, 1934, p. 6, IP.

41. Harold M. Skeels, "Mental Development of Children in Foster Homes," *JGP* 49 (1936): 91–106; see also Skeels, "The Relation of the Foster Home Environment to the Mental Development of Children Placed in Infancy," *CD* 7 (1936): 1–5; *DMR*, June 18, 1936.

42. Harold M. Skeels, "A Cooperative Orphanage Research," *JER* 30 (1936–37): 437–44; Skeels and Eva A. Fillmore, "The Mental Development of Children from Underprivileged Homes," *JGP* 50 (1937): 427–39.

43. The monograph in which the Davenport project was reported was Harold M. Skeels, Ruth Updegraff, Beth L. Wellman, and Harold M. Williams, *A Study of Environmental Stimulation: An Orphanage Preschool Project*, UISSCW, vol. 15, no. 4 (Iowa City: University of Iowa, 1938). The first public announcement of IQ loss was Wellman and Skeels, "Decreases in IQ of Children under an Unfavorable Environment," *PB* 35 (1938): 715.

CHAPTER SIX

1. See LeRoy Ashby, "Partial Promises and Semi-Visible Youths: The Depression and World War II," in Joseph M. Hawes and N. Ray Hiner, eds., *American Childhood: A Research Guide and Historical Handbook* (Westport, Conn.: Greenwood Press, 1985), 489–532, a perceptive historiographical essay with many valuable bibliographical leads. Hawes, *The Children's Rights Movement. A History of Advocacy and Protection* (Boston: Twayne Publishers, 1991), 66–79, has a fine summary of these programs. See also Robyn Muncy, *Creating a Female Dominion of Reform, 1890–1935* (New York: Oxford University Press, 1991), which has many excellent insights and many valuable bibliographical leads.

2. Barry D. Karl and Stanley N. Katz, "The American Philanthropic Foundation and the Public Sphere," *Minerva* 19 (1981): 236–70, a seminal essay. See also Alan I Marcus and Howard P. Segal, *American Technology: A Brief History* (San Diego, Calif.: Harcourt, Brace, Jovanovich, 1989), a book with much broader implications than the title suggests.

3. *Time*, Nov. 7, 1938; *DI*, Feb. 19, 1939; "Continuity for Broadcast in the 'Adventures of Science' Program by Watson Davis, Columbia Broadcasting System, Station WBBM Chicago, Mar. 2, 1939, 6:15 PM CTS," and "Supporting Materials for Broadcast of George D. Stoddard, Columbia Broadcasting System, March 2, 1939, 'Cultivating the Child's Mind,'" VF:GDS.

4. *DI*, July 7, 1939; see also George D. Stoddard, "Some New Light on Human Intelligence," *California Journal of Secondary Education* 14 (1939): 490–94.

5. Ronald Lippitt, evaluation of Kurt Lewin, May 10, 1967, p. 9, Folder 1, Box M944, KL.

6. Ronald Lippitt, *An Experimental Study of the Effect of Democratic and Authoritarian Group Structures*, in Studies in Topological and Vector Psychology II, *UISSCW*, vol. 18, no. 2 (Iowa City: University of Iowa Press, 1940), 45–195, quote at 190.

7. Kurt Lewin, Ronald Lippitt, and Ralph K. White, "Patterns of Aggressive Behavior in Experimentally Created 'Social Climates,'" *JSP* 10 (1939): 271–99; Dan L. Adler, Lippitt, and White, "An Experiment with Young People under Democratic, Autocratic, and Laissez-Faire Atmospheres," in National Council of Social Work, *Proceedings of the National Council of Social Work, Selected Papers, Sixty-Sixth Annual Conference Buffalo, New York, June 18–24, 1939* (New York: Columbia University Press, 1939), 66:152–299. See also *DI*, Dec. 14, 1940; *Boston Herald*, Feb. 17, 1941; *New York Sunday Times Magazine*, Dec. 15, 1940.

8. Kurt Lewin to Horace M. Kallen, Dec. 3, 1937, Folder 767, HMK; Lewin and Ronald Lippitt, "An Experimental Approach to the Study of Autocracy and Democracy: A Preliminary Note," *Sociometry* 1 (1938): 292–300; Lewin, "Experiments on Autocratic and Democratic Atmospheres," *Social Frontier*, 4 (1938): 316–19; Lewin, "Field Theory and Experiment in Social Psychology: Concepts and Methods," *American Journal of Sociology* 44 (1939): 868–96; Lippitt, "Field Theory and Experiment in Social Psychology: Autocratic and Democratic Group Atmospheres," *American Journal of Sociology* 45 (1939): 26–49; Lewin, "Experiments in Social Space," *Harvard Educational Review* 9 (1939): 21–32.

9. Marie Skodak, *Children in Foster Homes: A Study of Mental Development, UISSCW*, vol. 16, no. 1 (Iowa City: University of Iowa, 1939), quotes at 131–32.

10. Harold M. Skeels and Harold Dye, "A Study of the Effects of Differential Stimulation on Mentally Retarded Children," *Proceedings of the American Association of Mental Deficiency* 44 (1939): 114–36. See also Skeels, "A Study of the Effects of Differential Stimulation on Mentally Retarded Children: A Follow-Up Report," *American Journal of Mental Deficiency* 46 (1942): 340–50.

11. Benjamin R. Simpson, "The Wandering I.Q.: Is It Time for It to Settle Down?" *JPsy* 7 (1939): 351–67; Simpson, "The Wandering I.Q.: Fact or Statistical Illusion?" *SS* 50 (1939): 20–23; Simpson, "The Wandering I.Q.: A Continuation," *JPsy* 9 (1940): 31–48; Beth L. Wellman, "The IQ: A Reply," *JPsy* 8 (1939): 143–55; Wellman, "The IQ Illusion," *SS* 50 (1939): 733.

12. "Conversation between Mr. [Albert E.] Wiggam and Dr. [Harold M.] Skeels," Apr. 21, 1939; "Conversation between Mr. Wiggam and Dr. [Beth L.] Wellman," Apr. 21, 1939; "Conversation between Mr. Wiggam, Dr. [George D.] Stoddard, and Dr. Skeels, Iowa City, Apr. 21, 1939"; all in VF:BLW; copies also in VF:HMS and VF:GDS.

13. See *New York Times*, Oct. 26, 1939; *Oakland Tribune*, Oct. 31, 1939.

14. Robert R. Sears, *Your Ancients Revisited: A History of Child Development* (Chicago: University of Chicago Press, 1975), 52–53, briefly discusses the California institute; a compendium of the institute's more important papers is Mary Cover Jones, Nancy Bayley, Jean Walker Macfarlane, and Marjorie P. Honzik, *The Course of Human Development* (Waltham, Mass.: Xerox Publishing Company, 1971).

15. H. O. O'Neill, "Variations In the Intelligence of 105 Children," *CD* 8 (1937): 357–63; Donald Syngg, "The Relation between the Intelligence of Mothers and of Their Children Living in Foster Homes," *PSJGP* 52 (1938): 401–6; Jessie Wells and Grace Arthus, "Effect of Foster-Home Placement on the Intelligence Ratings of Children of Feeble-Minded Parents," *Mental Hygiene* 23 (1939): 277–85; Sara Salzman, "The Influence of Social and Economic Background on Stanford-Binet Performance," *JSP* 12 (1940): 71–81; George S. Speer, "The Intelligence of Foster Children," *PSJGP* 57 (1940): 49–55.

16. The literature on these matters is enormous. See, for example, C. L. Nemzek, "The Constancy of the I.Q.," *Peabody Journal of Education* 9 (1931): 123–24; Nemzek, "The Constancy of the I.Q.'s of Gifted Children," *JEP* 23 (1932): 607–10; Nemzek, "The Constancy of the I.Q." *PB* (1933): 143–67; Nancy Bayley, "Mental Growth during the First Three Years: A Developmental Study of Sixty-One Children by Repeated Tests," *Genetic Psychology Monographs* 14 (1933): 1–92; Bayley and Harold E. Jones, "Environmental Correlates of Mental and Motor Development: A Cumulative Study from Infancy to Six Years," *CD* 8 (1937): 329–41; Marjorie Honzik, "The Constancy of Mental-Test Performance during the Preschool Period," *PSJGP* 52 (1938): 285–302; Gertrude H. Hildreth, *The Resemblance of Siblings in Intelligence and Achievement*, Teachers College Contributions to Education, no. 186 (New York: Teachers College, 1925); P. Stocks and M. N. Karn, "A Biometric Investigation of Twins and Their Brothers and Sisters," *Annals of Eugenics Cambridge* 5 (1933): 1–55; H. J. Muller, "Mental Traits and Heredity," *Journal of Heredity* 16 (1925): 433–48; S. K. Richardson, "The Correlation of Intelligence Quotients of Siblings of the Same Chronological Age Levels," *JJR* 20 (1936): 186–98.

17. Guy M. Whipple, "Editorial Impression of the Contribution to Knowledge of the Twenty-Seventh Yearbook," *JEP* 19 (1928): 392; Barbara Stoddard Burks, "The Relative Influence of Nature and Nurture upon Mental Development: A Comparative Study of Foster Parent–Foster Child Resemblance and True Parent–True Child Resemblance," in Guy M. Whipple, ed., *National Society for the Study of Education, Twenty-Seventh Yearbook*, pt. 1, *Nature and Nurture: Their Influence upon Intelligence* (Bloomington, Ill.: Public School Publishing Company, 1928), 219–316; Lewis M. Terman, "The Influence of Nature and Nurture upon Intelligence Scores: An Evaluation of the Evidence in Part I of the 1928 Yearbook of the National Society for the Study of Education," *JEP* 19 (1928): 362–69.

18. Bird T. Baldwin, "Heredity and Environment—Or Capacity and Training?" *JEP* 19 (1928): 405–9; see also *ICPC*, Mar. 16, 1927; *Oskaloosa Daily Herald*, Sept. 27, 1927; *Mankato Tribune*, Oct. 7, 1927; *Literary Digest*, Jan. 17, 1928.

19. On Stoddard's role in the National Association for Nursery Education, see, for example, *DI*, Nov. 18, 1931, Nov. 5, 1935, Oct. 27, 1937; on his role in the John Dewey Society, see, for example, William Heard Kilpatrick to George D. Stoddard, Oct. 8, 1936; Stoddard to Kilpatrick, Nov. 12, 1936; William Heard Kilpatrick, "To Members of the Yearbook Committee," Nov. 30, 1936 (broadside for John Dewey Society); "The John Dewey Society: The Teacher and Society" (broadside), n.d.; all in VF:GDS. On Stoddard's views in these years, see, for example, *DI*, Mar. 9, Aug. 26, 1932, Nov. 5, 1933, Jan. 10, Apr. 4, 12, May 4, 5, 1935, Mar. 17, 18, May 8, June 24, 1936, Mar. 10, 18, 24, 1937; *Daily*

Texan, Nov. 5, 1936; *DMR*, Feb. 10, Mar. 24, 1935, Apr. 26, May 24, June 18, Nov. 22, 1936, Feb. 4, 1937; *DMT*, Nov. 22, 1936; *ICPC*, Dec. 20, 1932, July 2, 1936; *New York Times*, Oct. 18, 1932, Mar. 3, 1935.

20. See *DI*, Sept. 24, 1937; see also Guy M. Whipple, ed., *The Thirty-Ninth Yearbook of the National Society for the Study of Education*, 2 vols. (Bloomington, Ill.: Public School Publishing Company, 1940), 1:xvii–xviii.

21. Dorothea McCarthy to Florence L. Goodenough, Feb. 2, 1938; Goodenough to McCarthy, Feb. 11, 1938; both in Folder 2, FLG.

22. Florence L. Goodenough to Dr. Amanda Herring, May 1, 1939, Folder 2, FLG. Many of the above generalizations are based on the rich correspondence in Folder 2, FLG, and in Folders 12–14, Box 14, LMT.

23. Lewis M. Terman to Arnold Gesell, Dec. 20, 1938; Florence L. Goodenough to Gesell, Dec. 1, 1938; Gesell to Goodenough, Dec. 6, 1938; Gesell quote in Gesell to Terman, Jan. 5, 1939; all in AG. Barbara Stoddard Burks to Terman, Feb. 14, 1939; Terman to Burks, Feb. 21, 1939; both in Folder 24, Box 13, LMT.

24. *Time*, July 17, 1939; *DMT*, July 5, 1939; *Los Angeles Examiner*, July 4, 1939; *DMR*, July 8, 1939; *ICPC*, July 7, 1939; *Cedar Rapids Gazette*, July 7, 1939; *Mason City Globe-Gazette*, July 9, 1939.

25. Florence L. Goodenough to John E. Anderson, Aug. 7, 1939; E. Lowell Kelley to Goodenough, Nov. 15, 1939; both in Folder 2, FLG. Goodenough to E. L. Kelley, Oct. 25, 1939, Folder 13, Box 14, LMT. See correspondence between Goodenough and Lewis M. Terman, Oct–Nov. 1939, Folder 13, Box 14, LMT; all detail setting up the Columbus meeting. See also Goodenough to Terman, Sept. 26, 1939, Folder 2, FLG. On other matters, including Goodenough's speech at Columbia, see Terman to Goodenough, Nov. 2, Nov. 9, 1939, Folder 2, FLG.

26. John E. Anderson, "The Limitations of Infant and Preschool Tests in the Measurement of Intelligence," *JPsy* 8 (1939): 351–79.

27. Florence L. Goodenough to Lewis M. Terman, Feb. 23, 1940, Folder 13, Box 14, LMT; Goodenough, "Look to the Evidence! A Critique of Recent Experiments on Raising the I.Q.," *Educational Method* 19 (1939–40): 73–79; Goodenough, "Can We Influence Mental Growth? A Critique of Recent Experiments," *Educational Record* 21 (1940), supp. 13, 120–43; Goodenough and Katherine M. Maurer, "The Relative Potency of the Nursery School and the Statistical Laboratory in Boosting the I.Q.," *JEP* 31 (1940): 541–49.

28. Whipple, *Thirty-Ninth Yearbook*. An interesting perspective on the controversy is in Henry L. Minton, *Lewis M. Terman: Pioneer in Psychological Testing* (New York: New York University Press, 1988), 191–201.

29. George D. Stoddard, "Intellectual Development of the Child: An Answer to the Critics of the Iowa Studies," *SS* 51 (1940): 529–36.

30. Quinn McNemar, "A Critical Examination of the University of Iowa Studies of Environmental Influence upon the IQ," *PB* 37 (1940): 63–92. Their response is Beth L. Wellman, Harold M. Skeels, and Marie Skodak, "Review of McNemar's Critical Examination of Iowa Studies," *PB* 37 (1940): 93–111. Many of the individuals whom Dr. Milton J. E. Senn interviewed remembered the controversy over the Iowa findings, and without exception they reported that it was the statistical criticisms that hit home and dissuaded them from looking more closely.

31. See, for example, Mandel Sherman, *Hollow Folk* (New York: W. W. Norton and Company, 1932); Sherman and C. B. Key, "The Intelligence of Isolated Mountain Children," *CD* 3 (1932): 279–90; D. K. Hallowell, "Stability of Mental-Test Ratings for Pre-

school Children," *PSJGP* 40 (1932): 406–21; D. B. Lithauer and Otto Klineberg, "A Study of the Variation in I.Q. of a Group of Dependent Children in Institution and Foster Home," *PSJGP* 42 (1933): 236–42; E. J. Asher, "The Inadequacy of Current Intelligence Tests for Testing Kentucky Mountain Children," *PSJGP* 46 (1935): 480–86.

32. See Hamilton Cravens, *The Triumph of Evolution: The Heredity-Environment Controversy, 1900–1941* (1978; reprint, Baltimore, Md.: Johns Hopkins University Press, 1988), xvii–xvi and 269–74.

33. See, for example, the correspondence between Clark Hull and Kenneth W. Spence, as in Folders "Spence-Hull Correspondence, 1940," and "Spence-Hull Correspondence, 1943," Box M937, Kenneth W. Spence Papers, Archives of the History of American Psychology, University of Akron, Akron, Ohio.

34. See, for example, Harold M. Skeels, "A Study of the Effects of Differential Stimulation on Mentally Retarded Children: A Follow-Up Report," *American Journal of Mental Deficiency* 46 (1942): 340–50; Beth L. Wellman and Edna Lee Pegram, "Binet IQ Changes of Orphanage Preschool Children: A Re-Analysis," *PSJGP* 65 (1944): 239–63. See also W. A. Saucier, "Lack of Scientific Attitude in Psychology," *SS* 53 (1941): 670–71; Evelyn Katz, "The Constancy of the Stanford-Binet IQ from Three to Five Years," *JPsy* 12 (1941): 159–81; Jessie Batley Rhinehart, "Some Effects of a Nursery School–Parent Education Program on a Group of Three-Year-Olds," *PSJGP* 61 (1942): 153–61; James W. Layman, "IQ Changes in Old-Age Children Placed for Foster-Home Care," *PSJGP* 60 (1942): 61–70; Mary Elizabeth Allen and Florene M. Young, "The Constancy of the Intelligence Quotient as Indicated by Retests of 130 Children," *Journal of Applied Psychology* 27 (1943): 41–60: Katherine P. Bradway, "An Experimental Study of the Factors Associated with Stanford-Binet IQ Changes from the Preschool to the Junior High School," *PSJGP* 66 (1945): 107–28.

35. Beth L. Wellman and E. L. Pegram, "Binet IQ Changes of Orphanage Preschool Children: A Reanalysis," *JGP* 64 (1944): 239–63.

36. Quinn McNemar, "Note on Wellman's Re-Analysis of IQ Changes of Orphanage Preschool Children," *JGP* 67 (1945): 215–18.

37. I am very indebted to Dr. Bernadine Barr, of Stanford University, for many lengthy discussions of these and related problems. See Bernadine Courtright Barr, "Spare Children, 1900–1945: Inmates of Orphanages as Subjects of Research in Medicine and in the Social Sciences in America," Ph.D. diss., Stanford University, 1992, a brilliant study.

CHAPTER SEVEN

1. LeRoy Ashby, "Partial Promises and Semi-Visible Youths: The Depression and World War II," in Joseph M. Hawes and N. Ray Hiner, eds., *American Childhood. A Research Guide and Historical Handbook* (Westport, Conn.: Greenwood Press, 1985), 490. Ashby's essay covers the pertinent secondary literature to date of publication very well indeed.

2. In addition to the various reports of the White House Conferences, useful insights on these conferences can be gained in Papers of the White House Conferences on Child Health and Protection, 1909–50, Hoover Institution Archives, Stanford University, Stanford, California.

3. White House Conference on Children in a Democracy, *Final Report* (Washington, D.C.: Government Printing Office, 1940), 357–78.

4. For a general discussion of these developments, see Hamilton Cravens, "Child-Saving in the Age of Professionalism, 1915–1930," in Hawes and Hiner, *American Childhood*, 415–

88; and Robert R. Sears, *Your Ancients Revisited: A History of Child Development* (Chicago: University of Chicago Press, 1975).

5. Arnold L. Gesell, with H. M. Halverson, Helen Thompson, Frances L. Ilg, B. M. Castner, Louise B. Ames, and Catherine Amatruda, *The First Five Years of Life: A Guide to the Study of the Preschool Child*, Yale University Clinic of Child Development, 9th ed. (New York: Harper, 1940), for an example of Gesell's gift for popularization. More technical works are Gesell, *An Atlas of Human Behavior: A Systematic Delineation of the Forms and Early Growth of Human Behavior Patterns*, Yale University Clinic of Child Development, 2 vols. (New Haven, Conn.: Yale University Press, 1934); and Gesell and Amatruda, *Developmental Diagnosis: Normal and Abnormal Child Development. Clinical Methods and Pediatric Application* (New York: Paul B. Hoeber, 1941).

6. Sears, *Your Ancients Revisited*, 21–22; here Sears was speaking directly from personal experience.

7. Kurt Lewin to Horace M. Kallen, Oct. 11, 1941, Folder 767, HMK; news of Stoddard's appointment is in *ICPC*, Sept. 19, 1941; *DI*, Aug. 14, 1941; *DMR*, Sept. 20, 1941.

8. Virgil M. Hancher to George D. Stoddard, Dec. 5, 1941, and attached Stoddard to Hancher, Dec. 4, 1941, and Mark A. May to Stoddard, Dec. 1, 1941 (copy); Hancher to Robert R. Sears, June 4, 1942; all in IP; Sears interview, by Hamilton Cravens, May 30, 1984, pp. 1–5, Stanford University Archives, Stanford, California, and University of Iowa Archives, Iowa City, Iowa.

9. Howard H. Kendler, "The Iowa Tradition," in Joan H. Cantor, ed., *Psychology at Iowa: Centennial Essays* (Hillsdale, N.J.: Lawrence Erlbaum Associates, 1991), 1–17; for Hull's system, see C. L. Hull, *Principles of Behavior* (New York: Appleton Century, 1943).

10. See, for example, Robert R. Sears to Kurt Lewin, Mar. 8, 22, 1937, Apr. 29, May 18, 1938; Lewin to Sears, Apr. 27, May 3, 25, 1938; all in RRS.

11. Robert R. Sears, "Studies of Projection," pt. 1, "Attribution of Traits," *JSP* 7 (1936): 151–63. See Sears to Sigmund Freud, Jan. 25, 1934, RRS.

12. On Sears's recruitment to Yale, see, for example, Roswell P. Angier to Sears, Apr. 21, May 5, 11, 1936; Clark Hull to Sears, May 7, 1936; all in RRS. Sears interviews, May 30, 1984, pp. 1–15; June 2, 1984, pp. 85–106; and June 4, 1984, pp. 107–15; all by Hamilton Cravens, Stanford University Archives, Stanford, California, and University of Iowa Archives, Iowa City, Iowa; Carl Iver Hovland and Sears, "Minor Studies of Aggression," pt. 6, "Correlation of Lynching with Economic Indices," *JPsy* 9 (1940): 301–10. See also Sears, "Experimental Studies of Projection," pt. 2, "Ideas of Reference," *JSP* 8 (1937): 389–400; Sears, "Initiation of the Repressive Sequence by Experienced Failure," *JExpP* 20 (1937): 570–80; Sears, Hovland, and Neal E. Miller, "Minor Studies of Aggression," pt. 1, "Measurement of Aggressive Behavior," *JP* 9 (1940): 275–95; Robert R. Sears and Pauline Snedden Sears, "Minor Studies of Aggression," pt. 5, "Strength of Frustration-Reaction as a Function of Strength of Drive," *JP* 9 (1940): 297–300.

13. John Dollard, Leonard Doob, Neal E. Miller, O. H. Mowrer, and Robert R. Sears, in collaboration with Clellan S. Ford, Carl Iver Hovland, and Richard T. Sollenberger, *Frustration and Aggression* (New Haven, Conn.: Yale University Press, 1939).

14. Neal E. Miller and John Dollard, *Social Learning and Imitation* (New Haven, Conn.: Yale University Press, 1941). On Kroeber, see Cravens, *The Triumph of Evolution*, 110.

15. Interviews with Robert R. Sears, June 2, 1984, pp. 85–106; June 4, 1984, pp. 107–15; Mar. 12, 1985, pp. 14–20; all by Hamilton Cravens, Stanford University Archives, Stanford, California, and University of Iowa Archives, Iowa City, Iowa.

16. Robert R. Sears to Mark A. May, Dec. 24, 1942; Sears to Irwin Child, Dec. 24, 1942;

Sears to Dr. and Mrs. Carl I. Hovland, Nov. 13, 1942; Sears to Don Marquis, Sept. 25, 1942; Sears to Lewis M. Terman, Nov. 28, 1942; Sears, "The Family's Part in National Defense," Sept. 29, 1942; Sears, "Conscience as a Psychological Problem," Oct. 13, 1942; Sears, "Unrest of Youth in War Time," Feb. 8–12, 1943; Sears, "Children in War Time" (radio transcription); Sears, "Building for the Post-War World," n.d. [1943]; Sears, "Social Psychological Factors in Post-War Europe" (typescript), n.d. [1943]; Sears to A. T. Jersild, May 31, 1943; Sears to Virgil M. Hancher, June 28, 1943; Beth Wellman, "Memorandum on Proposed Study of Children in Occupied Countries" (typescript), June 1943; Kurt Lewin, "Post-War Research in Occupied Countries," June 16, 1943; Patrick M. Malin to Sears, July 12, 1943; Myres S. McDougal to Sears, July 14, 1943; John M. Begg to Sears, July 24, 1943; Sears to Malin, July 5, 1943; Sears to Jersild, July 28, 1943; Jersild to Sears, July 26, 1943; Hajo Holborn to McDougal, July 22, 1943; all in RRS. See also "Tentative Plan for a Course in the Use of Statistical Machines," Sept. 8, 1942; and the summaries of staff meetings for Sept. 8, 14, 21, 28, Oct. 12, 17, 19, 24, 26, 31, Nov. 2, 7, 9, 14, 21, 1942; all in CW.

17. Robert R. Sears to President Virgil M. Hancher, Aug. 28, 1943, and attached confidential memorandum from Sears to Hancher, "Child Welfare Research Station, A Report and a Program," Aug. 25, 1943, IP.

18. Edwin B. Wilson to Robert R. Sears, Aug. 27, 1942; Sears to Wilson, Sept. 9, 1942; both in RRS. Sears, "Child Welfare Research Station, A Report and a Program," 21, IP. Harold M. Skeels to Sears, Nov. 7, 1945; Sears to Skeels, Nov. 14, 1945; Skeels, "Mental Development in Adoptive Homes," Nov. 21, 1945; Sears to R. H. Singleton, Dec. 19, 1945; Singleton to Sears, Mar. 3, 1946; all in ICBD:HMS.

19. Sears, "Child Welfare Research Station, A Report and a Program," 6–7.

20. Kurt Lewin, "Remarks to Mr. Hull's Supplementary Note" (typescript), n.d. [1943], Folder "Spence-Hull Correspondence, 1943," Box M937, Kenneth W. Spence Papers, Archives of the History of American Psychology, University of Akron, Akron, Ohio (hereafter cited as Spence Papers).

21. Kendler, "The Iowa Tradition," 4–7.

22. See, for example, Kenneth W. Spence to Clark Hull, July 16, 1942, Folder "Miscell. Corresp.," Spence Papers. See also correspondence between Hull and Spence, Jan.–Apr. 1943, Folder "Spence-Hull Correspondence, 1943," Box M937, Spence Papers. On Lewin and Sears, see interview with Robert R. Sears, by Hamilton Cravens, Mar. 12, 1985, pp. 14–20.

23. Kurt Lewin, "Cooperative Project in Child Psychology and Psychoanalysis," Jan. 13, 1939, CW; DI, Oct. 13, 1939; George D. Stoddard and Franz Alexander to Robert J. Havighurst, June 15, 1940, and attached Dan L. Adler, Thomas M. French, and Lewin, "Report on Cooperative Research, Child Welfare Research Station, State University of Iowa and Institute for Psychoanalysis, Chicago" (typescript), n.d.; Robert A. Lambert to Havighurst, June 25, 1940; Stoddard to Lambert, June 28, 1940; Lambert to Stoddard, July 1, 1940; "Grant in Aid: New York, RA MS 4012," July 8, 1940, and "Detail of Information, RA MS 4012"; Lambert to Stoddard, July 9, 1940; Stoddard to Lambert, July 13, 1940; all in Record Group 1.2, Series 200A, Folder 1110, Box 92, RF.

24. Kurt Lewin to George D. Stoddard, memo, Dec. 27, 1939, and attached Lewin, "The Iowa Child Welfare Research Station, the University of Iowa, Iowa City, and the Chicago Park District, Chicago, Cooperative Project, An Experimental Study of Individual and Group Life within Selected Community Cultures" (typescript), n.d. [1939], IP. Stoddard to Joseph H. Willits, Jan. 2, 10, 1940; correspondence between Lewin and Willits, Jan.–May

1940; Donald Young to Willits, May 16, 1940; Willits to Young, May 21, 1940; Willits to Stoddard, May 24, 1940; Willits to Chester I. Barnard, May 27, 1940; Barnard to Willits, May 29, 1940; Willits to Stoddard, June 6, 1940; Willits to Barnard, June 4, 1940; Willits, notes, June 26, 1940; all in Record Group 1.2, Series 200A, Folder 1110, Box 92, RF.

25. Alex Bavelas, "Evaluation of Kurt Lewin, May 31, 1967," p. 5, Folder 1, Box M944, KL. Kurt Lewin, memorandum to Dr. [George D.] Stoddard, June 18, 1941; Lewin to Stoddard, Nov. 4, 1941; both in VF:KL. Lewin, memorandum to Stoddard, July 24, 1941; Fred O. Erbe to Lewin, July 23, 31, 1941; Julia B. Mayer to Lewin, July 1, 1941; Lewin, memorandum to Stoddard, July 31, 1941, and enclosed Thomas Rickman, Jr., to Lewin, July 26, 1941; Lewin to Rickman, July 31, 1941; Lewin, memorandum to Stoddard, Aug. 2, 1941; all in ICBD:KL. Bavelas and Lewin, "Training in Democratic Leadership," *JASP* 37 (1942): 115–19; Bavelas, "Civilian Morale: Leaders Can Be Made," *Frontiers of Democracy* 9 (Nov. 15, 1942): 47–48, 61; *DI*, Feb. 18, 1942. Lewin to Horace M. Kallen, Nov. 4, 1940; Kallen to Lewin, Nov. 8, 1940, Nov. 7, 28, 1941; Lewin to Kallen, Dec. 5, 1941; all in Folder 767, HMK.

26. Carl E. Guthe, "History of the Committee on Food Habits," in Margaret Mead, ed., *The Problem of Changing Food Habits: Report of the Committee on Food Habits, 1941–1943*, National Research Council Bulletin no. 108 (Washington, D.C.: National Academy of Sciences, 1943), 9–19. See also Committee on Food Habits, "Provisional Program of Action, February 28, 1941" (memo), quote at p. 1; Mead, "Informal Report to the Executive Committee Members Committee on Food Habits," Aug. 3, 1942; Committee on Food Habits, "Not for Publication"; all in Folder "Activities File, 1942–1945," Papers of the Committee on Food Habits, Archives of the National Research Council, Washington, D.C. (hereafter cited as Papers of the Committee on Food Habits).

27. William S. Graebner, *The Engineering of Consent: Democracy and Authority in Modern America* (Madison: University of Wisconsin Press, 1987), brilliantly discusses these issues.

28. Kurt Lewin, "The Relative Effectiveness of a Lecture Method and a Method of Group Decision for Changing Food Habits" (mimeograph), June 1942; Lewin, "A Group Test for Determining the Anchorage Points of Food Habits, A Preliminary Report for the Committee on Food Habits"; both in Folder "Report File, 1942–1945," Papers of the Committee on Food Habits. Lewin, "Forces beyond Food Habits and Methods of Change," in Mead, *The Problem of Changing Food Habits*, 35–65; "List of Projects, Studies, Researches Conducted by the Committee on Food Habits (Prepared for the Executive Meeting, Nov. 18–19, 1944) Exhibit B. Attitude Studies Conducted by The Committee on Food Habits," Folder "Activities File, 1942–1945," Papers of the Committee on Food Habits.

29. Goodwin Watson, ed., *Civilian Morale: Second Yearbook of the Society for the Psychological Studies of Social Issues* (Boston: Houghton-Mifflin Company, 1942), 7.

30. Kurt Lewin to Horace M. Kallen, June 6, 1941, Folder 767, HMK; Lewin, "Personal Adjustment and Group Belongingness," *Jewish Social Service Quarterly* 17 (1941): 362–66; Lewin, "Self-Hatred among Jews," *Contemporary Jewish Record* 4 (1941): 219–32; Lewin, "Changes in Social Sensitivity in Child and Adult," *CE* 19 (1942): 53–57; Lewin, "Psychology and the Process of Group Living," *JSP, SPSSI Bulletin* 17 (1943): 113–31, quote at 113; Lewin, "Cultural Reconstruction," *JASP* 38 (1943): 166–73; Lewin, "The Special Case of Germany," *Public Opinion Quarterly* 7 (1943): 555–66; Lewin, "The Dynamics of Group Action," *Educational Leadership* 1 (1943–44): 195–200. For a sophisticated and provocative discussion of Lewin's work in larger context, see William S. Graebner, *The Engineering of Consent: Democracy and Authority in Twentieth Century America* (Madison: University of Wisconsin Press, 1987), 75–78, 105, 109, 127, 136–37, 144.

31. On the Boy Scout project, see, for example, *State University of Iowa News Bulletin*, Jan. 1943; Kurt Lewin, memo to Dr. [Beth L.] Wellman, n.d. [Summer 1942], and attached Lewin to Charles E. Hendry, July 21, 1942; Hendry to Lewin, July 27, 1942; Wellman to Robert R. Sears, Aug. 5, 1942; all in ICBD:KL. "Grant from the Boy Scouts of America Scoutmaster Training Project, 12 Months Basis," n.d. [1943], IP. Officials of the Boys Scouts of America informed me that there were no surviving files on this project. On Lewin's consulting, see Alfred J. Marrow, *The Practical Theorist: The Life and Work of Kurt Lewin* (New York: Basic Books, 1969), 141–52. For Lewin's perspectives on the CCI, see, for example, Lewin, "Proposal for the Study of the D.P. Problem by the Jewish Research Institute for the Study of Human Relations" (typescript), n.d., Folder 22, Box M946, KL. Graebner discusses the CCI and Lewin's role in *The Engineering of Consent*, 144.

32. Robert R. Sears, *Survey of Objective Studies of Psychoanalytic Concepts*, Committee on Social Adjustment, bulletin 51 (New York: Social Science Research Council, 1943).

33. Robert R. Sears to John Dollard, Nov. 1, 1943, RRS; Dorwin Cartwright, "Relation of Decision-Time to the Categories of Response," *AJP* 54 (1941): 174–96; Cartwright, "Decision-Time in Relation to the Differentiation of the Phenomenal Field," *PR* 48 (1941): 425–42; Leon Festinger, "Wish, Expectation, and Group Standards as Factors Influencing Level of Aspiration," *JASP* 37 (1942): 184–200; Festinger, "A Theoretical Interpretation of Shifts in Level of Aspiration," *PR* 49 (1942): 235–50; Festinger, "An Exact Test of Significance for Means of Samples Drawn from Populations with an Exponential Frequency Distribution," *Psychometrika* 8 (1943): 205–10; Cartwright and Festinger, "A Quantitative Theory of Decision," *PR* 50 (1943): 595–621; Festinger, "Development of Differential Appetite in the Rat," *JExpP* 32 (1943): 226–34; Festinger, "Studies in Decision," pts. 1 and 2, *JExpP* 32 (1943): 291–306, 411–23.

34. Kurt Lewin, Charles E. Meyers, Joan Kalhorn, Maurice L. Farber, and John R. P. French, *Authority and Frustration*, Studies in Topological and Vector Psychology III, *UISSCW*, vol. 20 (Iowa City: University of Iowa Press, 1944).

35. See correspondence between Kurt Lewin and Robert R. Sears, Oct.–Nov. 1944, ICBD:KL; *ICPC*, Dec. 15, 1944. Gardner Murphy to Horace M. Kallen, Nov. 8, 1943; Kallen to Murphy, Nov. 11, 1944; both in Folder 767, HMK. Sears to George D. Stoddard, Nov. 16, 1944; Stoddard to Sears, Nov. 22, 1944; both in ICBD:GDS. Marrow, *The Practical Theorist*, 156–65; Lewin, "The Research Center for Group Dynamics at Massachusetts Institute of Technology," *Sociometry* 2 (1945): 126–36. On the Research Center at MIT, see the enormous file "Dean of Humanities, 1944, 1945, 1946, 1947," Kurt Lewin Papers, Archives, Massachusetts Institute of Technology, Cambridge, Massachusetts; and Marrow, *The Practical Theorist*, 166–219.

36. Sears's characterizations of the old research in child development permeates the interviews I conducted with him.

37. Cravens, interview with Robert R. Sears, Mar. 12, 1985, pp. 14–20, quote at p. 16; Sears, "Research in Child Welfare," *The Baconian Lectures on Aims and Progress of Research in the State University of Iowa, 1945: General Theme. Global Trends in Research*, Series on Aims and Progress of Research, no. 80, Study Series 415 (Iowa City: University of Iowa, 1945); Sears, "Experimental Analysis of Psychoanalytic Phenomena," in J. McVicker Hunt, ed., *Personality and the Behavior Disorders*, 2 vols. (New York: Ronald Press, 1944), 306–32; Sears, "Personality and Motivation," *RER* 14 (Dec. 1944): 368–80. See also Joan W. Swift, "Reliability of Rorschach Scoring Categories with Preschool Children," *CD* 15 (1944): 207–16; Swift, "Relation of Behavioral and Rorschach Measures of Insecurity in Preschool Children," *Journal of Clinical Psychology* 1 (1945): 196–205; Melanie Klein, *The Psycho-*

analysis of Children (New York: W. W. Norton and Company, 1932); Cravens, interview with Sears, p. 31,

38. George R. Bach, "Young Children's Play Fantasies," *Psychological Monographs* 59, no. 2, whole no. 272 (1945); Ruth Phillips, "Doll Play as a Function of the Realism of the Materials and the Length of the Experimental Session," *CD* 16 (1945): 123–43; Elizabeth F. Robinson, "Doll Play as a Function of the Doll Family Constellation," *CD* 17 (1946): 99–119; M. H. Pintler, "Doll Play as a Function of Experimenter-Child Interaction and Initial Organization of Materials," *CD* 16 (1945): 145–66.

39. Barbara Merrill, "A Measurement of Mother-Child Interaction," *JASP* 41 (1946): 37–49; Cravens, interview with Robert R. Sears, Mar. 12, 1985, pp. 40–41, 33–34; Margaret H. Pintler, Ruth Phillips, and Robert R. Sears, "Sex Differences in the Projective Doll Play of Preschool Children," *JPsy* 21 (1946): 73–80; Robert R. Sears, Margaret H. Pintler, and Pauline S. Sears, "Effect of Father Separation on Preschool Children's Doll Play Aggression," *CD* 17 (1946): 219–43; George R. Bach, "Father Fantasies and Father-Typing in Father-Separated Children," *CD* 17 (1946): 63–80.

40. Robert R. Sears to Alan Gregg, Feb. 7, 1944; Gregg to Sears, Feb. 14, 1944; Gregg, memorandum of interview, Feb. 23, 1944; all in Record Group 1.1 [Projects], Series 200A (U.S.—Medical Sciences), Folder 1111, Box 92, RF. Sears to Carl I. Hovland, Apr. 10, 1946; Joseph H. Willits to Sears, June 28, 1946; Gregg, interoffice correspondence, Dec. 20, 1946; Sears to Hovland, Jan. 10, 1947, and attached "Proposal for Research Investigation of Social and Cultural Factors Influencing Child Development"; Sears to Hovland, Mar. 3, 1947, and enclosed Virgil M. Hancher to Willits, Mar. 3, 1947; all in Record Group 1.2, Series 200S (U.S.—Social Sciences), Folder 4483, Box 524, RF. For Sears's recruitment of Vincent Nowlis and John Whiting, see Nowlis to Sears, Nov. 10, 19, Dec. 7, 21, 1945, Jan. 2, 1946; Sears to Nowlis, Nov. 17, 28, Dec. 18, 1945; Whiting to Sears, Apr. 21, 1947; Sears to Whiting, Apr. 23, May 14, 1947; all in RRS. On the grant, see, for example, Record of Motion, RF47032, Apr. 2, 1947; Norma S. Thompson to Hancher, Apr. 2, 1947, Record Group 1.2, Series 200S (U.S.—Social Sciences), Folder 4483, Box 524, RF.

41. On the project as it developed, see, for example, "SOHP Interview: Robert R. Sears with Hamilton Cravens, Mar. 13, 1985," pp. 1–9, Stanford University Archives, Stanford, California, and University of Iowa Archives, Iowa City, Iowa; Sears to Leland C. DeVinney, July 14, 1948, and attached "Iowa Child Welfare Research Station, State University of Iowa, Annual Report, July 1, 1947–June 30, 1948" (typescript), Record Group 1.2, Series 200S (U.S.—Social Sciences), Folder 4483, Box 524, RF. See also Sears to Lewis M. Terman, June 3, Dec. 8, 1947, RRS. Documents pertaining to the project once Sears had moved to Harvard in 1950 are in Record Group 1.2, Series 200S (U.S.—Social Sciences), Folders 4359–61, Box 510, RF.

42. Sears outlined his general position in 1947 in "Personality Development in Contemporary Culture," *Proceedings of the American Philosophical Society* 92 (1947): 363–70. The monograph is Robert R. Sears, J. W. M. Whiting, V. Nowlis, and P. S. Sears, in collaboration with E. K. Beller, J. Carl Cohen, E. Hollenberg Chasdi, H. Faigin, J. L. Gewirtz, M. Sperry Lawrence, and J. P. McKee, "Some Child-Rearing Antecedents of Aggression and Dependency in Young Children," *Genetic Psychology Monographs* 47 (1953): 135–236.

43. Robert R. Sears to Lawrence K. Frank, Oct. 4, 1947; Frank to Sears, Oct. 13, 1947; Sears to Frank, Oct. 17, 1947; Frank to Sears, Oct. 28, 1947; all in RRS. H. Davis, R. Sears, H. Miller, and A. Brodbeck, "Effects of Cup, Bottle, and Breast Feeding on Oral Activities of Newborn Infants," *Pediatrics* 2 (1948): 549–58.

44. Robert R. Sears to Roger G. Barker, June 3, 1947, RRS; *DMR*, Mar. 11, 1947;

Sears, "Clinical Psychology in the Military Services," *PB* 41 (1944): 502–9; Sears, "Graduate Training Facilities," *American Psychologist* 1 (1946): 135–50; Sears, "Clinical Training Facilities, 1947," *American Psychologist* 2 (1947): 199–205. Sears, "The Family's Part in National Defense," Sept. 29, 1942; Sears, "Unrest of Youth in Wartime," Feb. 8–12, 1943; Sears, "Children in Wartime," June 19, 1943; Sears, "Building for the Post-War World"; all in RRS. Sears, "Training for Dissemination in Child Welfare," *JConP* 8 (1944): 238–40.

45. On the reorganization of the SRCD see, for example, Carroll E. Palmer, "To Members of the Society for Research in Child Development," Sept. 11, 1946; Palmer, "Memorandum about the Boston Meeting, 27–28 December, 1946," and attachments; Palmer, "Report of the Business Meeting, Hotel Bradford, Boston, Massachusetts, Dec. 27, 1946"; Robert R. Sears to Robert J. Havighurst, May 12, 1947; Havighurst to Sears, May 12, 1947; Sears to Lester Sontag, May 22, 1947; Beulah Brewer to Sears, May 27, 1947; Havighurst to Sears, June 16, 1947; Sears to Palmer, Jan. 2, 1948; all in RRS. On the reorganization of the CCD, see, for example, Committee on Child Development, National Research Council, Minutes, 6 March 1948; George K. Bennett to Sears, May 27, June 16, 1948; Sears to Bennett, June 18, 1948; A. Irving Hallowell to Sears, July 20, 1948; Hallowell to Alfred Washburn, July 20, 1948; Sears to Hallowell, Oct. 18, Nov. 20, 1948; Katherine Bain to Sears, Nov. 30, 1948; Sears to John L. Gillin, Dec. 1, 1948; "Meeting of the Committee on Research in Child Development of the National Research Council, acting in an advisory capacity to the Children's Bureau, Federal Security Building . . . December 6–7, 1948"; Sears, "Committee on Child Development, National Research Council, Annual Report," n.d. [1948]; all in RRS.

46. Robert R. Sears to J. McVicker Hunt, Dec. 4, 1948, Joseph McVicker Hunt Papers, University Archives, University of Illinois at Champaign-Urbana (hereafter cited as Hunt Papers).

47. Robert R. Sears to Lewis M. Terman, Aug. 25, 1948; Sears to Martha Eliot, Nov. 29, 1948; both in RRS. J. McVicker Hunt to Sears, Nov. 22, 1948; Sears to Hunt, Nov. 29, 1948; Hunt to Sears, Dec. 1, 1948; Sears to Hunt, Dec. 4, 1948; Hunt to Sears, Dec. 8, 1948, Jan. 25, 1949; Sears to Hunt, Jan. 27, 1949; all in Hunt Papers.

48. Martha M. Eliot to Robert R. Sears, Jan. 13, 1949; Katherine Lenroot to Sears, Jan. 17, 1949; J. McVicker Hunt to Sears, Jan. 25, 1949; J. Donald Kingsley to Lewis M. Terman, Jan. 27, 1949; "National Child Research Act," 81st Cong., 1st sess., S. 904, Feb. 10, 1949; Sears, "Testimony on S. 904, May 11 [1949] before the Subcommittee of Senate Labor and Public Welfare Committee"; all in RRS.

49. Robert R. Sears, "Addendum" to oral history interviews with Hamilton Cravens, Aug. 5, 1988, pp. 1–4, Stanford University Archives, Stanford, California, and University of Iowa Archives, Iowa City, Iowa.

50. Clark Hull to Kenneth Spence, Mar. 5, 1949, Folder "Miscellaneous Correspondence," Box M937, Spence Papers; Stow Persons, *The University of Iowa in the Twentieth Century: An Institutional History* (Iowa City: University of Iowa Press, 1990), 136–74.

51. Kenneth W. Spence, "Memorandum Concerning the Relation of the Child Welfare Station to the Department of Psychology," Feb. 8, 1949; Orvis C. Irwin to Dean Harvey H. Davis, Apr. 28, 1949; Robert C. Kammerer to Davis, Apr. 29, 1949; May Pardee Youtz to Davis, n.d. [April 1949]; Howard V. Meredith, "To the Committee on Future Station Policy and Program," May 2, 1949; Anne Graham Nugent to Davis, May 2, 1949; Vincent Nowlis to Davis, May 2, 1949; Ruth Updegraff, "Statement Regarding Major Activities of Ruth Updegraff as Staff Member, 1948–49, Iowa Child Welfare Research Station," May 2,

1949; Ralph H. Ojemann to Davis, May 2, 1949; Beth Wellman to Davis, May 5, 1949; Davis to President Virgil Hancher, July 8, 1949; all in CW.

52. The above comments on the distribution of research interests and publications at the station derived from my examination and statistical analyses of the information in Charles L. Spiker, comp., *The Institute of Child Behavior and Development: Fifty Years of Research, 1917–1967* (Iowa City: University of Iowa Press, 1967).

53. See the large file "Advisory Committee Institute of Child Behavior and Development—1974," IP, in which there is much revealing information on why the institute was closed. Perhaps the most common criticism made of the institute was the narrowness of its research, according to its critics. Whether true or not, this perception stuck. Many in the profession with whom I have talked about the institute shared this perception of the institute's on-campus critics. That perception is clearly very different from the common view of the Iowa station in the 1930s and 1940s, that the researchers there had very broad and exciting (if controversial) theories and arguments.

EPILOGUE

1. Edward B. Fiske, "Head Start: Ten Years Old and Planning Experiments," *New York Times*, June 8, 1975, sec. 1, p. 40.

2. There is a large literature on Head Start. A useful introduction is Edward Zigler and Jeanette Valentine, eds., *Project Head Start: A Legacy of the War on Poverty* (New York: Free Press, 1979).

3. See, in particular, such brilliant and moving works as Robert Coles, *Children of Crisis*, 5 vols. (Boston: Houghton-Mifflin, 1964–78). In the absence of a general history of children and childhood in America, see the useful compilation Joseph M. Hawes and N. Ray Hiner, eds., *American Childhood: A Research Guide and Historical Handbook* (Westport, Conn.: Greenwood Press, 1985), which has numerous useful essays and many bibliographical citations.

4. James Gilbert, *A Cycle of Outrage: America's Reaction to the Juvenile Delinquent in the 1950s* (New York: Oxford University Press, 1986). On the shift from the interwar to the modern eras and related matters, see, for example, Hamilton Cravens, "History of the Social Sciences," in S. G. Kohlstedt and M. W. Rossiter, eds., *Historical Writing on American Science. Problems and Prospects* (Baltimore, Md.: Johns Hopkins University Press, 1986), 183–207; Peter Clecak, *America's Quest for the Ideal Self: Dissent and Fulfillment in the 60s and 70s* (New York: Oxford University Press, 1983); William S. Graebner, *The Age of Doubt: American Thought and Culture in the 1940s* (Boston: Twayne, 1991); Douglas Tallack, *Twentieth-Century America: The Intellectual and Cultural Context* (New York; Longman, 1991).

5. J. McVicker Hunt, *Intelligence and Experience* (New York: Ronald Press, 1961).

6. Benjamin Bloom, *Stability and Change in Human Characteristics* (New York: Wiley and Sons, 1964).

7. Ellen Condliffe Lagemann, *The Politics of Knowledge: The Carnegie Corporation, Philanthropy, and Public Policy* (Middletown, Conn.: Wesleyan University Press, 1989), 180–215.

8. Harold M. Skeels, *Adult Experiences of Children with Contrasting Early Life Experiences: A Follow-Up Study*, Monographs of the Society for Research in Child Development, vol. 31, no. 3 (Chicago: University of Chicago Press, 1966), quote at p. 55.

9. See Zigler and Valentine, *Project Head Start*, pp. 3–155.

10. Arthur R. Jensen, "How Much Can We Boost I.Q. and Scholastic Achievement?" *Harvard Educational Review* 39 (1969): 1–123; Russell Kirk, "False Start for Head Start in Michigan," *National Review* 18 (Sept. 6, 1966): 886.

11. Fiske, "Head Start"; The Westinghouse Learning Corporation study is Victor G. Circirelli, *The Impact of Head Start: An Evaluation of the Effects of Head Start on Children's Cognitive and Affective Development*, 2 vols. (Washington, D.C.: National Bureau of Standards, Institute for Applied Technology, 1969), and the following discussion of that report and the Nixon administration's reaction to it: *New York Times*, Apr. 20, 1969, sec. 4, p. 11; Apr. 27, 1969, sec. 1, p. 44. For Head Start's status as of the early 1990s, see, for example, James L. Hymes, Jr., *Early Childhood Education: Twenty Years in Review. A Look at 1971–1990* (Washington, D.C.: National Association for the Education of Young Children, 1991); U.S. Department of Health and Human Services, Administration for Children, Youth, and Families, Head Start Bureau, *Head Start, A Child Development Program: 25 Years. Building America's Future* (Washington, D.C.: Government Printing Office, 1990); see also *New York Times*, Feb. 14, 1990, Mar. 30, 1990, May 6, 13, 1990, Oct. 2, 1990, Nov. 4, 1990; *Washington Post*, Jan. 27, 1990, sec. A, p. 4, col. 1; Jan. 30, 1990, sec. A, p. 6, col. 5; *Los Angeles Times*, Jan. 27, 1990, sec. A, p. 1, col. 5; Feb. 4, 1990, sec. M, p. 7, col. 1; Mar. 15, 1990, sec. A, p. 3, col. 1.

12. Irving Lazar and Richard Darlington et al., *Lasting Effects of Early Education: A Report from the Consortium for Longitudinal Studies*, Monographs of the Society for Research in Child Development, vol. 47, nos. 2–3 (Chicago: University of Chicago Press, 1982), ix–x, 1–77.

13. See William Graebner, *The Engineering of Consent: Democracy and Authority in Twentieth Century America* (Madison: University of Wisconsin Press, 1987).

INDEX

Action, psychology of: research on, 224–25, 235–37

Addams, Jane, 3, 30

Adler, Daniel L., 166, 190–91

Adolescence: research program in, 153. *See also* General Education Board

Adult Status of Children with Contrasting Early Life Experiences: A Follow-Up Study (Skeels), 256–57

"Adventures in Science" (radio program), 187

Aid to Dependent Children (ADC), 185

Albany (N.Y.) Board of Public Education, 68

Allen, Garland E., 89

Allport, Gordon, 236

American Association for the Advancement of Science, 204

American Association for the Study of the Feeble-Minded, 34

American Association of School Administrators, 165

American Jewish Congress. *See* Congress on Community Interrelations

American Parents Committee, 246

American Psychological Association, 165, 245

Amherst H. Wilder Child Guidance Clinic (St. Paul, Minn.), 198

Anatomy and the Problem of Behavior (Coghill), 92–93

Anderson, Harold H., 129, 138–39, 140

Anderson, John E., 64, 98–99, 129, 154, 170, 191, 205, 207, 210; *Experimental Child Study*, 98–99, 101, 128, 170–71

Angell, James Rowland, 62

Anthropological theory, 227

Ashby, LeRoy, 217

Association tests, 130

Atmospheres projects, at Iowa station, 213, 233

Atwater, W. O., 25

Authority and Frustration (Lewin et al.), 238–39

Bach, George, 241

Baldwin, Bird T., 27–29, 35–37, 40–43, 51–54, 59, 68–69, 72–88; *The Psychology of the Preschool Child*, 102–3; 104, 106, 108–10, 118, 124–25, 139, 155–56, 230, 240; as critic of 1928 *Yearbook* of National Society for the Study of Education, 103, 230, 240

Baldwin, Patricia, 201

Bank Street College of Education (New York, N.Y.), 46

Barker, Roger, 162, 163, 166

Barrett, Helen, 97, 98, 131

Bavelas, Alex, 166, 233–35, 236

Bayley, Nancy, 66, 99–100, 103, 198, 205, 209

Beard, Charles, 152

Beard, Mary, 152

Beatles, the, 253

Bergmann, Gustave, 165

Berkeley Growth Study, 66, 99–100, 198, 209

Berkeley Guidance Study, 66–67, 197–98, 209

Berne, Esther Van Cleve: pioneering personality study, 125

Bestor, Arthur E., Jr., 254

Better Homes and Gardens, 220

Binet-Simon intelligence test, 5, 22, 95–105, 106, 130–31, 170; design of, 199–200

Binet, Alfred, 23, 106, 130, 188

Birney, Mrs. Theodore, 6

Bliss, A. Ione, 85

Bloom, Benjamin, 254, 256, 257; *Stability and Change in Human Characteristics*, 254

Boas, Franz, 21, 22

Bowditch, Henry Pickering, 21, 22

Boynton, Bernice, 115

Boy Scouts of America, 236

Bronfenbrenner, Urie, xii–xiii

Bronner, Augusta Fox, 32

Bruner, Jerome, 255

Bryn Mawr College: topological psychology conference at, 165

Buffalo State Teachers College, 68

Bureau of Educational Experiments, 46

Burks, Barbara Stoddard, 201, 203

California Congress of Parent-Teacher Associations, 64

California Department of Public Instruction, 65

Canadian National Committee for Mental Hygiene, 104

Carmichael, Leonard, 101, 111, 202, 207, 220, 245; and maturation theory, 91, 92, 93, 94; debates Irwin over learning versus maturation, 121–22

Carnegie, Andrew, 39

Carnegie Corporation, 255, 257

Carnegie Institution of Washington, 33

Caroline Zachry Foundation, 152

Caroline Zachry Institute, 244

Cartwright, Dorwin, 166, 238

Caste and Class in a Southern Town, (Dollard), 225

Center for Cognitive Studies (Harvard University), 255

Century of the Child, The (Key), 1–2

Chapin, F. Stuart, 170

Chapin Scale for Rating Living Room Equipment, 170, 171

Chicago Park District, 233

Child anthropology, 228

Child development, x–xii, 45–105, 109–35, 151–53, 156–84, 188–250

Child guidance movement, 219. *See also* Mental hygiene

Child labor legislation, federal, 185

Children: scientific work on before 1920, 17–38

Children at risk: as ideology, 250

Children's Year (1919), 36

Child scientists, 5

Child study, 1–5, 17–29

Child welfare, 1–5, 6–7, 9, 29–35, 42. *See also* Hillis, Cora Bussey; Rogers, Josephine Rand

Child welfare advocates, 3, 4, 29–32

Civil Works Administration (CWA), 139

Civilian Conservation Corps (CCC), 185

Coffey, Hubert S., 172, 173, 174, 175

Coffman, Lotus D., 63–64

Coghill, George E., 91–94, 111, 220; *Anatomy and the Problem of Behavior*, 92–93

Columbia Broadcasting System, 187

Commission on Community Interrelations (CCI): of American Jewish Congress, 237

Committee on Child Development, Division of Anthropology and Psychology, National Research Council, 68–69, 153, 245, 246; conferences, 69, 100

Committee on Child Welfare, Division of Anthropology and Psychology, National Research Council, 41

Committee on Food Habits, Division of Biology and Agriculture, National Research Council, 234–35

Commonwealth Fund, 40–42, 83, 89

Conant, James B., 254

Conditioned reflex, 122

Conference of the Iowa Council on Child Study and Parent Education, 137, 151, 156

Conservatives: in Iowa Republican party, 15–16

Cook County Juvenile Court, 30, 32

Cornell University, 68

Council Bluffs, Iowa: parent education experiment in, 57–58

Country life movement: ideology of, 43

Courthouse faction: in Iowa Republican party, 14

Covariance method, in statistics, 214–16

Cox, James, 95

Criminal Imbecile, The (Goddard), 35

Culture-personality dichotomy, 227

Cummins, Albert Baird, 6, 7, 10

Cummins progressives: in Iowa Republican party, 10, 14

Curti, Merle, 39

Daniels, Amy L., 35, 36, 60, 74–75, 77, 84, 85, 109; and maturation theory, 111–13; retires, 155

Darlington, Richard, 259

Darwin, Charles, 12

Davenport, Charles B., 34, 37

Davenport orphanage project, 176–84; difficulties with, 182–83; 191–93, 215–16

Davis, Mary Dabney, 136

Dearborn, Walter F., 116

Declaration of Independence (U.S.), 221

Dembo, Tamara, 163, 166

Democratic social engineering, 236, 260–61

Department of eugenics: at Iowa station, 36–38

Department of Family Life, Child Development, and Parent Education, Cornell University, 67

Der Begriff Des Genese in Physik, Biologie,

und Entwicklungsgeschichte (Lewin), 158–59

Des Moines, Iowa: parent education experiment in, 57–59

Des Moines Jewish Community Center, 233

Des Moines public schools: and parent education, 60

Des Moines Register, 155

Des Moines Register and Leader, 14

Des Moines Women's Club, 7

Dewey, John, 46, 47, 110, 111, 135, 136, 152

Division of Anthropology and Psychology, National Research Council, 41

Dodge, Raymond, 62–63

Dollard, John, 225, 237, 238; *Caste and Class in a Southern Town*, 225

Doll play: as research method, 240–42

Du Bois, W. E. B., 2–3

Dummer, Ethel S., 32

Dye, Harold S., 194, 204, 256

Early childhood intervention, 259–60

Economic Opportunity Act of 1964, 251

Education, of parents. *See* Parent education

Elementary and Secondary Education Act of 1965, 257

Eliot, Martha May, 246, 247

Emergency Committee in Aid of Displaced German Scholars, 162

Emergency nursery schools, 138, 139, 141

Erikson, Erik (Erik Homberger), 165, 245

Eugenics, 2, 89; popular meaning of, 2, 78; popular notions of among women activists, 37; at Iowa station, 77, 86

Eugenics Record Office (Cold Spring Harbor, Long Island, N.Y.), 34

Euthenics: popular meaning of, 78

Experimental Child Study (Goodenough and Anderson) 98, 99, 101; Updegraff criticizes, 128; deterministic arguments of, 170–71

Fair Labor Standards Act (1938), 185

Fales, Evaline, 128

Farber, Maurice, 166, 238–39

Faris, Ellsworth, 36, 76
Farm Children: An Investigation of Rural Child Life in Selected Areas of Iowa (Fillmore and Hadley), 104–5
Farrand, Max, 41
Federal child research institute: political campaign for, 246–48
Federal Emergency Relief Administration (FERA), 137, 138, 141
Feebleminded Club, 33, 34
Festinger, Leon, 166, 238
Fillmore, Eva Abigail, 104; *Farm Children: An Investigation of Rural Child Life in Selected Areas of Iowa*, 104–5
Flexner, Simon, 41
Foundations, 39–71; Russell Sage Foundation, 30; Commonwealth Fund, 40, 41, 42, 83, 89; Rockefeller Foundation, 40, 41, 70, 162, 163, 219, 221, 233, 241, 242; Laura Spelman Rockefeller Memorial, 41–45, 47, 48, 49, 52, 59, 60, 67, 69, 70, 104, 107, 108, 119, 151, 153, 155, 180, 197, 229, 247, 250; General Education Board, 138, 153, 162, 163, 221; Caroline Zachry Foundation, 152. *See also* Frank, Lawrence K.; Ruml, Beardsley; Woman's Christian Temperance Union
Frank, Lawrence K., 45–50, 51–54, 59; and child development, 60–71; 74, 104, 107–8, 138, 154, 156–57, 163, 197, 221, 244–45, 250; role in professionalization of child development, 70–71; political views of, 151–54; *See also* Child development; Foundations; Parent education
French, John R. P., 166, 239
Freud, Sigmund, 222, 223, 225, 237, 245
Frustration and Aggression (Sears et al.), 224–25
Frustration and regression study (by Kurt Lewin), 166–69, 188, 213
Fundamentals of Child Study, The (Kirkpatrick), 19

Gardner, John W., 162, 256, 257
General Education Board (GEB), 138, 152, 153, 157, 162, 163, 221

Genetic psychology, 26
Genetic Studies of Genius (Terman et al.), 83, 96, 132, 219
George, William R., 31
Gesell, Arnold L., 5, 62–63; *The Normal Child and Primary Education*, 27, 28; and maturation theory, 93–94; *The Mental Growth of the Preschool Child* and *Infancy and Growth*, 94, 111, 203, 204, 208, 213, 219, 220–21
Gesell, Beatrice Chandler, 27, 28
Gestalt psychology, 158–60
Gilbert, James B., 253
Goddard, Henry H., 5, 21–23, 24, 29, 33, 34, 90, 95, 96; *The Criminal Imbecile*, 35; *The Kallikak Family*, 35
Goodenough, Florence L., 64, 98–99, 103, 129, 170, 175, 191, 202–8, 210, 213, 214, 229; *Experimental Child Study*, 98, 99, 101, 128, 170, 171
Gordon, Anna E., 81
Graebner, William S., 236
Gregg, Alan, 242
Grigsby, Olive J., 124
Group atmospheres projects, 188–91
Group dynamics research, 127, 227–28, 236–37

Hadley, Lora, 104; *Farm Children: An Investigation of Rural Child Life in Selected Areas of Iowa*, 104–5
Hall, G. Stanley, 7, 8, 19–20, 22, 26, 27, 29, 33
Hancher, Virgil M., 222, 248, 249
Handbook of Child Psychology (Murchison): 1st edition, 101; 2d edition, 101–2, 121, 160–61
Harding, William L., 15
Harrington, Michael, 252
Hart, Hastings Hornell, 30, 31
Hart, Hornell, 43, 86
Harter, Genevieve L., 123–24
Harvard Growth Study, 116, 219
Harwood Corporation, 236
Hattwick, LaBerta A., 128
Head Start, xii–xii, 251–52, 259, 261; history of, 257–59
Healy, William, 32

Hearst, Phoebe, 6
Hecht, George, 246, 247
Hendry, Charles, 236
Heredity-environment controversy, 89; *See also* Nature-nurture controversy
Herring, Amanda, 203
Hicks, James Allen, 122–23
Hillis, Cora Bussey, 7–17, 19, 30, 32, 35–38, 40–42, 64, 76–77, 84, 107, 135, 139, 246, 250; death of, 59
Hillis, Issac Lea, 7
Hitler, Adolf, 162, 213
Hitler *Jugend*, 138
Hollingworth, Leta S., 202, 207, 208
Home economics, 25
Honzik, Marjorie, 209
Hoover, Herbert, 186, 218
Hope Farm, 61
Hopkins, Harry L., 137
Horack, Frank, 85
Houtchens, H. Max, 130
Hovland, Carl E., 242
Hull, Clark L., 214, 222–23, 224, 231–32, 248, 249, 250
Hull House, 3, 30
Human Biology, 117
Hunt, J. McVicker, xv–xvi, 246, 247; *Intelligence and Experience*, 253–54, 255–57

Idiots: as diagnostic category, 34
Illinois Board of Public Charities, 30
Illinois Children's Home and Aid Society, 30
Imbeciles: as diagnostic category, 34
Influence of Stuttering on the Personality, The (Johnson), 126
Innate IQ, 91, 95–105, 209, 231, 238, 253
Instincts: psychology of, 26
Institute for Psychoanalysis (Chicago), 232–33
Institute of Child Behavior and Development (University of Iowa), 250
Institute of Child Welfare (Teachers College, Columbia University), 49, 51, 61–62, 95; closed, 154
Institute of Child Welfare (University of

California, Berkeley), 64–67, 70, 99, 128, 133, 153, 154, 155 198, 219, 247, 255
Institute of Child Welfare (University of Minnesota), 63–64, 70, 95, 98, 128, 219, 247; parent education at, 64, 154
Institute of Human Relations (Yale University), 70, 95, 222–24, 247
Institute of Psychology (Yale University), 62–63
Intelligence: single and multiple factorial theories of, 99; *See also* Binet-Simon test; IQ; IQ constancy; IQ inconstancy; Stanford-Binet Measuring Scale of Intelligence
Intelligence and Experience (Hunt), 253–54
International Congress of Child Welfare (1908), 9
International Congress of Psychology (1929), 160
Introduction to Social Psychology, An (McDougall) 26
Iowa Chapter, American Association of University Women, 55
Iowa Child Study Society, 7, 10
Iowa Child Welfare Commission, 50–51
Iowa Child Welfare Research Station, x–xiii, 11–16, 25, 27, 36–38, 51, 53–57, 70–71, 74, 84, 102, 105, 108–9, 111, 113, 219, 225–28, 237, 243, 244, 247, 248, 249, 250; political campaign for, 9–17; legislative founding of, 17; LSRM grants to, 43–45, 51, 53–60; publications of faculty and students, 74–75, 109, 249–50; preschool founded, 77; WCTU grant for, 77; fosters new ideas of children, 102–5; Stoddard becomes director of, 106; budgets, 108, 154; growth in faculty, 108–9; graduate degrees conferred by, 109, 249–50; challenges to orthodoxy in field, 110–41; research on sex differences at, 128, 242, 243; GEB grant for, 153; reorganization, 154–55; *Time* magazine story about, 186–87; transformation of, 239–40; closing of, 248–50; significance of, 260–61
Iowa Congress of Mothers, 8, 9–10, 15

Iowa Congress of Parents and Teachers, 55, 107
Iowa Farm Bureau, Woman's Division, 55
Iowa Federation of Women's Clubs, 10, 16, 54–55
Iowa General Assembly, 17
Iowa Placement Tests, 106
Iowa Republican party, 10, 155
Iowa Soldiers' Orphans' Home (Davenport), 175, 176, 193, 216
Iowa State Board of Control, 175, 176, 193
Iowa State Board of Education, 41, 53, 54
Iowa State Board of Regents, 250
Iowa State College of Agriculture and Mechanic Arts, 9–14, 50, 53–55, 57, 60, 140
Iowa State Conference on Child Study and Parent Education (1936), 177
Iowa State Council of Child Study and Parent Education, 54–55, 107, 108; summer conference, 55–56, 177
Iowa State Highway Commission, 14
Iowa State School for the Feebleminded (Glenwood), 192, 193, 194, 201
Iowa State Teachers College, 53–55, 60
Iowa Woman's Christian Temperance Union, 8, 10, 13, 15–16, 54
IQ: idea of first articulated, 130
IQ constancy: idea of, 96–102; criticized, 103–4, 130; scientific justification of, 130–31; Iowa station and, 130–41; reasons for belief in, 199–200
IQ inconstancy: research on, at Iowa station, 170–84, 188, 191–99; idea of, 181; claimed by Wellman and Skeels, 184
Irwin, Orvis C., 108, 109, 118–22

Jack, Lois M., 127, 188
James, William, 18–19
Jensen, Arthur, 258
Jessup, Walter A., 15, 35, 41–43, 59, 74, 76, 106, 107, 248
John Dewey Society, 202
Johnson, Lyndon B., 257, 258
Johnson, Wendell, 108, 125–27, 155; *Influence of Stuttering on Personality*, 126–27

Johnstone, E. R., 33
Jones, Alma H., 57
Jones, Harold E., 66, 202
Judge Baker Foundation (Boston), 32
Juvenile court, 4; campaign for, in Iowa, 9

Kalhorn, Joan, 166, 238
Kallen, Horace, 163, 164, 191, 221, 234; as Zionist, 163
Kallikak Family, The (Goddard), 35
Karl, Barry D., 186
Katz, Stanley N., 186
Kelley, Truman Lee, 99
Kephart, Newell C., 130
Key, Ellen Karolina Sofia, 1–3; *The Century of the Child*, 1–2
Kirk, Russell, 258
Kirkpatrick E. A., 19
Klein, Melanie, 241
Klineberg, Otto, 211
Knott, Virginia B., 115, 118
Koch, Helen, 97, 98, 131
Koffka, Kurt, 158
Köhler, Wolfgang, 158
Kounin, Jacob, 166
Kroeber, Alfred L., 225, 226
Kuhlmann-Binet test, 97, 176

Lagemann, Ellen Condliffe, 254
Lathrop, Julia, 30, 31
Laughlin, Harry H., 37
Laura Spelman Rockefeller Memorial (LSRM), 41–45, 47, 48, 49, 50, 51, 52, 59–60, 67, 69, 104, 107, 108, 118, 151, 153, 155, 180, 197, 229, 247, 250; dissolved, 70; final grants of, 70. *See also* Foundations; Frank, Lawrence K.; Ruml, Beardsley
Lazar, Irving, 259, 260
Lazar-Darlington study, 259–60
Leahy, Alice M., 171–72
Lewin, Kurt, 109, 110, 124, 137, 157–69, 183, 184, 213, 221, 223, 226, 227, 228, 229, 230, 231, 232–37, 238, 240, 242, 243, 244, 245, 248, 252, 261; conferences on topological psychology, 157, 165; early life in Germany, 158–62; and Gestalt psychology, 158–60; ideas of, in

Berlin, 158–62; *Der Begriff Des Genese in Physik, Biologie, und Entwicklungs-geschichte*, 158–59; and action psychology, 159–60; article in Murchison's *Handbook of Child Psychology*, 160–61; and *vergleichenden Wissenschaftslehre*, 161, 162; critique of traditional American psychology, 161–63; and Nazism, 162, 164, 165; and Palestine, 163, 164; as Zionist, 163, 164; project on frustration and regression, 166–69; group atmospheres research, 188–91; research at Iowa station, 229–31; *Authority and Frustration*, 238–39; dies, 239; and small group dynamics, 260–61
Lewin, Leopold, 158
Lewin, Recha, 158
Lincoln, Mrs. S. E., 107, 108, 110
Lindsey, Ben B., 9
Lippitt, Ronald, 166, 236; research of, 188–90

MacBride, Thomas Houston, 11–13, 15
McCandless, Boyd, 249, 250
McCloy, Charles H. 108, 113, 117, 118, 155
McCollum, E. V., 25
McDougall, William, *Introduction to Social Psychology, An*, 26
Macfarlane, Jean Walker, 65, 66, 196–97, 199, 200, 206, 209, 211
MacLean, George, 10, 11
McNemar, Quinn, 211, 214–16
Man in the Gray Flannel Suit, The (Wilson), 252
Marrow, Alfred J., 236
Marshall, Everett L., 118
Matched pair method, in child study, 178, 183
Maturation theory, 91–95, 110–24, 209, 220–21, 231, 240, 253; holistic theory of, 91–95; dissemination of, 94–95; Iowa station and, 110–25; and Amy L. Daniels, 111–13; and T. W. Richards, 122; and Lois Jack, 127; and Kurt Lewin, 238
May, Mark A., 222, 224
Mead, Margaret, 157, 158, 234, 235, 245

Medicare, 259
Mendel, Gregor, 21
Mendel, Lafayette B., 35
Mendelian heredity, 18, 21; multiple factorial theories of, 99
Mengert, Ida G., 125
Mental hygiene, 89, 90, 129, 245; ideology of, 153; *See also* Child guidance; Commonwealth Fund
Meredith, E. T., 15
Meredith, Howard, 109, 113–17, 154, 155, 229, 250
Merrill-Palmer, Lizzie, 67
Merrill-Palmer School (Detroit, Mich.), 51, 67, 219
Metheny, Eleanor, 117, 118
Meyer, Adolf A., 89–90
Meyers, Charles E., 166, 238
Miller, Neal E., 225, 237, 238
Mills Brothers, the, 253
Mills College, (Oakland, Calif.) 67
Minnesota Occupational Scale, 170, 171, 173, 191
Minnesota State Board of Charities and Corrections, 30
Mitchell, Lucy Sprague, 46, 47
Mitchell, Wesley Clair, 47
Moore, Elizabeth Skelding, 130
Morale, civilian: research on, 235–36
Morons: as diagnostic category, 34
Mothers and Parent-Teacher Association of Mason City, Iowa, 72
Murchison, Carl, 101–2, 121, 160–61

Nash, Roderick, 39
National Association for Nursery Education (NANE), 113, 165, 197, 202, 204; 1931 conference, 132, 173; 1937 conference, 151–52
National Committee for Mental Hygiene, 90. *See also* Comonwealth Fund; Mental hygiene
National Conference of Christians and Jews, 187
National Congress of Mothers (NCM), 6–8, 19
National Congress of Parents and Teachers, 6

National Education Association (NEA), 175
National Institute of Mental Health, 248
National Institutes of Health, 248
National Research Council, 68, 69. *See also* Committee on Child Development; Committee on Child Welfare; Committee on Food Habits
National Society for the Study of Education, 200, 202, 206; 1928 *Yearbook*, 103, 206; 1940 *Yearbook*, controversy over, 200–215
National Youth Authority (NYA), 185
Nature-nurture controversy, 188. *See also* Heredity-environment controversy
Nazism, 162, 164, 165, 213
New Deal, 110, 185, 217–19
New Jersey Association for the Study of Children and Youth, 33
New mathematics, 255
New School for Social Research (New York, N.Y.), 47
New York: child development and parent education in, 67–68
New York Department of Education, 68
New York Orphan Asylum, 31
New York Society for the Prevention of Cruelty to Children, 30
New York Telephone Company, 46
Nixon, Richard, 258
Normal child: Seashore's conception of, 17; Gesells' definition of, 27–28; Baldwin's definition of, 28, 80, 81; as alternative to child welfare, 38; holistic notions of, 88–105
Normal Child and Primary Education, The, (Gesell and Gesell) 27, 28
Nowlis, Vincent, 242
Nursery schools: Stoddard advocates national system of, 136–41, 157
Nursery school studies of IQ, 207–8
Nutrition, science of, 24–26, 84, 85; at Iowa station, 111–13; closed down at Iowa station, 155

Office of Economic Opportunity (OEO), 251, 259
Ohio Bureau of Juvenile Research, 90, 95

Ojemann, Ralph H., 108, 109, 140, 156
O'Neill, H. O., 198
Organization Man, The (Whyte), 252
Origin of Species (Darwin), 12
Orphans: research on, 191–96
Other America, The: Poverty in the United States (Harrington), 252

Palestine, 163, 164
Palmer, Louvenia, 251
Parent education, 47–50, 51, 52–60, 60–61, 63, 64, 65, 66, 67, 68, 70–71, 107, 140–41, 154–56, 221, 228
Parents Magazine, 70, 220, 244, 246, 247, 250; and Lawrence K. Frank, 70; and George Hecht, 246, 247
Patrick, George T. W., 8
Pavlov, Ivan, 122
Perkins, Frances, 46
Personality, research on: at Iowa station, 124–30, 227–28, 237–42; at Harvard University, 227–28
Personality-culture dichotomy, 227
Philadelphia Child Guidance Clinic, 198
Philadelphia Negro, The (Du Bois), 2–3
Phillips, Ruth, 241
Physical growth, research in: at Iowa station, 81, 82, 83, 102, 103, 113–17, 155–56
Piaget, Jean, 253
Pintler, Margaret, 241
Popular Science Monthly, 75
Population genetics: and child science, 100
Preschool: founded at Iowa Station, 51–52, 77; opens, 78; routine at, 78–80
Principles of Psychology, The (James), 18–19
Professionalism, female, 3; in child development, 84
Progressive education, 46
Progressive education movement, 84
Progressive Education Society, 165
Projection, research on, 223–24
Psychodynamics, research on: at Iowa station, 231–44
Psychological Review, 121
Psychologische Forschung, 160
Psychology of action, 159–60

Psychology of the Preschool Child, The (Baldwin and Stecher), 102–3
Psychopathic Clinic of Cook County Juvenile Court, 32

Quin, Barbara S., 42

Radio Child Study Club, 55, 73, 140, 156
Reagan, Ronald, 259
Reeder, Rudolph, 31
Research Center for Group Dynamics (Massachusetts Institute of Technology), 239
Richards, Ellen, 3, 25
Richards, Theodore W., 120, 122
Richardson, Anna E., 53, 54, 57
Richardson, W. S., 41, 42
Rickover, Hyman, 254
Rise of American Civilization, The (Beard and Beard), 152
Roberts, Katherine E., 208
Robinson, Elizabeth, 241
Rockefeller, John D., 39, 41
Rockefeller Foundation, 40–41, 70, 162, 163, 233, 241, 242
Rogers, Josephine Rand, 64
Rohrschach tests, 240
Roosevelt, Franklin D., 46, 137, 186
Roosevelt, Theodore, 39, 42
Ross, Edward A., 43
Rubner, Max, 25
Ruml, Beardsley, 43, 45, 47, 51, 62–63, 106–8
Rural child project: at Iowa station, 45, 104, 105
Russell, James E., 61, 62
Russell Sage Foundation, 30

Saint Louis Congress of Arts and Sciences, 19
Scammon, Richard, 64
Schlesinger, Arthur M., Jr., 79
Schlesinger, Arthur M., Sr., 79
Schlossman, Steven, 154
Schoff, Hanna, 9
Sears, Jesse Brundage, 222
Sears, Pauline Snedden, 227, 242
Sears, Robert R., 109, 162, 222–32, 239–

49; *Frustration and Aggression*, 224–25; research at Iowa station, 229–31; *Survey of Objective Studies of Psychoanalytic Concepts*, 237–38; resigns as director of Iowa station, 247; and social learning theory, 260
Seashore, Carl E., 8, 11–15, 17, 35–37, 40–42, 68, 69, 77, 81, 106, 156, 198
Second International Congress of Eugenics, 81
Semple, Ellen Church, 3
Sex, research on: at Iowa station, 128, 241–42
Sheppard-Towner Maternity and Infancy Act, 4, 50
Sherman, Mandel, 211
Shriver, R. Sargent, 258, 259
Simon, Theodore, 23, 106, 130
Simpson, Benjamin R., 195
Skeels, Harold M., 109, 176, 177, 178, 180, 181, 182, 183, 184, 188, 191, 195, 196, 198, 199, 203, 205, 210, 212, 213, 214, 228, 229, 240, 252, 255–56, 260; on the Davenport project, 177–78; research at Iowa State Home for the Feebleminded, 192, 193, 194, 204; *Adult Status of Children with Contrasting Early Life Experiences*, 256–57
Skinner, B. F., 13
Skodak, Marie, 191, 192, 198, 212
Smith, Afton, 156
Smith, Lois Z., 123
Smith-Lever Act (1915), 49
Social learning theory, 225, 237–38, 240–43
Social Security, 259
Social Security Act of 1935, 185
Society for Research in Child Development (SRCD), 69, 221, 245, 246
Society for the Psychological Study of Social Issues (SPSSI), 235
Spearman, Charles, 99
Speer, George, 199
Spence, Kenneth W., 222, 231–32, 248, 249, 250
Spiker, Charles, 250
Stability and Change in Human Characteristics (Bloom), 254

Stanford University, 65
Stanford-Binet Measuring Scale of Intelligence, 24, 83, 176, 240, 260
Starkweather, Elizabeth K., 208
State University of Iowa, x, 9, 10, 11, 12, 14, 50, 55, 69, 140
State University of New York at Albany, 68
Station for Experimental Evolution (Cold Spring Harbor, Long Island, N.Y.), 34
Stecher, Lorle I., 78, 79, 83
Steinbeck, John, 222
Stern, Wilhelm, 130
Stinchfield, Sara, 85
Stoddard, George D., 97, 101, 106, 107, 108, 109, 110, 113, 118 138, 139, 141, 152, 155, 156–57, 159, 163, 172, 175, 176, 181, 183, 194, 195, 196, 199, 200, 202, 203, 204, 210, 211, 213, 219, 221–22, 223, 226, 228, 229, 230, 234, 240, 252, 260, 261; director of Iowa station, 108–10, 135–41, 155–57, 175–84, 186–88, 194–96, 202–16; on mental growth and IQ, 132, 135–37; views of Hillis, 135; political activities of, 135–41; political ideas of, 156–57, 186–88; advocates nursery schools, 157; and IQ inconstancy, 175; and Davenport project, 177–78; speaks on "Adventures in Science" radio program, 187; resigns as director, 221, 222
Stolz, Herbert R., 65, 66, 106
Stumpf, Carl, 157, 158
Successful Farming, 15
Survey of Objective Studies of Psychoanalytic Concepts (Sears), 237–38
Syngg, Donald, 198

Terman, Lewis M., 5, 20–22, 24, 29, 35, 83, 95, 96, 175, 191, 202–4, 206–7, 210, 213, 229, 247; *Genetic Studies of Genius*, 83, 96, 132, 219; editor of *Yearbook* of National Society for the Study of Education, 103, 200–201; and Kurt Lewin, 162
Thomas Wood–Bird T. Baldwin Age-Weight-Height Table, 118
Thorndike, Edward Lee, 61

Thorndike, Robert L., 99
Time magazine, 186–87
Todd, Arthur J., 35
Tolman, Edward C., 165
Topological psychology, 213, 238; conferences on, 157, 165
Toronto Infants Home and Mental Hygiene Clinic, 198
Town, Clara, 85–86

U.S. Children's Bureau, 4, 30, 39, 40, 76, 218, 246
United States Commission on Country Life, 42, 43
U.S. Department of Education, 136
United States Office of Experiment Stations, 25
U.S. Office of Scientific Research and Development, 237
U.S. War Industries Board, 46
University of California, 187–88
University of Cincinnati, 68
University of Georgia, 68
University of Iowa Series in Child Welfare (monograph series), 81
Updegraff, Ruth, 86–88, 108, 109, 123, 129, 227; ideas on environment, 128

Veblen, Thorstein, 46
Vergleichenden Wissenschaftslehre: and Kurt Lewin, 158, 159, 161, 162
Vincent, George E., 41
Vineland Association, 33
Vineland Training School, 5, 21, 33, 90

Walden Two (Skinner), 13
Walter Reed Army Hospital, 76
War on Poverty, 257–58
Watson, John B., 111, 119, 120, 122, 220, 245; and maturation theory, 91, 92, 93; stimulus-response formula of, 119, 245; behaviorism of, 120; criticized, 125, 130
Weiss, Albert Paul, 118–19
Welfare state: in America, 185–86
Wellman, Beth L., 109, 122, 123, 124, 163, 172, 173, 174, 175, 176, 183, 184, 188, 195, 196, 198, 199, 201, 202, 203, 205, 207, 208, 210, 213, 214–15, 227,

228, 229, 240, 250, 260; on mental growth and IQ, 132–35; Wellman-Coffee study, 172–75
Wenger, M. A., 121
Wertheimer, Max, 158
Westinghouse Learning Corporation: study of Head Start, 258
Whipple, Guy M., 200–201
White, Ralph K., 166, 190–91
White House, 139
White House Conference on Child Health and Protection (1930), 113, 218
White House Conference on Child Health and Protection (1940) 217
White House Conference on the Care of Dependent Children (1909), 4, 39
White House conferences on children, 217–18
Whiting, John, 242
Whiting, Phineas W., 37, 86
Whyte, William, 252
Wiggam, Albert E., 195, 196
Wilson, Sloan, 252
Wilson, Woodrow, 36, 40, 95

Wishy, Bernard, ix
Wissler, Clark, 62–63
WOI (radio station, Ames, Iowa), 140
Woman's Christian Temperance Union, 36, 38, 51, 78, 81, 108; grant to ICWRS, 51, 78, 86, 108. *See also* Iowa Woman's Christian Temperance Union
Woodworth, Robert S., 68, 69, 245
Woolley, Helen Thompson, 62, 94, 98–99, 101, 131, 211; study of IQ inconstancy, 97
World War II, 221
Wright, Herbert F., 163, 166
WSUI (radio station, Iowa City, Iowa), 140

Yale University Psycho-Clinic, 49, 219
Yearbook, of National Society for the Study of Education. *See* National Society for the Study of Education
Year of the Child, 218
Yerkes, Robert M., 35, 62–63
Youtz, May P. 51, 53, 54, 57, 107, 108, 109, 140, 156